Challenges and Opportunities for the Convergence of IoT, Big Data, and Cloud Computing

Sathiyamoorthi Velayutham
Sona College of Technology, India

A volume in the Advances in Web Technologies
and Engineering (AWTE) Book Series

Published in the United States of America by
IGI Global
Engineering Science Reference (an imprint of IGI Global)
701 E. Chocolate Avenue
Hershey PA, USA 17033
Tel: 717-533-8845
Fax: 717-533-8661
E-mail: cust@igi-global.com
Web site: http://www.igi-global.com

Library of Congress Cataloging-in-Publication Data

Names: Sathiyamoorthi, Velayutham., 1983- editor.
Title: Challenges and opportunities for the convergence of IoT, big data,
  and cloud computing / Sathiyamoorthi Velayutham, editor.
Description: Hershey, PA : Engineering Science Reference, 2021. | Includes
  bibliographical references and index. | Summary: "This book focuses on
  the applications, issues, and challenges in the convergence of the
  internet of things, big data, and cloud computing"-- Provided by
  publisher.
Identifiers: LCCN 2019048560 (print) | LCCN 2019048561 (ebook) | ISBN
  9781799831112 (h/c) | ISBN 9781799831129 (s/c) | ISBN 9781799831136
  (eISBN)
Subjects: LCSH: Internet of things. | Big data. | Cloud computing. |
  Convergence (Telecommunication)
Classification: LCC TK5105.8857 .C53 2021 (print) | LCC TK5105.8857
  (ebook) | DDC 004--dc23
LC record available at https://lccn.loc.gov/2019048560
LC ebook record available at https://lccn.loc.gov/2019048561

This book is published in the IGI Global book series Advances in Web Technologies and Engineering (AWTE) (ISSN: 2328-2762; eISSN: 2328-2754)

British Cataloguing in Publication Data
A Cataloguing in Publication record for this book is available from the British Library.

For electronic access to this publication, please contact: eresources@igi-global.com.

Advances in Web Technologies and Engineering (AWTE) Book Series

Ghazi I. Alkhatib
The Hashemite University, Jordan
David C. Rine
George Mason University, USA

ISSN:2328-2762
EISSN:2328-2754

MISSION

The **Advances in Web Technologies and Engineering (AWTE) Book Series** aims to provide a platform for research in the area of Information Technology (IT) concepts, tools, methodologies, and ethnography, in the contexts of global communication systems and Web engineered applications. Organizations are continuously overwhelmed by a variety of new information technologies, many are Web based. These new technologies are capitalizing on the widespread use of network and communication technologies for seamless integration of various issues in information and knowledge sharing within and among organizations. This emphasis on integrated approaches is unique to this book series and dictates cross platform and multidisciplinary strategy to research and practice.

The **Advances in Web Technologies and Engineering (AWTE) Book Series** seeks to create a stage where comprehensive publications are distributed for the objective of bettering and expanding the field of web systems, knowledge capture, and communication technologies. The series will provide researchers and practitioners with solutions for improving how technology is utilized for the purpose of a growing awareness of the importance of web applications and engineering.

COVERAGE

- Software agent-based applications
- Human factors and cultural impact of IT-based systems
- Data analytics for business and government organizations
- Mobile, location-aware, and ubiquitous computing
- Security, integrity, privacy, and policy issues
- Integrated user profile, provisioning, and context-based processing
- Data and knowledge validation and verification
- Ontology and semantic Web studies
- Web systems performance engineering studies
- Knowledge structure, classification, and search algorithms or engines

IGI Global is currently accepting manuscripts for publication within this series. To submit a proposal for a volume in this series, please contact our Acquisition Editors at Acquisitions@igi-global.com or visit: http://www.igi-global.com/publish/.

Titles in this Series

For a list of additional titles in this series, please visit: http://www.igi-global.com/book-series/advances-web-technologies-engineering/37158

Building Smart and Secure Environments Through the Fusion of Virtual Reality, Augmented Reality, and he IoT

Nadesh RK (Vellore Institute of Technology, India) Shynu PG (Vellore Institute of Technology, India) and Chiranji Lal Chowdhary (School of Information Technology and Engineering, VIT University, Vellore, India)
Engineering Science Reference • © 2020 • 300pp • H/C (ISBN: 9781799831839) • US $245.00

The IoT and the Next Revolutions Automating the World

Dinesh Goyal (Poornima Institute of Engineering & Technology, India) S. Balamurugan (QUANTS Investment Strategy & Consultancy Services, India) Sheng-Lung Peng (National Dong Hwa University, Taiwan) and Dharm Singh Jat (Namibia University of Science and Technology, Naibia)
Engineering Science Reference • © 2019 • 340pp • H/C (ISBN: 9781522592464) • US $255.00

Integrating and Streamlining Event-Driven IoT Services

Yang Zhang (Beijing University of Posts and Telecommunications, China) and Yanmeng Guo (Chinese Academy of Sciences, China)
Engineering Science Reference • © 2019 • 309pp • H/C (ISBN: 9781522576228) • US $205.00

Semantic Web Science and Real-World Applications

Miltiadis D. Lytras (The American College of Greece, Greece) Naif Aljohani (King Abdulaziz University, Saudi Arabia) Ernesto Damiani (Khalifa University, UAE) and Kwok Tai Chui (The Open University of Hong Kong, Hong Kong)
Information Science Reference • © 2019 • 399pp • H/C (ISBN: 9781522571865) • US $195.00

Innovative Solutions and Applications of Web Services Technology

Liang-Jie Zhang (Kingdee International Software Group Co., Ltd., China) and Yishuang Ning (Tsinghua University, China)
Engineering Science Reference • © 2019 • 316pp • H/C (ISBN: 9781522572688) • US $215.00

Dynamic Knowledge Representation in Scientific Domains

Cyril Pshenichny (ITMO University, Russia) Paolo Diviacco (Istituto Nazionale di Oceanografia e di Geofisica Sperimentale, Italy) and Dmitry Mouromtsev (ITMO University, Russia)
Engineering Science Reference • © 2018 • 397pp • H/C (ISBN: 9781522552611) • US $205.00

701 East Chocolate Avenue, Hershey, PA 17033, USA
Tel: 717-533-8845 x100 • Fax: 717-533-8661
E-Mail: cust@igi-global.com • www.igi-global.com

Table of Contents

Detailed Table of Contents

    Mutwalibi Nambobi, Islamic University, Uganda
    Kanyana Ruth, Kampala International University, Uganda
    Adam A. Alli, Islamic University of Technology, Bangladesh
    Rajab Ssemwogerere, Islamic University, Uganda

The age of autonomous sensing has dominated almost every industry today. Our lives have been engaged with multiple sensors embedded in our smartphones to achieve sensing of all sorts starting from proximity sensing to social sensing. Our possessions (cars, fridges, oven) have sensors embedded in them. The art of autonomous IoT has shifted from a mere detection of events or changes in the environment to dominant systems for social sensing, big data analytics, and smart things. Recently, sensing systems have adapted connectivity resulting in input mechanisms for big data analytics and smart systems resulting in pervasive systems. Currently, a range of sensors has come to existence, for example, mobile phone sensors that measure blood pressure at patients' figure tip, or the sensors that be used to detect deforestation. In this chapter, the authors provide a technical view upon which autonomous IoT devices can be implemented and enlist opportunities and challenges of the same.

    Rashmi S., Dayananda Sagar College of Engineering, India
    Roopashree S., Dayananda Sagar University, India
    Sathiyamoorthi V., Sona College of Technology, India

Cloud computing and internet of things (IoT) are two disparate technologies that can be united for a common purpose as in an operating profit. The technologies are integral parts of modern sophisticated human life. In the future, it is destined to proliferate boundlessly covering utmost spheres. This chapter describes the challenges faced in adopting the two technologies. Edge computing includes both computing and processing the information are carried at the edge of the IoT devices where vast information gathered instead of relying on the central location. Benefits include avoiding latency issues, improving the performance of the application, and cost effectiveness as it reduces the data volume to be processed in cloud/centralized location. In the advent of IoT devices, edge computing is a vital step in building any of its application which sends and receives enormous information to and from the cloud over the course of operations. Applications such as virtual reality and smart systems are benefited by edge computing as they expect higher rate of response and processing speed. A case study on video surveillance is done in this chapter.

Chapter 3

Shaila S. G., Dayananda Sagar University, India
Monish L., Dayananda Sagar University, India
Lavanya S., Dayananda Sagar University, India
Sowmya H. D., Dayananda Sagar University, India
Divya K., Dayananda Sagar University, India

The new trending technologies such as big data and cloud computing are in line with social media applications due to their fast growth and usage. The big data characteristic makes data management challenging. The term big data refers to an immense collection of both organised and unorganised data from various sources, and nowadays, cloud computing supports in storing and processing such a huge data. Analytics are done on huge data that helps decision makers to take decisions. However, merging two conflicting design principles brings a challenge, but it has its own advantage in business and various fields. Big data analytics in the cloud places rigorous demands on networks, storage, and servers. The chapter discusses the importance of cloud platform for big data, importance of analytics in cloud and gives detail insight about the trends and techniques adopted for cloud analytics.

Chapter 4

Sivakumar V., Dayananda Sagar Academy of Technology and Management, India
Swathi R., Sree Abiraami College for Women, Thiruvalluvar University, Vellore, India
Yuvaraj V., Shenzhen Center Power Tech Co. Ltd., Shenzhen, China

The current methods of energy monitoring and metering in India are extremely labor-intensive and prone to human errors. The system the authors propose will incorporate an automatic energy reading meter system (AERM) which will aid in the collection of data accurately and efficiently. Additionally, power companies find it hard to withstand the power requirement of a consumer because of a surge in industries, buildings, and population. The usage of electrical appliances has drastically increased over time. As per as energy balance maintains between the energy demand and supply for the power companies are bearing in mind an energy supervision technique. Therefore, there is adoption for load scheduling or load shifting to reduce the electricity bill. So consequently, the authors look into various optimization algorithms for load-shifting.

Chapter 5

Rinat Galiautdinov, Independent Researcher, Italy

The chapter describes the new approach in artificial intelligence based on simulated biological neurons and creation of the neural circuits for the sphere of IoT which represent the next generation of artificial intelligence and IoT. Unlike existing technical devices for implementing a neuron based on classical nodes oriented to binary processing, the proposed path is based on simulation of biological neurons, creation of biologically close neural circuits where every device will implement the function of either a sensor or a "muscle" in the frame of the home based live AI and IoT. The research demonstrates the developed nervous circuit constructor and its usage in building of the AI (neural circuit) for IoT.

Chapter 6

Anchitaalagammai J. V., Velammal College of Engineering and Technology, India
Kavitha S., Velammal College of Engineering and Technology, India
Murali S., Velammal College of Engineering and Technology, India
Padmadevi S., Velammal College of Engineering and Technology, India
Shanthalakshmi Revathy J., Velammal College of Engineering and Technology, India

The internet of things (IoT) is rapidly changing our society to a world where every "thing" is connected to the internet, making computing pervasive like never before. It is increasingly becoming a ubiquitous computing service, requiring huge volumes of data storage and processing. Unfortunately, due to the lack of resource constraints, it tends to adopt a cloud-based architecture to store the voluminous data generated from IoT application. From a security perspective, the technological revolution introduced by IoT and cloud computing can represent a disaster, as each object might become inherently remotely hackable and, as a consequence, controllable by malicious actors. This chapter focus on security considerations for IoT from the perspectives of cloud tenants, end-users, and cloud providers in the context of wide-scale IoT proliferation, working across the range of IoT technologies. Also, this chapter includes how the organization can store the IoT data on the cloud securely by applying different Access control policies and the cryptography techniques.

Chapter 7

Chellaswamy C., Kings Engineering College, Chennai, India
Sathiyamoorthi V., Sona College of Technology, India

Currently, cities are being reconstructed to smart cities that use an information and communication technology (ICT) framework alongside the internet of things (IoT) technology to increase efficiency and also share information with the public, helping to improve the quality of government services citizens' welfare. This large, diverse set of information called big data is obtained by ICT and IoT technologies from smart cities. This information does not have any meaning of its own but a high potential to make use of smart city services. Therefore, the information collected is mined and processed through use of big data analytic techniques. The environmental footprints in smart cities can be monitored and controlled with the help of ICT. Big data analytic techniques help enhance the functionalities of smart cities and the 4G and 5G network provides strong connectivity for professional devices.

Chapter 8

Karthika K., Adhiyamaan College of Engineering, Hosur, India
Devi Priya R., Kongu Engineering College, Erode, India
Sathishkumar S., Adhiyamaan College of Engineering, Hosur, India

Various unimaginable opportunities and applications can be attained by the development of internet-connected automation. The network system with numerous wired or wireless smart sensors is called as

IoT. It is showing various enhancement for past few years. Without proper security protection, various attacks and threats like cyberattacks threat causes serious disaster to IoT from the day it was introduced. Hence, IoT security system is improvised by various security and the management techniques. There are six sections in security management of IoT works. IoT security requirement is described intensively. The proposed layered of security management architecture is being defined and explained. Thus, this proposed architecture shows the security management system for IoT network tight security management for a network of the IoT which is elaborately explained with examples and about GDPR. In information security, intrusion recognizable proof is the showing of placing exercises that attempt to deal the protection, respectability, or availability of a benefit.

Chapter 9
Shaila S. G., Dayananda Sagar University, India
Bhuvana D. S., Dayananda Sagar University, India
Monish L., Dayananda Sagar University, India

Big data and the internet of things (IoT) are two major ruling domains in today's world. It is observed that there are 2.5 quintillion bytes of data created each day. Big data defines a very huge amount of data in terms of both structured and unstructured formats. Business intelligence and other application domains that have high information density use big data analytics to make predictions and better decisions to improve the business. Big data analytics is used to analyze a high range of data at a time. In general, big data and IoT were built on different technologies; however, over a period of time, both of them are interlinked to build a better world. Companies are not able to achieve maximum benefit, just because the data produced by the applications are not utilized and analyzed effectively as there is a shortage of big data analysts. For real-time IoT applications, synchronization among hardware, programming, and interfacing is needed to the greater extent. The chapter discusses about IoT and big data, relation between them, importance of big data analytics in IoT applications.

Chapter 10
Sathishkumar S., Adhiyamaan College of Engineering, Hosur, India
Devi Priya R., Kongu Engineering College, Erode, India
Karthika K., Adhiyamaan College of Engineering, Hosur, India

Big data computing in clouds is a new paradigm for next-generation analytics development. It enables large-scale data organizations to share and explore large quantities of ever-increasing data types using cloud computing technology as a back-end. Knowledge exploration and decision-making from this rapidly increasing volume of data encourage data organization, access, and timely processing, an evolving trend known as big data computing. This modern paradigm incorporates large-scale computing, new data-intensive techniques, and mathematical models to create data analytics for intrinsic information extraction. Cloud computing emerged as a service-oriented computing model to deliver infrastructure, platform, and applications as services from the providers to the consumers meeting the QoS parameters by enabling the archival and processing of large volumes of rapidly growing data faster economy models.

Chapter 11

Revathi Rajendran, SRM Valliammai Engineering College, India

Arthi Kalidasan, SRM Valliammai Engineering College, India

Chidhambara Rajan B., SRM Valliammai Engineering College, India

The evolution of digital era and improvements in technology have enabled the growth of a number of devices and web applications leading to the unprecedented generation of huge data on a day-to-day basis from many applications such as industrial automation, social networking cites, healthcare units, smart grids, etc. Artificial intelligence acts as a viable solution for the efficient collection and analyses of the heterogeneous data in large volumes with reduced human effort at low time. Machine learning and deep learning subspaces of artificial intelligence are used for the achievement of smart intelligence in machines to make them intelligent based on learning from experience automatically. Machine learning and deep learning have become two of the most trending, groundbreaking technologies that enable autonomous operations and provide decision making support for data processing systems. The chapter investigates the importance of machine learning and deep learning algorithms in instilling intelligence and providing an overview of machine learning, deep learning platforms.

Chapter 12

Selvaraj Kesavan, DXC Technology, India

Senthilkumar J., Sona College of Technology, India

Suresh Y., Sona College of Technology, India

Mohanraj V., Sona College of Technology, India

In establishing a healthy environment for connectivity devices, it is essential to ensure that privacy and security of connectivity devices are well protected. The modern world lives on data, information, and connectivity. Various kinds of sensors and edge devices stream large volumes of data to the cloud platform for storing, processing, and deriving insights. An internet of things (IoT) system poses certain difficulties in discretely identifying, remotely configuring, and controlling the devices, and in the safe transmission of data. Mutual authentication of devices and networks is crucial to initiate secure communication. It is important to keep the data in a secure manner during transmission and in store. Remotely operated devices help to monitor, control, and manage the IoT system efficiently. This chapter presents a review of the approaches and methodologies employed for certificate provisioning, device onboarding, monitoring, managing, and configuring of IoT systems. It also examines the real time challenges and limitations in and future scope for IoT systems.

Chapter 13

J. Fenila Naomi, Sri Krishna College of Engineering and Technology, India

Kavitha M., Sri Krishna College of Engineering and Technology, India

Sathiyamoorthi V., Sona College of Technology, India

For centuries, the concept of a smart, autonomous learning machine has fascinated people. The machine learning philosophy is to automate the development of analytical models so that algorithms can learn continually with the assistance of accessible information. Machine learning (ML) and deep learning (DL) methods are implemented to further improve an application's intelligence and capacities as the quantity of the gathered information rises. Because IoT will be one of the main sources of information, data science will make a significant contribution to making IoT apps smarter. There is a rapid development of both technologies, cloud computing and the internet of things, considering the field of wireless communication. This chapter answers the questions: How can IoT intelligent information be applied to ML and DL algorithms? What is the taxonomy of IoT's ML and DL and profound learning algorithms? And what are real-world IoT data features that require data analytics?

Chapter 14

Preethi Sambandam Raju, SRM Valliammai Engineering College, India
Revathi Arumugam Rajendran, SRM Valliammai Engineering College, India
Murugan Mahalingam, SRM Valliammai Engineering College, India

This chapter brings out the perspective outcomes of combining three terminologies: artificial intelligence, cloud, and internet of things. The relation between artificial intelligence, machine learning, and deep learning is also emphasized. Intelligence, which is the capability to attain and apply knowledge in addition to skills, is analysed in the following sections of the chapter along with its categories that include natural intelligence, artificial intelligence, and hybrid intelligence. Analysis of artificial intelligence-based internet of things system is deliberated on two approaches, namely criterion-based analysis and elemental analysis. Criterion-based analysis covers the parameter-based investigation to highlight the relation between machine learning and deep learning. Elemental analysis involves four main components of artificial intelligence-based internet of things system, such as device, data, algorithm, and computation. Research works done using deep learning and internet of things are also discussed.

Chapter 15

Shaila S. G., Dayananda Sagar University, India
Monish L., Dayananda Sagar University, India
Rajlaxmi Patil, Dayananda Sagar University, India

With the advancement of computation power and internet revolution, IoT, big data, and cloud computing have become the most prevalent technologies in present time. Convergence of these three technologies has led to the development of new opportunities and applications which solve the real time problems in the most efficient way. Though cloud computing and big data have an inherent connection between them, IoT plays a major role of a data source unit. With the explosion of data, cloud computing is playing a significant role in the storage and management. However, the main concern that accompanies IoT are the issues related to privacy, security, power efficiency, computational complexities, etc. Misinterpretation of data and security limitations are the bottlenecks of big data whereas the limitations of cloud computing involve network connection dependency, limited features, technical issues, and security. The chapter considers use cases to address their real time problems and discusses about how to solve these issues by combining these technologies.

Chapter 16

    Rohit Rastogi, ABES Engineering College, Ghaziabad, India

    Devendra Chaturvedi, Dayalbagh Educational Institute, India

    Parul Singhal, ABES Engineering College, Ghaziabad, India

The Delhi and NCR healthcare systems are rapidly registering electronic health records and diagnostic information available electronically. Furthermore, clinical analysis is rapidly advancing, and large quantities of information are examined and new insights are part of the analysis of this technology experienced as big data. It provides tools for storing, managing, studying, and assimilating large amounts of robust, structured, and unstructured data generated by existing medical organizations. Recently, data analysis data have been used to help provide care. The present study aimed to analyse diabetes with the latest IoT and big data analysis techniques and its correlation with stress (TTH) on human health. The authors have tried to include age, gender, and insulin factor and its correlation with diabetes. Overall, in conclusion, TTH cases increasing with age in case of males and not following the pattern of diabetes variation with age, while in the case of females, TTH pattern variation is the same as diabetes (i.e., increasing trend up to age of 60 then decreasing).

Preface

The Internet of Things (IoT) is becoming the next Internet-related revolution. It allows billions of devices to be connected and communicate with each other to share information that improves the quality of our daily lives. On the other hand, Cloud Computing provides on-demand, convenient and scalable network access which makes it possible to share computing resources; indeed, this, in turn, enables dynamic data integration from various data sources. Big Data has emerged in the past couple of years and with such emergence the cloud has become the architecture of choice. Most companies find it feasible to access the massive quantities of big-data via the cloud. However, the intersection of both Internet of things and big-data has created new challenges like data storage, integration and analytics.

All these emerging technologies that are already part of our life. Their adoption and use are expected to be more and more pervasive, making them important components of the future Internet. It is a novel paradigm where Cloud, Big-data and IoT are merged together to solve some real-time problems and seen as an enabler of a large number of application scenarios. Many works in the past have presented cloud computing, big-data computing and IoT separately. All those works were presented their main properties, features, underlying technologies and open issues. However, to the best of our knowledge, those books or works lack a detailed analysis of the new paradigm, which involves integration or convergence of these technologies to address issues or build new applications based on it.

Hence, from the above discussion, one can find the inter-dependency between the three mutually exclusive technologies. Here Cloud computing plays the role of a common workplace for IoT and big data where IoT is the source of data and big data as a technology for data analytics. The IoT generates a vast amount of data and this in turn puts a huge strain on Internet Infrastructure. As a result, it forces companies to find solutions to minimize the pressure and solve their problem of transferring large amounts of data. There are many issues standing in the way of the successful implementation and integration of these technologies. Hence, we need to leverage each of these technologies to find solutions to other problems. To bridge this gap, this book would provide a complete framework for integrating IoT with Cloud or IoT with Big-data or any other combination of these three technologies. It tries to identify open issues and future directions in these fields, which are expected to play a major role in the landscape of the future Internet.

To conclude, the convergence of the Internet of things, big data and cloud computing leverage a new horizon of decision support system. Moreover, the convergence of the IoT, big data and cloud computing can provide new opportunities and applications in all the sectors. This will also give an excellent career scope for professionals who are working on the individual technologies currently. Therefore, this book entitled *Challenges and Opportunities for the Convergence of IoT, Big Data, and Cloud Computing* would provide information on how these three technologies such as Internet of Things (IoT), Big-Data and Cloud Computing are related to each other and how these can be combined to address the major issues in real-time problems. Also, it focuses on the applications, issues and challenges while integrating these three technologies in real time problem solving.

OBJECTIVE

After reading this book, readers would be able to:

- Store and Analyze the data to discover potential information out of it
- Demonstrate the uses of various algorithms in the real-time data sets
- Apply learned concepts to solve the real-time problems
- Decompose the problem to solve using machine learning techniques
- Carry out their R & D works in an efficient way
- Propose solutions to issues in Integration emerging areas such as Internet of Things, Big-Data and Cloud Computing
- Integrate emerging technologies to solve real time problems/ societal problems
- Interpret data using analytics techniques and tools
- Demonstrate the tools and their Integration for the given problem
- Help alleviate talent gap

TOPICS COVERED

Prevailing knowledge and research issues in the following are covered through the contributed chapters by various authors of specific field expertise:

- Big-Data Data Analytics in Cloud Platform
- Cloud Based IoT and its Applications
- Big-Data Analytics and its Applications in IoT
- Challenges of Internet- and cloud-based IoT applications, and edge computing;
- Big data issues: gathering, governance, GDPR, security, and privacy;
- Machine & Deep learning techniques in IoT and cloud;
- Emerging trends and techniques in Cloud-based data analytics
- Other issues related to Integration of these three technologies- IoT, Cloud and Big-Data
- Real-time problems to be solved by the combination of these three technologies

With Regards

Sathiyamoorthi Velayutham
Sona College of Technology, India

Acknowledgment

I am very happy and thankful to IGI Global Inc., USA, for allowing me to produce this book entitled *Challenges and Opportunities for the Convergence of IoT, Big Data, and Cloud Computing*, which is highly needed in the present data-driven internet controlled world.

I express my deep sense of gratitude to Jan Travers, Lindsay Wertman, Maria Rohde, Michael Brehm, Jordan Tepper, Halle N. Frisco, Kayla Wolfe, Josh Christ, and other members of IGI Global who supported either directly or indirectly during book project development.

I am thankful to all authors who have contributed their valuable efforts and ideas in the form of chapters in our book. Also, I would like to express our sincere thanks to all my reviewers for their continuous support, guidance, and encouragement in bringing this book into success.

I am thankful to the management and faculty of my institute for their support and kindness while completing this book.

Also, I am much thankful to my family members for their support and encouragement in achieving this target in our academic career goal.

I dedicate this book to my Wife Ms. K Surya and my Lovely Son S. Vikash

With Regards

Sathiyamoorthi Velayutham
Sona College of Technology, India

Chapter 1
The Age of Autonomous Internet of Things Devices:
Opportunities and Challenges of IoT

Mutwalibi Nambobi
https://orcid.org/0000-0001-6822-616X
Islamic University, Uganda

Kanyana Ruth
Kampala International University, Uganda

Adam A. Alli
https://orcid.org/0000-0002-4066-1546
Islamic University of Technology, Bangladesh

Rajab Ssemwogerere
https://orcid.org/0000-0002-9786-8898
Islamic University, Uganda

ABSTRACT

The age of autonomous sensing has dominated almost every industry today. Our lives have been engaged with multiple sensors embedded in our smartphones to achieve sensing of all sorts starting from proximity sensing to social sensing. Our possessions (cars, fridges, oven) have sensors embedded in them. The art of autonomous IoT has shifted from a mere detection of events or changes in the environment to dominant systems for social sensing, big data analytics, and smart things. Recently, sensing systems have adapted connectivity resulting in input mechanisms for big data analytics and smart systems resulting in pervasive systems. Currently, a range of sensors has come to existence, for example, mobile phone sensors that measure blood pressure at patients' figure tip, or the sensors that be used to detect deforestation. In this chapter, the authors provide a technical view upon which autonomous IoT devices can be implemented and enlist opportunities and challenges of the same.

DOI: 10.4018/978-1-7998-3111-2.ch001

INTRODUCTION

The Internet of things (IoT) and their applications have increased pervasiveness, they have a great impact on our daily lives and change the way people interact with this physical world (Alli and Alam 2019). Autonomous sensing devices possess intelligent systems that are powered by machine learning, deep learning, communication systems, electrical and computational resources, smart algorithms for predictions and decision making. Bechtsis asserts that firms' production and performance are becoming data-driven, this can be enhanced through the utilization of autonomous and distributed devices (Bechtsis, Tsolakis et al. 2017). Additionally, incorporating the Internet of Things calls for the design and implementation of autonomous sensing devices to address the anticipated challenges in industries and homes (Alur, Berger et al. 2016). Therefore, autonomous sensing devices are getting more useful in the field of information engineering, robotics, and artificial intelligence.

Autonomous IoT devices can be categorized into service and rescue robots, exploring disaster areas and waste management (Birk and Carpin 2006). Looking at homes, these perform cleaning like Roomba vacuum cleaning robot, office delivery of goods and services like the FedEx unveils autonomous delivery robot and RP-VITA (Remote Presence Virtual + Independent Telemedicine Assistant) that is basically found in health public hospitals. Autonomous devices were created in the same architecture as a human, they use sensors, laser scanners, spectrometers, and vision cameras as their mechanism to perceive the environment in making quick and safety decisions. They possess an embedded system that makes a quick decision even without the notice of its brain called the computer. They also use actuators like motors display instructions such making the movement (Pratt and Williamson 1995). Considering this background, the purpose of this chapter is to detail the technical and theoretical aspects of autonomous sensing and connected devices. In order to achieve this aim, the specific objectives of this chapter are to;

i.   Highlight some of the components used to implement autonomous connected devices and how they are integrated.
ii. Present the system engineering perspective on the conceptual design and integration of the crucial tools used in the internet of things (IoT) to come up with autonomy ability.
iii. Present the importance of the internet of things in various sectors of applicability.
iv. Discuss the key challenges associated with the use of autonomous devices.
v.

Figure 1. shows data characteristics of good autonomous IoT devices

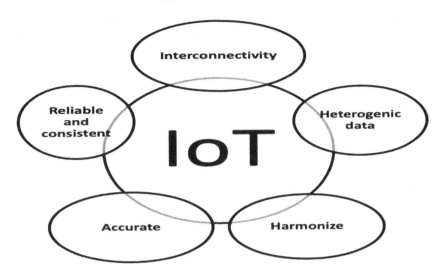

Explanation

To achieve the goal of autonomous sensing and connected devices, there has to be an Internet of Things infrastructure that connects the dots actuators. Data here is need for decision making. The fundamental characteristics of the autonomous sensing and connected devices are as follows (Barnaghi, Bermudez-Edo et al. 2015, Patel and Patel 2016);

The data obtained in the autonomous IoT devices is greatly inclined to the interconnectivity of the objects in the system. Communication occurs from people to object or object to object through wireless interactions, implanted circuits, and sensor technology. Through these techniques, anything can be connected with worldwide information and communication infrastructure. However, without the ability to interpret and transmit all the data collected by the sensors, IoT can't work.

Once the data is interconnected; it has to be made accurate. This means data collected by the sensor combined with computation techniques that separate the noise from the signals has to be accurate. The sensors generate a significant amount of data that is used for decision and policymaking, however, they are susceptible to damage in the rough environment which can affect the accuracy of the data collected by alternating its quality. This becomes challenging to differentiate meaningful and substantial data from trusted data with a sizable quantity of noise in the data. The accuracy of data can't be truly ensured unless it can be secured throughout the entire manipulation process in the autonomous IoT devices.

With IoT, a single set of data processed through different protocols can deliver a different result. At each layer, data is prone to a new external connection and security risks which in return affect the accuracy of the system output. However, if accuracy is to be maintained, machine learning logarithms can be used, these logarithms have the ability to sieve, normalize and apply data quality to deliver accurate and insightful data in near real-time. The information obtained from these connected devices in most cases free from a human error which helps one to allocate resources with greater agility and precision thus making profitable decisions.

Autonomous IoT devices produce heterogenic data. The data from these connected devices are produced by different objects with dissimilar hardware platforms, standards, and network. The final data is the combination and correlation of data from multiple sensors and other systems connected to the IoT structure. It doesn't have gaps in it. i.e raw data is accumulated at the central storage point subjects to cloud and data centers. These autonomous IoT devices have the ability to harmonize the data from different sensors. It is very critical to determine if the sensor data has arrived at the required point in the network or data point. This helps one to act on the data preventing incidences or anomalies in real-time since so much data is recorded.

Figure 2. shows a proposed sensing and connected devices architecture

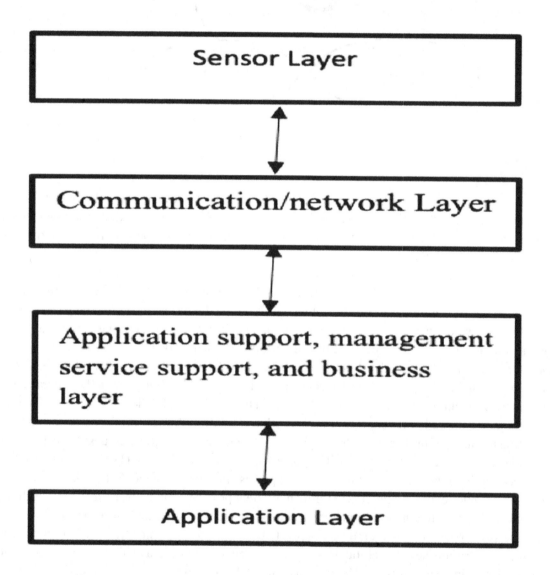

Data from the autonomous IoT device system must be reliable and consistent. This means the data coming from the sensors must be accurate, with patterns over a specific time. The sensor readings are unto precision and repeatability means the sensor produces the same values with the same accuracy over the same location where the sensor is placed. Due to the high heterogeneity of data, the system can be filled with ubiquitous data considering technologies like machine learning that make use of this for making a prediction in the sensing devices.

Sensor Layer

This is the lowest layer of the autonomous IoT devices and it consists of sensors integrated into smart objects. The sensors are connected to the gateways through different platforms, for instance, ultrasonic sensors, RFID, infrared, Bluetooth. However, WAN can be used for the sensor that doesn't necessitate connectivity to sensor aggregators (Zhu, Wang et al. 2010, Ma, Wang et al. 2013). These sensor aggregators allow real-time information to be gathered and processed enabling interconnection of the physical and digital worlds. These sensors are designed for various purposes. Some have the ability to take measures such as air quality, humidity, pressure, temperature, and radiation. The sensor technology used here has the ability to store data to a certain degree and also convert physical properties to signal that can be interpreted by the instruments. It is also important to note that they are classified according to their unique purpose like body sensors, home appliances, and environmental.

Communication /Network Layer

In this layer, the network infrastructure of wired or wireless high-performance communication systems is used as a transport medium for the massive volumes of data produced by the sensors. The different protocols tied within the current network support machine-to-machine communication (Rajandekar and Sikdar 2015, Rossi, de Souza et al. 2019). This layer is regarded as the pillar of autonomous IoT devices with routing, subscribing and publishing as the major services associated with this layer. The application layer and the various operating activities use the communication layer as a channel between them with the capabilities of representing the data link layer. A suitable network connection between the physical devices and the nodes is set up in this layer so that data is shared by the two parties. This is done by the protocols that are configured within the layer.

Application Support, Management Service Support, and Business Layer

This is where the processing of information is made possible through security control protocols, analytics, device management, and process modeling (Ma, Wang et al. 2013). It acts as the manager of the entire system because it's configured with the ability to control application, profit models and business.it also control how information is created, changed and stored however this layer is very vulnerable and prone to attacks from hackers because it allows misuse of the application when business logic is avoided. The business logic is responsible for the management and control of information flow from the user and supporting databases of an application once there is programming flow, the information is susceptible to misuse by the attackers.

The business and process rule engines in this layer filter and route data to the post-processing system to enable calculated decision making in the systems (Malche and Maheshwary 2015). For instance, the data collected has different levels of urgency, some data triggers instant response while others can be stored and used later on for decision making. The rule engines, therefore, automate the processing of data and permit more responsive systems.

Relevant information is extracted using analytics tools from the enormous quantity of raw data and processed at a considerably faster rate. The in-memory facilitates faster decision making and save time for the query. Streaming analytics is another platform where the data flowing in the system is analyzed in real-time and decisions are made promptly.

Application Layer

The definitive goal of this layer is to guarantee the utilization of IoT applications with simplicity and high reliability such as smart cities, homes, cars (Yang, Yue et al. 2011). 2011. Conversely, these services may vary from application to application because they greatly depend on the data collected by the sensor devices. However, the application layer has issues in its functioning and security. Whenever the system is not secure, there are threats that make the entire system vulnerable on both the inside and outside. This means designers at this layer have to be aware of logic errors and buffer (Singla and Sachdeva 2013).

The Challenges Faced by Autonomous IoT Devices

1. Data quality and Management

The main challenge facing data quality and management comes from the implementation of data provenance techniques (Liono, Jayaraman et al. 2019). With IoT, the employment of security to provenance data is still a puzzle because it involves putting in place security measures such as signed hashes. However, as far as communication is concerned, data should be secure. if this is not dealt with, the exposition of sensitive data can occur causing a security breach in the system. Therefore, data provenance must be confidential in that only authorized users can access it (Gouru and Vadlamani 2019).

Applying data provenance in scenarios where the meta-data used to regulate information provenance is bigger than the main data is very challenging because the system produces an enormous amount of data which makes tracing the provenance of an object in big-data very difficult.at the same time collecting evidence from various sources to determine the causes and effect of the un-normally is very problematic.in addition, Provenance data requires unnecessary resource consumption on the network since the meta-data must be broadly accessible and updated so often. The updated made may consume an IoT of bandwidth on the network which can result in slowing down the system performance. The data produced from complete provenance is so huge which makes querying very challenging because different users tend to use different features and values found in the metadata yet the indexing structure in the sensor data storage cannot handle it.

The accessibility and packing of data in the IoT system need to be flexible since real-time sensor data is perhaps of greatest value to the collector who gets in immediately and other parties who may archive it for later use (Feng and Wang 2019). However, expecting this entire request is not possible.it is not enough to use provenance data to spot lineage and the derivation of data. Methodology for flexible query tools that are aimed at assisting next-generation cybersecurity systems must be enabled by the usage of provenance data because users need to trace and track specific records within a particular context or better still detect their discretion. The processing of data through the different layers of the system can result in an alteration of the quality of data since different data formats are introduced at each layer. However, sketching provenance data need to be accessible consequently in order to track the changes induced on the transformation process

The ability to interoperate the different objects connected to the system from different vendors is still a challenge in developing the IoT data quality due to the heterogenic and dynamic nature of autonomous IoT devices (Janssen, Luthra et al. 2019). All objects must be integrated, linked and have the ability to re-use each other's content. However, the use of diverse protocols for communication and application of different data formats makes tracing provenance and data propagation path in the autonomous IoT device very challenging. Error in the measurement of data collected from the different devices can enormously affect the quality of the data got from an IoT system (Côrte-Real, Ruivo et al. 2019). If Information obtained from integration and combination of data from different devices is processed, the final result could not be accurate since there is a variation between the data collected from the individual source and one processed from multiple data. It is essential to annotate the provenance of the information in order to be able to accurately select the origin of information and the processing for each separate application.

Another factor that can greatly after the quality of data in the autonomous IoT device system is the noise in the environment in which the sensors are located. Noise can be any form that can temper with the normal operation of the sensor system. When this happens, the sensor is susceptible to picking wrong signals which later result in errors in the data collected which can be further amplified in the processing application.

2. Privacy and Security Concerns Associated With IoT

The network connection through which IoT operates presents a threat to the security of the system. There is a likely hood of the personal information leakage out through a loophole which may be taken advantage of by malicious people (Hwang 2015). And these threats can originate from outside the network or within. Internal attacks are more serious since they can expose private information. Data flow is spontaneous over the autonomous IoT environment and it involves the use of public networks, therefore an end to end protection of the data should be carefully applied over the whole IoT system (Golchay, Mouël et al. 2011, Hudaib and Albdour 2019). For instance, in smart homes where the user can monitor, manage and compute power usage via the internet, device service providers may gain access to the system and monitor the behavioral pattern of the user with or without their permission which possesses a potential threat to the user's privacy. These service providers may be interested in using the available data for marketing and research purposes. This means when information is leaked at the provider's point, this may cause a threat.

However, end encryption data frameworks can be used to help control and manage data flow within the system thus protecting the user's privacy. The different devices are connected to each other which later presents a threat when they are dynamically moved from one location to another or replaced by a new one. In such a scenario, security protocols in connected things should be kept by the things so that a loophole is not created (Aman, Chua et al. 2019). For example, all the things on the network should operate in the same security procedure thus securing communication between the devices.

IoT environment contains many different devices in various sizes and operations. Most of these devices have different abilities such as storage, constrained batteries and power to process information. However, this can greatly affect the entire system when the security of one thing is breached because it propagates to the other things in the system and in the end it hard to guarantee security with many things. This calls for redesigning the levels of security used depending on the capabilities, roles, and capacities of the devices used in IoT since the same security design cannot be used on these different devices. Most of the end-users don't really know much about the configuration of the IoT systems because it seems so complex to a layman which can cause a security threat to the entire system. However, if an automatic way of applying security policy is put in place it will become much easier for the end-user to secure their privacy.

The integration of RFID and wireless transmission in objects enables tracking using a smartphone and one of the parameters it should have access to is the geo-location of the object and the customers (Ouadou, Sahbani et al. 2019). This violates the privacy of an individual in case the network is hacked and his location exposed. For example, if one is monitoring his/her goods from the manufacturer, malicious people can trace the RFID tags and collapse it within a short time or captures private information about the consumer which permits the misuse of private data.

Sensors, cameras, and RFID technology are widely used in IoT (Schmidt, Petrov et al. 2019) however, IoT is also widely used in providing safety for the public. Since it offers cheap and effective alternatives to human deployment it is enormously used. The more the units on the IoT increases, it becomes a bit hard for an individual to control them which calls for government intervention. This allows the government agencies to follow up on an individual without their permission. This subjects the public to serious infringement to their private security. Most of the above-mentioned challenges are intruder model based, in such a model the challenges are caused by external factors. The communication is intercepted between the IoT devices and hubs during transmission (Askar 2019). Sometimes the machines themselves can impose a challenge on the IoT system. This kind of attack makes the network information and resources unavailable to its deliberate users. This can be due to low storage and limited computation power.

3. Lack of Interpolation, Standardization, and Protocol

For connectivity to be fully realized, faultless programmability should be created through interoperation. Interoperation is characterized by the ability of the devices to be compatibility with the one they communicate with and this is attended when they follow common communication protocols and standards (Kamilaris and Ostermann 2018). However, interoperation is still a big challenge in IoT systems and for it to be dealt with one has to look at it in different dimension i.e technical interoperability: this is about the protocols used in communication between devices as well as their software and physical compatibility. Another dimension is concerned with the format through which the message is communicated; it is referred to as syntactical interoperability (Xiao, Guo et al. 2014). In addition to the above two, semantic interoperability is also key to having a great IoT system; it is characterized by common standards and units of measurement. For instance, different sensors like temperature and radiation sensors should be able to semantically communicate with each other.

The challenge facing interoperation is the proprietary technology that is on a rise. Giant software companies make their devices incompatible with other manufacturer devices (Gilchrist 2016). The varying data produced by heterogeneous devices present an obstacle in the communication between the devices in the IoT systems as there is no data semantics and ordinary standard to interpret the meaning of the data. Also, application programming interfaces (APIs) of different devices are incompatible and need a common API management system layer, which can remove the complexities of involved in smart devices. This complexity is a major setback in device interoperability. Creating a secure communication line is key to every manufacturer of IoT sensing devices but the increase in connectivity of the devices poses a challenge in the autonomous IoT device system and privacy.

The interoperability issues of the IoT devices have metamorphosed in dynamics and operation as more and more devices are getting connected to the IoT ecosystem. The is a need for creating an open application programming interface available for testing, monitoring, and maintenance for regular sensing devices. During the process of implementing, interoperation resources are consumed greatly especially when implementing security. Since different devices have different APIs, software interfaces that bridge the communication gap between these devices present a hurdle to systems with many IoT sensing devices.

Furthermore, the availability of diverse operating systems, data structure and programming languages, platform interoperability challenges. Manufacturers are developing single user/single-tasking operating for specific IoT devices with unique data structure and programming languages. This creates multitasking and uniformity difficult for the application developers to come up with a platform that cuts across all the technologies used in the different IoT devices.

The Opportunities Associated With Autonomous IoT Devices

Predictive Maintenance

The internet of things has emerged from many different trends with the ubiquity of the internet and the cost of productivity involved in devices. These devices are becoming more powerful covering a wide range of industries creating smarter machines. These machines are becoming connected to the internet. The major facility of IoT is that we have to understand the state of our devices in order to improve the current business models and human experience that is to say in smart homes. In the industrial setting, with the emergence of IoT means, managers can understand the operations of the industry better and integrating data-driven decisions is made quicker. The manufacturers can reduce processes through these evidence-based decisions which created a high return on investment and improve the safety of the environment. The vision of most of these industries is smarter factories with an adaptable mechanism to operate with high efficiency and productivity.

The BCG predicts that by 2020 the IoT market will be more than $ 267 Billion (Assante, Romano et al. 2018). These estimates indicate a rapidly growing arena for the internet of things devices. This causes a disruption where industries have to evolve to creating predictable maintenance of IoT devices, predictive quality, and asset conditioning monitoring. In this chapter, the researchers highlight more on predictive maintenance. Industries are interested in increasing operational reliability and reduce costs. This is done by performing regular checks which may pose a challenge on knowing when to perform the check. With predictive maintenance, industrialists estimate the optimal time for failure. This maximizes pieces of equipment lifetime and quality maintenance of the products.

Figure 3. showing the prosed predictive maintenance infrastructure in the internet of things

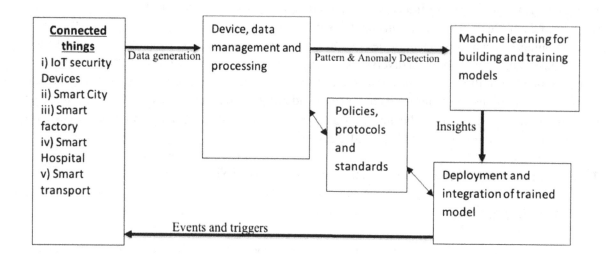

Today, machines are generating lots of data. This calls for the great infrastructure of machine learning integration with IoT to take advantage of this data to generate insights for predictive maintenance and product scalability. This integration of machine learning helps to build and train the model to predict when devices are going to fail. This means the trained model will be deployed to work in the industrial facility, IoT deployment center like smart cities or in homes. This means these devices can be operated locally with their triggers available for anomaly detection. The data is analyzed for predictive quality or failure of different industrial devices/equipment to reduce costs, prevent unplanned production outages and optimize maintenance work schedules.

This creates an intelligent connected IoT concerns

- Device security (keep devices and data secures)
- Downtime (operated at top performance even without cloud connectivity)
- Legacy equipment (onboard greenfield and brownfield devices)
- Security policies

IoT helps to improve the maintenance of systems by enabling a user to monitor the parameters of the system in real-time thus lowering labor cost and improving production (Gopalakrishnan, Kar et al. 2019, Pecht and Kang 2019). This maintenance is made up of a small electronic circuit that is attached to systems, these are usually sensors fixed for the parameter being monitored. Sometimes, antennas help in sending information to the gateway. The gateway then relays the data collected by the sensor to the analytic platform where the data is analyzed and the decision made accessible according to the configurations. This system can be made to send data autonomously in real-time.

For IoT to be used in predictive maintenance, it is calibrated in a way that when a certain critical value of the parameter being monitored is triggered, data transfer is immediately sent out to the maintenance team to act accordingly. The system can also be configured to initiate a certain protocol to prevent further damage to the system. For example, the IoT attachment system can automatically shut down the machine operation when the wear and tear of some parts are detected. With is the incidence, there is increased safety, efficiency and productivity in areas or places of operations where predictive maintenance cannot be easily realized by human visibility. For example, in mines where it's hard to realize developing cracks in the rocks or concrete walls. Autonomous IoT devices are connected to the Rock bolts which are equipped with a strain sensor which detects if the bolt is still attached to the wall or not, it then monitors the wall in real-time to give readings about the force, strain, and stress experienced by the wall under different conditions. This information helps the maintenance team to take on the necessary precaution to prevent damage through predicting the patterns developed from the autonomous assistant or system.

IoT technologies can also be integrated into conveyor belts to monitor the rolling speed and direction. In case the belt has a defect, the operators are able to change it during maintenance thus optimizing productivity. This approach allows systems to be installed rapidly reducing the installation cost because transmission is automated. By using IoT attached systems, the status information from the sensor can be used to activate reinforcement in predictive maintenance thus enhancing customer care and also improve the reputation of the product.

Operations and Supply Chain Management

There is a great deal of excitement around the internet of things and its emphasis on many organizations due to its performance and autonomous application infrastructure it possesses. This is an opportunity for the supply chain alterations and simplicity at all levels in the chain through turning the supply chain objective into intelligent and communication devices like sensors places to devices, the sensor collects data through internet communication (Neelakandan, Tyagi et al. 2019). The supply chain delivers products from raw materials to customers using the internet of things to engineer the flow of information, distribution of products and flow of money. The figure shows the flow of products, information from all stakeholders in the supply chain and integration of information repository with the help of IoT devices like RED (I) product flow can be materials, finished products, services, returns, and replacements, recycling, and disposal (ii) The information can be informed of former information, invoices, orders, sales literature, technology, and product specification and policies governing trade The researcher used a clothing business supply chain as an example of an opportunity bought about the involvement of IoT in supply chain management (Naskar, Basu et al. 2020).

The use of RFID was adopted in the proposal model of designing the infrastructure of IoT to enable efficiency in the supply chain. RFID uses radio waves to read and capture information stored on an RFID tag. This information is then stored in the cloud to be used by all stakeholders in the supply chain using an RFID reader. This facilitates asset tracking, reduces the time for holding stock and monitors the operational Excellency of the product in the supply chain. The cloud can be used in the designing of process automation and visibility by integrating tools like machine learning for pattern prediction

Figure 4. shows the implementation architecture in operations and supply chain management

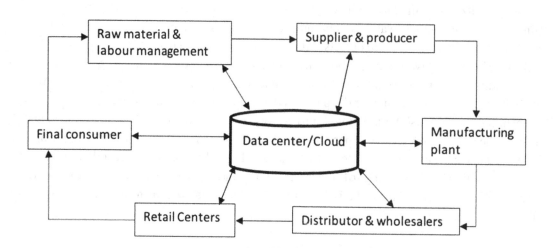

Internet-based information transfer between customers, suppliers, and companies has greatly improved over the years since the invention of the internet. Information integration, mechanism coordination, and sharing have become effective and efficient in the supply chain with the use of the internet. However, real-time information flows and material flows is still a gap in the supply chain. With the introduction of the internet of things, this gap is narrowed. It enables automatic information collection, real-time processing, the omnipresent connection between inventory and Information flows and ubiquitous computing.

IoT greatly uses Auto Identification based on devices like RFID which is of low cost to identify the unique identity number on the inventory. The RFID readers extract the identity number and synchronize it with the networked databases; this is done without human aid thus saving operation costs and producing more accurate results with fewer misreading. The IoT provides information technology infrastructure which facilitates a secure and reliable means of exchange of material and information. It makes it possible to link things irrespective of time and location. The unique identification number read by the RFID reader is linked to the database which contains information about the inventory thus saving time

Internet of things captures information more accurately and in real-time which speeds up information flow compared with the internet. The accuracy of this system in the business process provides a viable advantage in terms of process maximization. The ability of the RFID tags to be read simultaneously onto the computer from different orientation anywhere as long as they are within the range speeds the operation process in the supply chain. With the continuous capturing of the information about the items, a more responsive and lively fashion is created in the supply chain.

It also enables the tracking and tracing of the material flow of every supply chain. The manufacturer, supplier, and customer are able to get information about the products' location, transportation, and state in the real-world and reconcile it with information in the databases which were created at the time of fabrication. Through the IoT, the current status and the history of an item can be monitored continuously and the supply chain is improved based on the accessibility of dynamic, accurate data. Since every inventory's tag has the history of the items and particular information about the items, there is no need to open the container which saves time.

Application of IoT in Homes and how it Enhances our Home

Every day, new development is happening in the technology world. integrating IoT in homes is one of the areas that are greatly developing. Almost everything is automated to make life easier thus improving productivity and quality of life which in return optimizes the use of home systems (Miori and Russo 2014, Kumar, Shen et al. 2019). With just a simple click on your smartphone, you are able to control your entire home thanks to IoT. This helps one to manage things conveniently, effectively and efficiently. There are several applications in homes where this technology is greatly utilized to satisfy behavioral values for the user.

IoT system is used in AC systems. It monitors the rate at which the air is saturated by pollutants using things a sensor. The information is then sent to the database which is configured to have a threshold value beyond which appropriate ventilation can be established, this is termed as data analysis. This application helps to improve air quality in the building in real-time thus saving power consumption. Market value, as well as the brand image of the building, is also greatly enhanced.

IoT has enormously improved power consumption, the end-user is able to get reliable power services from the power distribution companies. This technology is in cooperated in the meter thus automating its operation. The technology is able to sense power outrage and send data to the server where it is processed and analyzed. The information got from the processed data is able to help in detecting the source of the outrage at the individual level. The monitoring done with this technology saves time and its effective in restoring power quickly in case of any disconnection due to unknown reasons. IoT can also be used to automatically control the lighting system of a home thus cutting the cost of power consumption.

With the use of IoT, one can easily implement predictive maintenance for home appliances. For example, one is able to get collect data about the operation of a dishwasher or others that fall in that category. The analyzed information is able to point out points in the machine that is likely to get a malfunction in the future. This gives the end-user time to do preventive maintenance before the machine completely breaks down. It is cost-effective and saved time.

CONCLUSION

In this chapter, we detailed the technical and theoretical aspects of autonomous sensing by detailing the characteristics of IoT sensing, connectivity, applications and challenges. The integration of autonomous robots and humans will support functional and operational developments that will help various sectors expand their capabilities and services. It may also create positive awareness among the readers towards integrating different autonomous devices in their societies to ease work and live a simplified. Industrial sectors especially the logistics company, mining industry will use this chapter to increase and improve productivity, better monitoring, and improving the safety of people by reallocating them from risk work. Policymakers or the government will get useful information in this book chapter. Future research has to consider including the current progress, 802.11ah, 802,11ax, ieee fog standard, ieee mec standards.

REFERENCES

Alli, A. A., & Alam, M. M. (2019). SecOFF-FCIoT: Machine learning-based secure offloading in Fog-Cloud of things for smart city applications. *Internet of Things*, *7*, 100070. doi:10.1016/j.iot.2019.100070

Alur, R. (2016). *Systems computing challenges in the Internet of Things*. arXiv preprint arXiv:1604.02980

Aman, M. N. (2019). Hardware Primitives-Based Security Protocols for the Internet of Things. In Cryptographic Security Solutions for the Internet of Things. IGI Global.

Askar, A. (2019). *Internet of things (IoT) device registration*. Google Patents.

Assante, D. (2018). Internet of Things education: Labor market training needs and national policies. In *2018 IEEE Global Engineering Education Conference (EDUCON)*. IEEE. 10.1109/EDUCON.2018.8363459

Barnaghi, P. M. (2015). Challenges for Quality of Data in Smart Cities. *J. Data and Information Quality, 6*(2-3), 6:1-6:4.

Bechtsis, D., Tsolakis, N., Vlachos, D., & Iakovou, E. (2017). Sustainable supply chain management in the digitalisation era: The impact of Automated Guided Vehicles. *Journal of Cleaner Production*, *142*, 3970–3984. doi:10.1016/j.jclepro.2016.10.057

Birk, A., & Carpin, S. (2006). Merging occupancy grid maps from multiple robots. *Proceedings of the IEEE*, *94*(7), 1384–1397. doi:10.1109/JPROC.2006.876965

Côrte-Real, N. (2019). Leveraging internet of things and big data analytics initiatives in European and American firms: Is data quality a way to extract business value? *Information & Management*.

Feng, P., & Wang, P. (2019). Matching Technology of Internet of Things Based on Multiple Linear Regression Model in Urban Management. *In The International Conference on Cyber Security Intelligence and Analytics*. Springer.

Gilchrist, A. (2016). *Industry 4.0: the industrial internet of things*. Apress. doi:10.1007/978-1-4842-2047-4

Golchay, R. (2011). *Towards bridging IOT and cloud services: proposing smartphones as mobile and autonomic service gateways*. arXiv preprint arXiv:1107.4786

Gopalakrishnan, P. K. (2019). Live Demonstration: Autoencoder-Based Predictive Maintenance for IoT. In *2019 IEEE International Symposium on Circuits and Systems (ISCAS)*. IEEE. 10.1109/IS-CAS.2019.8702230

Gouru, N., & Vadlamani, N. (2019). DistProv-Data Provenance in Distributed Cloud for Secure Transfer of Digital Assets with Ethereum Blockchain using ZKP. *International Journal of Open Source Software and Processes*, *10*(3), 1–18. doi:10.4018/IJOSSP.2019070101

Hudaib, A., & Albdour, L. (2019). Fog Computing to Serve the Internet of Things Applications: A Patient Monitoring System. *International Journal of Fog Computing*, *2*(2), 44–56. doi:10.4018/IJFC.2019070103

Hwang, Y. H. (2015). Iot security & privacy: threats and challenges. In *Proceedings of the 1st ACM Workshop on IoT Privacy, Trust, and Security*. ACM. 10.1145/2732209.2732216

Janssen, M., Luthra, S., Mangla, S., Rana, N. P., & Dwivedi, Y. K. (2019). Challenges for adopting and implementing IoT in smart cities. *Internet Research*, *29*(6), 1589–1616. doi:10.1108/INTR-06-2018-0252

Kamilaris, A., & Ostermann, F. (2018). *Geospatial Analysis and Internet of Things in Environmental Informatics.* arXiv preprint arXiv:1808.01895

Kumar, D. (2019). All things considered: an analysis of IoT devices on home networks. *28th {USENIX} Security Symposium ({USENIX} Security 19.*

Liono, J., Jayaraman, P. P., Qin, A. K., Nguyen, T., & Salim, F. D. (2019). QDaS: Quality driven data summarisation for effective storage management in Internet of Things. *Journal of Parallel and Distributed Computing*, *127*, 196–208. doi:10.1016/j.jpdc.2018.03.013

Ma, M. (2013). Data management for internet of things: Challenges, approaches and opportunities. In *2013 IEEE International conference on green computing and communications and IEEE Internet of Things and IEEE cyber, physical and social computing.* IEEE. 10.1109/GreenCom-iThings-CPSCom.2013.199

Malche, T., & Maheshwary, P. (2015). Harnessing the Internet of things (IoT): A review. *International Journal (Toronto, Ont.)*, *5*(8).

Miori, V., & Russo, D. (2014). Domotic evolution towards the IoT. In *2014 28th International Conference on Advanced Information Networking and Applications Workshops.* IEEE. 10.1109/WAINA.2014.128

Naskar, S. (2020). A literature review of the emerging field of IoT using RFID and its applications in supply chain management. In Securing the Internet of Things: Concepts, Methodologies, Tools, and Applications. IGI Global.

Neelakandan, S. (2019). *Robotic process automation for supply chain management operations.* Google Patents.

Ouadou, M, (2019). A Data-Filtering Approach for Large-Scale Integrated RFID and Sensor Networks. In *International Conference on Mobile, Secure, and Programmable Networking.* Springer. 10.1007/978-3-030-22885-9_7

Patel & Patel. (2016). Internet of things-IOT: definition, characteristics, architecture, enabling technologies, application & future challenges. *International Journal of Engineering Science and Computing, 6*(5).

Pecht & Kang. (2019). *Predictive Maintenance in the IoT Era.* Academic Press.

Pratt, G. A., & Williamson, M. M. (1995). Series elastic actuators. In *Proceedings 1995 IEEE/RSJ International Conference on Intelligent Robots and Systems. Human Robot Interaction and Cooperative Robots.* IEEE. 10.1109/IROS.1995.525827

Rajandekar, A., & Sikdar, B. (2015). A survey of MAC layer issues and protocols for machine-to-machine communications. *IEEE Internet of Things Journal, 2*(2), 175–186. doi:10.1109/JIOT.2015.2394438

Rossi, F. D. (2019). Network Support for IoT Ecosystems. In Enabling Technologies and Architectures for Next-Generation Networking Capabilities. IGI Global.

Schmidt, M. (2019). Wireless power supply for a RFID based sensor platform. In *Smart Systems Integration; 13th International Conference and Exhibition on Integration Issues of Miniaturized Systems.* VDE.

Singla, A., & Sachdeva, R. (2013). Review on security issues and attacks in wireless sensor networks. *International Journal of Advanced Research in Computer Science and Software Engineering, 3*(4).

Xiao, G. (2014). User interoperability with heterogeneous IoT devices through transformation. *IEEE Transactions on Industrial Informatics, 10*(2), 1486–1496. doi:10.1109/TII.2014.2306772

Yang, Z. (2011). Study and application on the architecture and key technologies for IOT. In *2011 International Conference on Multimedia Technology*. IEEE. 10.1109/ICMT.2011.6002149

Zhu, Q. (2010). Iot gateway: Bridgingwireless sensor networks into internet of things. In *2010 IEEE/IFIP International Conference on Embedded and Ubiquitous Computing. IEEE*. 10.1109/EUC.2010.58

Chapter 2
Challenges for Convergence of Cloud and IoT in Applications and Edge Computing

Rashmi S.
Dayananda Sagar College of Engineering, India

Roopashree S.
 https://orcid.org/0000-0003-1327-1267
Dayananda Sagar University, India

Sathiyamoorthi V.
 https://orcid.org/0000-0002-7012-3941
Sona College of Technology, India

ABSTRACT

Cloud computing and internet of things (IoT) are two disparate technologies that can be united for a common purpose as in an operating profit. The technologies are integral parts of modern sophisticated human life. In the future, it is destined to proliferate boundlessly covering utmost spheres. This chapter describes the challenges faced in adopting the two technologies. Edge computing includes both computing and processing the information are carried at the edge of the IoT devices where vast information gathered instead of relying on the central location. Benefits include avoiding latency issues, improving the performance of the application, and cost effectiveness as it reduces the data volume to be processed in cloud/centralized location. In the advent of IoT devices, edge computing is a vital step in building any of its application which sends and receives enormous information to and from the cloud over the course of operations. Applications such as virtual reality and smart systems are benefited by edge computing as they expect higher rate of response and processing speed. A case study on video surveillance is done in this chapter.

DOI: 10.4018/978-1-7998-3111-2.ch002

INTRODUCTION

Cloud Computing and Internet of Things (IOT) are two disparate technologies that can be united for a common purpose as in an operating profit. The two technologies are integral parts of modern sophisticated human life. In future, it is destined to proliferate boundlessly covering utmost spheres. Edge computing for IoT enhances the deployments of IoT devices by processing the data closer to end devices. Non-IoT edge computing is much different when compared to IoT edge. IoT devices possess limited capability with respect to processing and storing the voluminous unstructured data generated by them. The edge environment will in-turn overcome the above limitations and also reduces the cost of the device as it can off-load the computation and storage to edge. Some of the industries that would benefit from edge computing are manufacturing, retail, oil and gas and healthcare. Some of consumer benefits would be in gaming, Augmented Reality / Virtual Reality and healthcare.

SIGNIFICANCE OF CLOUD IN IoT APPLICATIONS

IOT devices used in large scale industrial applications such as software actuators, sensors and other computer devices give rise to enormous data every second. Enterprises face problems is managing aforesaid data. Microsoft Azure and Amazon Web Services (AWS) are the most common platforms that provide a solution to applications by endowing themselves as a Cloud Backend for storage as well as for analysis and computation. This enhances the power of IOT and also simplifies interfacing with mobile and web apps.

COMPARISON BETWEEN IoT AND CLOUD

An inquiry of the essential characteristics of the Cloud and IOT gives an insight on the whole idea of integration (Atlam et al, 2017) as shown in Figure 1. To start with, in terms of Mobility, IOT refers to Pervasive computing (Low Mobility) whereas Cloud refers to ubiquitous Computing (High Mobility). Pervasive Computing includes devices that can be fit in any required place. Ubiquitous Computing can happen anywhere and everywhere irrespective of the location, device and format. IOT mainly uses real physical components such as sensors, RFID tag etc., Cloud is mainly dependent on virtual resources. Processing and storage capacities of IOT is either bounded or nil which conflicts with Cloud having boundless capacities with respect to processor and storage capacity. Internet plays a significant role in both domains, but Cloud uses it to deliver its services and IOT as a seamless point of connection. Though, both IOT and Cloud contributes to Big data but in a different way. IOT serves as a data generator for Big data applications. Cloud serves as one of the best platforms for handling the Big Data.

Figure 1. Comparison between IoT and cloud

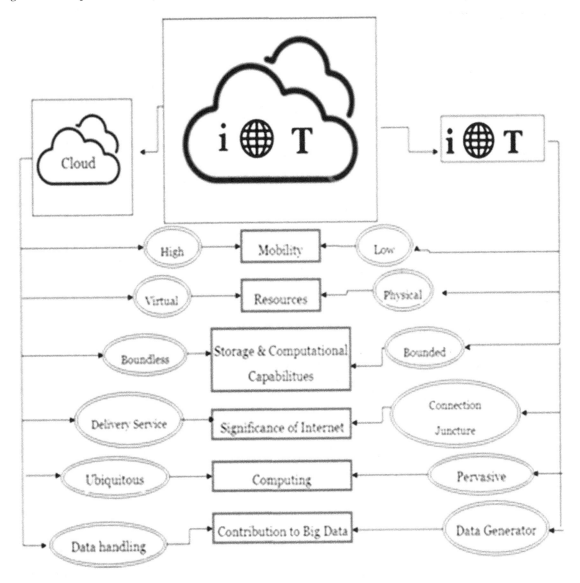

CHALLENGES AND ISSUES IN IoT AND CLOUD

IoT CHALLENGES

The skeleton of a sample IOT system consists of the following steps as shown in Figure 2. Another notion is a layered approach. Various researchers and experts have arrived at conventional architecture 3-layer, 4-layer and 5-layer architecture. Figure 3 shows a 5-layered approach (Said & Masud, 2013), (Liu et al, 2016). The lowermost Perception layer involves identifying the information in the real world and gather them using RFID, different sensors, GPS, IR, Actuators etc., Network layer is concerned with safe and authentic transmission of information across distributed networks. Support Layer deals mainly with Data

Processing, Storage and Analytics. Application Layer refers to Industrial and consumer Applications. The topmost Layer, Business Layer, deals with system management and business models.

Figure 2. Sample IoT System

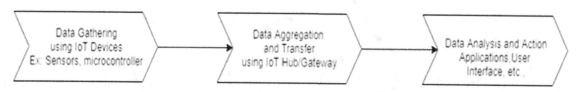

Figure 3. A 5-layered approach

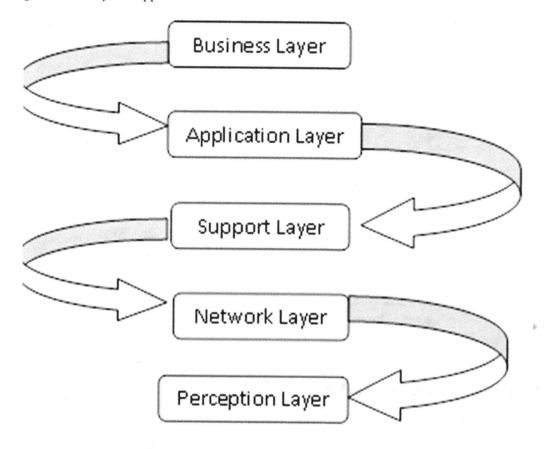

Security: Security (Vijayalakshmi & Arockiam, 2016), (Laeeq & Shamsi, 2015) is considered to be the most noteworthy challenge in most IoT applications. IoT basically is a galaxy of connected entities. Increase in connected space by addition of new nodes actually increases prospects for the hackers to enter into the system. Incompetent designs of the IoT based system gives way for the malicious users causing serious threats. As an example of Smart Healthcare, an Electronic Health Record is a convenient arrangement between the patient and the guardian or any well-wisher to keep a constant watch on the health condition using a connected device. If designed and used appropriately, it helps a medical practitioner on a clinical decision in case of an emergency. However, the health information may be used for a business purpose by an insurance agent breaching the confidentiality. Use of automated insulin pumps, drug infusion pumps that can be controlled remotely can also be misused.

In terms of the 5-layered IOT architecture shown in Figure 3, the Perception layer is prone to Denial of Service attack, malicious data/node attack, collusion attack, reply attacks, jammers etc., As the next layer is concerned with secure transmission, DOS attack and man-in-the-middle attack, computer viruses, eavesdropping, susceptible network servers, false routing etc., are the challenges to be faced. The support layer is also susceptible to DOS attack and malicious insider attack. Application layer faces challenges in dealing with mass data, cross site scripting which is an injection attack, malicious code attack and privacy protection. The Business layer is subject to business logic attack and zero day attack.

Privacy: Smart devices such as cell phones, smart watches, Smart TV, Smart Toaster etc., contribute majorly to compromise with private information. Technological changes have made possible to track location information of smart Phones although GPS services are not active. Some sensors and time zone information aid in this regard. It also helps to predict the lifestyle and pattern of the community. Such data may fall into wrong hands violating privacy law (Sun et al, 2017), (Salas-Vega et al, 2015).

Privacy issues can be classified as:

Location Privacy: Location based services play a vital role in the smart systems and social media. While the users are habituated with the conveniences provided by these services, it also has the threat of disclosing geo-localized history of users

Data Protection: As shown in the sample IOT system (Figure 2), the first step includes data collection which involves huge data. This data has to be protected from Data Falsification, Device manipulation, theft of identity, data and IP, cyber crime and network manipulation

Consumer Trust: Different challenges in IOT further dispirit the customers to procure smart devices. That disposes another challenge to keep up the true potential of IOT

Governing Laws: Smart systems based on IOT have customers distributed globally across the world. As the governing laws vary across regions, the data controllers in IOT system affected and expected to adapt to the regional laws accordingly.

Interoperability Issues: Many researchers and developers have felt a dearth of Interoperability Technology standards (Konduru & Bharamagoudra, 2017). Interoperability perks up the monetary benefit of the device/product in question in the market. The main concerns are dealing and handling with data while inter-switching between heterogeneous systems. Many organizations such as IETF, ITU, and IEEE are working towards the same. IT giants such as Microsoft, Apple, Google etc., have their share in this contribution. An interoperability framework needs to be designed at different levels.

Machine Level: In order to establish interconnectedness between different machines, compatibility in their software and hardware configurations has to be ensured

Data Level: Information from different IOT devices (sensors/actuators) is in different formats. When an application uses a collection of such devices, some conversion and computing is needed to arrive at a common data format.

Technology Level: IOT uses short, medium and large range communication technologies such as RFID, WiFi, QR code, Ethernet, GPS, Satellite etc., Interaction and communication between these technologies is a challenge.

Intelligent Analysis and Actions: A part of the IOT implementation is to mine information for testing and scrutiny. The technologies that assist in analysis of data collected from IOT devices are Computer Vision, Natural-Language processing and speech recognition. Oddity or insufficient data may lead to imprecise analysis causing false positives or false negatives. This limits the algorithmic efficiencies. IOT essentially deals with unstructured and real-time data. Some traditional applications use outdated former systems that are not well versed with data interaction in unstructured format. Managing real time dynamic data also becomes a challenge in such case.

Advanced analytics is the source of intelligent actions.IOT data demands instant action without which data becomes outdated. Rapid changes in data require new calibration and calculation in a continuous manner. This requires advanced machine serviceability. Some applications build machines that persuade human behaviour. Deep Learning tools are nowadays dominating the area. However, the impulsive behaviour of machines in unpredictable conditions is a challenge. This also affects the trust in application and as a consequence the acceptance rate decelerates.

CLOUD CHALLENGES

Cloud computing and cloud technologies are another giant in the new era that has spread its wings far and wide across domains. The sub-headings under the challenges in cloud are mostly similar to that IOT. Some of the common challenges are

Security: Various security risks and threats are discussed in (Shuijing, 2014), (Wadhwa & Gupta, S,2015), (Dooley et al, 2018). Distributed Denial-Of-Service (DDOS) attacks are common in a networked environment. Widely used yahoo website had suffered from DDOS attack in the year 2000. A Cloud Service Provider (CSP) needs to ensure availability, confidentiality and integrity. However, if a CSP is attacked by DDOS attack, it becomes hard to maintain availability. The different types of DOS and DDOS attacks on cloud can be Bandwidth attack, Amplification attack, ICMP Flood, DNS Flood, HTTP GET Flood, Reflector Attack etc., (Alotaibi, 2015) Man-in-the-middle (MITM)and playback attacks (**Amazon, 2015**). also contributes to IP Spoofing. CSP are threatened by attacks such as Guest-hopping, SQL injection, Side channel, malicious insider and data storage security (Turab, 2013). In addition to these, there are other security issues. Cloud users are given an opportunity to interact with CSP directly through Application Programming Interfaces (APIs). Security protocols must beamalgamated with APIs if not the interaction channel becomes unsafe. Simple registration procedures and interfaces may be misused by spammers to gain access to the services and stealthily discover passwords. This leads to hijacking of accounts and services. Data crash and unlawful access to confidential data is another threat.

Privacy (Liu et al, 2015), (Takabi et al, 2010), (Lar et al, 2011): Data Protection is one of the major fear factors that Cloud Service Users (CSU) faces. CSU panic to store confidential data away from their premises, the reason being loss and violation of data. In order to ensure that there is no loss of data, multiple copies of data had to be maintained by the CSP. This further increases the risk of data violation and breaches. As the security protocols are heterogeneous, the attackers now had to find the weakest link where one of the copies was available. Data synchronization among all the copies was an additional overhead. Most importantly, whenever there is a request to delete data, CSU must be sure that the corresponding CSP has completed deleted all of its copies. This requires an external auditing procedure. Data transmission in the distributed environment during proliferation is a concern. Data centres are geographically distributed and local laws and regulations may not be sufficient. As per the news stated in "The New York Times" in March 2010(Steve Lohr, 2010), Netflix cancelled its $1 Million contest over privacy concerns raised by Federal Trade Commission (FTC). The contest would help to enrich its business by building better ways for movie recommendations. However, it was blamed to disclose anonymous information of its clients that could be used to identify them.

Virtualization Issues (Han et al, 2015): Virtualization is the core of cloud environment that allows its computing resources such as memory, storage, operating systems, and networks to be virtualized. As it consists of multiple devices, both physical and virtual, privacy concerns arise as to whether all the diverse devices should be given equal privileges. User roles should be clearly defined and granular separation of roles and responsibilities has to be made to address this concern. A hypervisor controls multiple VMs. An attack on hypervisor would be hazardous to all VMs under it. All VMs creation and initiation procedures are stored in hypervisor. In addition, configuration files, status of all VMs (active or dormant) are also stored here. An attack to this location would break all VMs.

Interoperability (Mezgár & Rauschecker, 2014), (Rashidi et al, 2013): As known, CSPs are flexible in terms of usage but the process of integration and migration to cloud services has not been evolved at a greater extent. The organizations face difficulty in switching their services from one vendor to another vendor. There might exist some interoperability issues along with some system support uses during the migration to cloud platform. For example, applications developed on Linux Platform might not function properly on the Windows platform. The barriers involved in transition of an application from one cloud to another are:

i)   Restructuring the application stack on the new cloud
ii)   Establishing the network environment on the new cloud to provide uninterrupted services
iii) Set up security protocols similar to earlier cloud
iv)   Management of applications in the new cloud
v)   Encryption and decryption of data before and after transition between clouds

Furthermore, interoperability among heterogeneous data formats is difficult. To address the interoperability issue, different types of alliances can be formed by the CSPs. Federated clouds and Hybrid clouds are among them. Federated clouds are those in which the CSPs arrive at a mutual agreement and build a trust boundary that helps to scale and backup during a disaster. Hybrid Clouds allows applications to select resources/services from different clouds simultaneously by using crossed trust boundaries between CSPs.

Sky Computing (Keahey et al, 2009) is a secure way to access a remote resource by a user. It congregates a distributed trusted environment and enables users to manage remote resources. Multitier, e-commerce applications or databases swarmed on different clouds can benefit from sky computing. To facilitate Sky computing, a high-quality network connectivity is expected from CSP and CSU. Other issues include Performance and Service Level Agreements. To deal with these issues, a Virtual Network (ViNe) was used. ViNe router (VR) is the machine where ViNe software is installed. A virtual cluster is deployed with ViNe. VR is made available in every LAN section. APIs are put forward by the providers for virtual networking. In case ViNe services are unavailable, the VP can manage traffic across LAN sections. An association is established between IaaS providers, Application providers and Deployment orchestrators to uphold trust. However, the challenge of differentiated SLAs on varied infrastructure levels still exist.

With all the challenges taken to consideration, both IOT and Cloud computing has its own benefits and gains, and they are considered to be the future of Information and Communication Technology (ICT). The two main domains can be converged in two ways. IOT features and services can be brought into Cloud or Cloud services can be brought into IOT. Convergence of IOT and Cloud may give rise to a new set of challenges.

CHOICE OF COMMUNICATION PROTOCOLS FOR CONNECTING IoT AND CLOUD

The essence of IOT lies in its ability to connect and communicate with other devices/elements to deliver worthy business. One of the key factors to achieve this includes deploying an appropriate communication protocol. A communication protocol defines a set of rules for interaction between two or more elements of the system. It may include syntax, semantics, error recover methods, synchronization procedures etc., The requirements for IOT communication covers a broad spectrum. A possibility of all-in-one approach is fairy lesser. For instance, a smart home application requirement includes Wi-Fi, Ethernet or Bluetooth connections where as a smart farming or any remote application may require satellite network or mobile network. Consequently, the challenge here is to understand the requirements during the initial architectural and technological decisions. The communication protocols used in Application Layer in Figure 3 are MQTT, CoAP, AMQP and HTTP.

Message Queuing Telemetry Transport Protocol (MQTT): MQTT (Akbar et al, 2017) is Machine-to-Machine (M2M) communication protocol. It enables communication between low bandwidth networks over an unreliable network. It has a publish-subscribe method of communication. Its actors are broker, publisher and subscriber. The communication is initiated by the publisher by publishing the message with a specific Key-name. The broker is the intermediary that puts all such messages in queue. All subscribers for that Key-name gets the message with a push notification. Many IOT systems has used MQTT protocol in the area of robotics, medical, education, social media etc.,

Constrained Application Protocol (CoAP): The protocol has been designed by a working group called Constrained RESTful Environments (CoRE) in IETF. CoAP (Lerche et al, 2012) is apt for low bandwidth networks. It has compatibility with HTTP and can use its GET, POST, DELETE and PUT methods. However, it requires that the transport layer protocol to be UDP and not TCP.

CoAP has two layers: The upper Request/Response and the lower Messaging Layer. The Request/Response layer operates on resources using the earlier mentioned HTTP's methods. The messaging layer is responsible for ensuring reliability and also duplicate message detection. A message can be of four types:

1. Confirmable- A message where acknowledgment is needed
2. Non-Confirmable- A message for which no acknowledgment is needed
3. Acknowledgment- An acknowledgment message sent in response to Confirmable message
4. Reset- A message that could not be processed

CoAP has the following features as well:

1. Resource observation: it uses best effort mechanism by publish/subscribe method to track resources and its clients
2. Block Transfers: Data is transferred to and from the devices in blocks.
3. Multicast: A part of IP multicast feature is supported to enable group communication

4.   Resource Discovery: CoRE Link format contains the resource information. CoAP identifies them through a URI

Table 1. (Naik, 2017). Comparison of Communication Protocols

Sl No	Characteristic	Lowest	Lower	Average	High
1	Message Overhead	CoAP	MQTT	AMQP	HTTP
2	Power Consumption	CoAP	MQTT	AMQP	HTTP
3	Resource Requirements	CoAP	MQTT	AMQP	HTTP
4	Latency	CoAP	MQTT	AMQP	HTTP
5	Interoperability	MQTT	AMQP	CoAP	HTTP
6	Reliability	HTTP	CoAP	AMQP	MQTT
7	Security	MQTT	CoAP	HTTP	AMQP
8	Standardisation	MQTT	AMQP	CoAP	HTTP
9	IOT usage/ M2M	HTTP	CoAP	AMQP	MQTT

CoAP provides security using a transport layer protocol called Datagram Transport Layer Security (DTLS). The key features of DTLS are integrity, confidentiality, authentication, anti-replay protection and non-repudiation. It is a version of Transport Layer Security (TLS) that is meant for end-to-end communication securely using cryptography. CoAP has 4 modes of security (Dragomir et al, 2016):

1.   NoSec: Security (DTLS) is disabled. Packet transmission takes place with UDP over IP
2.   PreSharedKey: Security is enabled. Symmetric shared keys are used for either one-to-one or multicast communication.
3.   RawPublicKey:Security is enabled. Asymmetric shared keys are used.
4.   Certificates:Security is enabled. A X.5009 certificate is supplemented with a pair of asymmetric keys.

CoAP in combination with DTLS, uses Elliptic Curve cryptography (ECC) for RawPublicKey and Certificates. Elliptic Curve Digital Signature Algorithm (ECDSA) and Elliptic Curve Diffie-Hellman Algorithm (ECDHE) is also employed for authentication and key agreement techniques.

Advanced Message Queuing Protocol (AMQP): AMQP (Vinoski, 2006), (Fernandes et al, 2013) is a standard messaging protocol. AMQP supports a c convenient message transmission in different language/ platform. It can transmit either using publish/subscribe model or point-to-point communication model. It uses a TCP connection ensuring at-least-once, at-most-once and exactly-once message delivery. Two kinds of messages bare and annotated are carried, the one sent and the one actually received. Similar to CoAP, AMQP also uses TLS over TCP. And hence implementation on IOT devices is intricate.

As Hyper Text Transfer Protocol (HTTP) is a much commonly used protocol, detailed discussion is not made here (Naik, 2017) gives a comparative study based on different parameters. Table 1 shows a comparison of the above discussed protocols based on different parameters.

The protocols, HTTP, AMQP and MQTT use TCP whereas CoAP use UDP. UDP transmits in datagrams and hence has a lower response time when compared to other protocols. Bandwidth utilization and latency is lowest is case of CoAP and then MQTT, AMQP and HTTP in increasing order. The HTTP offers highest levels of interoperability but lags behind in reliability. With respect to security, MQTT may rely on simplest username and password mechanism. COAP works with DTLS and IPSec that takes care of integrity, authentication and encryption. HTTP has HTTP Basic and HTTP Digest as authentication methods. AMQP has the robust security with single-port TLS, pure TLS and Tunnel TLS models.

Figure 4. Protocols used in each layer of the Internet model

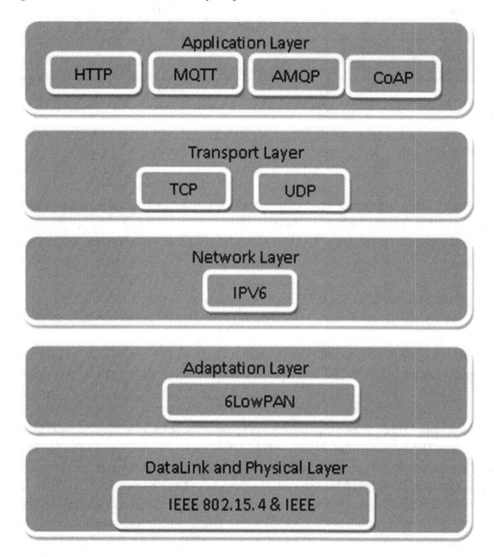

CoAP has a set of extended services based on the IOT requirement. In order to build a more secure IOT system, a combination of these protocols can be used.

IPv6 over Low Power Wireless Persona Area Networks (**6LowPAN**) (Sha et al, 2013): 6LowPAN operates in the network layer. It was introduced with an intention to support IPV6 in low power small embedded wireless devices. It is the most favourable method for enabling IOT based IP communication across smart devices. Specifically, it uses IEEE 802.15.4 of physical and MAC layers. It brings in a new layer between network and MAC layer called Adaptation Layer. This layer helps in interoperability with existing or obsolete networks. Some implementations of 6LowPAN work with a technique called Low Power Listening (LPL) that are apt for noisy environments. The Table 1 and Figure 4 shows the protocols commonly used in each layer of the Internet model.

CLOUD_BASED IoT SYSTEMS

Until now, IOT and Cloud challenges were discussed separately. However, it need not be particularly emphasized that Cloud-based IOT combines challenges of both. Fusion of these two imperative domains has as much benefits as there are issues. IOT and Cloud can be brought together in two ways. Cloud –based IOT that incorporates IOT components into Cloud and IOT-based Cloud that fits in cloud modules into IOT system. Security, Privacy, Interoperability, Reliability concerns continue to exist on either way implemented.

For protection against security, fierce authentication techniques have to be chosen that provides protection against attacks such as DOS and MITM. CoAP, DTLS protocols mentioned above can be used when web transfers are involved in IOT system. IDS and firewalls can be used to detect desirous and malicious traffic based on rules and alert other nodes. This helps to prevent IP Spoofing.Encryption algorithms give individuals control over their confidential data to some extent. But the confusion is about who should take on the responsibility whether CSP or CSU. A CSP can take up the responsibility of encrypting and managing data as with one of the options available in Amazon S3 (Michael Wittig 2018), but the problem is the threat associated with malevolent insiders of CSP. A solution can be to involve a third party to verify whether the CSP abides by the SLA. The method is called Third Party Auditing. Tech giants such as Google are coming up with interoperability solutions with its recent release, Android Things platform. The Android Things Developer Preview 6 (DP6) enhances its IOT functionality by providing Android development tools and Google APIs to ease the potential of the developers. Below mentioned are a few frameworks (da Cruz et al, 2018), (Masek et al, 2016) for interoperability.

IOTivity – is a framework that facilitates direct connection among millions of devices. It is an open source platform supported by Open Connectivity Foundation (OCF). It uses CoAP block transfer and also provides secure connections using DTLS.

AllJoyn (Masek et al, 2016) is another software framework that enables interoperability among the software applications that runs on Linux, Windows, iOS, and Linux-based Android platforms. AllJoyn also works in collaboration with OCF.

Apple HomeKit -Though not as compatible as Google and Amazon's solution, it is growing at a faster rate. It is a framework which enables us to configure, communicate and control home automation accompaniments.

Google Weave- is a communication platform to single handily deal with IoT from Android and Google cloud. It provides features such as better security, internet agnostic and bug fixing.

Figure 5. IoT applications and Edge Computing Architecture

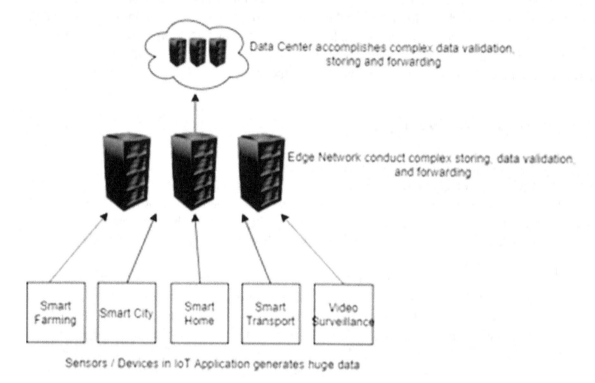

EDGE COMPUTING

It is a new paradigm emerging to solve computing needs of IoT. Like cloud computing it migrates both storage or computation of data to the edge of the network near the end users. This ensures that the distributed nodes across the network offload the computation stress and reduce latency in exchange of message. In IoT, this distributed structure can well balance the network traffic and also reduce transmission latency between edge servers and the end users. This extends the lifetime of the individual nodes as the communication and computation are transferred from limited battery supply to nodes with significant power resources.

The IoT technologies such as smart city, smart health care impact the potential users, interests of US by 2025 (The national intelligence council sponsor workshop, 2008) by increasing billions of interconnected physical devices (The national intelligence council sponsor workshop, 2008), (Gubbi J. et.al., 2013), (Rose, K. et. al., 2015). Hence, IoT devices are main source for big data. The three communication models of IoT are machine to machine, machine to cloud and machine to gateway communication. In machine to machine communication, the devices communicate over different type of networks (not limited to Internet or IP networks) (Wortmann, F. & Flüchter, K. 2015) to achieve requirements of QOS. Applications include smart homes. Compatibility between various device communications is the issue of this model (Al-Fuqaha, et. al., 2015). In Machine to cloud, the different IoT devices seek cloud service for both application and storage (Jararweh, Y. et. al., 2016). The main limitations are on bandwidth and network resources. The Machine to gateway model consists of an intermediary gateway with protocol or data translation algorithm running between the cloud and IoT devices. Thus, increases flexibility and security and reduces power consumption of IoT devices. The sensors in IoT devices provide diverse types of measurement data. IoT gateways connect cloud servers and sensor network. The gateways collect and aggregate data from sensors to cloud servers and forward the processed results in cloud servers back to the end users. The cloud servers perform the data processing using its varied storage and computation capacity.

The Figure 5 illustrates the basic architecture between IoT and edge computing. Edge computing servers are closer to the end users than the cloud. Rapid increase in usage of mobile devices has made the cloud computing struggle for QoS whereas edge computing provides better Quality of Service to end users. The sensors / end devices provide good response to the end users than cloud. Most of the storage and data computation are computed in edge network. Deployed farthest to end devices are cloud servers provide massive storage and computation such as big data, machine learning etc.

Edge computing technology typically follow two types of models such as Hierarchical model and Software-defined model. Hierarchical model defines the functions built on distance and resources hence suitable to describe the edge computing network structure. (Jararweh, Y. et. al., 2016) propose a hierarchical model integrating cloudlet and edge computing servers. Software defined model would be an ideal solution to deal with complexity management of edge computing. (A. Ahmed and E. Ahmed, 2016) proposed a software defined model which reduces administration and management cost.

Comparing the characteristics of Cloud, IoT and edge computing is shown in Table 2.

Table 2. Features of Cloud, IoT and Edge computing

	Cloud	**IoT**	**Edge**
Components	Virtual Resources	Physical Devices	Edge Nodes
Storage	Unlimited	Small	Limited
Computation	Unlimited	Limited	Limited
Deployment	Centralised	Distributed	Distributed

CHALLENGES OF EDGE COMPUTING IN IoT

Edge computing is a heterogeneous system as it includes various network topologies, platforms and servers. The heterogeneous platform probes for challenges such as (Varghese, B., 2016), (Raychaudhuri, D., 2012) and (Zhang, L., 2010). The challenging issues are (Gennaro, R., 2010) is the discovery of edge nodes which runs the required server-side programs as the devices of IoT are unaware of the available platforms. Another challenge address on the data management as many storage servers run on different operating system platforms. The huge IoT devices generates and uploads data, the naming of the data resources is also a challenge to be faced. Yet another problem is regarding the security and privacy of the computational tasks to be uploaded. (Clemens, J., 2016) introduced verifiable computing, which enables the untrusted node to offload the tasks of computation. These computational nodes use and maintains the verifiable results to compare with the results of the trusted nodes of computation. As computation is moved from cloud to edge, a trust between IoT devices and edge servers without third party intervention in security must be maintained. (Schütze M, 2011) propose a solution to extend integrity of the end-devices under constrained operating systems.

VIDEO SURVEILLANCE – A CASE STUDY

Video surveillance is a process of observing the scenes/image frames for specific improper/illegal behaviours and revealing its existence or emergence in scenes. Video surveillance are mostly used in public areas such as Railway station, airports etc. and public events too. The whole procedure incorporates identifying the concerned area using groups of cameras where the output quality depends mainly on the quality of the captured image.

Surveillance used in health care is for deterrence in psychological conditions than on physical control. Many health organizations intend to use surveillance to keep intruders away from secured areas, monitoring critical areas ensuring the non-usage of dummy or non-working cameras. The recordings of the surveillance system are retained in the library for minimum of 10 days.

Common recommended areas for cameras in health-care environment are:

1. Entrance of waiting and emergency rooms
2. Reception / Admission area
3. Garages, parking lot and many more.

The higher the resolution of the camera, the images tend to be sharper. The cameras with IR (Infrared Technology) are best suited for a good night vision which is an important feature for outdoor security.

Many developed countries use video surveillance also known as Closed-circuit television for inpatient psychiatry (Vartiainen, H. & Hakola, P., 1994), (Olsen D. P., 1998), (Warr, J. et. al., 2005), (Stolovy, T. et. al., 2015), (Due, C. et. al., 2012), (Nolan, K. A., & Volavka, J., 2006) and (Desai, S., 2010) to increase in security for both patients and staff. A serious concern in psychiatric institutions is about the violence among patients, staffs or even between patients and staff. The surveillance would recognise, prevent and document sexual assaults, violence and any undesirable behaviours.

Disaster rescue can be benefited from camera captured images. But there are two limitations in this rescuing effort. They are the constraints on the bandwidth and increase in consumption of the energy. During the disaster ECV's (Energy Communication Vehicle) provide communication services through satellites as the original communication would be congested or interrupted. The emergency communication in disaster areas are unstable and very poor (Manoj, B. S., & Baker, A. H., 2007).

Currently, IoT with its various sensors or mobile devices used in several applications such as detection of fire (Genovese, A., 2011) and in controlling industrial systems. Edge computing an emerging technology in which a bridge is constructed by edge servers between cloud and resource constrained mobile devices. Thus, forwarding the services to the edge network. MOCHA – Mobile Cloud Hybrid Architecture (Soyata, T., et. al., 2012) is a real-time face recognition using mobile-cloudlet cloud architecture. It distributes the load of computation among the cloud and cloudlets. In edge-based disaster rescue, ECV's are used edge servers by taking the advantage of storage capacity and large computing power.

Video surveillance are expected to grow widely in both developed and developing countries. This growth promotes for real-time video analytics, edge, public and private cloud / clusters in much demand. Added to the above, the huge need to increase in the computing power to analyse the security, traffic, and crime. An architecture of camera, edge and cloud is shown in Figure 6. A good solution will be a Geo-Distributed architecture for cloud, clusters, edge, and video cameras to meet the real-time constraints of video analytics, bandwidth, and latency.

Figure 6. Architecture for video surveillance in edge

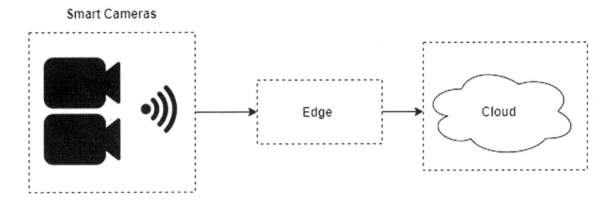

An example of a health care with IoT-edge-cloud based services where a variety of sensors are used to sense the human body, collect the information, and deliver to health broker for its authentication with hospital. The broker initiates a recommendation on family doctor, or any emergency as required. As noticed a lot of computation is involved. Hence, the usage of efficient edge devices will be able to perform the required computation much rapidly by minimizing the risk of user transmission of data. The author Uddin, M. Z. (2019) focuses on processing the health-related data on a fast edge device such as laptop (along with GPU). Some of the sensors incorporated in the experiment are accelerometer, gyroscope, electrocardiograph (ECG) and magnetometer. The Figure 7 depicts a schematic diagram of a health care system using IoT-edge-cloud services.

Figure 7. A schematic diagram of a health-care smart system

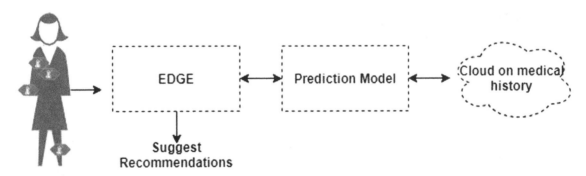

Some of the operational issues to be taken care are (1) Improvement in processing speed, production optimization and asset performance. (2) Reduction in security issues and latency issues.

CONCLUSION

Internet of Things (IoT) and Cloud Computing are amongst the booming technologies that have become an indivisible part of our lives. The chapter ponders over the challenges and issues to be addressed while integrating IoT and Cloud. It also summarises on the choice of a communication protocol to be adopted. A significant potential gain to both consumers and industries are offered by IoT edge. Many verticals such as smart cities, intelligent transport system and smart factories can benefit from storage and data processing at edge. Deploy of IoT edge and cloud would create new opportunities with new services such as electric car linked to smart grid and intelligent public transport (bus) routed to stop with large group of people waiting for its service. Edge computing in IoT is gaining momentum as an exciting domain.

REFERENCES

Ahmed, A., & Ahmed, E. (2016, January). A survey on mobile edge computing. *Proc. 10th Int. Conf. Intell. Syst. Control (ISCO)*, 1-8.

Akbar, S. R., Amron, K., Mulya, H., & Hanifah, S. (2017, November). Message queue telemetry transport protocols implementation for wireless sensor networks communication—A performance review. In *2017 International Conference on Sustainable Information Engineering and Technology (SIET)* (pp. 107-112). IEEE. 10.1109/SIET.2017.8304118

Al-Fuqaha, A., Guizani, M., Mohammadi, M., Aledhari, M., & Ayyash, M. (2015). Internet of things: A survey on enabling technologies, protocols, and applications. *IEEE Communications Surveys and Tutorials*, *17*(4), 2347–2376. doi:10.1109/COMST.2015.2444095

Alotaibi, K. H. (2015). Threat in Cloud-Denial of Service (DoS) and Distributed Denial of Service (DDoS) Attack, and Security Measures. *Journal of Emerging Trends in Computing and Information Sciences*, *6*(5), 241–244.

Amazon, A. W. S. (2015). *Amazon Web Services Overview of Security Processes*. Author.

Atlam, H., Alenezi, A., Alharthi, A., Walters, R., & Wills, G. (2017). Integration of cloud computing with internet of things: challenges and open issues. Academic Press.

Clemens, J., Pal, R., & Philip, P. (2016, October). Extending trust and attestation to the edge. In *2016 IEEE/ACM Symposium on Edge Computing (SEC)* (pp. 101-102). IEEE. 10.1109/SEC.2016.29

da Cruz, M. A., Rodrigues, J. J. P., Al-Muhtadi, J., Korotaev, V. V., & de Albuquerque, V. H. C. (2018). A reference model for internet of things middleware. *IEEE Internet of Things Journal*, *5*(2), 871–883. doi:10.1109/JIOT.2018.2796561

Desai, S. (2010). Violence and surveillance: Some unintended consequences of CCTV monitoring within mental health hospital wards. *Surveillance & Society*, *8*(1), 84–92. doi:10.24908s.v8i1.3475

Dooley, R., Edmonds, A., Hancock, D. Y., Lowe, J. M., Skidmore, E., Adams, A. K., ... Knepper, R. (2018). *Security best practices for academic cloud service providers*. Academic Press.

Dragomir, D., Gheorghe, L., Costea, S., & Radovici, A. (2016, September). A survey on secure communication protocols for IoT systems. In *2016 International Workshop on Secure Internet of Things (SIoT)* (pp. 47-62). IEEE. 10.1109/SIoT.2016.012

Due, C., Connellan, K., & Riggs, D. (2012). *Surveillance, security and violence in a mental health ward: an ethnographic case-study of an Australian purpose-built unit*. Academic Press.

Fernandes, J. L., Lopes, I. C., Rodrigues, J. J., & Ullah, S. (2013, July). Performance evaluation of RESTful web services and AMQP protocol. In *2013 Fifth International Conference on Ubiquitous and Future Networks (ICUFN)* (pp. 810-815). IEEE. 10.1109/ICUFN.2013.6614932

Gennaro, R., Gentry, C., & Parno, B. (2010, August). Non-interactive verifiable computing: Outsourcing computation to untrusted workers. In *Annual Cryptology Conference* (pp. 465-482). Springer. 10.1007/978-3-642-14623-7_25

Genovese, A., Labati, R. D., Piuri, V., & Scotti, F. (2011, September). Wildfire smoke detection using computational intelligence techniques. In *2011 IEEE International Conference on Computational Intelligence for Measurement Systems and Applications (CIMSA) Proceedings* (pp. 1-6). IEEE. 10.1109/CIMSA.2011.6059930

Gubbi, J., Buyya, R., Marusic, S., & Palaniswami, M. (2013). Internet of Things (IoT): A vision, architectural elements, and future directions. *Future Generation Computer Systems, 29*(7), 1645–1660. doi:10.1016/j.future.2013.01.010

Han, B., Gopalakrishnan, V., Ji, L., & Lee, S. (2015). Network function virtualization: Challenges and opportunities for innovations. *IEEE Communications Magazine, 53*(2), 90–97. doi:10.1109/MCOM.2015.7045396

Jararweh, Y., Doulat, A., AlQudah, O., Ahmed, E., Al-Ayyoub, M., & Benkhelifa, E. (2016, May). The future of mobile cloud computing: integrating cloudlets and mobile edge computing. In *2016 23rd International conference on telecommunications (ICT)* (pp. 1-5). IEEE. 10.1109/ICT.2016.7500486

Jararweh, Y., Doulat, A., Darabseh, A., Alsmirat, M., Al-Ayyoub, M., & Benkhelifa, E. (2016, April). SDMEC: Software defined system for mobile edge computing. In *2016 IEEE International Conference on Cloud Engineering Workshop (IC2EW)* (pp. 88-93). IEEE.

Keahey, K., Tsugawa, M., Matsunaga, A., & Fortes, J. (2009). Sky computing. *IEEE Internet Computing, 13*(5), 43–51. doi:10.1109/MIC.2009.94

Konduru, V. R., & Bharamagoudra, M. R. (2017, August). Challenges and solutions of interoperability on IoT: How far have we come in resolving the IoT interoperability issues. In *2017 International Conference On Smart Technologies For Smart Nation (SmartTechCon)* (pp. 572-576). IEEE. 10.1109/SmartTechCon.2017.8358436

Laeeq, K., & Shamsi, J. A. (2015). A study of security issues, vulnerabilities and challenges in internet of things. *Securing Cyber-Physical Systems, 10*.

Lar, S. U., Liao, X., & Abbas, S. A. (2011, August). Cloud computing privacy & security global issues, challenges, & mechanisms. In *2011 6th International ICST Conference on Communications and Networking in China (CHINACOM)* (pp. 1240-1245). IEEE.

Lerche, C., Hartke, K., & Kovatsch, M. (2012, September). Industry adoption of the Internet of Things: A constrained application protocol survey. In *Proceedings of 2012 IEEE 17th International Conference on Emerging Technologies & Factory Automation (ETFA 2012)* (pp. 1-6). IEEE. 10.1109/ETFA.2012.6489787

Liu, X., Lam, K. H., Zhu, K., Zheng, C., Li, X., Du, Y., . . . Pong, P. W. (2016). *Overview of spintronic sensors, Internet of Things, and smart living.* arXiv preprint arXiv:1611.00317

Liu, Y., Sun, Y. L., Ryoo, J., Rizvi, S., & Vasilakos, A. V. (2015). A survey of security and privacy challenges in cloud computing: Solutions and future directions. *Journal of Computing Science and Engineering: JCSE, 9*(3), 119–133. doi:10.5626/JCSE.2015.9.3.119

Manoj, B. S., & Baker, A. H. (2007). Communication challenges in emergency response. *Communications of the ACM, 50*(3), 51–53. doi:10.1145/1226736.1226765

Masek, P., Fujdiak, R., Zeman, K., Hosek, J., & Muthanna, A. (2016, April). Remote networking technology for IoT: Cloud-based access for AllJoyn-enabled devices. In *2016 18th Conference of Open Innovations Association and Seminar on Information Security and Protection of Information Technology (FRUCT-ISPIT)* (pp. 200-205). IEEE.

Mezgár, I., & Rauschecker, U. (2014). The challenge of networked enterprises for cloud computing interoperability. *Computers in Industry, 65*(4), 657–674. doi:10.1016/j.compind.2014.01.017

Michael Wittig. (2018). https://cloudonaut.io/encrypting-sensitive-data-stored-on-s3/

Naik, N. (2017, October). Choice of effective messaging protocols for IoT systems: MQTT, CoAP, AMQP and HTTP. In *2017 IEEE international systems engineering symposium (ISSE)* (pp. 1-7). IEEE.

Nolan, K. A., & Volavka, J. (2006). Video recording in the assessment of violent incidents in psychiatric hospitals. *Journal of Psychiatric Practice, 12*(1), 58–63. doi:10.1097/00131746-200601000-00010 PMID:16432448

Olsen, D. P. (1998). Ethical considerations of video monitoring psychiatric patients in seclusion and restraint. *Archives of Psychiatric Nursing, 12*(2), 90–94. doi:10.1016/S0883-9417(98)80058-7 PMID:9573636

Rashidi, B., Sharifi, M., & Jafari, T. (2013). A survey on interoperability in the cloud computing environments. *International Journal of Modern Education and Computer Science, 5*(6), 17–23. doi:10.5815/ijmecs.2013.06.03

Raychaudhuri, D., Nagaraja, K., & Venkataramani, A. (2012). Mobilityfirst: A robust and trustworthy mobility-centric architecture for the future internet. *Mobile Computing and Communications Review, 16*(3), 2–13. doi:10.1145/2412096.2412098

Rose, K., Eldridge, S., & Chapin, L. (2015). The internet of things: An overview. *The Internet Society (ISOC), 80.*

Said, O., & Masud, M. (2013). Towards internet of things: Survey and future vision. *International Journal of Computer Networks*, 5(1), 1–17.

Salas-Vega, S., Haimann, A., & Mossialos, E. (2015). Big data and health care: Challenges and opportunities for coordinated policy development in the EU. *Health Systems and Reform*, 1(4), 285–300. doi:10.1080/23288604.2015.1091538 PMID:31519092

Schütze, M. (2011). *Examination of the Attitudes of Mental Health Patients Towards Video Monitoring on a Secure Psychiatric Ward* (Doctoral dissertation). Bochum, Germany, Ruhr University Bochum Faculty of Medicine. http://www-brs.ub.ruhruni-bochum.de/netahtml/HSS/Diss/SchuetzeMorana/diss.pdf

Sha, M., Hackmann, G., & Lu, C. (2013, April). Energy-efficient low power listening for wireless sensor networks in noisy environments. In *Proceedings of the 12th international conference on Information processing in sensor networks* (pp. 277-288). 10.1145/2461381.2461415

Shuijing, H. (2014, January). Data security: the challenges of cloud computing. In *2014 Sixth International Conference on Measuring Technology and Mechatronics Automation* (pp. 203-206). IEEE. 10.1109/ICMTMA.2014.52

Soyata, T., Muraleedharan, R., Langdon, J., Funai, C., Ames, S., Kwon, M., & Heinzelman, W. (2012, May). COMBAT: mobile-Cloud-based cOmpute/coMmunications infrastructure for BATtlefield applications. In Modeling and Simulation for Defense Systems and Applications VII (Vol. 8403, p. 84030K). International Society for Optics and Photonics.

Steve Lohr. (2010). *The New York Times*. Retrieved from https://www.nytimes.com/2010/03/13/technology/13netflix.html

Stolovy, T., Melamed, Y., & Afek, A. (2015). Video surveillance in mental health facilities: Is it ethical? The Israel Medical Association journal. *The Israel Medical Association Journal*, 17(5), 274–276. PMID:26137651

Sun, G., Chang, V., Ramachandran, M., Sun, Z., Li, G., Yu, H., & Liao, D. (2017). Efficient location privacy algorithm for Internet of Things (IoT) services and applications. *Journal of Network and Computer Applications*, 89, 3–13. doi:10.1016/j.jnca.2016.10.011

Takabi, H., Joshi, J. B., & Ahn, G. J. (2010). Security and privacy challenges in cloud computing environments. *IEEE Security and Privacy*, 8(6), 24–31. doi:10.1109/MSP.2010.186

The national intelligence council sponsor workshop. (2008). *Intelligence, S. C. B., 2008. Disruptive Civil Technologies. Six Technologies with Potential Impacts on US Interests out to 2025*. Available: https://fas.org/irp/nic/disruptive.pdf

Turab, N. M., Taleb, A. A., & Masadeh, S. R. (2013). Cloud computing challenges and solutions. *International Journal of Computer Networks & Communications*, 5(5), 209–216. doi:10.5121/ijcnc.2013.5515

Uddin, M. Z. (2019). A wearable sensor-based activity prediction system to facilitate edge computing in smart healthcare system. *Journal of Parallel and Distributed Computing*, 123, 46–53. doi:10.1016/j.jpdc.2018.08.010

Varghese, B., Wang, N., Barbhuiya, S., Kilpatrick, P., & Nikolopoulos, D. S. (2016, November). Challenges and opportunities in edge computing. In *2016 IEEE International Conference on Smart Cloud (SmartCloud)* (pp. 20-26). IEEE. 10.1109/SmartCloud.2016.18

Vartiainen, H., & Hakola, P. (1994). The effects of TV monitoring on ward atmosphere in a security hospital. *International Journal of Law and Psychiatry*, *17*(4), 443–449. doi:10.1016/0160-2527(94)90019-1 PMID:7890477

Vijayalakshmi, A. V., & Arockiam, L. (2016). A study on security issues and challenges in IoT. *International Journal of Engineering Sciences & Management Research*, *3*(11), 1–9.

Vinoski, S. (2006). Advanced message queuing protocol. *IEEE Internet Computing*, *10*(6), 87–89. doi:10.1109/MIC.2006.116

Wadhwa, A. V., & Gupta, S. (2015). Study of security issues in cloud computing. *International Journal of Computer Science and Mobile Computing IJCSMC*, *4*(6), 230–234.

Warr, J., Page, M., & Crossen-White, H. (2005). *The appropriate use of CCTV observation in a secure unit*. Bournemouth University.

Wortmann, F., & Flüchter, K. (2015). Internet of things. *Business & Information Systems Engineering*, *57*(3), 221–224. doi:10.100712599-015-0383-3

Zhang, L., Estrin, D., Burke, J., Jacobson, V., Thornton, J. D., Smetters, D. K., ... Papadopoulos, C. (2010). Named data networking (ndn) project. Relatório Técnico NDN-0001. *Xerox Palo Alto Research Center-PARC*, *157*, 158.

Chapter 3
Emerging Trends and Techniques in Cloud-Based Data Analytics

Shaila S. G.
Dayananda Sagar University, India

Monish L.
Dayananda Sagar University, India

Lavanya S.
Dayananda Sagar University, India

Sowmya H. D.
Dayananda Sagar University, India

Divya K.
Dayananda Sagar University, India

ABSTRACT

The new trending technologies such as big data and cloud computing are in line with social media applications due to their fast growth and usage. The big data characteristic makes data management challenging. The term big data refers to an immense collection of both organised and unorganised data from various sources, and nowadays, cloud computing supports in storing and processing such a huge data. Analytics are done on huge data that helps decision makers to take decisions. However, merging two conflicting design principles brings a challenge, but it has its own advantage in business and various fields. Big data analytics in the cloud places rigorous demands on networks, storage, and servers. The chapter discusses the importance of cloud platform for big data, importance of analytics in cloud and gives detail insight about the trends and techniques adopted for cloud analytics.

DOI: 10.4018/978-1-7998-3111-2.ch003

1. Why Cloud Platform for Big Data?

Big data refers to storage of bulk data whereas cloud computing deals with storage and computing. Big data in computing environment can be managed by using distributed storage. Traditional storage method is not sufficient for storing big data. Hence, cloud evolved to provide the solution. The expansion of big data storage is done by cloud through virtual machines and makes big data more accessible. Initially, big data and cloud are used in various ways. Many investors decided to join the two techniques to make a maximum business outcome. Both the technologies aimed to reduce the investment cost and increase the income of the organizations. Microsoft, Google, amazon are successful in using big data in cloud platform. The world runs online. People surf data and leave data online. For example: people use internet in various ways like social media such as Facebook, twitter etc., for ecommerce websites like flipkart, amazon, etc, to get any valuable information they can use Google search engine and so on and leave data online. A new survey found that 42 percent of Americans use the internet several times a day. Companies gather all this data and utilize accordingly to provide better products to satisfy customer requirements and increase their business turn over (Singh and Reddy, 2014). The grouping of these two techniques led to the drastic changes and improvements. It gave huge advantage to analysts and changed the decision-making process for companies, and their outcome is improved.

Cloud technology is a fast-growing field as it offers services to the consumers on a pay-as-you-go model. Instead of storing a data in personal computer or local servers the data is stored in cloud which is easy to manage and provide security. Cloud offers the features such as pay as you-go model, storing, processing, etc. Another feature is that cloud supports large network access in which user from any location can access and upload information to the cloud using their devices. These capabilities are accessible over the network. Availability of the cloud makes it extensible based on requirements. Based on user necessities extra cloud storage (small amount) is provided for their usage. The most important feature of any cloud platform is security. It is one of the best features of cloud platform. The data is safeguarded even if one of the server goes down because cloud creates snapshot of data that is stored. The data that is stored in cloud is neither hacked nor exploited by the intruder, because data is stored within the storage devices with high security. Another feature in cloud is it support data analytics. Cloud offers three primary service models which consist of Platform as a Service (PaaS), Software as a Service (SaaS), and Infrastructure as a Service (IaaS). Platform as a Service uses public, private and hybrid clouds. PaaS does not include hosting, but it provides open source software. The Cloud contributor provide resources like object storage, runtime, queuing, databases, etc. Customers are able to develop, run and manage applications by using this platform. Ex: Google App Engine, Herokus, etc. SaaS is known as on-demand software or web-based software or hosted software. This service provides all the necessary settings and infrastructure in place. There are two types of SaaS that is, Vertical SaaS and Horizontal SaaS. Ex: Salesforce Customer Relationship Management (CRM). IaaS is high-level APIs and is provided through the internet. It offers resources such as virtual-machine, disk-image library, IP addresses and virtual local area networks. This service provider provides whole structure along with the related tasks such as Amazon Elastic Compute Cloud (EC2).

The benefit of using cloud platform is that user need not have to develop the infrastructure from the scratch for storage. Apart from this if companies needs to do some analysis, they can create the virtual copies for analytics. Analytics speed up the process and helps in achieving goals. Cloud simplifies the connectivity within an organization which gives employee access to relevant analytics. The recovery solutions and backups are also implemented within cloud. Agility is yet another advantage because storing and managing data in database by using traditional method is becoming outmoded. Installing a server and setting up new structure will take few weeks. Therefore, this can be compensated by using cloud instead of storing information by using traditional method. Pliability is that storage space of cloud platform is increasing accordingly with growing data. Once the organizations find a pattern from obtained information then, based on their requirements the storage space can be increased or reduced to accommodate the data. As per the survey of new vantage partners, the enterprises focus on advanced techniques to drive the innovative ideas. To give a better competition spirit enterprise successfully implement techniques that can keep away from their competitors. Even though organizations are boosting up the systems, all the data may not be fitted into a single system. This is where cloud platform is used. There are various types of cloud analytics such as private, public and hybrid. Private cloud is a cloud that is dedicated to a single organization. This cloud can be accessed by only one company. The highest priority is given to security and data privacy. Public cloud is available to the public. IT systems will not share the data (Sharma and Navdeti, 2014). This reduces cost and burden on companies. Hybrid cloud results in grouping of both private and public clouds. The crucial data is placed in a private cloud and non-sensitive data that can be accessed by public is placed in public cloud.

2. Role of Analytics in Cloud

Approximately every day two billion emails are sent and the numbers of Google searches are around one billion per day. Instagram photos posted for every minute is around 65,972 and 4, 48,800 tweets are composed. By the end of 2020, the number of mobile user could reach to some billions. Accenture study performs a survey and reveals that the co-operate executives may lose their position if they are not focused on big data, further analysis said that most of the companies takes a project on big data either to increase their profit and to lose their competitive position. Thus the data within the enterprise is increasing exponentially which creates a huge impact on storage. One of the survey conducted by forester research in 2017 revealed the solutions of big data along with cloud has increased about 7.5 times (Manju Sharma et al, 2016). Big data in a cloud platform is a perfect combination as it provides an accessible and cooperative solution for business analytics. Lot of efforts have been put in developing the techniques, where all data is easily accessible at one place and the whole world is getting benefit from that information. Social media generates a bulk of unstructured information. This information has to be analysed and processed by using big data in cloud and this should be accessible to small, medium and large enterprise. Reducing complexity and enhancing the productivity of big data analysis is done by providing an option to automate these components by cloud computing (Nathiya, 2017). The advantages of business analytics such as data processing in which gathering and analysing of big data in an effective way is more demanding task. It is a complex process of examining the bulk data for identifying customer preferences, hidden arrangements, market styles that help investors to improve the return on investment. Organizations take prior decisions by analyzing the historic data sets. The data collected is processed by organization and remodeled to NoSQL database such as Hadoop and others. Analytical tools such as Pig, Hive, Spark, and MapReduce and so on are applied on collected big data (Jayashree et al, 2013).

Lot of criteria's such as integration, visualization and scalability are considered while selecting Big Data analytical tools. Integration is a statistical tool that is required to conduct analysis by organizations. Visualization refers to displaying data in visual or graphical format, often makes it more usable. Scalability is yet another feature to be considered because data has a tendency to grow even bigger. Organizations need to consider the analytical tools based on the data size and structure they choose.

There are multiple types of analytics capabilities such as path analysis, link analysis, predictive mining. Analyses do not involve collaboration. Getting data in and out from various tools is difficult task and the tools of big data should be considered priory. The challenges faced in applying analytics on data are Security and privacy, storage and quality of data, getting bulk data into the cloud platform, and need for synchronization across disparate data sources. Even though there are various problems faced in analytics it is still widely used because it has improved operational efficiency, diverse marketing ideas, maintains the customer relation and runs profitable business. The role of analytics in big data plays vital role as the organizations have a special goal to extract relevant data to make profit, instead of collecting huge amount of unstructured data. Big data uses advanced tools such as automation tools and parallel computing tools and data analytics use statistical and predictive modelling which is relatively simple.

Cloud analytics model is used to extract the meaningful and useful data by applying various analytical tools and techniques available at web browser. Various tools used in respective stages in data storage and retrieval are Hadoop, Map Reduce for data storage, Pig and Hive. Data analyst and Data scientist study different types of data that is stored in cloud platform. Analytics are done to improve business for attracting new customers and to provide better offers for existing customer. Analytics provide environment for companies to take actions and stay competitive. The most popularly used cloud platforms are Amazon Web 7Service (AWS), Google cloud platform, Microsoft Azure, Alibaba, etc.

Benefits of Cloud Analytics gives ease of access to the cloud by employees, stockholders from anywhere and anytime. Internal management of network is done, as cloud accepts data from different data sources. Cloud also allows to scale up when there is a sudden demand for analytics in cloud. The number of customers increases day-by-day. This leads to changes in analytics. Users can easily transfer files and collaborate in real time when they view analytics in the cloud anywhere in the world. The evolution of cloud analytics leads to increase in identifying data from various sources. Organizations do not need to purchase hardware for cloud analytics. The challenges faced in cloud analytics is data security. Proper training in security can reduce risk of data loss. The best approach for cloud analytics is hybrid approach. Availability of cloud experts is costly because of shortage of professionals with this skillset. Companies find difficulty for hiring and training the right person, who can manage analytics operation. Cloud splits the data and data is stored in various locations. Computing in cloud environments are used to provide flexibility on demand. Thereby cloud platform plays a vital role in big data. Nowadays most of the emerging business-oriented company's implements technologies used in big data with cloud platform to take faster decision and adapt to future trends and behaviour. Amazon Web Services is a leading company in e-commerce and it provides various cloud computing platforms such as storage, data analysis and so on. Amazon provides its services to government, individuals and companies. Google cloud platform offers its services to public. It provides storage facility and also supports the data processing and analysis using machine learning, networking for predicting decisions. All services provided by them can be accessible by using internet. Microsoft Azure also offers cloud services that prove to be trustworthy. The Chinese market offers cloud services in the name of Alibaba. Blue mix is a platform offered by IBM for sharing infrastructure as service (IaaS) (Aydin et al, 2015).

There are various cloud analytics such as Microsoft power Bi, Tableau, Zoho analytics etc., Microsoft power Bi is a graphical business analytical service provided by Microsoft. Users can find patterns to find out relation to their business. Instead of DAX formulae, users are more comfortable with excel to control this analytical tool. Power Bi premium plan is based on capacity pricing. Power bi desktop plan is suitable for single user. It includes connectivity to various sources. Tableau offers an array of tools to provide intelligence and business analytics reports for individual analysts, embedded analytics, associations and teams (Bala et al, 2017). For individuals, creator offers something from each to create a suite of products for analytics from which user can prepare data for conception. The toolkits can involve desktop, prep, server and online forms. It offers a range of API to allow user to modify and integrate analytics for customers using OpenID Kerberos, using SAML. Embedded analytics allows user to embed this directly into application.Zoho is a software-based company in India. It sprouted in 2006. It gave several useful features, by using few clicks users can upload their data in their reporting centre. Along with this data, user can also upload tables and reports. The automation feature involved runs data without prompts. The data in columns can be inserted with Handy drag and drop feature. The data can be sorted with various filter techniques. Analyst can also run several number of SQL queries. The analytics application is a part of zoho software but can also works as a standalone package. The interface is user friendly. In domos users can view data relating multiple business areas. The dashboard works in real time. Users can manage all functions from main dashboards. It includes a large variety of plug-ins. It has its own App store. Cognos recommends the best chart types for visualizations. Charts can also be improved with other media such as voiceovers and interactive elements. Cognos analytics can be run from your premises or from cloud. Data in the form of spreadsheets can be uploaded to the program.

3. Trends of Cloud Analytics

Cloud analytics uses cloud computing tools for its analysis. The section presents a description of analytical tools and techniques that are used to extract useful information from massive data and offer the data in a more precise manner. Certain technologies and analytical tools are available to extract the valuable information (Talia, 2013). Cloud analytics aims in reforming the statistical data in a more precise manner via the web browser. Here are a few emerging cloud technology trends:

Hybrid Cloud Solution: Hybrid cloud is a prevailing cloud business model with a modern infrastructure having two or more delivery models. Hybrid cloud uses public, private and on-premise cloud to satisfy the needs. Hybrid cloud allows the enterprises to use the resources to work on the fluctuating data. To balance the demand, the cloud offers close monitoring. Hybrids clouds plays vital role in medical monitoring, by controlling the sensitive and confidential data. The organizations can choose their own storages to secure the data.

Artificial Intelligence Platform: The two demanding backings of Artificial Intelligence are data and computation. Efficiency of processing the data has increased. Blending the artificial intelligence with cloud has led to the development of "The Intelligent Cloud". Artificial Intelligence aims in providing improved business functionalities for future. Robotic Process automation has automated manual tasks in the organizations to reduce workloads. Artificial Intelligence focusses on hardware optimization by using wearable silicon chips.

Server less Computing: Server less architecture is event-driven. For each event, a state is generated and after the response, the state is destroyed. Server less computing is accessed using Private APIs and this hatches another layer in cloud Architecture called as Functions as a Service (FaaS). IOT web and mobile applications are incorporating serverless computing to amalgamate with the changing needs. This event-based programming spins only for few seconds to complete the task, thus reducing the cost.

Edge Computing: Edge computing is repositioning the computing functions to the edge (source). This enables interconnection making it easier to gather and analyse the data in real time. open-ended architecture in edge computing enables load sharing. It allows automatic decision making in the industries without human intervention. Edge computing is the building block for smart factories equipped with temperature, motion and climate sensors controlling the physical environment.

Backup and Disaster Recovery: As the technologies rely completely on data, there is a need to adopt the backup and disaster recovery software. The problem with hardware failure contrived to loss of confidential data. Disaster recovery software will overcome this problem. Data backup cannot be considered as a solution, as it requires regular maintenance and testing. The influence of cloud computing has made the recovery process automated. It occurs in few seconds. Cloud backup plays the role of antivirus without the intrusion of threats from external sources.

Cloud Security: Cloud computing security contains set of policies and control mechanisms running together to protect data and infrastructure of the cloud-based systems. Security of the cloud-based systems depends on the cloud service provider. Cloud security focus on securing the data and fighting against intruders. network security, physical security, measuring endpoint security and communication encryption are the types of security systems embedded in the cloud. Public channels are used for packet communication. For the data movement in the channel possible checks are implemented. Data integrity is maintained by using encryption techniques like SSL. With the technological innovation cloud computing is growing with rising trends. Better security, storage and better decision making is enabled only because of cloud computing technologies. The trends in cloud computing will ensure automation and reduce human intrusion. The companies are leveraging these cloud-computing trends to stay ahead of the competition.

4. Techniques of Cloud Analytics

APACHE HADOOP: Hadoop is open source software used to manage the data efficiently in a distributed environment and also solves various issues of large data sets by efficiently using massive number of computers. It uses map reduce programming model to store, access and manage the data sets. It is used in various applications such as you tube, amazon, Google etc. There are two basic components used for efficient processing of data are HDFS, Map Reduce. To increase the processing speed, Hadoop splits the files into n number of block which is of size 64 Megabytes or 128 megabytes and the blocks are circulated among the nodes of cluster and MapReduce is applied for processing data in nodes by executing parallelly in a system. There are ups and downs in applying MapReduce on information such as it increases scalability, fault-tolerance. However, the challenges faced is security, privacy and processing the information online. Larger datasets can be handled by using file distributed systems which is implemented by Google. The computation process is improved by storing large datasets in a multiple node through HTTP. HDFS is designed to run on commodity machines. These machines perform computation at low cost and are available as a computing component for parallel computing. Since it is a distributed system, routine maintenance of hardware breakdown is required. Name node is one of the component in HDFS to maintain namespace of files and operations performed by clients. Data node will keep track of the data blocks and replication factor. The major goal of this systems is detecting and recovering back from failures. HDFS was designed with POSIX4 semantics to improve the throughput. Write-once-read-many simplifies the data coherency issues. Once the task is spliced into smaller division, it passes through various stages. In first phase, the mapping of key k1 and value v1 is done. In second phase, the sorting and shuffle process yields the result. The shuffle process can optimize the communication service cost.

APACHE SPARK: Spark was released by apache software foundation to improve the computation process in Hadoop. This is different from Hadoop, as spark manages its own cluster. But spark uses

Hadoop in two ways such as storage and processing. Sparks supports different workloads like processing the queries iteratively, batch applications etc. Along with these workloads, it reduces the management overhead. Initially, Spark was developed as a sub project of Hadoop and it was open source in 2010. But later on, donated to apache and now it has become the top-level apache project. Since Hadoop follows Map-Reduce jobs thereby it takes hours to complete the jobs. In case of spark it runs on Hadoop and replaces the traditional Map-Reduce and will complete the task within a stipulated time.

APACHE PRESTO: Presto was developed by Facebook and it is an open source SQL query engine to process the queries on gigabyte data and return the results in seconds. It is considered to be a fastest query engine that is set up from scratch. The queries are executed in a parallel fashion among the machines by using a MPP SQL engine. Thereby the queries are executed at a higher speed. The architectures of presto fully abstracts the data sources. The presto connectors can be created until there exist a mapping between data into relational ideas such as columns, rows, tables. The data from different connectors can be processed and run queries at once by presto users after registering. The presto is easily accessible by using a current connector such as Mongo DB, MYSQL, S3. Data science has to perform extract, transform and load process using Presto. Presto consist of two types of nodes such as coordinate and worker nodes. Coordinate node does the parsing, optimization of query whereas processing of query is done by worker nodes. Once after planning, the co-ordinate node sends the plan to workers and starts executing the task. Meanwhile, it counts the splits and assigns to the task. The responsibility of splits is to read the data. Worker nodes process the splits during the execution of task, either from retrieving data from external source or the results from another worker. Worker nodes uses multitasking concept to execute queries concurrently and data is shared properly among the task. It as a capability of returning the results before all the task is executed and store it in intermediate buffer. Presto are extensible and plugins are used to communicate with external data stores through available APIs. It is composed of 4 parts such as metadata, data location, data source and data sink API. It does not make use of MapReduce instead message passing is used to process the quires. Example to show how client data is processed by Presto. Initially, the query from the client side is received at coordinate node and creates a plan according to query. The data is sent to the nearest worker node by scheduler to minimize the network traffic to transfer the data. The data plan is later on executed at worker node and return back the result to the coordinate and forward to the client. It can work with different data sources in a single query. It does not use Hadoop file distributed system for storage purpose.

APACHE FLINK: Apache Flink is an open source platform and one of the processing engines that process the data obtained from different sources. It is faster compared to Map-Reduce in processing the information. It works in a master slave fashion. The distributed computing is enhanced in Flink and it process data at high speed. Master splits the jobs and submits to the slaves in the cluster. There are two types of data available such as finite and infinite. So, Flink requires different APIs to apply on data. Dataset API is used for finite data and DataStream API for infinite data. These are not similar to DStream and RDD but the difference of this API is optimized by using an optimizer. The lambda architecture is implemented because only one message is handled at once. Bulk data means obtaining a stream or static data from different sources and processing such a large volume of data requires high computing clusters. Then it later on integrated with this lambda architecture to improve the speed.

HBase: HBase will handle large data sets using parallel computing. It supports high volume updates on table. It allows the clusters to scale horizontally. Data consistency is ensured while performing read and write. HBase follows an architecture which makes it possible to achieve load balancing and failures. HBase is powered using region servers. Sharing is a concept primarily used in HBase. HBase does splitting either manually or automatically. Scaling up of clusters is easy by adding n number of computers to the cluster. After adding, the region server starts to run and will rebalance by itself. HBase will focus on storing the data in columns rather than storing the data in rows as seen in relational database. It also supports easy operations by using command line tools. If user assume the records are stored in the pages of memory, off chance the pages are loaded into the memory only when needed and are not officially displayed in memory. Hence, to perform the page in and page out operations, it will cause the overhead and will result in delayed time.

Other Cloud Analytical Technologies:

a. AWS Analytics products:

I.   **Amazon Athena** is a query service used to analyse the data in Amazon S3 using standard SQL. Athena is serverless. Characteristic of Athena is that it does not contain any infrastructure. Athena is easy to use. Athena points to the data stored in S3 cloud. User can define a schema and can query using SQL. Results are available in seconds. ETL jobs are abolished. Analysis of large data sets are made easier with Athena. Anyone with the knowledge of SQL can easily use Athena to work on large data sets. Athena is integrated with AWS Catalog, that creates a metadata repository across various services, creep data sources to unearth schemas and populate the catalog with new and modified tables and schemas.

II.   **Amazon EMR** is the trending big data analytics platform, which is cost effective and quick in data processing. Using open source tools such as Apache Spark, Hive, HBase, Flink, Hudi, and Presto, are coupled with EC2 and S3, EMR gives analysts the elasticity to deal with Petabyte data. EMR gives the analysts flexibility to run the short-lived clusters that will scaleup to meet the demand on large scale data. If Apache Spark and Apache Hive, are installed on-premise then EMR cluster can be implemented on cloud to scaleup via outpost on cloud.

III. **Amazon Redshift** is an Internet hosting service provided by AWS. it is built on top of massive parallel processing (MPP) data warehouses. Redshift differs from Amazon's other services with the ability to handle large data sets stored on column-oriented database. Redshift can handle connections from other sources using ODBC and JDBC connections.

Google Cloud Analytics Products:

I.   **Google Big Query** is a well-managed serverless and analytical data warehouse. Big Query provides (Software as a Service)SaaS RESTful web service that analyse bulk datasets along with MapReduce. Big Query is scalable, *ad hoc* queries are used to perform read only operations. all the requests in Big Query must be authenticated.

II.   **Google Cloud Dataflow** is a unified beam, acting as a pipeline to provide services like data processing, pattern matching, ETL, batch computing and stream analytics. Cloud Dataflow evolved from MapReduce and technologies like Flume and Millwheel. The entire pipeline is written in java language.

III. **Google Cloud Dataproc** will manage Spark and Hadoop service, to process big datasets. Dataproc is fast, easy-to-use, it easily integrates with other Google Cloud Platform (GCP) services to give a powerful platform for data processing.

IV.   **Google Cloud Datalab** is used to gather and analyse the data and building machine learning models on the data. This will help in the research based on data science tasks. The system is scalable that deals with certain terabytes of data. Composer provides machine learning models that are used for predictions. Google Data Studio turns data into dashboards and reports that can be read, shared, and customized.

V.   **Google Cloud Dataprep** is a data service that can handle both structured and unstructured data. It visualizes, clean, prepare data for analysis by machine learning algorithms. Cloud Dataprep is serverless, so no need to deploy the architecture. Most of the steps in data preparation are done automatically to avoid time-consuming data profiling and focus on data analysis.

Related Azure Services and Microsoft Products

I.   **HDInsight** is a fully managed, open source, full-spectrum, analytical software provided by Azure cloud. HDInsight is a feature enabled in HDFS, YARN, and MapReduce programming model to process and analyse bulk data sets.

II.   **Data Lake Analytics** is a cloud based, distributed data processing feature by Azure. It pairs YARN and Hadoop system. Parallel processing of structured and unstructured data stored in existing data warehouse is. Lake analytics is designed using SQL and c#. It provides software service(SaaS). This feature is based on pricing per job not per hour.

III.   **Machine Learning Studio** is a software tool that aims at creating different Artificial Neural Network(ANN) and Machine Learning(ML) models. Frameworks like MXnet and TensorFlow have made this possible. This studio has made the development of the models easier just by drag and drop interface.

5. Pros and Cons of Cloud Analytics

To be in a competitive position organization develop big data projects and it requires additional infrastructure, which also known as CAPEX. By shifting to OPEX column, the expense of CAPEX is reduced by using IaaS model in cloud. Thereby organizations need not to invest in setting up data servers. Thus, dumping bulk data in cloud requires zero CAPEX and also supports in enhancing the scalability. Also, the cost of analytics is reduced and innovative culture is encouraged. The data received from various sources may be structured/unstructured, it requires very high storage capacity and servers require extra power to run. Scaling of infrastructure is easily done by using cloud. Setting up of on premise infrastructure, maintenance cost and physical damage to the systems are also reduced. Once the data is stored in cloud, companies need not to worry about the technical aspects of processing. The creativeness within enterprise should be cultivated to maximize their profit. Instead of focusing on servers and database, team should concentrate on analysing information so that it gives insights.

Storing big data in cloud rises with certain security issues in which the information obtained from internet consist of details of credit card, security numbers, and addresses of individual (Achariya and kauser Ahmed, 2016). This is one of the limitations. Thus, providing security is important. If a data loss occurs then there is a sudden loss to companies. Migrating the data to the cloud sometimes faces data loss and may cause discomfort. Another limitation is less control over agreement in which organizations migrating their information to cloud must think about compliance. The service provider provides set of rules and regulations to companies such as PCI, HIPAA and many more. Even though there are rules, organizations may not have a full control over their data. The service provider provides a security checks, organizations should be aware of few questions such as where the data is placed, who the actual owner is and who can access the data. Understanding the agreement, before migrating data to cloud is very important. With a poor internet connectivity and service interruptions may lead to improper accessing of data in cloud (Dan and Roger 2010). Since the data collected is in large size, it faces many latency issues. Before making an investment, the companies should analyze the extent of usage of cloud. Investing in cloud platform should bring a profit for organization, necessary planning has to be done. For new investors the volume of data growing may be devastating. However, using cloud to store data may overcome these issues.

CONCLUSION

Organizations can take faster decision by converging big data and cloud technologies to maximize their profit and adopt with future trends and behavior. The chapter discusses the importance of cloud platform for big data, importance of analytics in cloud and gives detail insight about the trends and techniques adopted for cloud analytics. Users can access their data remotely from anywhere at any time. Analytics on cloud avoids companies to build from scratch. Analytics on cloud helps business to stay competitive and as wide benefits.

REFERENCES

Achariya & Ahmed. (2016). A survey on big data analytics: challenges, open research issues & tools. *IJACSA, 7*(2).

Aydin, N. (2015). Cloud Computing for E-Commerce. *Journal of Mobile Computing and Application, 2*(1), 27–31.

Balachandra & Prasad. (2017). *Challenges and Benefits of Deploying Big data analytics in the cloud for business intelligence international conference on knowledge based & intelligent information & engineering systems.* Elsevier.

Dan, S., & Roger, C. (2010). Privacy and consumer risks in cloud computing. *Computer Law & Security Review, 26*(4), 391–397. doi:10.1016/j.clsr.2010.05.005

Jayashree, M. (2013). Data Mining: Exploring Big Data Using Hadoop and Map Reduce. *International Journal of Engineering Science Research, 4*(1).

Manju Sharma. (2016). Big data analytics challenges & solutions in cloud. *American Journal of Engineering Research, 6*(4), 46-51.

Nathiya, T. (2017). Reducing D DOS Attack Techniques in Cloud Computing Network Technology. *International Journal of Innovative Research in Applied Sciences and Engineering, 1*(1), 23–29. doi:10.29027/IJIRASE.v1.i1.2017.23-29

Sharma, P., & Navdeti, C. (2014). Securing Big Data Hadoop: A Review of Security Issues, Threats and Solution. *IJCSIT*, *5*(2), 2126–2131.

Singh & Reddy. (2014). A survey on platforms for big data analytics. *Journal of Big Data, 2.*

Talia, D. (2013). *Clouds for scalable big data analytics*. IEEE Computer Science. doi:10.1109/MC.2013.162

Chapter 4
An IoT–Based Energy Meter for Energy Level Monitoring, Predicting, and Optimization

Sivakumar V.

ⓘ https://orcid.org/0000-0003-1553-9562

Dayananda Sagar Academy of Technology and Management, India

Swathi R.

Sree Abiraami College for Women, Thiruvalluvar University, Vellore, India

Yuvaraj V.

Shenzhen Center Power Tech Co. Ltd., Shenzhen, China

ABSTRACT

The current methods of energy monitoring and metering in India are extremely labor-intensive and prone to human errors. The system the authors propose will incorporate an automatic energy reading meter system (AERM) which will aid in the collection of data accurately and efficiently. Additionally, power companies find it hard to withstand the power requirement of a consumer because of a surge in industries, buildings, and population. The usage of electrical appliances has drastically increased over time. As per as energy balance maintains between the energy demand and supply for the power companies are bearing in mind an energy supervision technique. Therefore, there is adoption for load scheduling or load shifting to reduce the electricity bill. So consequently, the authors look into various optimization algorithms for load-shifting.

INTRODUCTION

The Internet of Things is a moderately new model that describes a group of coordination, methods, objects, etc.., by way of Internet Protocol v6 support onto the Internet environment. In the existing method of power supply grid is setup with an IoT arrangement is mainly used to improve the complications faced

DOI: 10.4018/978-1-7998-3111-2.ch004

by various issues found by the consumers on a day-to-day base. For example, in the existing meter used by the users are getting the energy consumed details only once in a month using there is no control on the existing energy smart meter. Moreover, these energy bills can be problematic on user's consume data, but a user will not be able to access or modifications in their energy consumed on or after the most recent receipt. In furthermost circumstances, if some user is unsuccessful paying the receipt, then user connection power supply get disconnect on the next working day itself.

The IoT allows items to be sensed, shared data or controlled remotely within presented network structure, reduces people work and human interference creating opportunities for more integration of the physical world into computer-based systems, it will increases efficiency, accuracy and economic benefit. When IoT is augmented with sensors and actuators, the technology becomes an instance of the more general class of cyber-physical system, which also encompasses technologies such as smart grids, virtual power plants, smart homes and smart cities. Each thing is uniquely identified through its embedded system but is able to integrate inside the existing internet communications.

The Internet of Things (IoT) is the set of connections of substantial things or "objects" set in with hardware or electronics devices, sensors, network connectivity and including software, this enables these items to gather and transfer the energy data. IoT items agree to objects to be sensed and controlled via remotely from corner to corner from the presented network communications, it creating opportunities for more direct integration between the physical world and computer-based systems, and resulting in improved efficiency, accuracy and economic benefit. "Things," in the IoT sense, can refer to a wide variety of devices such as energy data monitoring, weather monitoring, health monitoring data, biochip transponders on farm animals, electric clams in coastal waters, vehicles with built-in sensors, agriculture monitoring or field operation devices that assist forest fire-fighters in search and rescue operations. These devices collect useful data with the help of various presented technologies and then transfer by the devices itself flow the data between other devices.

An IOT is a recent technology with internet connected user devices. More rapidly or presently each IT company is must to build a outline support to IOT. Power or energy related companies by now make use of networked sensors to determine vibrations in turbines. They enroll the data all the way through the network to calculate systems that analyses it to forecast while apparatus will need preservation and when they will fail. Smart driverless car manufacturers set in sensors that measure temperature, light, pressure, and other surroundings to improve their products for easy access.

Sensors bring together statistics from the environment or object under dimension and spin it into helpful information. This sensor layer is cover up the whole thing from legacy manufacturing components to automatic systems, water level detectors, air quality sensors, accelerometers, and heart bit rate monitors. The scope of the IOT is getting higher rapidly, thanks in part to low energy consumed wireless sensor network technologies, which make possible components on a wired or wireless LAN to operate without the need for an A/C power source.

Even with the modern consideration given to safety and security for IOT components, it can be simple to ignore the need for end to end security for an IOT platform. Every part of a platform should be analyzed for security prospects. From the internet links to the software applications, and components to the transfer, stored information. The particular most important non-functional constraint of an IOT platform is that it offers strong safety measures.

In a real-time scenario using an IOT framework with the deployment of sensor mechanism, the authors are able to get the precise energy consumed by user details. A user can make choices to manage connected loads. A coordination can able to give the best choice to the consumers an estimate of exactly how much energy is being used, or that users will agree to adjust their routines with able to reduce or lesser costs.

The residential consumers are allowed and this model will support the minimum amount of energy consumption efforts. In amongst within many approaches to build and design models, the statistical approaches are the best preference to avoid the problem connected to production methodologies based on the existing approaches and methodologies observed from the available existing data.

In linear and statistical regressions analysis shows results that are promising because of the relatively simple implementation and reasonable accuracy when associated with other existing approaches. In either simple linear regression analysis algorithm or multiple-linear analysis regression algorithms with a quadratic analysis regression were implemented going on daily and hourly records.

The investigation of unconventional schemes can be calculated over and done with simulations models in directive to regulate the furthermost well-organized and profitable or commercial preferences aimed at new construction or buildings. Energy intake or consumed demonstrating approaches can be categorized as an arithmetical modeling approach or black-box modeling, white-box modeling and crossbreed modeling.

The exactness of an approach is determined by available existing information aimed at the determination of the method. An arithmetical modeling method need measured information; on the other hand not constructions characteristics whereas the white-box approaches need building characteristics on the other hand not for information. In the regression techniques and statistical modeling approaches are worthy consideration due to:

- Moderately easiness to implement.
- Prerequisite of a smaller amount of computational control than further approaches.
- Adequate forecast capacity.
- Improved accessibility of data over smart energy meter.
- Manual Process reduced.
- User friendly.

In this book chapter, the authors also discuss a circulated energy management approach that targets to achieve uptown energy. The approaches that are recommended consider the neighborhood energy surpluses in order to shrinkage energy costs. This enhanced administration based on a set of dependence aspects that a customer outlines an own neighbor to evade worst energy procurements.

At present-day, power variations and burdens are the most important issues tackled by the consumer. The best essential action of the industry effectiveness remains to produce in addition generated electrical energy supply to consumer's real demand with a very little operational rate.

The most important stimulating responsibilities for the service supplier are to fulfill the end user consumption requirement. Consumer's energy demand is very high, at that time of peak hours. For that reason, an appropriate mechanism is essential to solving both the service provider and customer necessities.

Some leading intentions of a smart-grid are to proficiently practice the obtainable power by the customer. Customers, energy level usage charge is cheap by effective function the machines throughout the off-peak periods.

Background

The electricity field is developed by estimating with various approaches that have been proposed all over the years. The Internet of Things is a fresh idea that enlightens gathering of coordination, methods, objects etc.., over the of Internet Protocol v6 support in contradiction of the Internet atmosphere. Users are accessible by means of the energy spent particulars simply monthly once but no control over the existing available or installed smart meter. Additionally, these bills can be convoluted on how they existent a customer's usage data, but customers may possibly not be able to interpret modifications in their power usage from the latest receipt.

Anita Priscilla Mary et al. (2018) "Analysis and Forecasting Of Electrical Energy a Literature Review" this research proposes about the analysis of the various sources of electricity generation and to predict the electricity generation to meet the future demand on energy using different data mining techniques.

Audun, Josang.,&Jochen, Haller., (2007) "Dirichlet Reputation Systems" this paper discusses various probability distribution analysis and compute repute score based on the ratings from several different parties of the various sources of electricity generation and to predict the electricity generation to meet the future demand for energy-using different data mining techniques.

BasumataryJwngsar et al. (2018) "Demand Side Management of a University Load in Smart Grid Environment" this paper recommends a DSM technique. The authors are suggested a bottom-up load modeling procedure to learning the arrangement of electrical energy shortage in MNNIT Institute, Allahabad, India. Additional supporting, it recommends a load scheduling performance to form the shortage curvature by reorganizing the lecture schedules.

Birendrakumar, Sahani et al. (2017) "IoT Based Smart Energy Meter" proposes Arduino Uno board based energy meter. Authors explained with component in additionally webpage added to this smart energy meter.

Hlaing, Win et al. (2017) "Implementation of Wi-Fi-based single phase smart meter for Internet of Things (IoT)" proposes a system that utilizes the ESP8266 Wi-Fi Module in order to connect to the internet and transmit data as opposed to the previous paper which would require a stable mobile network. According to the paper, this meter can correctly and reliably read the energy meter parameters such as demand value, load profile, and total energy consumption.

Fumo, Nelson et al. (2015) "Regression Analysis for Prediction of Residential Energy Consumption" this research work, simple linear regression analysis and multiple linear regression analysis methods achieved in additionally a quadratic regression analysis be there implemented taking place daily or hourly records from a firm. The phase interval for the perceived statistics was shown to be a significant feature that well-defined the importance of the model.

Mhadhbi, Zeineb et al. (2018) "Validation of a Distributed Energy Management Approach for Smart Grid Based on a Generic Colored Petri Nets Model" this paper proposed the Petri Nets Model with an intelligent neighborhood-based energy management approach that proceeds assistance of neighborhood power leftover. The introduced approach allows consumers to insist on a dependence reason on their neighbors in order to control the preeminent alternate to fulfill their necessities.

Muralitharan, K., et al. (2015) "Multiobjective Optimization Technique for Demand Side Management with Load Balancing Approach in Smart Grid" in this paper they used a multi-objective evolutionary procedure, which outcomes in the charge saving for power convention and decreases the waiting time for machine performance.

K, C, Okafor et al. (2017) "Development of Arduino Based IoT Metering System for On-Demand Energy Monitoring" discuss the implementation of an Internet of Things based Energy meter using an Arduino Uno, Hall Effect Sensor and a SIM 800 L GSM Component data transmission. To connect the internet and data relay using GPRS, GSM technologies in real-time. This structure was shown to be popular in energy consumption, measuring energy and more over handling charges acquired by the consumer. These metrics are interconnecting charges to the cloud server and power depletion.

Pooja, Talwar, et al. (2016) "IOT Based Energy Meter Reading" discussed with ARM controller but author not mentioned any algorithm for transmission of data and computing data in this proposed work.

Rashika, Rajput. & Amit, Gupta. (2018) "Power Grid System Management through Smart Grid in India" in this research work concerted happening the inverter for system crossing point can effectively be assistance in the direction of accomplishing devolution of dynamic power acquired from the sustainable asset, stack quick to respond energy demand support, energy noises compensation next to PCC and energy unbalance and dispassionate present wage if around ought to be an existence of 3-stage 4-wire outline.

Ramanan, G et al. (2017) "Implementation of Machine Learning Algorithm for Predicting User Behavior and Smart Energy Management" this paper explores the preeminent varieties of methodologies that have been inspected to solve the load disaggregation badly behaved, specifically, the feedback data for efficient and improved energy management.

Xiaoou, Monica, Zhang et al. (2018) "Forecasting Residential Energy Consumption: Single Household Perspective" this paper investigates fifteen anonymous individual household's electricity consumption forecasting using SVR (support vector regression) modeling approach is pragmatic to both daily and hourly data granularity.

Discussion

In the existing electro mechanical energy meter consists of an aluminum disc placed between two electro magnets, one of the coil is connected to the load and it is called as current coil next another coil electro-magnet is connected to the voltage supply. The interaction between the fluxes between the two coils is responsible for providing a torque to the disc, which starts rotating, with the revolutions proportional to the load current. The counter records the number of revolutions and displays them, which indicates the energy consumed. In the existing system different model was available for the energy theft identification. Meanwhile existing papers above mentioned under background chapter have both advantages and disadvantages.

For the advantages many authors have proposed IOT based energy meter integrate with different types of components. Authors have different types of algorithms used to compute the energy meter reading and reduce the human intervention to collect the energy utilization data in each area by area. In each day 8 hours to spend a time to do this work it will take more than 10 days to 15 days for collecting this energy utilization data in each area. Authors are proposed to reduce this manual reading data. Each author has different idea and algorithm used in this energy meter. But authors are not mentioned which algorithm is more useful for compute energy utilization, data transform to the server and transfer message to the consumer regarding energy utilization. Each author have different proposed model for compute energy utilization, data transform to the server and transfer message to the consumer regarding energy utilization.

This system will improve monthly energy meter reading without any disturbance to the consumer and there is no necessary of human intervention from the electricity board department to read the meter readings in each area, company or house. This can be achieved by the use of Arduino board unit that constantly monitor and records the energy meter reading and store it in the memory location. This system constantly records the energy meter reading and the live meter reading can be displayed on webpage to the consumer on request. This system also can be used to disconnect the power supply of the industry or house when needed.

Some of the authors are discussed energy meter based on cloud but authors not develop any application for the consumers. Authors developed an application for digital watt meter with cloud infrastructure platform for storing their collected data in cloud server. The server can accessible for authorized electricity employees from both or either state government or central government. As per recent technology many authors are proposed and developed energy meter based on internet of things because of easy access the data and immediately collect the data via remotely and transfer the data to the server towards scheduled timing.

PROPOSED SYSTEM

The proposed model consists of Automatic Energy Reading Meter (AERM) capability with the assistance of the current sensor. The values are providing for the controller to calculate the usage of power. The server will generate the bill as per our monthly energy consumption according to the tariff rate.

A separate database is maintained in the server which encloses consumer particulars and their monthly consumption details. Thus, the authors can avoid human entry errors while entry in the energy meter card and also calculating the readings from AERM. To determining energy consumptions, calculate Microcontroller data from the server. Current sensors are detecting a power theft in an LCD Display for reading all the information on the consumer part. In the proposed model the authors which deal with Automatic Energy Reading Meter with power theft handling or control model.

The proposed work, the total power consumption from the power load terminal will be calculated by using a micro-controller and it is used to identify at all theft in the middle of the AERM and service supply line. This transfers the data from the AERM and it is stored in server after that as per electricity board computation rules for calculating the consumer usage cost later it send a SMS to the consumer about the bill amount and maybe if any other activities happen in this proposed system such as tempering, overloading, fault etc. IOT is the basis of communication between user and service provider. Internet of things devices is the universal network for the data transfer over and the always live connection between server location and IOT mobile devices. The cost of transferring data is much lesser than the SMS. In this proposed system power supply is provided to AERM energy meter. A GSM unit shows the interfacing with the Arduino Uno board based device. Each and every consumer has unique number provided by the electricity board authority.

The goal of creating more awareness about energy consumption would be optimization and reduction in energy usage by the user. This would reduce their energy cost as well as conserve energy Requirement of less computational power than other statistical approaches (genetic algorithms, neural networks, support vectors machine). Satisfactory prediction ability is also available. Data availability is increased through Automatic Energy Reading Meter System.

Normally a person comes from electricity board, standing in front of our house for taking reading data, whose duty is to read the energy meter for every month or two months once and handover the reading data to electricity board data entry people. This is nothing but manual entry for meter reading. According to that meter reading, consumers have to pay the bills amount. The main drawback of this system is that electricity board person has to go area by area and he has to read and write the meter of every company or house. Many times errors like extra bill amount or notification from electric board even though the bills are paid are common errors. To defeat this problem authors have come up with an idea which will remove the third party between the consumer and service provider, even the errors will be overcome.

Methodology

- A suitable Machine Learning Algorithm is to apply for learning energy usage data and predicting future usage. Several Machine Learning techniques can be used for this purpose having their own advantages and disadvantages.
- Support vector machines essentially consist of kernel and optimizer algorithm. Kernel divides non-linear data into high-dimensional space and makes data linearly separable.
- The optimizer algorithm is applied to solve the optimization problems. The multiple linear regression, or univariate multiple regression, is the generalization of the simple linear regression model. The model in multiple linear regression allows more than one predictor variable.
- In this proposed will incorporate an Automatic Energy Reading Meter which will aid in the collection of data accurately and efficiently.
- Additionally, power companies find it hard to with stand the power requirement of a consumer because of a surge in industries, buildings and population. The usage of electrical appliances has drastically increased overtime. In order to maintain a balance between the supply and demand the power companies are considering a demand side management approach. As a result, there is adoption of for load shifting or scheduling their loads into off-peak hours to reduce their electricity bill. So therefore, consider various optimization algorithms for load-shifting.

Automatic Energy Reading Meter (AERM)

AERM, where power and telecommunication infrastructure work together with automatic, is also provided with a payment facility and it gives from top to bottom safety in all the transfer. In this proposed model the power is determined in units and the data is forwarded to remote servers where the application is used to produce a bill for energy consumption. Meter reader transmits a handheld laptop or any data gathering device with an analysis, collects the readings from a smart meter by placing the read inquiry in close nearness to a reading coil attached in the touchpad. When the button is clicked, an interrogate signal is sent by the review analysis to the touch segment in order to accumulate them reading. Figure 1shows an IOT Energy Meter schematic structure.

Energy meter or watt-to-hour meter is an electrical device that calculates the amount of electrical energy used by the consumers. Utilities is one of the electrical departments, which install these instruments at every place like homes, industries, organizations, commercial buildings to charge for the electricity consumption by loads such as lights, tube lights, fans, washing machines, iron box, refrigerators and other home appliances. Energy meter measures the rapid voltage and currents, calculate their product and give instantaneous power. This power is integrated over a time period, which gives the energy utilized over that time period. An AERM smart energy meter is an electronic circuit device that records the energy consumption of electrical energy in based on the sometime intervals of an hour or less and communicates that information at least daily back to the utility for monitoring and billing Smart meters enables two-way communication between the meter and central system.

Benefits or Advantages of AERM

- AERM reading will get accurate and improved billing mechanism.
- Very less financial encumbrance while correcting mistakes.
- Energy management will be able to view by data analytical graphs.
- Tamper detection improved security and equipment.
- Cost of meter reading have clearness while reading the data
- In any circumstances of deficiencies or shortages utility function will be able to supply allocation or manage.
- Very less ensued expenses
- Better-quality attaining power and yet more right data
- Fastening of usage and enhanced billing method.

Figure 1. IOT Energy Meter schematic structure

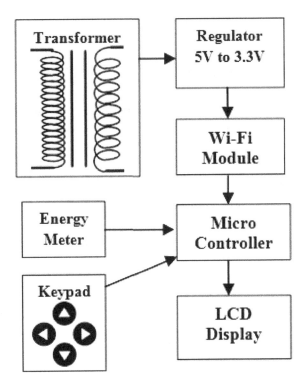

Energy Stealing or Theft Identification

Digital energy meter will calculate the energy consumed from the supply load ended a period of time. It sending information that is in a part of the energy utilized. Digital wireless data transmitter supports the energy consumed details transmit to the server. The data receiver taking place the opposite end system backbone collects data sent by the spreader from the supply load meter. The data receiver will send it to the micro-controller. The digital meter will calculate the power transmitted through line1 and be responsible for proper data handover to the micro-controller. Here and now microcontroller has two readings one is energy transmitted through line1 and another is energy spent by the load (L1&L2) respectively.

The electrical energy department as well contains a few issues similar to power stealing. Power theft is a determine offense and it moreover directly affects the country economy. Power Transmission, production and supply of electricity include the loss of electricity. To keep away from the losses must require monitoring the energy utilization and losses, so that resourcefully make use of the generated power. Energy Meter tempering is another division of power stealing and also against the law offense which can reduce. Energy consumed billing is a method in common the human electricity operator goes to visit every user's home or company then as long as bill it will get lot of time. To determination these problems authors developed AERM metering system on the base of IOT energy meter reading.

If any tapping is done through any illegal persons on that particular line to connect home or company appliances then it will get traced and informed to the server. The difference will be calculated in the middle of AERM reading and pole meter reading.

The micro-controller matches the two reading standards and if the restrained evaluation level on the pole is more than the level sent by the meter by some tolerance then the authors can say that energy stealing is happening taking place that particular route. Illegal stealing or tapping of the precise location is display in the effective terminal mode.

The Benefit of the Proposed System

- The smart automated process as a replacement for physical labor work.
- Optimize the maintenance and Careful information collect from network load.
- Custom-built billing rates and customized date of billings
- Efficient high bill inquiries.
- Faster recovery from power failure
- Outage statistics will be automatic.

  Advantages of the Proposed System

- An evaluation has been automated.
- The hazard of human error and corruption will get reduced.
- In particular due to bad weather environments like rain, snow, storm, etc. The system will not impede on bring together. Illegal Social activities avoided (Power Theft, tampering...)

WORKING MODEL

Working of ACS712 Current Sensor

Before the authors initiate to building this development it is especially necessary to know the functioning of ACS712 energy sensor. This one is an important part of determining current exclusively AC current. It is all the time a threatening job appropriate to the noise cooled with its inaccurate insulation will make it into difficulty, etc. on the other hand with the help of this ACS712 sensor the authors perform works taking places the standard of Hall-effect. Affording to this standard, while the current-carrying rod is positioned into a magnetic field, a voltage is generated across its ends upright to both the magnetic field and current.

Figure 2. ACS712 30A Current Sensor Module
Source: electronicscomp.com

Let us not acquire in addition profound interested in the idea apart from humbly use a hall-sensor to compute the magnetic-field just about a current-carrying rod. This calculation will be made in terms of millivolts which is called hall-voltage. This considered hall-voltage is comparative to the current from end to end the conductor. The most important benefit of the ACS712 current sensor is that it can determine both DC and AC current. It also provides inaccessibility among the measuring part i.e. micro-controller unit and AC/DC load unit. Figure 2 as shown below have the pins on the sensor component have ground, Vout and Vcc correspondingly.

A hall-effect sensor module is working under 5 voltage. The ground pin is connected to the ground coordination. The Vout pin has an offset voltage of 2500millivolts. The current flowing is positive value while the current is flowing through a fastidious cable at that point the voltage output will be 2500mv. The flow of current is negative while voltage greater than 2500mv. The electrical energy will be less mm than 2500mv using Arduino pin to understand the output voltage of the module, which will be 2500mv there is no current flowing over the cable. This measured value will decrease as the current flow in a negative direction and will increase as the current movements in the positive route.

Figure 3. Circuit of an IOT Energy Meter

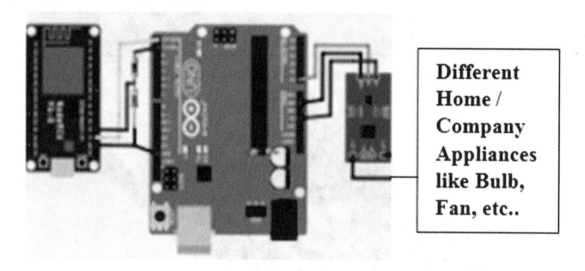

This above Figure 3 shown is based on energy meter using NodeMCU and Arduino. At hand is one analog pin presented popular the NodeMCU ESP12. That analog pin from the ESP sequence is able to get a maximum of 3.3 volts on their pins. The authors are using a current sensor that can give up to 5volts, it will be able to damage the WIFI component that's why the authors are not using outside NodeMCU to put together the output of the current sensor 3.3v as an alternative of 5v. So that the authors cannot usage the voltage separator circuit in the middle of an analog pin of NodeMCU and current sensor. For the reason that the current sensor to facilitate at 2.5Volts output, so Arduino will read the current sensor details over an analog pin, transfer the details to the Wi-Fi component, ESP12 by means of a serial message. Use voltage divider circuit at receiver pin in nodeMCU, accordingly with the aim of receive pin can change up to 3.3voltage level. Figure 4 shows the Model of an IOT Energy Meter.

Materials Required to the Proposed System

1. Arduino Uno board
2. ESP12/Node MCU
3. Current / energy sensor
4. Male-female wires

5.   Any ac appliances

Figure 4. Model of an IOT Energy Meter
Source: circuitdigest.com

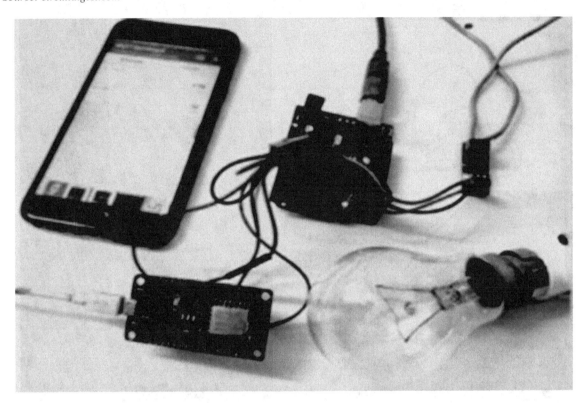

Arduino board is the heart of our proposed system. Complete execution of proposed method depends on this Arduino board. Arduino reacts to the 5v supply given by opto-coupler and keeps on counting the supply and then calculates the power consumed and also the cost. This data, it continuously stores on server, so that users can visit any time and check their consumption. It even reacts accordingly as per programmed, to the situations like message sending during threshold value etc. Arduino is a microcontroller based board. It is based on ATmega328P. This arduino board consists of 14 digital I/O pins. From this 6 input pins out of 14 are used as PWM outputs, remaining 6 input pins out of 14 as analog inputs, and quartz crystal of 16MHz. This board having USB port connection, power supply and reset button. Easily everyone able to connect this Arduino board to any device or computer using USB port connection to utilize the data. As per compare Arduino UNO board with other it differs from the proceeding board which doesn't use FTDI because it is USB to Serial communication. Instead of that the ATmega8U2 is programmed as USB to serial conversion.

Figure 5. Implementation an IOT based AERM

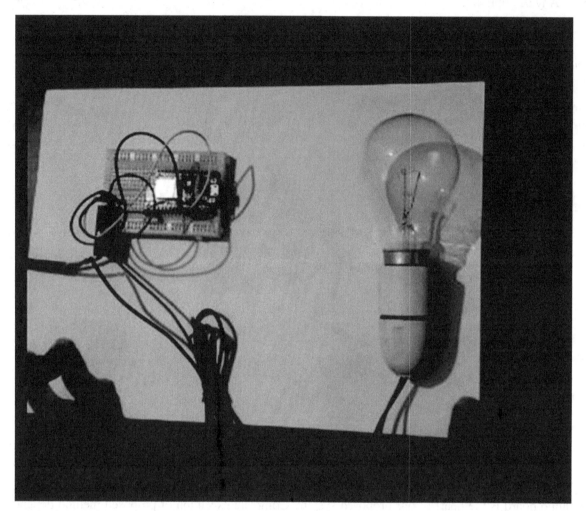

EXPERIMENTAL RESULTS

In Figure 5 shows that IOT based AERM implementation. In this chapter authors have developed android application. This android application has two login, one is for consumer login and other one is electricity data entry login. In consumer login have energy utilization data for each month, bill amount and payment option details. Authors displaying the information about the energy consumed in terms of units, about the bill amount. For this reason every user can check the information anywhere from the worldwide. This android application is used for displaying the information of the consumer details. Figure 6 shows front design of the application for consumer. Figure 7 shows consumer energy utilization data as per AERM energy meter and as well as energy utilization price.

Figure 6. Front Design of a Consumer Application

Smart Meter Reading

Customer Login

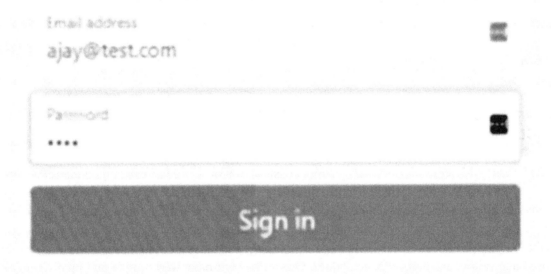

Figure 7. Consumer Payment Details

Payment History		
Date	**Amount**	**Meter Reading**
22-Jun-2020	Rs. 136.45	43.22 units
25-Jul-2020	Rs. 154	102.56 units

FUTURE RESEARCH DIRECTIONS

In future work, the total component will make for commercial purpose with less cost. The AERM should be available in very less size compare with the existing devices. AERM meter details will be stored on the database server; this data will be useful for the future enhancement using recent effective data analytics algorithms.

CONCLUSION

The IOT Energy Meter now collects the energy consumption data and uploads it onto the server using the ESP8266 Wifi Module. Using the data collected from the meter and by applying certain machine learning algorithms to it. The system can now fairly accurately predict the future energy consumption needs of the household. Using various optimization techniques author will also be able to balance and shift the load across various areas so as to minimize wastage and maximize efficiency of the model among the used algorithms, methods and techniques. Our framework empowers simple and precise ongoing following and checking of vitality utilization at family units. It additionally diminishes the repetitive expense of work included. Gives specialists the capacity to anticipate future vitality utilization and plan as needs be. Furnishes clients with the capacity to track and screen their vitality utilization, consequently empowering them to adjust and spare vitality. In this book chapter, authors have considered various approaches to building an IoT based AERM Energy Meter, forecasting future energy consumption and efficient strategies for optimizing the current load supplied to the area. Our system enables easy and accurate real time tracking and monitoring of energy consumption at households. It also reduces the recurring cost of labor involved provides authorities the ability to predict future energy consumption and plan accordingly. It provides users with the ability to track and monitor their energy consumption, hence enabling them to adapt and save energy. As per this work carried by the authors have considered various approaches to building an IoT based AERM Energy Meter, forecasting future energy consumption and efficient strategies for optimizing the current load supplied to the area. The authors have also attempted to analyze these approaches and identify the advantages and disadvantages of each methodology.

ACKNOWLEDGMENT

This research received no specific grant from any funding agency in the public, commercial, or not-for-profit sectors. Author's expresses thanks to Shreyas.N, Ajay.R, Anusha.A, Chaitra.A for their support in this work.

REFERENCES

Anita, P., Mary, M., & Josephine, M.S. (2018). Analysis and Forecasting Of Electrical Energy a Literature Review. *International Journal of Pure and Applied Mathematics*, *119*(15), 289–293.

Audun, J., & Jochen, H. (2007, April). *Dirichlet Reputation Systems*. Paper presented at the Second International Conference on Availability, Reliability and Security (ARES'07), Vienna, Austria

Basumatary, Pratap, Singh, Brijendra, & Gore. (2018, January). *Demand Side Management of a University Load in Smart Grid Environment*. Paper presented at the Workshops ICDCN '18, Varanasi, India.

Birendrakumar, S., Tejashree, R., Akibjaved, T., & Ranjeet, P. (2017). IoT Based Smart Energy Meter. *International Research Journal of Engineering Technology*, *4*(4), 96–102.

Fumo, N., & Biswas, R. (2015). Regression analysis for prediction of residential energy consumption. *Elsevier Renewable and Sustainable Energy Reviews*, *7*(47), 332–343.

Hao, H., & Rongxing, L., & Zonghua, Z. (2015, December). *Vtrust: A robust trust framework forrelay selection in hybrid vehicular communications*, Paper presented at the IEEE Global Communications Conference, GLOBECOM 2015, San Diego, CA.

Hlaing, W., Thepphaeng, S., Nontaboot, V., Tangsun, N., Sangsuwan, T., & Chaiyod, P. (2017, March). *Implementation of WiFi-based single phase smart meter for Internet of Things (IoT)*. Paper presented at the International Electrical Engineering Congress (iEECON), Pattaya, Thailand.

Mhadhbi, Z., Zairi, S., Gueguen, C., & Zouari, B. (2018). Validation of a Distributed Energy Management Approachfor Smart Grid Based on a Generic Colored Petri Nets Model. *Journal of Clean Energy Technologies*, *6*(1), 20–25.

Muralitharan, K., Sakthivel, R., & Shi, Y. (2015). Multi objective Optimization Technique for Demand Side Management with Load Balancing Approach in Smart Grid. *Elsevier Neurocomputing*, *177*, 110–119.

Okafor, K. C., Ononiwu, G. C., & Precious, U. (2017). Development of Arduino Based IoT Metering System for On-Demand Energy Monitoring. *International Journal of Mechatronics. Electrical and Computer Technology*, *7*(23), 3208–3224.

Pooja, T. D., & Kulkarni, S. B. (2016). IOT Based Energy Meter Reading. *International Journal of Recent Trends in Engineering & Research*, *2*(6), 586–591.

Rajeshwari, S., Santhoshs, H., & Varaprasad, G. (2015). Implementing Intelligent Traffic Control System for Congestion Control, Ambulance Clearance, and Stolen Vehicle Detection. *IEEE Sensors Journal*, *15*(2), 1109 – 1113.

Rajput, R., & Gupta, A. (2018). Power Grid System Management through Smart Grid inIndia. *International Journal on Recent Technologies in Mechanical and Electrical Engineering*, *5*(1), 17–26.

Ramanan, R. G., Manikandaraj, S., & Kamaleshwar, R. (2017, February). *Implementation of Machine Learning Algorithm for Predicting User Behavior and Smart Energy Management*. Paper presented at the International Conference on Data Management, Analytics and Innovation, Pune, India.

Rashmi, H., Rohith, S. R., & Indira, M. S. (2013). RFID and GPS based automatic lane clearance system for ambulance. *International Journal of Advanced Electrical and Electronics Engineering, (IJAEEE)*, *2*(3), 102–107.

Vignesh, G., Vishal, N., Prakash, S., & Sivakumar, V. (2016, May). *Automated Traffic Light Control System and Stolen Vehicle Detection*. Paper presented at the 2016 IEEE International Conference on Recent Trends in Electronics, Information & Communication Technology (RTEICT), Bangalore, India.

Zhang, M. X., Grolinger, K., & Capretz, A. M. (2018, December). *Forecasting Residential Energy Consumption: Single Household Perspective*, Paper presented at the 17th IEEE International Conference on Machine Learning and Applications (ICMLA), Orlando, FL.

ADDITIONAL READING

Li, Z., & Dong, B. (2017). A new modeling approach for short term prediction of occupancy in residential buildings. *Building and Environment*, *121*, 277–290.

Lusis, P., Khalilpour, K. R., Andrew, L., & Liebman, A. (2017). Short-term residential load forecasting: Impact of calendar effects and forecast granularity. *Applied Energy*, *205*, 654–669.

Miller, R., Golab, L., & Rosenberg, C. (2017). Modeling weather effects for impact analysis of residential time of use electricity pricing. *Elsevier Energy Policy*, *105*, 534–546.

Tascikaraoglu, A., Boynuegri, A., & Uzunoglu, M. (2014). A demand side management strategy based on forecasting of residential renewable sources: A smart home system in turkey. *Elsevier Energy and Buildings*, *80*, 309–320.

KEY TERMS AND DEFINITIONS

Arduino Uno: Arduino Uno is a micro-controller board support by ATmega model. It includes the whole thing needed to maintain the microcontroller, computer able connect it with a USB wire or power get through AC to DC adapter or battery.

Automatic Energy Reading Meter: Automatic energy reading meter is a new equipment of without human intervention gather the energy consumption details data from energy metering device and transfer that particular data to a database server for billing and analyze.

Energy Management: Energy management consists of energy production preparation and operation and energy consumption details.

Energy Theft: Energy theft is the illegal perform of electrical power theft. As per law it is an offense and is liable to be punished by fines or imprisonment.

Internet of Things: Internet of things is a technique of interconnected devices with individual identifier for each device and capability to transmit data over a group of nodes no need of human or computer interaction.

Machine Learning: Machine learning is a next level of artificial intelligence that gives systems capability to learn without human intervention and improve from practice without any human programming. It targets on the program development; it can be able data access and data learning for themselves.

NodeMCU: NodeMCU is an open source Internet of Things development platform. The NodeMCU term by default refers to the firmware. It uses a variety of open source projects.

Chapter 5
Artificial Intelligence Based on Biological Neurons:
Constructing Neural Circuits for IoT

Rinat Galiautdinov
https://orcid.org/0000-0001-9557-5250
Independent Researcher, Italy

ABSTRACT

The chapter describes the new approach in artificial intelligence based on simulated biological neurons and creation of the neural circuits for the sphere of IoT which represent the next generation of artificial intelligence and IoT. Unlike existing technical devices for implementing a neuron based on classical nodes oriented to binary processing, the proposed path is based on simulation of biological neurons, creation of biologically close neural circuits where every device will implement the function of either a sensor or a "muscle" in the frame of the home based live AI and IoT. The research demonstrates the developed nervous circuit constructor and its usage in building of the AI (neural circuit) for IoT.

INTRODUCTION

Although the concept of the "Internet of Things" (IoT) has been around for a long time, it, especially in the light of our rapid technological development, is constantly evolving. We can say that IoT is the embodiment of the gradual merger of the physical and digital worlds, as data is collected from an ever-growing number of devices and then combined into so-called "big data." The number of such devices of the "Internet of things", according to experts and analysts, will reach 50 billion by 2020.

However, when you try to transfer the data collected by IoT devices to a centralized storage, such as a cloud, there is a problem with the delay in their transmission. In many respects, even though the connection speed is constantly increasing, the characteristics of this process do not correspond to the available data growth. If you transfer the "raw" data, that is, unprocessed, all in a row, the delay will increase and, therefore, the overall system performance will suffer.

DOI: 10.4018/978-1-7998-3111-2.ch005

Data processing is one of those areas in which AI can make a significant contribution. In addition, it opens the way to the introduction of technological innovations in various fields, from optimizing the movement of urban transport to improving public safety and improving the provision of financial services.

Implementing AIoT requires components that can cope with complex and diverse conditions at the edge of the network. The periphery, as you know, can be literally anything - from airborne vehicles and aircraft to factories or oil installations in the desert. All this requires a flexible and adaptable approach to the production of components to solve this problem. An important point is that AI promises to eliminate the influence of the human factor on decision-making as much as possible. This puts more pressure on system integrators: they need to provide special control over the quality of the functioning of the system, since an accident in systems with artificial intelligence does not always have an obvious culprit or a visible reason.

Another difficulty we face with is related to the fact that we always have to tune something in the settings and in some cases we might want the devices to work in one mode in another in the other one, so as a result we'd constantly have to spend our time on tuning, changing, updated and doing lots of work. Besides it would take lots of time to read the instructions, to learn how to use some software, etc.

One more problem is enclosed in the fact that what we call "Artificial Intelligence" is not really the AI, it provides extremely narrow functionality which only allows to select the proper "answer" based on multi-criteria condition. Such the AI can not really think, evolve with time. Such the AI will require the constant installation of the new and new modules for processing new tasks and the abilities of such the AI can't be compared with the abilities of even the most primitive creature.

A good example of the scope of limited AI is the recognition of text, images and speech, which we can implement using neural networks and machine learning. During training, such artificial intelligence remembers thousands, if not millions, of various iterations of data and is able to correctly determine the image or an object located in the zone of its action. No matter how complex the predictions of such an AI become, it is still limited by a narrow function. If something goes beyond the given parameters, the AI becomes almost useless. For example, artificial intelligence, trained to recognize written numbers, can master this task and easily push people out of this sphere of activity, because it will work more efficiently, without fatigue and interruptions, but it will be completely useless if it is given to it without retraining such tasks as e.g. letter identification.

As for the concept of border (peripheral) computing, the initial idea of IoT was that the data for processing and subsequent analysis was sent to some central device or to the cloud. However, as the number of devices increases exponentially, many applications have already reached the limit of their capabilities, and all this large amount of data transferred back and forth leads to problems with unacceptable delays in decision making and response.

Border computing solves this problem by processing "big data" directly on the edge of the network. Thus, the device can independently determine what needs to be sent to the cloud and what can be filtered out like digital garbage. In fact, this concept offers the movement of computing power to the "edge" of the network - to where the Internet connects to various devices.

And here we come to another problem which is enclosed in neural computation.

A model approach to research allows us to overcome the limitations and difficulties that arise when setting up a laboratory experiment, due to the possibility of conducting so-called numerical experiments, and to study the response of the system under study to changes in its parameters and initial conditions.

In this regard, computer simulation is widely used in all natural sciences. Neuroscience or the science of the brain, whose task is to study the functioning of the brain and nervous system. The brain is a complex object consisting of a large number of different types of cells, including the main signal cells - neurons (cells that generate and transmit electro-chemical impulses that can form networks through contacts called synapses), glial cells that regulate metabolism, blood vessel cells, etc. Modeling such systems, complex in internal connections and large in the number of elements, using modern personal computers is extremely difficult, due to the large th computing capacity derived models.

However, the use of supercomputer technologies allows the use of more diverse modeling methods. One of such the methods is called large-scale modeling. Large-scale modeling is one of the directions in supercomputer modeling. This method is intended for the development and conduct of numerical experiments with global computer models of multidimensional systems in which macro and micro models that simulate the interconnected functioning of multilevel systems are integrated. This direction arose relatively recently due to significant progress in the technology of manufacturing microcircuits, parallel computing, and the increased processing power of supercomputer systems, which became available with the advent of specialized software. Large-scale modeling is based on the principle of hierarchical reduction, which assumes that any complex system consists of hierarchically subordinate subsystems (levels of organization). A high-level organization system consists of lower-level systems, and a combination of low-level organization systems forms a higher-level system. Application of this principle to modeling in neuroscience allows us to represent the brain in the form of several 4 interacting independently described subsystems. The hierarchy of the model allows you to achieve the level of detail required by research, by increasing or decreasing the number of organization levels considered. However, with an increase in the number of levels of organization, the number of parameters describing the system increases, which greatly complicates the task of creating a realistic model that reproduces the phenomena observed in a laboratory experiment. An increase in the number of model parameters leads to an increase in the amount of input data required to determine them, data that are difficult to measure and often do not have a sufficient degree of accuracy. In this regard, abstraction is used when creating models - an approach that allows you to discard parameters that are unimportant for research in the framework of the task, with the aim of solving which the model was developed. Thus, the task of abstracting is to preserve only what is important for the construction and analysis of models at different levels of the organization without losing the convenience of manipulation. The considered modeling method provided researchers with a set of neural network simulators that can greatly simplify research in the field of neuroscience.

Additionally to that it's very important to have the ability of virtual construction of neural circuit both for researching goals and the applied ones in the sphere of Artificial Intelligence and IoT. As a result the author describes the major features of such the neural constructor and represents it, showing how it was applied in simulation of the neural circuit of Aplysia(the mollusk) and Planarian(Tricladida) and how it could be used in the next generation of the IoT where all the smart devices are represented as the sensors and the constructed neural circuit processes the signals the way the nervous system processes the signals coming from the sensors of any live creature.

PROBLEMS

The Limits of the IoT Technology

IoT devices in their pure form collect data with only small or specifically specified amounts of computation. For further analysis, data is sent to the cloud. However, in such premises not all data has the same value. Take, for example, video materials for a security system: the system needs frames in which people or objects move, while images of an unchanging background are clearly not of particular interest. Sending all the data obtained during shooting to the cloud for analysis will lead to the occupation of the transmission channel bandwidth, which could be used to greater advantage.

Computing Power and Harsh Work

The transfer or implementation of AI to the periphery may require a lot of computing resources. Standard storage and memory devices will help provide the required performance, but the problem is that commercially available components of this type are generally poorly adapted to work in the harsh environments typically found in borderline applications. For example, when monitoring traffic at the location of IoT devices, cyclical changes in temperature are possible during the transition from day to night and from summer to winter. In addition, automotive systems must withstand shock and vibration, while industrial systems must withstand increased levels of pollution, etc.

Disadvantage of the Artificial Neuron

Currently in the AI sphere we use so called Artificial Neuron, which is basically represents extremely primitive and limited ability of the biological neuron.

Let's consider some of the disadvantages of usage of the artificial neuron vs biological neuron (here and after under the term "artificial neuron" we should understand the classical representation of the artificial neuron and under the term "biological neuron" we should understand the simulated biological neuron, for example the one which is represented in the Neural constructor of Rinat Galiautdinov):

- A weak signal can't initiate a reaction of an artificial neuron. However if we consider biological neuron, in certain conditions the weak signal can initiate the reaction, as an example it could be seen in the processes called "Summation", "Long-Term Potentiation". Here's the simple example which illustrates this: a dripping tap. A single drop of water initiate extremely weak signal which might repeat not so frequently. So if we have only one sensor which is responsible only for listening of the sounds then it will not activate the system based on the artificial neurons used at the moment simply because such the signal want pass to another neuron. However if we use the simulated biological neurons (represented in the Neural constructor of Rinat Galiautdinov) then we will see that a single drop of water will not initiate a signal, however the series of weak and repeatable signals will initiate the signal and eventually it will be passed to another neuron. Such the process is called "Summation" and we can simulate such the process only if we use biological neurons.

- The artificial neuron can't distinguish the power of signals. So the artificial neuron there is no difference between the power of signals for such the processes as "dripping tap" and our memories of some positive or negative feelings we had during the day. However all that changes when we consider a biological neuron: in some cases it can't or can initiate a signal and in the other cases even a week signal can immediately initiate a reaction if there was a strong enough signal during a day. In our life we constantly face with such the examples: let's say you found 5 dollars, it creates strong enough positive signal in your brain and then during the day you will memorize this even from time to time. Or you spilled coffee in the morning: it created a strong enough negative signal and from time to time you will memorize this event during the day. Most probably you will forget about these events next day or the day after that. Such the process is called "Long-Term Potentiation" (LTP) and it can be simulated only if we use biological neurons.

- The artificial neurons can't automatically change the architecture of the neural network, they can only change the weights. The biological neurons can change the architecture of the neural network. So the artificial network built on the basis of the biological neurons can evolve with time and adjust itself to the new environment.

- The neural network based on the artificial neurons can't really include and use the new devices/sensors which this network does not know: simply speaking the neural network's developers never taught the network to use some new unknown device/sensor. In the same situation the neural network built on the basis of the neural circuits based on the biological neurons can include the new device/sensor into the system and learn how to use it.

BACKGROUND

Artificial Neuron

The artificial or programming neuron used in Computer Science partially simulates the biological neuron. Such the artificial neuron receives the number of the signals as the input data and each of these signals is in fact the output of another neuron. Each input gets multiplied by the appropriate weight (simulating the synaptic strength) then we can sum all the values and define the level of neuron activation. The final result of this operation would be either 0 or 1 (Michie D., Spiegelhalter D., Taylor C., & Campbell J., 1994).

There are different kind of the neural networks but all of them are based on the above described configuration. There are multiple input signals for the artificial neuron: $x_1, x_2,...,x_n$. These input signals correspond to the input signal in the synapses of biological neurons. Each signal gets multiplied by the appropriate weight $w_1, w_2,..,w_n$, and then all they gets redirected to the summation block marked with a symbol $\sum$. Each weight corresponds to the power of a single biological synapse. The summation block which corresponds to the body of the biological element, arithmetically sums the inputs and creates the output R.

Figure 1. Illustrates the Artificial neuron

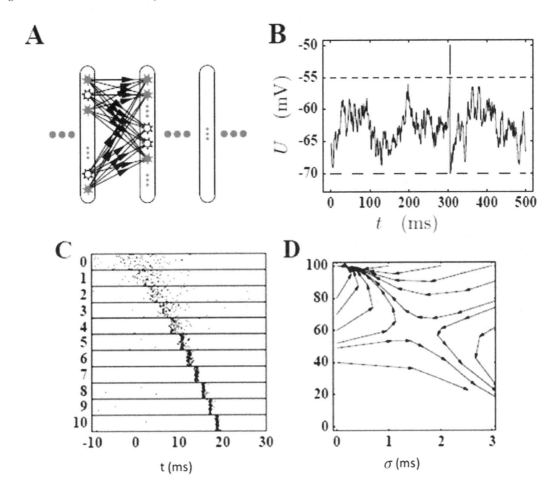

Such the description can be defined with the following formula:

$$R = \sum_{i=1}^{n} W_i X_i + W_0$$

Where:

W$_0$ – is a bias

W$_i$ – is the weight of the ith neuron

x$_i$ - is the exit of the ith neuron

n – is the number of the neurons, which serve as the input for the processing neuron. And this was already described in the article of Abbott L.F. and Kepler T.B. (1990).

The signal W$_0$ which has a name "bias" represents the shift limit function. This signal allows you to shift the origin of the activation function, which subsequently leads to an increase in the learning speed. This signal is added to each neuron, it learns like all other scales, and its feature is that it connects to the +1 signal, and not to the output of the previous neuron. The received signal R gets processed by the activation function and returns the output signal X (Figure 2).

Figure 2. Illustrates the artificial neuron with the activation function

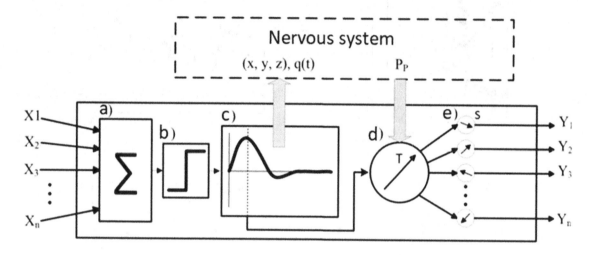

Figure 3. Type of logistic/sigmoidal activation function

$$\begin{cases} C\dfrac{dV}{dt} = I - g_L(V - V_L) - g_{Ca}M_{SS}(V - V_{Ca}) - g_K N(V - V_K) \\ \qquad\qquad \dfrac{dN}{dt} = \dfrac{N - N_{SS}}{\tau_N}, \end{cases}$$

$$M_{SS} = 0.5(1 + \tanh[\frac{V - V_1}{V_2}]),$$

$$N_{SS} = 0.5(1 + \tanh[\frac{V - V_3}{V_4}]),$$

$$\tau_N = 1/(\phi \cosh[\frac{V - V_3}{2V_4}]),$$

In the case if the activation function narrows the range of variation X the way so that for each value of R the value of X belongs to some range – the final interval, then the function F is called a function which narrows. For this it's usually used logistic function. This function can be described in the following way:

The major advantage of such the function is that it has a simple derivative and differentiates along the abscissa. The graph of the function looks in the following way: (Figure 3).

The function increases the weak signals and reduces "too strong" signals.

Another function that is also often used is hyperbolic tangent. It resembles a sigmoid in shape and is often used by biologists as a mathematical model of nerve cell activation. It looks in the following way:

Like the logistic function, the hyperbolic tangent is S-shaped, but it is symmetrical with respect to the origin, and at the point of R = 0 the value of the output signal X = 0

The graph shows that this function unlike logistic one accepts the values of the different signs, what could be a beneficial for a certain type of neural networks.

Figure 4.

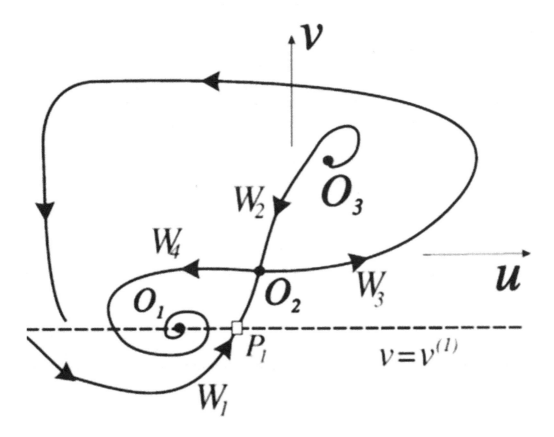

The considered model of an artificial neuron ignores many properties of a biological neuron. For example, it does not take into account time delays that affect the dynamics of the system. Input signals immediately generate the source. But despite this, artificial neural networks composed of the considered neurons reveal the properties that are inherent in the biological system (Abdelbar A. M. & S. M. Hedetniemi, 1998).

Models of Synaptic Plasticity

Unlike an isolated cell, network-connected neural oscillators capable of forming various kinds of connections between themselves, the nature of which will determine the properties of the network as a whole. One of the characteristic features of a neural network is the ability to learn, which is manifested in the modification of the parameters of elements or connections in response to external stimulation. This modification can lead to a change in the dynamic behavior of the network as different input stimuli are presented. On the other hand, the spread of impulse activity in such networks affects the current state of interelement connections.

Most of the cells of the nervous system possess plastic connections (Nicholls J.G. et al, 2001).

Thus, it is clear that synaptic contact is not just a place of neurons connecting with each other, but an independent dynamic system with, often, more complex functioning mechanisms than neurons themselves. For example, many model works devoted to the study of the dynamics of plastic networks consisting of simple neuron-like generators deal with synaptic contacts that are more complex than neurons (Izhikevich E.M., Gally J.A., & Edelman G.M., 1991).

Synaptic plasticity was first proposed as a mechanism for learning and memory based on theoretical analysis (Gong P.& Van Leeuwen C., 2007). Plasticity rule proposed by Hebb, argues that when one neuron activates another neuron, the connection between these neurons is enhanced. Theoretical analysis shows that there is not only Hebb's synaptic potentiation, but also depression between two neurons that are not sufficiently coactivated (Stent G.S., 1973). The experimental correlates of these theoretically proposed forms of synaptic plasticity are called long-term potentiation(LTP) and long-term depression (LTD). Let us analyze two main classes of synaptic plasticity models built on the basis of phenomenological correspondence and description of biophysical mechanisms.

Phenomenological models are characterized by a description of the process that regulates synaptic plasticity as a "black box". The Black Box accepts a set of variables as input, and produces output changes in synaptic efficiency. There are two different classes of phenomenological models (Morrison A. et al., 2008) that change the efficiency of signal transmission through the synapse depending on either the frequency of the pulses or the ratio of the times of the appearance of pulses, and differ in the type of input variables.

Many of the phenomenological models of synaptic plasticity that have been proposed in recent years, based on the dependence of the properties of synaptic transmission on the pulse frequency (Dayan P. & Abbott L.F., 2001). In these models, it is assumed that the frequency of pre-synaptic and postsynaptic pulses measured over a period of time determines the sign and magnitude of synaptic plasticity. This rule can be formulated as follows:

$$\frac{dW_i}{dt} = f\left(x_i, y, W_i, \ldots\right)$$

Where:

W_i - synapse efficiency

i, x_i - pulse frequency of the pre-synaptic neuron,

y is the frequency of the postsynaptic neuron.

A simple example of a frequency-based model is as follows:

$$\frac{dW_i}{dt} = \eta \left(x_i - x_0 \right) \left(y - y_0 \right)$$

Where:

η is the learning rate, which is assumed to be relatively low,

x_0, y_0 are some constants.

The discovery of the dependence of synaptic efficiency on the ratios of pulse arrival times at the synapse (Spike-timing dependent plasticity (STDP)) aroused interest in creating a new class of models. Most of these models depend only on the relative time between pairs of pulses; however, models have recently appeared that depend on the arrival times of three pulses (Pfister J.P. & Gerstner W., 2006).

Under certain assumptions about the statistics of the appearance of presynaptic and postsynaptic pulses, and the duration of pulsed overlap, these models can be averaged and reduced to frequency models (Kempter R. et al., 1991).

In the simplest case, the STDP effect is described by a simple curve, as shown in Figure 5.

Figure 5. Illustrates STDP curve

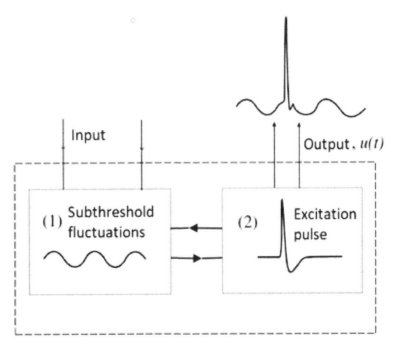

The direct sequence of impulses "presynaptic-postsynaptic"
leads to an increase in bond weight (LTP potentiation effect). If the order of appearance of the pulses at the synapse is reversed, then the effect of depression (LTD) occurs. STDP also depends on many other factors, such as the frequency of activation of neurons at which pairs of impulses arise (Markram H. et al., 1997), the level of local postsynaptic depolarization, or the initial state of synapses. Biophysical models, in contrast to phenomenological models, are based on modeling biochemical and physiological processes that lead to synaptic plasticity. A simple dynamic system that implements the hypothesis of controlling bond strength by changing the concentration of calcium is:

$$\frac{dW_i}{dt} = \eta(Ca)\big(O(Ca) - lW_i\big)$$

Another important type of synaptic plasticity is short-term frequency-dependent plasticity, at which the signal transmission efficiency depends on the frequency of the pulses followed. A model of such plasticity was proposed in the article of Tsodyks M. et al. (2000). It describes the kinetics of the release of a neurotransmitter (synaptic resources) using a 4th-order dynamic system. Short-term ductility depends on incoming pulses at time scales of tens of milliseconds. Using this model, in particular, it was possible to describe the mechanism of occurrence of population burst discharges in neural networks (Tsodyks M. et al., 2000). In various aspects of neurodynamics, other models of short-term plasticity have been proposed that have varying degrees of biophysical detailing (Abbott L.F. et al., 1997). Relying, as a rule, on the description of specific experimental phenomena, plasticity models remain essentially poorly studied from the point of view of nonlinear dynamics of transmission and conversion of pulsed excitations between neurons via plastic synaptic connections.

Formally, the short-term plasticity model discussed above is written as follows:

$$\frac{dx}{dt} = \frac{z}{\tau_{rec}} - \sum_{i=1}^{N} ux\delta(t - t_i)$$

$$\frac{dy}{dt} = \frac{-y}{\tau_1} + \sum_{i=1}^{N} ux\delta(t - t_i)$$

$$\frac{dz}{dt} = \frac{y}{\tau_1} - \frac{z}{\tau_{rec}}$$

$$\frac{du}{dt} = -\frac{u}{\tau_{fac}} + \sum_{i=1}^{N} U(1 - u)\delta(t - t_i)$$

Where:

t_i – the time of occurrence of the i-th presynaptic impulse,

N – total number of impulses,

$x,\ y,\ z$ – variables describing the shares of synaptic resources in restored, active and inactive states, respectively.

u – a variable responsible for synaptic depression or exacerbation.

τl, τrec, τfac - characteristic times of synapse dynamics.

The type of synapse is determined by a set of parameters, for example, for the exciting type of communication between two exciting neurons, it is proposed to take the synapse parameters:

A=1.8 mV, U=0.5, τ_{rec}=800 ms, τ_{fac}=0 ms, τ_1=3 ms.

The postsynaptic current in this model is described using the weighted synaptic variable y.

Each presynaptic impulse causes a jump in the variable y, after which y drops to zero in a relatively short time. The effect of synaptic depression (a decrease in the effective binding strength) is manifested in the fact that with each subsequent input pulse, the value of the jump in the variable y decreases if the interval between presynaptic pulses is not large enough for the synapse to return to its original state. Therefore, the higher the frequency of presynaptic pulses, the stronger and faster the strength of the bond decreases. Moreover, for the case of a periodic input action, the stationary value of the jumps is determined by the nonlinear function of the frequency of the input action.

In addition to synaptic plasticity, the dynamic organization of inter-element interactions in networks of neural oscillators is based on the so-called structural plasticity, which consists in the formation and destruction of connections between network elements. So in the process of operation of a neural system, the architecture of inter-element communications can change depending on the dynamics of the entire network. When recording new information, new relationships may reflect other propagation paths of pulsed signals. In conclusion, it should be noted that the basis of many computational properties, amazing efficiency and noise immunity in the processing of information and the high adaptive performance of neural networks is the dynamic organization of inter-element interactions, which is provided, inter alia, by various mechanisms of synaptic plasticity.

SOLUTIONS

Artificial Intelligence Platform

Speaking of a symbiosis called AIoT, we usually mean an AI platform located on the periphery of the network. Typically, this decision takes the form of a small industrial computer (IPC) with an integrated industrial-class processor. However, for real-time data analysis, such a processor needs adequate support in the form of flash memory and a disk drive.

Memory and Data Storage

To solve the problems of implementing AI in borderline applications, as mentioned above, industrial-grade data and memory storage devices are needed. First of all, it is necessary to study and identify the risks present in each specific place of data collection. This will allow the components to be implemented in accordance with the clear requirements of a particular application.

Overview of Modern Neural Network Simulators

Due to the increasing availability of computing resources, studies using computer modeling are becoming increasingly popular.

The use of a model approach really looks promising, since in modern neuroscience there are a number of issues that can only be solved using modeling. However, there is a problem that the results of such studies are difficult to verify and reproduce. To this end, carefully tested, documented simulators of neural networks are being developed for a wide range of users. These software tools allow you to standardize the code, which simplifies the interaction of research groups, and also contain built-in parallel programming tools, ensuring the availability of modern information technology.

These simulators are widely used in the construction of large-scale models of neural networks. There are several types of simulators:

- Simulators with a simple neuron model: PCSIM, NEST, Brain and NCS.
- Simulators with a neuron model consisting of several compartments: NEURON, GENESIS, SPLIT and MOOSE
- Event driven simulators: MVASPIKE
- Dynamic systems analysis systems: XPP
- Neural constructor simulator of Rinat Galiautdinov, which uses the simulated biological neurons and allows to build neural circuits and explore their behavior.

Along with the software for modeling cellular networks, simulators with hardware-implemented neural networks are widely used.

An example of such simulators is FACETS, a platform simulating the operation of approximately 106 neurons located on several connected boards, each of which houses analog network cores (ANCs), which are the main element of the FACETS architecture, which consists of neurons and synaptic connections (on average, each neuron this system has with 1 thousand contacts with others).

NEST

NEST is a software simulator used to model networks, biologically realistic elements and relationships. The program is optimized to simulate large neural networks and is currently capable of processing a

Figure 6. Illustrates example of a structured model of a neural network(a) and its representation (b)

$$\begin{cases} \varepsilon_1 \dot{u} = f(u) - v - y; \\ \dot{v} = \varepsilon_2(u + I), \\ \dot{x} = y, \\ \dot{y} = (\gamma(1 + \alpha I + \beta u) - lx^2)y - \omega_0^2 x, \end{cases}$$

model consisting of 100,000 elements (neurons) and approximately one billion connections (synapses) between them. In the simulation environment, a descending (top-down) approach to the description of the neural network is implemented, which is a kind of large-scale modeling. In accordance with the principle of hierarchy, neural networks are considered as multi-level structures that can be represented in the form of trees.

Obviously, the depicted neural network contains a large number of components with numerous common connections. The entire network is subdivided into structures that describe various levels of system organization: the retina and two model brain regions, V1 and V2. The model diagram in NEST is shown in Figure 6 (b). A network model is constructed using nodes and links. The nodes can be neurons, devices, and subnets that can exchange (receive and send) events of various types, for example, spikes or currents. The NEST software package contains built-in models of neurons, devices, synapses, and the use of the modular principle of application organization allows the user to create their own models.

Most of the implemented neuron models consist of a small number of compartments, which reduces the degree of detail of the described biophysical processes and morphological features of a single cell. Neurons form a network through the so-called synaptic contacts, for each of which its own dynamics can be determined.

The simplest model of communication between nodes is characterized by weight (determines the strength of interaction between nodes) and delay time (time required for transition

signal from one node to another). The simulator has built-in synapse models with implemented mechanisms of plasticity, synaptic depression and recovery, and also provides functions for creating various topological communication schemes and structuring large networks.

The main components of the system: the core and the interpreter of the simulation system. The interpreter interacts with the graphical interface and the modeling language with the core of the system. The

Figure 7. Illustrates modeling of a neural network in NEST. (a) absolute runtime; and (b) acceleration as a function of the number of processors involved.

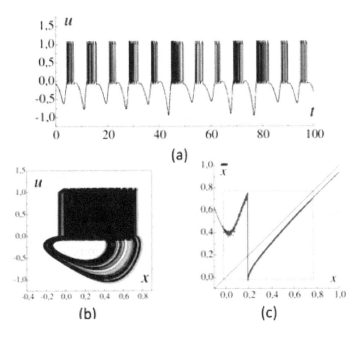

principles of organization of the NEST application contribute to the efficient use of computing resources of computers with a multi-core processor, multiprocessor computers and clusters. When modeling on a computing cluster or multiprocessor computers, each computer or processor recreates part of the network and stores information about the synaptic contacts of only its neurons. To distribute tasks to all computers (processors), NEST uses the Instant Messaging Interface (MPI) and POSIX threads (pthreads).

The graphs shown in Figure 7 demonstrate the dependence of NEST performance on the number of processors involved in calculating the network consisting of 12,500 elements described by the integrate-and-fire model (80% of the total number relates to exciting neurons and 20% inhibitory) each of which receives a signal from 10% of all neurons. The total number of synapses in the moody is 1.56×107. Neurons are initialized by random membrane potentials and are further stimulated by irregular exposure.

Examples of using NEST:

- Models for processing sensory information (visual, auditory, etc.)
- Models of the dynamics of neural network activity
- Training and plasticity in models of processing sensory information.
- Spike synchronization models in Synfire Chains networks.

The results of the study of spike synchronization in Synfire Chains networks using the NEST simulator are presented in Figure 8.

Figure 8.

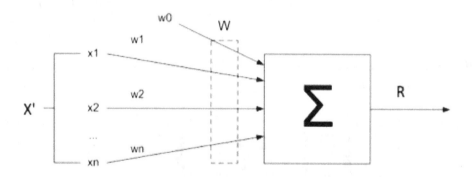

Figure 8 Illustrates:

(A) a diagram of a neural network known as a synfire chain. Groups of neurons are connected in a chain structure. Each neuron of the layer forms contacts (most of them exciting) with all neurons of the next layer, and receives a signal from all neurons of the previous layer.

(B) Fluctuations in the membrane potential of an individual neuron obtained by simulation.

(C) The result of neural network modeling is shown, where the first group of the chain is stimulated by a wide packet of incoming spikes. Subsequently, the phenomenon of spike synchronization is observed. (D) Phase portrait synchronization in synfire chain.

Neural Constructor of Rinat Galiautdinov for Simulating the Neural Circuits

The neural constractor of Rinat Galiautdinov for simulating the neural circuits is fully based on simulation of biological neurons, including all the processes running inside of the neuron, which includes but not limited to: simulation of the AP(action potential), opening of the calcium channels, moving of the calcium ions inside of the nerve cell, catching the calcium ions by the vesicles, movement of the vesicles with the neurotransmitters, calcium pump, effect of the neurotransmitters on the receptors, different kind of the protein receptors(NMDA, Non-NMDA), ability to simulate the processes such as Summation, Long-Term Potentiation, ability to construct the neural circuits based on the different types of the neurons such as: sensor neurons, inter-neurons, motor-neurons, ability to connect sensor neurons to the sensors and motor-neurons to the simulated muscles. Such the constructor is surely an innovative approach in science and allows both: research of the work of the constructed nervous system and simulation of behavior of the different kind of creatures. Eventually such the neural constructor could be the basis for the next generation computing systems.

The Main Modern Works in the Field of Modeling Brain Functions

The approach to the study of the brain of mammals using computer simulation is one of the most promising today. The following are the most significant results:

- A model of visual attention (Silvia Corchs, Gustavo Deco). The model consists of interconnected modules that can be connected by different areas of the dorsal and ventral paths of the visual cortex.
- Model II / III layers of the neocortex (Mikael Djurfeldt, Mikael Lundqvist et al.)
- This model was implemented on a Blue Gene / L supercomputer. It includes 22 million neurons, 11 billion synapses and corresponds to the cerebral cortex of a small mammal.
- Self-sustaining irregular activity in a large-scale model of the hippocampal region (Ruggero Scorcioni, David J. Hamilton and Giorgio A.Ascoli). The model consists of 16 types of neurons and 200,000 neurons. The number of neurons and their connections correspond to the anatomy of the rat brain. In the project, the authors analyze the emerging activity of the network and the effect on it of a decrease in the size or relationships of the network model.
- Blue Brain Project (Markram H. et al.)
- Model of the mammalian thalamocortical system (E.M. Izhikevich and G.M. Edelman, 2007).
- Neural constructor of Rinat Galiautdinov.

MATHEMATICAL MODEL OF BIOLOGICAL NEURON

Imagine the beginning vector, which is located in the center of the active stand, and the end is directed to the pattern point defined for a given neuron. Denote as the vector of the preferred direction of propagation of the excitation (T, trend). In the biological neuron, the vector T can manifest itself in the structure of the neuroplasm itself, perhaps these are the channels for the movement of ions into the body of the cell, or other changes in the structure of the neuron. A neuron has the property of memory, it can memorize

Figure 9.

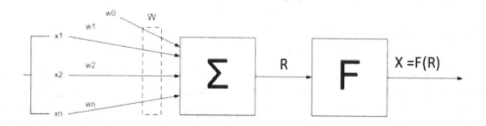

the vector T, the direction of this vector, can change and overwrite depending on external factors. The degree to which the vector T can undergo changes is called neuroplasticity (Choi Y.B. et al., 2014).

This vector, in turn, affects the functioning of the neuron synapses. For each synapse, we define the vector S beginning, which is located in the center of the cell, and the end is directed to the center of the target neuron with which the synapse is connected. Now the degree of influence for each synapse can be determined as follows: the smaller the angle between the vector T and S is, the more the synapse will be amplified (Boyen X. & Koller D., 1998); the smaller the angle, the stronger the synapse will weaken and may possibly stop the transmission of excitation. Each synapse has an independent memory property; it remembers the meaning of its strength. The indicated values change with each activation of the neuron, under the influence of the vector T, they either increase or decrease by a certain value.

The input signals $(x_1, x_2, \dots x_n)$ of the neuron are real numbers that characterize the strength of the synapses of the neurons that affect the neuron.

A positive value of the input means a stimulating effect on the neuron, and a negative value means an inhibitory effect.

For a biological neuron, it does not matter where the signal exciting it came from, the result of its activity will be identical. A neuron will be activated when the sum of the effects on it exceeds a certain threshold value. Therefore, all signals pass through adder (a), and since neurons and the nervous system work in real time, therefore, the effect of the inputs should be evaluated in a short period of time, that is, the effect of the synapse is temporary. The result of the adder passes the threshold function (b), if the sum exceeds the threshold value, then this leads to neuron activity. When activated, a neuron signals its activity to the system, advanced information about its position in the space of the nervous system and the charge that changes over time (c). After a certain time, after activation, the neuron transmits excitation along all the available synapses, previously recounting their strength. The entire activation period of the neuron ceases to respond to external stimuli, that is, all the effects of synapses of other neurons are ignored. The activation period also includes the recovery period of the neuron.

The vector T (d) is adjusted taking into account the value of the pattern point Pp and the level of neuroplasticity. Next, there is a reassessment of the values of all synapse forces in the neuron (e).

Note that blocks (d) and (e) run in parallel with block (c).

The next simplification of the Hodgkin-Huxley model is the MorrisLecar model, proposed in 1981. This system of equations describes the complex relationship between the membrane potential and the activation of ion channels in the membrane. Mathematically, the model is written as follows:

The open state probability functions, MSS (V) and WSS (V), are obtained from the assumption that in equilibrium the open and closed states of the channels are delimited, according to the Boltzmann distribution. Changes in the external current, I, are accompanied by a saddle-node bifurcation, leading

Figure 10.

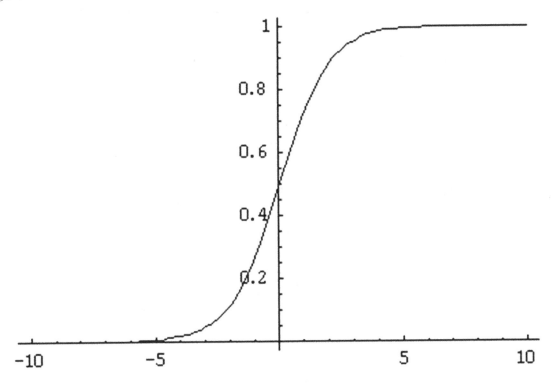

to the birth of a limit cycle. In the field of theoretical modeling of neural oscillators the author as an independent researcher developed the number of new math models of neural dynamics (Cheng, J. and Druzdzel M., 2000).

One of the most interesting developments is the model of the modified FitzHugh-Nagumo generator, which is a simplified version of the Hodgkin-Huxley model. This model has a separatrix threshold manifold that separates signals into subthreshold oscillations and suprathreshold excitation pulses, which are further used for communication between neurons. In addition, the model simultaneously possesses the properties of an integrative response typical of threshold systems and resonance characteristics similar to oscillatory systems. In other words, there is a fundamental possibility of simultaneously performing both frequency and phase encoding and decoding of information.

Previously, the authors of the model of the modified FitzHugh-Nagumo generator proposed a model of a neuron with spontaneous periodic oscillations below the excitation threshold. Such neurons, in particular, play a crucial role in the problem of coordination of movements of the brain, setting the universal rhythm of muscle contractions. The model is based on well-known dynamic systems and is described by a system of fourth-order differential equations.

The first block describes subthreshold oscillations and can be implemented as a Van der Pol generator in a soft excitation mode. The second block is responsible for the formation of an impulse and is implemented as an excitable FitzHugh-Nagumo element. When introducing a nonlinear connection between the blocks, we obtain that the dynamics of the model can be described by the following 4th-order system

Where:

the variables x and y describe the dynamics of the first block,

Figure 11. Phase plane of the FitzHugh-Nagumo model with a threshold manifold

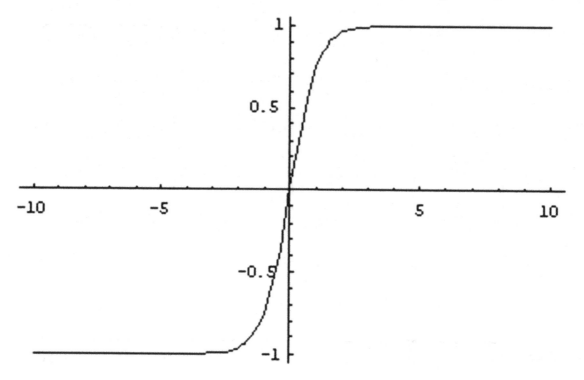

Figure 12. Model of an excitable element with subthreshold oscillations. Functional diagram.

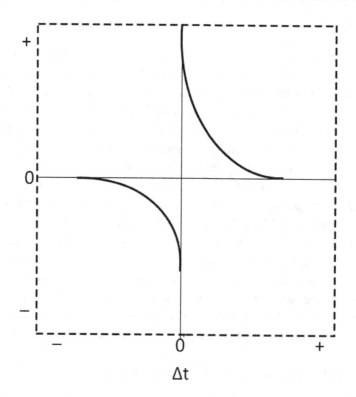

Figure 13.

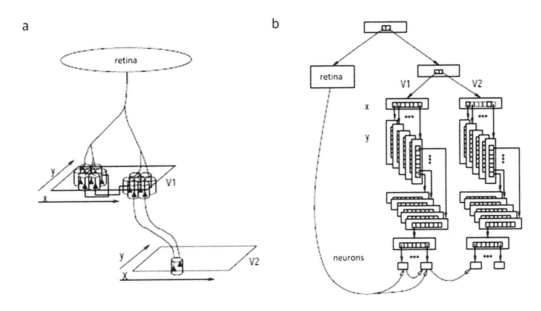

u, v – of the second one,

f(u) – nonlinear function of cubic form,

ε1, ε2 – small positive parameters

I – constant external stimulus

γ, β, 1 > 0, α < 0 – the parameters characterizing the dynamics of Van der Pol variables and the relationship between blocks.

Note that the dynamics of the variable u in the model qualitatively reflects the evolution of the membrane potential of a neuron, the variables x, y, and v show the dynamics of ion currents, parameter I determines the level of depolarization of the neuron. The introduction of two small parameters ε1, ε2 into the system is necessary for matching the characteristic time scales of blocks (pulse duration and period of subthreshold oscillations). Note that in the model two nonlinear systems interact with fundamentally different dynamic properties. Communication between the blocks is as follows. Oscillations close to harmonic from the first block (x, y) change the state of the second in the variable u. In turn, the change in the amplitude of subthreshold oscillations depends on the membrane potential u and external stimulus I.

Figure 14.

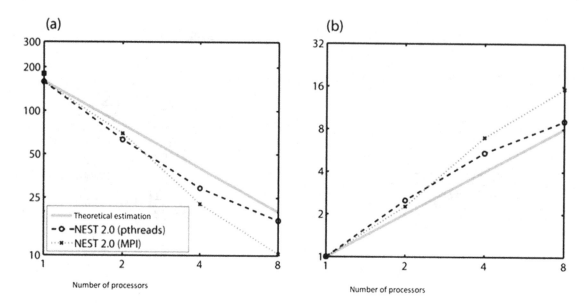

Chaotic Burst Vibrations in a Model I=-0.027. (a) Membrane potential evolution. (b) Phase trajectory in the projection onto the plane (x,u). (c) Poincare map corresponding to a chaotic attractor.

Note that for a certain ratio of the characteristic time scales of the model blocks, the oscillations are in the form of bursts, which can be both regular and chaotic. An example of a chaotic temporal realization and the Poincaré map corresponding to a chaotic attractor are presented in the figure.

EXPERIMENTS

Programming Implementation and AI Based Constructor's Experiments

The programming model of the artificial neuron which is based on the biological model contains the following key features:

- Each artificial biological neuron has generic list of the Queues for dendrites (input signals) and axons (output signals)
- Each synapse can generate the vesicles containing different type o neurotransmitters (in my research I used only 2 neurotransmitters: Glu, GAMA). The generation of the vesicles starts when the neuron receives the AP which can be instantiated based on the signals received from the Qeue(s) of dendrite(s). Such the signal is not constant and depends on the quantity of neurotransmitters caught by the synaptic membrane (for the case if summation process runs – Non-NMDA receptors were triggered) or it's constant enough even with the small quantity of neurotransmitters for the case when NMDA receptors were targeted and one of the initial signals was strong enough (Jin I. et al., 2012). The values of the signals and detailed work of the processes were described in the research of Galiautdinov Rinat (2020)

- Each axon can have only one type of neurotransmitters.
- The programmable synapse can generate the calcium ions coming inside and simulate the process of interaction with the vesicles, which effects on simulation of moving of the vesicles towards the synaptic membrane and emission of neurotransmitters into the synaptic cleft which will effect on initiation of the signal in another neuron.
- The emitted neurotransmitters do not effect directly on another neuron, they effect on the synaptic membrane which is programmatically represented as an input object of the dendrite connected with another neuron. The emission result fully depends on the type of the receptors and the whether NMDA receptor (if this is a case) is "turned on"(what could be caused by the initial strong signal)

Such the approach was used by the author in creation of the neuron based constructor in the beginning of 2016. This neuro-constructor allows to construct the neural circuits including the virtual muscles and virtual sensors (Galiautdinov Rinat et al., 2019A; Galiautdinov Rinat et al., 2019B). The virtual sensors serve as a triggering mechanism effecting on the neural circuit and the virtual muscles serve as outcome. Each neuron and each synapse generate the logs, which includes the data of the APs, the number of emitted calcium ions, the number of instantiated vesicles with neurotransmitters, the number of emitted neurotransmitters, the type of the receptors and the data related to the newly generated signals. This constructor allows to move the experiments on biological objects (such as Aplysia – the mullusc) into the virtual sphere where no animal is necessary for exploring of the work of the nervous system. More important, it allows to construct extremely complex virtual neural circuits and research its behavior. Such the approach allows to simulate the nervous system even of the complex creatures. During the experiment, with the help of the author's neuro-constructor, the author virtually created the nervous system of Aplysia and Planarian(Tricladida). The generated neural circuit was able to simulate the work and behavior of the natural creatures.

The usage of such the approach could be considered as revolutionary as it fully simulates all the processes of the nervous system and inside of each neuron. It fully simulates the behavior of a biological creature. And eventually this could be used not only in simulation of the nervous systems.

The major idea and solution in the frame of the title of the article is that every device can be used as a sensor or "muscle" connected to the "live" constructed neural circuit which will behave as a single live creature providing the owner of the neural circuit with all the benefits as if it was a live loving creature.

SUMMARY

Artificial intelligence has already become the norm in our world, and as its role in the Internet of Things is becoming increasingly important, we need to look for "smart" solutions that will facilitate their merger. In addition, AI will soon be ready to oust the human operator from many areas of activity, which further emphasizes the need for reliable systems that can cope with any problem corresponding to this ecosystem.

The use of AI platforms along with solutions for storing data and memory of an industrial class is a way to ensure that the equipment is ready to fulfill its tasks, and this is one of the key points in creating the "Internet of things" of the future.

However the most important thing in the context of usage of the AI along with the IoT is enclosed in the usage of the simulated biological neurons and neural circuits which allow to convert the area with the things into a single live creature having its own nervous system and using any device either as a sensor of the neural circuit or as a "muscle".

In the article the author described the math model of the biological neuron and suggested the new approach in Artificial Intelligence and the next generation of the AI. The author described created by him the neuro-constructor and the received results of simulation of the work of the virtually created neural circuits of Aplysia (the mollusc) and Planarian(Tricladida) showing that the same solution can be applied to the IoT. The author showed that AIoT based on simulation of the biological nervous systems could be more effective in all the tasks related to the sphere of Artificial Intelligence and simulation of the biological processes.

REFERENCES

Abbott, L. F. (1997). Synaptic depression and cortical gain control. *Science*, *275*(5297), 220–224. doi:10.1126cience.275.5297.221 PMID:8985017

Abbott, L. F., & Kepler, T. B. (1990). Model neurons: From hodgkin-huxley to Hopfield. *Statistical Mechanics of Neural Networks*, *18*, 5–18.

Abdelbar, A. M., & Hedetniemi, S. M. (1998). The complexity of approximating MAP explanation. *Artificial Intelligence*, *102*, 21–38. doi:10.1016/S0004-3702(98)00043-5

Boyen, X., & Koller, D. (1998). Tractable inference for complex stochastic processes. *UAI98 – Proceedings of the Fourteenth Conference on Uncertainty in Uncertainty in Artificial Intelligence*, 33–42.

Cheng, J., & Druzdzel, M. (2000). AIS-BN: An adaptive importance sampling algorithm for evidential reasoning in large Bayesian networks. *Journal of Artificial Intelligence Research*, *13*, 155–188. doi:10.1613/jair.764

Choi, Y. B., Kadakkuzha, B. M., Liu, X. A., Akhmedov, K., Kandel, E. R., & Puthanveettil, S. V. (2014). Huntingtin is critical both presynaptically and postsynaptically for long-term learning-related synaptic plasticity in Aplysia. *PLoS One*, *9*(7), e103004. doi:10.1371/journal.pone.0103004 PMID:25054562

Dayan, P., & Abbott, L. F. (2001). Theoretical Neuroscience: Computational and Mathematical Modeling of Neural Systems. *Neuroscience*, *39*(3), 460.

Gong, P., & Van Leeuwen, C. (2007). Dynamically maintained spike timing sequences in networks of pulse-coupled oscillators with delays. *Physical Review Letters. APS.*, *98*(4), 048104. doi:10.1103/PhysRevLett.98.048104 PMID:17358818

Izhikevich, E. M., Gally, J. A., & Edelman, G. M. (2004). Spike-timing dynamics of neuronal groups. Cerebral Cortex, 14(8), 933–944. doi:10.1093/cercor/bhh053

Jin, I., Udo, H., Rayman, J. B., Puthanveettil, S., Kandel, E. R., & Hawkins, R. D. (2012). Spontaneous transmitter release recruits postsynaptic mechanisms of long-term and intermediate-term facilitation in Aplysia. *Proceedings of the National Academy of Sciences of the United States of America, 109*(23), 9137–9142. doi:10.1073/pnas.1206846109 PMID:22619333

Kempter, R., Gerstner, W., & Van Hemmen, J. (1999). Hebbian learning and spiking neurons. *Physical Review E. APS, 59*(4), 4498–4514. doi:10.1103/PhysRevE.59.4498

Markram, H. (1997). Regulation of synaptic efficacy by coincidence of postsynaptic APs and EPSPs. *Science. AAAS., 275*(5297), 213–215. doi:10.1126cience.275.5297.213 PMID:8985014

Michie, D., Spiegelhalter, D., Taylor, C., & Campbell, J. (1994). *Machine Learning, Neural and Statistical Classification*. Ellis Horwood.

Morrison, A., Diesmann, M., & Gerstner, W. (2008). Phenomenological models of synaptic plasticity based on spike timing. *Biological Cybernetics, 98*(6), 459–478. doi:10.100700422-008-0233-1 PMID:18491160

Nicholls, J.G. (2001). *From Neuron to Brain*. Academic Press.

Pfister, J. P., & Gerstner, W. (2006). Triplets of spikes in a model of spike timing-dependent plasticity. *Journal of Neuroscience. Social Neuroscience, 26*(38), 9673–9682. PMID:16988038

Rinat, G. (2020). *Brain machine interface: the accurate interpretation of neurotransmitters' signals targeting the muscles. International Journal of Applied Research in Bioinformatics.* doi:10.4018/IJARB.2020 0102

Rinat, G., & Vardan, M. (2019A). Math model of neuron and nervous system research, based on AI constructor creating virtual neural circuits: Theoretical and Methodological Aspects. In V. Mkrttchian, E. Aleshina, & L. Gamidullaeva (Eds.), *Avatar-Based Control, Estimation, Communications, and Development of Neuron Multi-Functional Technology Platforms* (pp. 320–344). IGI Global. doi:10.4018/978-1-7998-1581-5.ch015

Rinat, G., & Vardan, M. (2019B). Brain machine interface – for Avatar Control & Estimation in Educational purposes Based on Neural AI plugs: Theoretical and Methodological Aspects. In V. Mkrttchian, E. Aleshina, & L. Gamidullaeva (Eds.), *Avatar-Based Control, Estimation, Communications, and Development of Neuron Multi-Functional Technology Platforms* (pp. 345–360). IGI Global. doi:10.4018/978-1-7998-1581-5.ch016

Stent, G. S. (1973). A physiological mechanism for Hebb's postulate of learning. *Proceedings of the National Academy of Sciences of the United States of America, 70*(4), 997–1001. 10.1073/pnas.70.4.997

Tsodyks, M., Uziel, A., & Markram, H. (2000). Synchrony generation in recurrent networks with frequency-dependent synapses. The Journal of Neuroscience, 20(1).

Chapter 6
Best Practices:
Adopting Security Into the Cloud–Based Internet of Things

Anchitaalagammai J. V.
Velammal College of Engineering and Technology, India

Kavitha S.
Velammal College of Engineering and Technology, India

Murali S.
Velammal College of Engineering and Technology, India

Padmadevi S.
Velammal College of Engineering and Technology, India

Shanthalakshmi Revathy J.
https://orcid.org/0000-0003-1724-7117
Velammal College of Engineering and Technology, India

ABSTRACT

The internet of things (IoT) is rapidly changing our society to a world where every "thing" is connected to the internet, making computing pervasive like never before. It is increasingly becoming a ubiquitous computing service, requiring huge volumes of data storage and processing. Unfortunately, due to the lack of resource constraints, it tends to adopt a cloud-based architecture to store the voluminous data generated from IoT application. From a security perspective, the technological revolution introduced by IoT and cloud computing can represent a disaster, as each object might become inherently remotely hackable and, as a consequence, controllable by malicious actors. This chapter focus on security considerations for IoT from the perspectives of cloud tenants, end-users, and cloud providers in the context of wide-scale IoT proliferation, working across the range of IoT technologies. Also, this chapter includes how the organization can store the IoT data on the cloud securely by applying different Access control policies and the cryptography techniques.

DOI: 10.4018/978-1-7998-3111-2.ch006

Figure 1. Illustration of Cloud based IoT

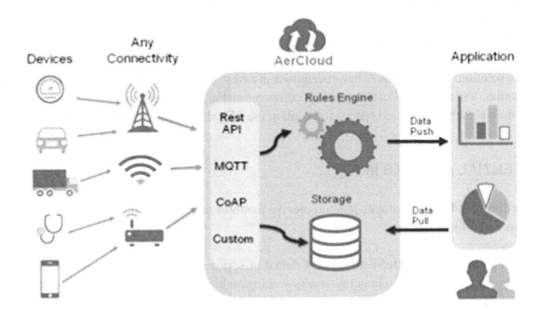

INTRODUCTION

IoT is an interconnection of everyday objects in a network, which are usually equipped with tremendous intelligence level. IoT has increased the usage of Internet gigantically by integrating every object for interaction through embedded systems, which leads to a highly dispersed network of devices communicating with human beings as well as electronic devices which support internet. IoT is a promising phenomenon which will improve the quality of our lives. In the recent past, IoT has been the center of attraction of researchers and practitioners from all over the world. IoT is a device which is capable of capturing data, storing and processing it. It can also visualize services, monitor and manage various devices.

There is a need of an advanced prototype for security, which considers the security issues from a holistic perspective comprising the advanced users and their intercommunication with this technology. Internet is primary of IoT hence there can be security loophole. Intercommunication paradigms are developed based on sensing programming for IoT applications, evolving an intercommunication stack to develop the required efficiency and reliability. Securing intercommunication is a crucial issue for all the paradigms that are developing based on sensing programming for IoT applications(Choudhury et al., 2017). If we provide good software which insures about security of the cloud storage system and communication between IoT device and cloud, then there is a no problem to accept cloud storage to store IoT data.

Data generated by the IoT devices is massive and therefore, traditional data collection, storage, and processing techniques may not work at this scale. Furthermore, the sheer amount of data can also be used for patterns, behaviors, predictions, and assessment. Additionally, the heterogeneity of the data generated by IoT creates another front for the current data processing mechanisms. Therefore, to harness the value of the IoT-generated data, new mechanisms are needed. In this context, Machine Learning (ML) is considered to be one of the most suitable computational paradigms to provide embedded intelligence in the IoT devices (Hussain et al., 2019). ML can help machines and smart devices to infer useful knowledge from the device or human-generated data. It can also be defined as the ability of a smart device to vary or automate the situation or behavior based on knowledge which is considered as an essential part for an IoT solution. ML techniques have been used in tasks such as classification, regression and density estimation. Variety of applications such as computer vision, fraud detection, bio-informatics, malware detection, authentication, and speech recognition use ML algorithms and techniques.

POTENTIAL ATTACKS IN IOT

A handful of IoT-related attacks seem to receive the most attention in the popular press which few of them are as follows.

a) **Denial of Service (DoS) Attacks:** A denial-of-service (DoS) attack deliberately tries to cause a capacity overload in the target system by sending multiple requests. Unlike phishing and brute-force attacks, attackers who implement denial-of-service don't aim to steal critical data. However, DoS can be used to slow down or disable a service to hurt the reputation of a business. For instance, an airline that is attacked using denial-of-service will be unable to process requests for booking a new ticket, checking flight status, and canceling a ticket. In such instances, customers may switch to other airlines for air travel. Similarly, IoT security threats such as denial-of-service attacks can ruin the reputation of businesses and affect their revenue.

b) **Side-Channel Attack:** A side-channel attack is the IT equivalent to spotting a liar by their nervous behavior while fibbing rather than what they say. In other words, the attacker can infer which encryption is used without having access to either plain or ciphertext. There are myriad ways this might work. An attacker might study a device's power use or optical or radio emanations. A hacker could even observe the sounds coming from the electronic components within a device and use that information to crack its encryption key.

c) **Pure Software Attacks:** This category includes malware variants such as viruses and trojans and worms. Also in this category is fuzzing, in which random data is thrown at software to see how it reacts. Distributed Denial of Service (DDoS) attacks can be software-based as well, although they can also occur at lower levels of the OSI Model. One potential example of an IoT-related DDoS risk would be safety-critical information such as warnings of a broken gas line that can go unnoticed through a DDoS attack of IoT sensor networks.

d) **Man-in-the-Middle Cryptographic Attacks:** In a Man-in-the-Middle (MiTM) attack, a hacker breaches the communication channel between two individual systems in an attempt to intercept messages among them. Attackers gain control over their communication and send illegitimate messages to participating systems. Such attacks can be used to hack IoT devices such as smart refrigerators and autonomous vehicles.

e) **Identity and Data Theft** Multiple data breaches made headlines in 2018 for compromising the data of millions of people. Confidential information such as personal details, credit and debit card credentials, and email addresses were stolen in these data breaches. Hackers can now attack IoT devices such as smart watches, smart meters, and smart home devices to gain additional data about several users and organizations. By collecting such data, attackers can execute more sophisticated and detailed identity theft.

Attackers can also exploit vulnerabilities in IoT devices that are connected to other devices and enterprise systems. For instance, hackers can attack a vulnerable IoT sensor in an organization and gain access to their business network. In this manner, attackers can infiltrate multiple enterprise systems and obtain sensitive business data. Hence, IoT security threats can give rise to data breaches in multiple businesses.

f)   **Inside-Job:** Here person, employee or staffs who have the knowledge of system can attack the cloud system.

IOT SECURITY AND MACHINE LEARNING

In this section, we discuss various machine learning algorithms and their applicability in IoT applications.

A.   **Basic Machine Learning Algorithms:** The ML algorithms can be classified into four categories; supervised, unsupervised, semi-supervised, and reinforcement learning algorithms (Fig. 2).

Supervised Learning: Supervised learning is performed when specific targets are defined to reach from certain set of inputs. For this type of learning, the data is first labeled followed by training with labeled data (having inputs and desired outputs). It tries to identify automatically rules from available datasets and define various classes, and finally predict the belonging of elements (objects, individuals, and criteria) to a given class.

Unsupervised Learning: In unsupervised learning, the environment only provides inputs without desired targets. It does not require labeled data and can investigate similarity among unlabeled data and classify the data into different groups. Supervised learning and unsupervised techniques mainly focus on data analysis problems while reinforcement learning is preferred for comparison and decision-making problems. This categorization and choice of ML technique depends on the nature of available data. When the type of input data and the desired outputs (labels) are known, supervised learning is used.

In this situation, the system is only trained to map inputs to the desired outputs. Classification and regression are the examples of supervised learning techniques where regression works with continuous and classification works with discrete outputs. Various regression techniques such as Support Vector Regression (SVR), linear regression, and polynomial regression are commonly used techniques. On the other hand, classification works with discrete output values (class labels). Common examples of classification algorithms include K-nearest neighbor, logistic regression, and Support Vector Machine (SVM). Some algorithms can be used for both classification and regression such as neural networks. When outputs are not well-defined and the system has to discover the structure within the raw data, unsupervised learning methods are used to train the system. Unsupervised learning includes clustering which groups objects based on established similarity criteria such as K-means clustering. The degree of precision of the predictive analytics depends on how well the respective ML technique has used past data to develop models and, how well is it able to predict the future values. Algorithms such as SVR, neural networks, and Naive Bayes are used for predictive modeling.

Semi-Supervised Learning: In the previous two types, either there are no labels for all the observation in the dataset or labels are present for all the observations. Semi-supervised learning falls in between these two. In many practical situations, the cost to label is quite high, since it requires skilled human experts to do that. So, in the absence of labels in the majority of the observations but present in few, semi-supervised algorithms are the best candidates for the model building. Reinforcement Learning: In Reinforcement Learning (RL), no specific outcomes are defined, and the agent learns from feedback after interacting with the environment. It performs some actions and makes decisions on the basis of the reward obtained. An agent can be rewarded for performing good actions or punishment for bad actions and use feedback criteria to maximize the long term rewards. It is greatly inspired by learning behaviors of humans and animals. Such behaviors make it an attractive approach in highly dynamic applications of robotics in which the system learns to accomplish certain tasks without explicit programming (Ambedkar, 2017). It is also very important to choose the suitable reward function because the success and failure of the agent depends on the accumulated total reward (Wirth et al., 2017).

B. **Deep Learning (DL) and Deep Reinforcement Learning (DRL) Deep Learning:** DL is a machine learning technique originated from ANN. The neural network is comprised of neurons (considered as variables) connected through weighted connections (considered as parameters). To achieve the desired set of outputs, supervised or unsupervised learning technique is associated with the network. The learning is carried out by using labeled and unlabeled data from supervised or unsupervised learning techniques, respectively followed by the iterative adjustment of the weights among each pair of neurons. Therefore, while discussing about DL, we refer to large deep neural networks where the term deep refers to the number of layers in that network (L., 2014), (L, 2015). DL is known for distributed computing and, learning and analysis of sheer amount of unlabeled, un-categorized, and unsupervised data. It develops a hierarchical model of learning and feature representation motivated by layered learning process in the human brain (Wang et al., 2017). DL models contribute to various ML applications such as speech recognition, computer vision and NLP by providing improved classification modeling and generating better data samples. Furthermore, these models also benefit the data compression and recovery, both in time and spatial domains because of its effectiveness in extracting patterns and features from large amounts of data and extracting relationships within time-dependent data. The different DL architectures available in literature include, Convolutional Neural Networks (CNN), Recurrent Neural Networks (RNN),

Boltzmann Machine (BM), Long-short Term Memory (LSTM) Networks, Generative Adversarial Networks (GAN), Feed forward Deep Networks (FDN) and Deep Belief Networks (DBN). CNN (used in spatially distributed data) and RNN (used in time series data) are the most widely used deep learning architectures.

Deep Reinforcement Learning: DL is one type of ML techniques used for function approximation, classification, and prediction whereas RL is another type of ML techniques used for decision making in which a software agent learns about optimal actions by interacting with an environment over various states. DL and RL come into play together in situation when the number of states and data dimensionality are very large and the environment is non-stationary. Therefore, traditional RL is not efficient enough. By combining DL and RL, agents can learn by themselves and come up with a good policy to obtain maximum long-term rewards. In this approach, RL obtains help from DL to find the best policy and DL performs action values approximation in order to find the quality of an action in a given state. Furthermore, RL and DL benefit from each other. DL is capable of learning from complex patterns but is prone to mis-classification. In this situation, RL has a powerful capability to automatically learn from environment without any feature crafting and helps DL in efficient classification. DRL integrates RL's decision making and DL's perception.

Figure 2. Classification of Machine Learning algorithms

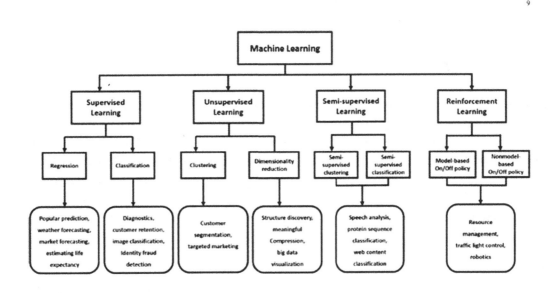

LERANING BASED SECIRTY TECHNIQUES IN IOT

Below Figure 3 illustrates the machine learning approach for threat model in IoT. This section includes solution for Authentication, Malware detection, IoT Offloading with learning and Access control (Xia et al., 2018).

Figure 3. Machine Learning Approach for threat model in the IoT

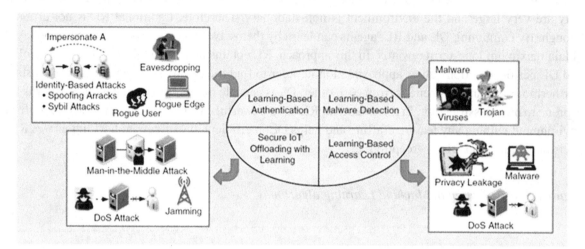

Learning-Based Authentication

Traditional authentication schemes are not always applicable to IoT devices with limited computation, battery and memory resources to detect identity-based attacks such as spoofing and Sybil attacks. Physical (PHY)-layer authentication techniques that exploit the spatial decorrelation of the PHY-layer features of radio channels and transmitters such as the received signal strength indicators (RSSIs), received signal strength (RSS), the channel impulse responses (CIRs) of the radio channels, the channel state information (CSI), the MAC address can provide light-weight security protection for IoT devices with low computation and communication overhead without leaking user privacy information (Xiao, Li, Han et al, 2016).

Figure 4. Performance of PHY-layer authentication system with different number of antennas at each landmark

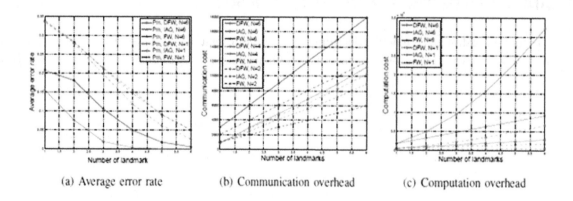

(a) Average error rate (b) Communication overhead (c) Computation overhead

PHY-layer authentication methods such as (Xiao, Li, Han et al, 2016) build hypothesis tests to compare the PHY-layer feature of the message under test with the record of the claimed transmitter. Their authentication accuracy depends on the test threshold in the hypothesis test. However, it is challenging for an IoT device to choose an appropriate test threshold of the authentication due to radio environment and the unknown spoofing model. As the IoT authentication game can be viewed as a Markov decision process (MDP), IoT devices can apply RL techniques to determine the key authentication parameters such as the test threshold without being aware of the network model.

Figure 5. ML-based authentication in IoT systems

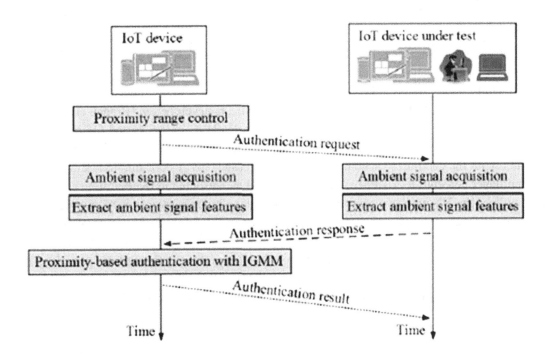

Supervised learning techniques such as Frank-Wolfe (dFW) and incremental aggregated gradient (IAG) can also be applied in IoT systems to improve the spoofing resistance. For example, the authentication scheme in (Xiao, Li, Han et al, 2016) applies dFW and IAG and exploits the RSSIs received by multiple landmarks to reduce the overall communication overhead and improve the spoofing detection accuracy. As shown in Fig. 4, the average error rate of the dFW-based authentication and the IAG-based scheme are 6‰ and less than 10−4, respectively, in the simulation with 6 landmarks each equipped with 6 antennas. The dFW-based authentication saves the communication overhead by 37.4%, while the IAG saves the computation overhead by 71.3% compared with the FW-based scheme in this case (Xiao et al., 2018).

Unsupervised learning techniques such as IGMM can be applied in the proximity based authentication to authenticate the IoT devices in the proximity without leaking the localization information of the devices. For instance, the authentication scheme as proposed in (Xiao et al., 2018) uses IGMM, a non-parameteric Bayesian method, to evaluate the RSSIs and the packet arrival time intervals of the ambient radio signals to detect spoofers outside the proximity range. This scheme reduces the detection error rate by 20% to 5%, compared with the Euclidean distance based authentication (Xiao et al., 2013) in the spoofing detection experiments in an indoor environment.

Learning Based Access Control

It is challenging to design access control for IoT systems in heterogeneous networks with multiple types of nodes and multisource data (Abu Alsheikh et al., 2014). ML techniques such as SVMs, K-NNs, and NNs have been used for intrusion detection (Buczak & Guven, 2015). For instance, the DoS attack detection as proposed in (Tan et al., 2013) uses multivariate correlation analysis to extract the geometrical correlations between network traffic features. This scheme increases the detection accuracy by 3.05% to 95.2% compared with the triangle-area-based nearest-neighbors approach using the KDD Cup 99 data set (Tan et al., 2013). IoT devices such as outdoor sensors usually have strict resource and computation constraints, yielding challenges for anomaly intrusion detection techniques and thus degrading the intrusion detection performance for IoT systems.

ML techniques help build lightweight access control protocols to save energy and extend the lifetime of IoT systems.For example, the outlier detection scheme as developed in (Branch et al., 2013) applies K-NNs to address the problem of unsupervised outlier detection in WSNs and offers flexibility to define outliers with reduced energy consumption. This scheme can save the maximum energy by 61.4% compared with the centralized scheme with similar average energy consumption (Branch et al., 2013). The multilayer perceptron (MLP)-based access control as presented in (Kulkarni & Venayagamoorthy, 2009) utilizes the NN with two neurons in the hidden layer to train the connection weights of the MLP and compute the suspicion factor that indicates whether an IoT device is the victim of DoS attacks. This scheme utilizes backpropagation (BP) that applies the forward computation and error BP and particle swarm optimization (PSO) as an evolutionary computation technique that utilizes particles with adjustable velocities to update the connection weights of the MLP. The IoT device under test shuts down the MAC- and PHY-layer functions to save energy and extend the network life if the output of the MLP exceeds a threshold.

Supervised learning techniques such as SVMs are used to detect multiple types of attacks for Internet traffic and the smart grid (Ozay et al., 2015). For instance, a lightweight attack-detection mechanism as proposed in (Yu et al., 2008) uses an SVM-based hierarchical structure to detect traffic flooding attacks. In the attack experiment, the data set collector system gathered Simple Network Management Protocol (SNMP) management information base data from the victim system using SNMP query messages. Experiment results show that this scheme can achieve an attack detection rate over 99.40% and classification accuracy over 99.53% (Yu et al., 2008).

Secure IoT Offloading with Learning

IoT offloading has to address the attacks launched from the PHY-layer or MAC layer attacks, such as jamming, rogue edge devices, rouge IoT devices, eavesdropping, man-in-the-middle attacks and smart attacks (Roman et al., 2018). As the future state observed by a IoT device is independent of the previous states and actions for a given state and offloading strategy in the current time slot, the mobile offloading strategy chosen by the IoT device in the repeated game with jammers and interference sources can be viewed as a MDP with finite states. RL techniques can be used to optimize the offloading policy in dynamic radio environments.

Figure 6. Illustration of the ML-based offloading

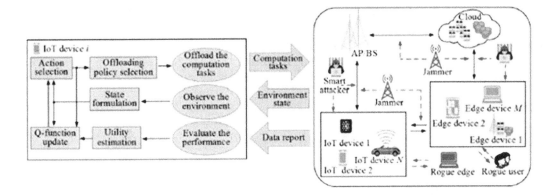

Q-learning, as a model-free RL technique, is convenient to implement with low computation complexity. As illustrated in Fig. 5, the IoT device observes the task importance, the received jamming power, the radio channel bandwidth, the channel gain to formulate its current state, which is the basis to choose the offloading policy according to the Q-function. The Q-function, which is the expected discounted long-term reward for each action-state pair and represents the knowledge obtained from the previous anti-jamming offloading. The Q-values are updated via the iterative Bellman equation in each time slot according to the current offloading policy, the network state and the utility received by the IoT device against jamming.

The IoT device evaluates the signal-to-interference-plus-noise ratio (SINR) of the received signals, the secrecy capacity, the offloading latency and energy consumption of the offloading process and estimates the utility in this time slot. The IoT device applies the ϱ-greedy algorithm to choose the offloading policy that maximizes its current Q-function with a high probability and the other policies with a small probability, and thus makes a tradeoff between the exploration and the exploitation. This scheme reduces the spoofing rate by 50%, and decreases the jamming rate by 8%, compared with a benchmark strategy as presented in (Xiao, Xie, Chen et al, 2016). As shown in Fig. 5, the IoT device observes the center frequency and radio bandwidth of each channel to formulate the state, and chooses the optimal offloading channel based on the current state and the Q-function. Upon receiving the computation report, the IoT device evaluates the utility and updates the Q values.

Figure 7. Illustration of the ML-based malware detection

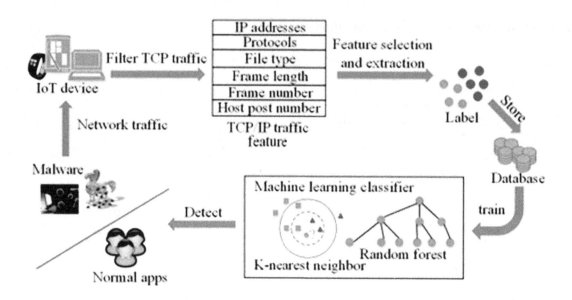

Figure 8. Illustration of the ML-based malware detection with offloading

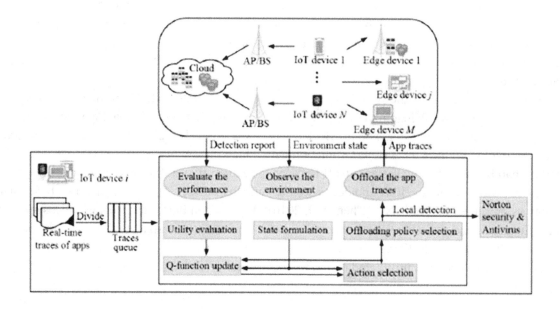

Learning-Based IoT Malware Detection

IoT devices can apply supervised learning techniques to evaluate the runtime behaviors of the apps in the malware detection. In the malware detection scheme as developed in (Narudin et al., 2016), an IoT device uses K-NN and random forest classifiers to build the malware detection model. As illustrated in Fig. 6, the IoT device filters the TCP packets and selects the features among various network features including the frame number and length, labels them and stores these features in the database. The K-NN based malware detection assigns the network traffic to the class with the largest number of objects among its K nearest neighbors. The random forest classifier builds the decision trees with the labeled network traffic to distinguish malwares. According to the experiments in (Narudin et al., 2016), the true positive rate of the K-NN based malware detection and random forest based scheme with MalGenome dataset are 99.7% and 99.9%, respectively.

IoT devices can offload app traces to the security servers at the cloud or edge devices to detect malwares with larger malware database, faster computation speed, larger memories, and more powerful security services. The optimal proportion of the apps traces to offload depends on the radio channel state to each edge device and the amount of the generated app traces. RL techniques can be applied for an IoT device to achieve the optimal offloading policy in a dynamic malware detection game without being aware of the malware model and the app generation model.

As shown in Fig. 7, the IoT device divides real-time app traces into a number of portions, and observes the user density and radio channel bandwidth to formulate the current state. The IoT device estimates the detection accuracy gain, the detection latency and energy consumption to evaluate the utility received in this time slot. This scheme improves the detection accuracy by 40%, reduces the detection latency by 15%, and increases the utility of the mobile devices by 47%, compared with the benchmark offloading strategy in (Xiao et al., 2017) in a network consisting of 100 mobile devices.

The Dyna-Q based malware detection scheme as presented in (Narudin et al., 2016) exploits the Dyna architecture to learn from hypothetical experience and find the optimal offloading strategy. This scheme utilizes both the real defense experiences and the virtual experiences generated by the Dyna architecture to improve the learning performance. For instance, this scheme reduces the detection latency by 30% and increases the accuracy by 18%, compared with the detection with Q-learning (Xiao et al., 2017).

To address the false virtual experiences of Dyna-Q especially at the beginning of the learning process, the PDS-based malware detection schemes as utilizes the known radio channel model to accelerate the learning speed. This scheme applies the known information regarding the network, attack and channel models to improve the exploration efficiency and utilizes Q-learning to study the remaining unknown state space. This scheme increases the detection accuracy by 25% compared with the Dyna-Q based scheme in a network consisting of 200 mobile devices (Xiao et al., 2017)

CONCLUSION

IoT security and privacy are of paramount importance and play a pivotal role in the commercialization of the IoT technology. Traditional security and privacy solutions suffer from a number of issues that are related to the dynamic nature of the IoT networks. ML and more specifically DL and DRL techniques can be used to enable the IoT devices to adapt to their dynamic environment. These learning techniques can support self-organizing operation and also optimize the overall system performance by learning and processing statistical information from the environment (e.g. human users and IoT devices). These learning techniques are inherently distributed and do not require centralized communication between device and controller.

However, the datasets needed for ML and DL algorithms are still scarce, which makes benchmarking the efficiency of the ML- and DL-based security solutions a difficult task. In this paper, we have considered the role of ML and DL in the IoT from security and privacy perspective. We have discussed the security and privacy challenges in IoT. We have described different ML and DL techniques and their applications to IoT security. We have also identified the IoT attack models and the learning based IoT security techniques, including the IoT authentication, access control, malware detections and secure offloading, which are shown to be promising to protect IoTs. Several challenges have to be addressed to implement the learning based security techniques in practical IoT systems.

REFERENCES

Abu Alsheikh, Lin, Niyato, & Tan. (2014). Machine learning in wireless sensor networks: Algorithms,strategies, and applications. *IEEE Commun. Surveys and Tutorials*, *16*(4), 1996–2018.

Ambedkar. (2017). Reinforcement Learning Algorithms: Survey and Classification. *Indian Journal of Science and Technology*, *10*, 1–8.

Branch, J. W., Giannella, C., Szymanski, B., Wolff, R., & Kargupta, H. (2013). In-network outlier detection in wireless sensor networks. *Knowledge and Information Systems*, *34*(1), 23–54. doi:10.100710115-011-0474-5

Buczak, & Guven. (2015). A survey of data mining and machine learning methods for cyber security intrusion detection. *IEEE Communications Surveys and Tutorials*, *18*(2), 1153–1176.

Choudhury, Gupta, Pradhan, Kumar, & Rathore. (2017). Privacy and Security of Cloud-Based Internet of Things (IoT). *2017 International Conference on Computational Intelligence and Networks*, 41-45.

Hussain, Hussain, Hassan, & Hossain. (2019). Machine Learning in IoT Security: Current Solutions and Future Challenges. Academic Press.

Kulkarni, & Venayagamoorthy. (2009). Neural network based secure media access control protocol for wireless sensor networks. *Proc. Int'l Joint Conf. Neural Networks*, 3437–3444.

L. (2014). Tagoram: Real-time tracking of mobile RFID tags to high precision using COTS devices. *ACM International Conference on Mobile Computing and Networking, 1*, 237–248.

L. (2015). DeepEar: robust smartphone audio sensing in unconstrained acoustic environments using deep learning. *ACM International Conference on Pervasive and Ubiquitous Computing, 1*, 283–294.

Narudin, F. A., Feizollah, A., Anuar, N. B., & Gani, A. (2016). Evaluation of machine learning classifiers for mobile malware detection. *Soft Computing*, *20*(1), 343–357. doi:10.100700500-014-1511-6

Ozay, Esnaola, Yarman Vural, Kulkarni, & Poor. (2015). Machine learning methods for attack detection in the smart grid. *IEEE Transactions on Neural Networks and Learning Systems*, *27*(8), 1773–1786. PMID:25807571

Roman, R., Lopez, J., & Mambo, M. (2018). Mobile edge computing, Fog et al.: A survey and analysis of security threats and challenges. *Future Generation Computer Systems*, *78*(3), 680–698. doi:10.1016/j.future.2016.11.009

Tan, Jamdagni, He, Nanda, & Liu. (2013). A system for Denial-of-Service attack detection based on multivariate correlation analysis. *IEEE Transactions on Parallel and Distributed Systems*, *25*(2), 447–456.

Wang, T., Wen, C.-K., Wang, H., Gao, F., Jiang, T., & Jin, S. (2017). Deep Learning for Wireless Physical Layer:Opportunities and Challenges. *IEEE China Communication*, *14*(11), 92–111. doi:10.1109/CC.2017.8233654

Wirth, Akrour, Neumann, & Frnkranz. (2017). A Survey of Preference-Based Reinforcement Learning Methods. *Journal of Machine Learning Research*, *18*, 1–46.

Xia, Wan, Lu, & Zhang. (2018). IoT Security Techniques Based on Machine Learning. Academic Press.

Xiao, Xie, Chen, & Dai. (2016). A mobile offloading game against smart attacks. *IEEE Access*, *4*, 2281–2291.

Xiao, L., Li, Y., Han, G., Liu, G., & Zhuang, W. (2016). PHY-layer spoofing detection with reinforcement learning in wireless networks. *IEEE Transactions on Vehicular Technology*, *65*(12), 10037–10047. doi:10.1109/TVT.2016.2524258

Xiao, L., Li, Y., Huang, X., & Du, X. J. (2017). Cloud-based malware detection game for mobile devices with offloading. *IEEE Transactions on Mobile Computing*, *16*(10), 2742–2750. doi:10.1109/TMC.2017.2687918

Xiao, L., Wan, X., & Han, Z. (2018). PHY-Layer Authentication With Multiple Landmarks With Reduced Overhead. *IEEE Transactions on Wireless Communications*, *17*(3), 1676–1687. doi:10.1109/TWC.2017.2784431

Xiao, L., Yan, Q., Lou, W., Chen, G., & Hou, Y. T. (2013). Proximity-based security techniques for mobile users in wireless networks. *IEEE Transactions on Information Forensics and Security*, *8*(12), 2089–2100. doi:10.1109/TIFS.2013.2286269

Yu, J., Lee, H., Kim, M.-S., & Park, D. (2008). Traffic flooding attack detection with SNMP MIB using SVM. *Computer Communications*, *31*(17), 4212–4219. doi:10.1016/j.comcom.2008.09.018

Chapter 7
Big Data IoT Analytics for Smart Cities With Cloud Computing Technique

Chellaswamy C.
https://orcid.org/0000-0002-2473-6042
Kings Engineering College, Chennai, India

Sathiyamoorthi V.
https://orcid.org/0000-0002-7012-3941
Sona College of Technology, India

ABSTRACT

Currently, cities are being reconstructed to smart cities that use an information and communication technology (ICT) framework alongside the internet of things (IoT) technology to increase efficiency and also share information with the public, helping to improve the quality of government services citizens' welfare. This large, diverse set of information called big data is obtained by ICT and IoT technologies from smart cities. This information does not have any meaning of its own but a high potential to make use of smart city services. Therefore, the information collected is mined and processed through use of big data analytic techniques. The environmental footprints in smart cities can be monitored and controlled with the help of ICT. Big data analytic techniques help enhance the functionalities of smart cities and the 4G and 5G network provides strong connectivity for professional devices.

INTRODUCTION

Cities of the world have become crowded and modern techniques and facilities incorporated into a city develop them into smart cities. City populations are slowly growing (Dohler et al. 2011) and the global population of urban areas is predicted to reach 70% in 2050; the incorporation of modern facilities would be needed to solve various problems. The World Health Organization has predicted the development of 37 cities into megacities by 2025, with 22 of them situated in Asia (Enbysk, 2013). Many world cities

DOI: 10.4018/978-1-7998-3111-2.ch007

are unable to manage this increase in population. The planning and operation of the expanded cities is inadequate and uncoordinated. In addition, most cities do not have real-time data capturing and processing techniques, and if it is captured, the data is analyzed effectively (Deloitte, 2015).

The development of a smart citiy extensivly improves facilities and quality of the life of its inhabitant. Moreover, the problems of those growing cities will reduce on achieving the status of smart cities. The Internet of Things (IoT) provides a good solution for managing complex situations. A huge amount of IoT devices are connected through high-speed communication networks, and monitoring and controlling is carried out by an intelligent system. It is estimated that, in 2019, 35 billion devices were connected to the internet and enormous volumes of data generated (Datameer, 2016). Gantz and Reinsel (2012) say that 40 Zettabytes of data will be comprised in the digital universe, doubling every two years. This huge amount of unstructured and structured data requires a capability to manage, store, analyze, and maintain security.

A machine learning technique is widely used for learning input data and the generalization of learned patterns of future unknown data (Najafabadi et al. 2015). The data received from different sensors and devices can be classified as unstructured, semi-structured, and structured (Chellaswamy et al. 2017; Datameer, 2013). This unstructured and semi-structured data can be analyzed to enable the provision of new opportunities, whereas the structured data can be accommodated only in a relational database. In the modern information era, the querying database is not a proper option for achieving accurate and suitable information. Big Data analytics provides a successful solution to scrutinize an enormous amount of structured and unstructured data and uses advanced correlation techniques and other insights (Vanolo, 2014).

The technological innovations of Big Data analytics show the way to create sustainable and scalable smart cities, while helping authorities in the assessment of situations and how to take relevant corrective measures. Urban development problems can be solved by introducing new smart cities, which can comprehensively gather information from different sensors and devices. It processes data efficiently and intelligently, and transmits the information safely and widely. It also provides urban monitoring and control, management and operational efficiency, promotes sustainable urban development, and improves urban service levels. Thus, the whole city can automatically sense and monitor and make effective self-decision techniques so city inhabitants can feel the intelligent services and applications available in the city (Neirotti et al. 2014).

In general, the major cities in the world are facing development problems relating to traffic congestion, environmental pollution, and energy shortage against rapid urbanization. Unban data computing based on IoT perception is a new concept related to modern data technology, big data mining, and data analysis technology (Hollands, 2015; Zheng et al. 2014; Yunhe et al. 2016). In urban computing, the units of perceived urban dynamics such as device, sensor, building, vehicle, and road in an urban space are considered (Salim and Haque, 2015). The cooperation of the citizen is a significant factor in the completion of the installation and provision of services. The foremost aim of computing in a smart city is to make elegant improvements in the lives of inhabitants and urban environment through data mining, urban perception, intelligent data extraction, and improved cyclical processes (Zheng et al. 2016; Mir et al. 2018). IoT based framework has been developed by Jin et al. (2017) for realizing smart cities. The framework contains complete information about the city, network support structure to data management systems, sensor-based cloud services, and expresses the way to transform from existing physical network systems (Jin et al. 2014). The remaining portion of this chapter is organized as follows: Section 2 describes the popular smart city technologies. Section 3 presents the Integration of big data, IoT, and cloud analytics in smart cities. In Section 4, the iKaaS software platform used in big data analytics is described. Section 5, provides the conclusion of the study.

POPULAR SMART CITY TECHNOLOGIES

Towns and cities are being reconstructed into smart cities. Smart cities incorporate IoT technology that uses sensors and actuators to connect the components in the city so that millions of connected devices and sensors send information to the cloud. The 4G/5G network provides connectivity for professionally working devices. This reconstruction provides detailed geographic data and location accuracy for urban planning. IoT technology remains the base for all smart city initiatives. The sensors and application used in IoT collect data from devices, which enables the technology to work effectively. Also, Big Data analytics are used to sort, analyze, and process large sets of data collected by IoT to implement smart city services.

5G Connectivity

Network connectivity between devices plays a vital role in smart cities. As the 5G network has a high data rate, it transfers the data quickly. Not only does it interconnect the people but it also controls the machines and devices. Automation has made all human activities easy, fast, and work is completed flawlessly. Digitalization makes human life smooth and safer through automation and manages resources and operations efficiently. This method has been introduced to many cities in the world. In automation, the role of sensors and actuators is vast. They collect a large set of data, sort it in a specific location where it is, analyzed, processed, and communicated to other devices or infrastructure to increase functionality of smart cities. A few applications include:

City lighting: In big cities like London, intelligent streetlights have been installed, which have sensors and actuators to provide a better life for residents. Other systems such as camera surveillance, charging unit for electric cars, the measurement of quality of air, and Wi-Fi hotspots are equipped to manage all their needs.

Public transport: Traffic data is automatically sent to the city transportation management centre where it will inform a real status such as expected time of arrival and departure, destination details, ongoing route details, and traffic congestion alerts etc.

Waste management: Various automatic systems have been introduced to manage waste in smart cities. For example, South Korea (Songdo district) introduced a smart garbage collection station that contains a smart sensing mechanism for identifying various types of garbage and sends them to the recycling centre. As a result, the noise pollution of garbage trucks is eliminated.

5G Possibilities

5G technology makes a drastic change to peoples' lives. It is designed to deliver high scalability, reliable connectivity, high data rate, low latency, and real-time fast transfer of data between the nodes. As a result, this technology enables devices in a smart city construction to share their data with other infrastructure rapidly, and make the changes easily. This helps new application function that was not possible before the evolution of 5G. Some of the examples of smart city enabled IoT are burglar alarm, automatic room light systems (ON/OFF), security and surveillance, etc. (Chellaswamy et al. 2018a, 2018b). 5G technology gathers information through various sensors and transfers them to a central unit, such as a server where all the data is stored and used for future needs.

Mobile Communication

Critical Machine Type Communication (CMTC) and Massive Machine Type Communication (MMTC) are part of 5G technology. MMTC is mainly used for IoT devices that are connected to large numbers and the data from sensors and actuators is transferred and shared effectively between devices. This can be seen and implemented in a smart building through water quality management, for example. CMTC is mainly used for applications in which the data is crucial in nature and needs accurate, delay-intolerant, and guaranteed transmission. This can be seen in remote monitoring systems, remote healthcare, autonomous vehicles, and traffic control. 5G technology is used in application and analytics where transmission of data has low delay and the data is shared with the cloud to download the processed information. Examples of use are:

- Machine learning techniques used in self-driving cars for analyzing huge data sets and make it suitable for the current situation.
- Video-monitoring producing large amounts of data and corresponding records. Edge computing permits important processing and allows high-reliability pattern recognition, remote monitoring, and motion detection.

Privacy and Integrity

Personal and critical calls are required to carefully handle secure communication. Privacy and integrity are fundamentals to smart city. Privacy is an important factor ensuring the safe transfer of data to the cloud, as well as to the public and infrastructure. This ensures no wrong calls and information shared with others is accessed by the right customer.

Integrity helps maintain consistency and accuracy of transferred data. Transferred data should not be wrongly decrypted or encrypted by unknown users. Thus, end-to-end transmission is secured with protection protocols and devices are connected to the network in a plug and play fashion. Designing the network with safe transmission of data, supports a variety of uses and satisfies all the requirements in a smart city environment.

Geospatial Technology

Geospatial technology in a smart city paves the way for location with the help of the maps is accessed through a smartphone with the help of an application. Before the evolution of this technology, people were dependant on paper maps and collected information from people to travel around the world. But, this technology allows people to wander around the world without the human assistance.

Remote sensing and geographic information systems allow smart cities to provide real-time information about the peoples' location. This technology is also used in the field of agriculture to gain information relating to the condition of the soil, plant disease, and climatic changes, which helps farmers profit.

Types of Geospatial Technology

Remote sensing is the collection of images and spatial data of the outlying people and the objects. It is classified into two kinds: 1) passive remote sensing and 2) active remote sensing. Passive remote sensing is what the sensor detects the reflection of the sun on the object, and the exposure from the sun reflects the sensor. Nowadays, geospatial technology provides detailed information about the images with a high resolution. The satellite images provide a clear picture of a particular location, location of human, etc.

Active remote sensing involves the transmission of signal done by the satellite or aircraft getting reflected by the object to the sensor on the satellite. An example of active remote sensing is Light Detection and Ranging (LiDar). It measures the distance between the objects by laser and the distance is calculated using the time taken for the laser to hit the object and reflect back.

Geographic Information System

Geographic Information System provides databases that gather data, monitor, store, analyze, and share the information. The system processes the data by the layers and has two types of information models, namely, 1) the raster model and 2) the vector model. The raster model splits the images into pixels and processes the information, and the vector model split the image into a series of points and then processes the data. Thus the layered map provides the environmental data in a structured manner. The cultural and physical details about the environment are easy to comprehend, scrutinize, and share it with the community.

Global Positioning System and Internet Mapping Techniques

The Global Positioning System (GPS) is a satellite navigation tool launched in 1973 by the US Military. It provides useful information to people and transmits a signal from the earth's satellites to the GPS receiver on the earth. Several countries and entities, namely, India, the European Union, Japan, Russia, and China use their satellite system for navigation purposes.

Robotics

Cloud robotics have played a vital role in today's robotics technique (Kehoe et al. 2015). The network-connected robots are enabled by cloud robotics to perform complex computation by parallel processing tasks and to share the data. The cloud robots make the individual robot intelligent and autonomous, and maintain good accuracy through the use of cooperative learning. With the advancement in the field of cloud computing and Big Data analytics, cloud robotics can break the barriers of the individual robots by including an Artificial Intelligence (AI) technique and acting as a centralized processor (Wan et al. 2016). The cloud robot has also the capability to add any other robot, which has limited resource, without updating the hardware (Gangid and Sharma, 2016). It eliminates the usage of sophisticated and complex processors and storage devices by the enormous backbone created by the cloud providers. The architecture of cloud robotics is shown in Figure 1.

In this Section, the Collaborative Cloud Robotics (C2RO) which supports a massive number of robots which are biologically distributed, distribute the resources dynamically, real-time processing on the cloud, and edge computing. Hybrid cloud robotics are engaged in the C2RO platform for dynamically distributed real-time processing (Satyanarayanan, 2017; Bilal and Erbad, 2017).

Figure 1. System architecture of cloud robotics

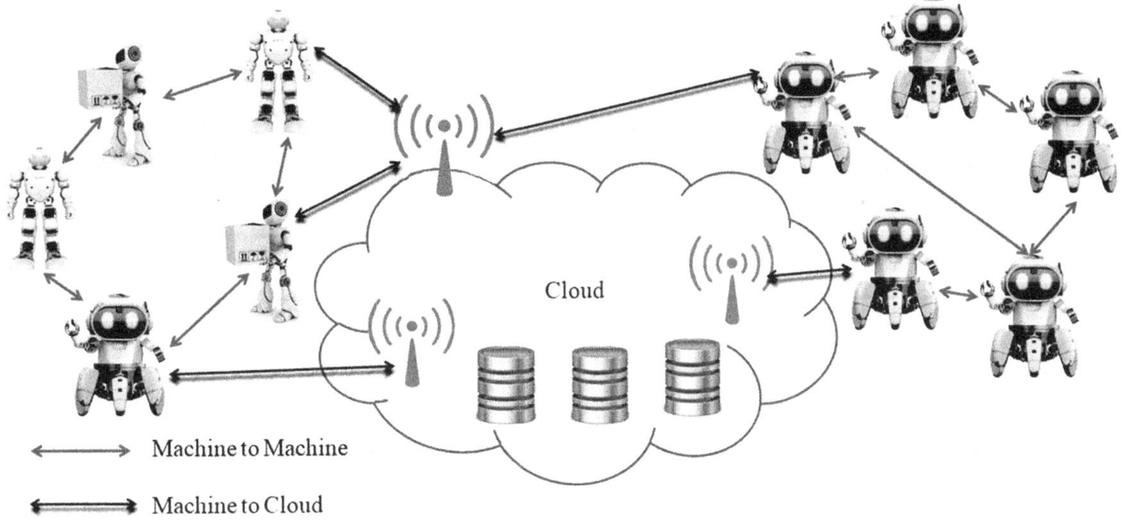

Machine to Machine

Machine to Cloud

C2RO Platform

C2RO has three layers, namely, the communication layer, the processing layer, and the service layer to process the real-time applications. It is shown in Figure 2. Both the data security layer and the communication layer do collection of the data from the sensors and provide the authentication to the platform, decoding and decompressing the data, and prepare it for processing. The central part of the C2RO platform is the processing layer that has a processing engine for real-time computation. It uses the parallel processing technology to process the received signals from the sensor and responds very fast (in terms of milliseconds). The third layer provides three different tasks, namely, analysis of sensor data, a collaboration of multi-robot, and AI with computer vision.

Processing Time

The processing time includes video decompression and processing latency on the cloud side and video capturing and video compression latency on the robot side of an application. Capturing time depends on the number of frames captured per second and the quality of the image improves with an increase in the number of captured frames. The compression method defines the bandwidth of the compressed video, the resolution of the image and the activity level. Fluctuations of bandwidth forth and back during compression increases CPU usage and complexity. C2RO includes an advanced compression method-H.264 (MPEG-4) to solve this problem and ensure high efficiency and low complexity (Balaji et al. 2017). A large number of sensors with cloud computing technology based on swarm robotics are used for mitigating process latency and real-time parallel processing applications (Kamburugamuve et al. 2015 and He et al. 2016). The processing time requires a few milliseconds, approximately, to compute data from different applications.

Figure 2. Different layers of C2RO

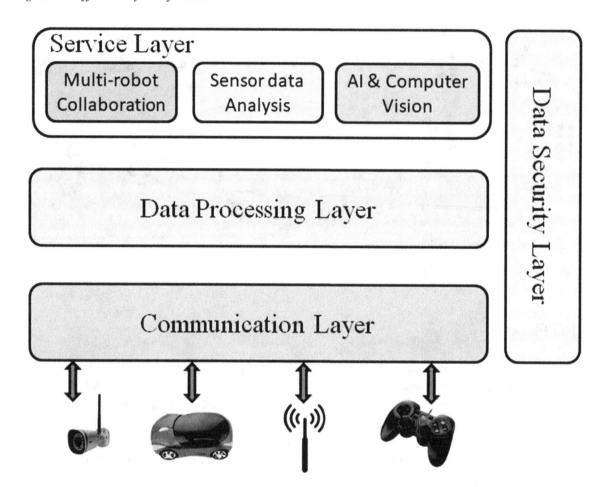

Response of the Network

The packets dropped and packet loss defines the performance of the network. If the latency of communication is more than the limit of application it degrades the Quality of Service (QoS). Some of the causes of latency in devices on the edge of the network (lower layers of communication) are packet loss, channel traffic, and retransmission of the packet. These can be overcome by introducing a protocol that supports QoS in a better way. To achieve QoS, IEEE 802.11e and mobile cellular networks such as Long Term Evolution (LTE) are introduced to meet the additional required performance for wireless communications to support QoS in delay-sensitive applications. To decrease the latency from the edge to the cloud (higher levels of the communication network), the data stream network can be employed. The C2RO provides DSN service in partnership with PubNub2.

The use of robots in daily life in many cities makes the lives and work of people easier, more simple, and perfect. It also improves operations performed in a city, including monitoring the area using drones, which is currently being practiced in Dubai and Tokyo. It is mainly used in security applications, hotel surveillance, and room services. Humanoid robots are to be used in the 2020 Tokyo Olympics to help with language translation.

INTEGRATION OF BIG DATA, IOT AND CLOUD ANALYTICS IN SMART CITIES

The internet of things has now acquired importance in the market through its application in society. From whether IoT is acknowledged by people to the race between IoT industry stakeholders, the IoT has grown cross all fields. The foremost part of IoT is in the collection of data from connected devices; it looks dynamic and heterogeneous. The impact of data in the cloud from the sensors is essential and this kind of processing of data helps modern intelligent and real-time applications.

The IoT and Big Data lead to an understanding of the content and services, real-time intuition, predictive knowledge, and optimization of performance. Cloud technologies provide scalable information and analytics and also data management. This section explains the large number of sensors connected with the devices and cloud-based IoT and the Big Data analytics and also their requirements and the architecture of IoT big data platform.

Table 1. Various tools used for monitoring and managing the cloud platform

Name of Tools	Functionalities
Amazon web services monitoring	• Analyze the performance of native services such as SNS, CloudFront, DynamoDB, RDS, EBS, EC2, ELB, ElastiCache, and SQS to optimize usage with CloudWatch. • Debug the performance issues of the native services.
Microsoft Azure Monitoring	• Track the performance of IaaS services, namely, PaaS services (Event Hubs, SQL database, and App Services) and virtual machines (VMs) and Kubernetes.
Google Cloud platform monitoring	• Monitoring the Google cloud platform includes monitor Google Kubernetes Engine, Google Compute Engine (GCE), Google App Engine (GAE), IAM, Cloud Audit Logging, VPC, Cloud Cloud SQL, BigQuery, etc. • Analyze the resource usage and check the availability of the complete Google Cloud platform stack.
Cisco Systems AppDynamics	• It provides cloud-based network monitoring tools for accelerating operations, assessing application performance, etc. It enables the users to learn their cloud applications in the real-time state. • It maximize the control and visibility of cloud applications in crucial PaaS/IaaS platforms, namely Amazon web services, Pivotal Cloud Foundry, and Microsoft Azure Monitoring.
BMC TrueSight Pulse	• BMC TrueSight Pulse helps to boost the performance of the multi-cloud operations and cost management. • It also used to monitor infrastructure resources, measure end-user experience, and identify the problems before it occurs.

Cloud Monitoring and Management Tools

Cloud monitoring utilizes both manual and automatic tools to monitor, manage, and evaluate various services, infrastructure, and cloud computing architecture. The cloud-based resources are monitored by allowing the administrator access to the cloud management strategies. It helps to identify the problem at the initial stage so one can prevent major issues. Various tools used for monitoring and managing the cloud platform are listed in Table 1. Other than that, various other monitoring and managing tools, such as, New Relic, Hyperic, Aternity, Redgate, Datadog, Solarwinds, ExoPrise, Retrace, Dynatrace, Sumo Logic, Stack Driver, Opsview, Logic Monitor, PagerDuty, Unigma are widely used.

Cloud Based IoT Platform

Based on standards created by the National Institute of Standards and Technology, cloud computing is defined as the tool for appropriate and on-demand network access to enable sharing a pool of computing resources that can be released with minimum management effort and interaction of a service provider. The cloud paradigm is delivered by three services like Platform as a Service (PaaS), Infrastructure as a Service (IaaS), and Software as a Service (SaaS). The cloud-based platform is a dynamic and flexible resource sharing tool that delivers IoT services and shares the scalable resources and service.

IaaS, PaaS and SaaS Paradigms

The cloud-based IoT platform should select any one of the services from SaaS, PaaS, and IaaS. These three service models distinguish the primary cloud computing service models. They are the important paradigms of cloud computing. As cloud computing can satisfy virtually any of the IT needs, these classifications indicate the role of a particular cloud service.

Infrastructure as a Service (IaaS)

IaaS helps the delivery of the computer infrastructure to support enterprise operations on an outsourcing basis. It is the low-level cloud service paradigm and the most important among all paradigms. The structure of IaaS is shown in Figure 3. IaaS preconfigured hardware resources are given to users via the virtual interface; it does not have any application or operating system. It merely provides access to the infrastructure which supports the software (Bineet et al. 2016). It provides storage access to corporate data backups, the network for a company website server and gives access to high-power computing. IaaS is mostly used by the Amazon EC2, IBM soft Layer, and Google's Compute Engine that power a large part of the backbone of the internet.

Figure 3. Infrastructure as a Service

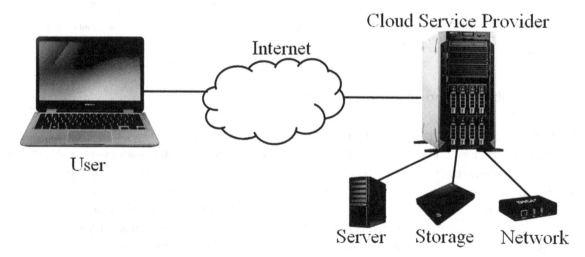

A server is used to process other programs and share the data or information with others through the internet (Fady et al. 2019). Servers are used for data sharing, data storing, and many more functions. The cloud vendor hosts the infrastructure as a service using the server. NVIDIA DGX server is used by the IBM cloud for hosting the infrastructure. The use of this server provides the ability to do things without any complex installation.

INTEL XEON is an Intel processor designed for empowering Amazon web services with the cloud providers. This processor has a high CPU performance and serves high-octane computing.

Some Benefits and Drawbacks of IaaS

Cost saving: Since the infrastructure is available on the internet, the maintenance of the hardware and the network devices do not require people. Thus, it saves lot of money spent on hardware devices. But the money is paid only for use of the service.

Several users: On a single server, more than one user can use the service from anywhere - including remotely - and at any time as the resources are available on the internet.

Quality of server: The data is spread over multiple servers. Hence, in the event of failure of a hardware device, the organization's infrastructure is not affected and IaaS can be operated even if the server goes down.

Various drawbacks of IaaS are:

Loss of data: Backup of data is done on an outdoor secured platform (data storage). Data may get lost at the providers' end.

Vulnerability: The interdependency of the system - increases vulnerability that may lead to leakage of the personal information.

Platform as a Service (PaaS)

Platform as a Service allows the customers to develop, run, and manage applications. The complexity in building and maintaining the infrastructure along with developing and implementing the application is removed. The structure of the PaaS system is shown in Figure 4. PaaS includes the base operating system and the applications' development tools. The need for building and organizing and maintaining the infrastructure is removed with PaaS. It is also called a middleware as it sits in between IaaS and SaaS.

PaaS technologies have problems and risks for service providers. The challenges relate to balance control, cost, the capacity of a PaaS-based service, creating audit trails, and implementing third-party services to PaaS (Stefania et al. 2017). Virtualization management, tuning the PaaS computer architecture, and the design of interoperability with other services should also be considered. The benefits of PaaS include faster time to market, a scalable environment, the rapid delivery of new capabilities, flexibility, speed, agility, and standardized middleware.

Figure 4. Platform as a Service

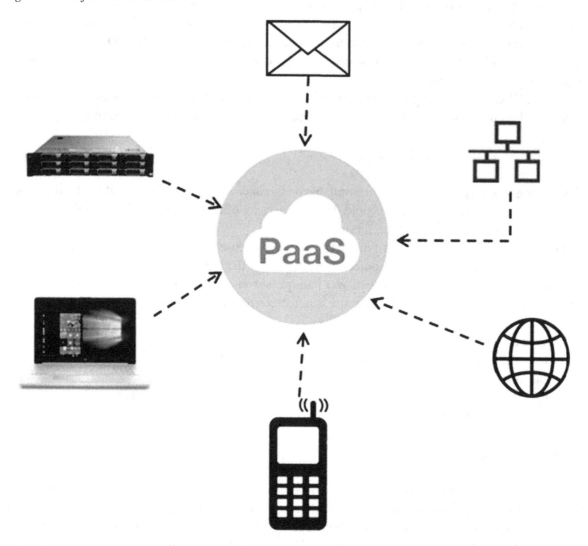

Software as a Services (SaaS)

The Software as a Service platform is a software licensing and delivery model. The software is allowed on a payment basis called on-demand software. The structure of the SaaS system is shown in Figure 5. Users access the SaaS using thin clients through the web browser. Cloud-based IoT platforms depend on the software as a service paradigm and users need to pay only for the use of the IoT-related service provided by the SaaS using a web interface. Initially, the sensor data is stored and then plotted as a graphics. But SaaS IoT platforms have limitations to their web services; developers cannot develop custom and complex applications but can extend the web services to user-provided callbacks. The resulting mechanism is not homogeneous, and maintenance is difficult. Developing an IoT Big Data is complex due to a large number of services for installation and configuration including: storage devices, message broker, and processing engines. The developer can note the needs of the real-time application in a specification file called the manifest. It is read by using the PaaS paradigm through the use of the PaaS platform.

Figure 5. Software as a Service

Various challenges of SaaS are:

The computing paradigm is unavailable to the unauthorized user's access and hacking in online domains. Risks like digital miscreants who target businesses that use the cloud to store their data by blocking their customer's access to weaken the online system. So that degrading the Software from the service provider's market value. So, service providers ensure authentication and security and give a guarantee to their customers and clients.

Other challenges of SaaS include secure and well-defined database, guaranteeing zero-downtime deployment, building a fully customizable SaaS system, managing the subscription lifecycle, and third-party payment integration, etc.

Requirements of IoT Big Data Analytics in Smart Cities

The IoT big data analytics in the smart cities should ensure dynamic management of the IoT data from the sensors and provide connectivity to the heterogeneous objects along with the interoperability issues. It extracts the information from the large set of IoT data received from the connected devices in the smart city (Ahmed, 2019). Big data analytics provides connectivity and accessibility to the users and diverse objects which are connected to each other for producing a massive amount of data hereby allowing the dynamic orchestration and management of users. It provides services to the users based on the requirements and preference allows personalization for users and services.

Intelligent and Dynamic: Components, applications, and the platform include autonomic and intelligent features for managing the functions and also, making real-time and smart decisions and dynamic implementation based on the understanding of the environment, users, and applications. Taking note of dynamic resources management of IoT and performance targets and constraints are provided which include the offloading of the workload from hosts or clients to the cloud.

Distributed: Functionalities like distributed intelligence, computing capabilities, distributed information processing, distributed data management capabilities, and distributed storage should be shared with smart city devices, servers, and a number of cloud environments.

Scalable: Data management, storage, and processing services require proper regulation and scalability of the platform for meeting the needs of different devices, services, and users.

Real-Time: The platform should provide real-time data derived from the devices quickly and the responses should be fast.

Programmable: The programming capacity of IoT supports data warehouse scheme, business and service logics, and service model of the platform.

Interoperable: The different IoT devices and the infrastructure should be interoperable. The APIs should strictly follow the standards. The components are made to operate as open-source software. The common model data exploits both unstructured and structured data. Raw data are replaced by the linked data and accept the relevant information for the creation of a multimodel and cross-domain smart application. It protects the platform and ensures security.

Functional Architecture of IoT Big Data Platform

The levels of the architecture of the IoT system:

End Devices (Things): Sensors, actuators, controllers, and peripheral devices are included in the end devices for the measurement and transfer of data to people. The data can be passed through any one of the protocols such as Serial, MODBUS, RS-485, BLE, CAN bus, OPC UA, Sigfox, WiFi, Bluetooth, and LoRaWAN. The volume of this information is small and called Little Data.

Gateways and hubs (Network): Routers act as a gateway for the transfer of the data from the connected devices to the cloud.

Cloud: A remote server in the data centre wherein data is stored safely and can be processed and analyzed. When the data from different devices is processed together, it becomes Big Data and thus the IoT becomes intelligent through the connection of the data analysis tools, namely, artificial neural network, and machine learning algorithms. Hence, the end devices are effectively controlled using the remote server. IoT system architecture in small and Big Data analytics is shown in Figure 6.

How the Internet of Things Collects Small Data

Sensors like temperature sensor, pressure sensor, vibration sensor, and level sensor measure temperature, pressure, vibration, and the level respectively and record the collected information and also the changes that occur in the devices. With less cost, the equipment can store a large number of data in it. Various wireless and wired networks have been used for data collection. As a result, the type and number of connections will increase. The following factors affect the selection of the data transfer protocol:

Figure 6. Three levels of IoT system architecture in small and big data analytic

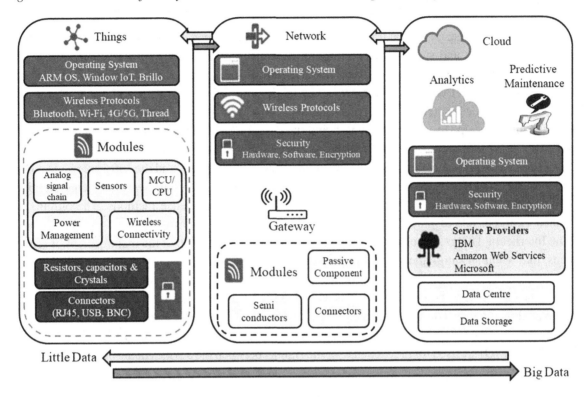

- Rate of transfer: It is the amount of data transferred in unit time.
- Frequency of data: The frequency of a particular data value is the number of times the data value occurs.
- Distance: The maximum distance required to transmit the data.
- Power consumption: It is the measure of end devices that operate in a single charge (without recharging).

Types of Sensors

There are two types of sensors used to transmit the data.

Active Sensor: It emits the signals and takes up their reflections. So, it requires more energy.

Passive Sensor: This type of sensor receives the signal only. So it consumes less power. Sensors operate on the wave principle, i.e., reception of sound (ultrasonic sensor), light, and heatwaves. Physical characteristics, namely, pressure, capacitances, and inductance are measured by different devices. The intelligence level and the quality of the sensor can be improved by combining different types of sensors with it.

How Internet of Things Works with Big Data

End devices in the industrial IoT cannot be accessed. But, gateways can connect the devices, equipment, intelligent processing, and storage systems. End devices use less power but transfer different formats of data to the gateways. The sensors connected to the end devices produce an analogue signal, which is then converted to digital values with the help of an analogue-to-digital converter. Then, the values are classified based on parameters called a tag. If the tag is complex, then the peripheral processor is more powerful. This tag helps to reduce bandwidth and the data transferred to the cloud and, as a result, the speed of the process is increased.

Now the data collected as tags is sent to the cloud cluster via gateways, and the software use Big Data tools to process and mine information. The data from the devices on the cloud server is then systemized and analyzed using machine learning algorithms and artificial intelligence methods. The outputs are presented as graphs and displayed on the user interface of the IoT platform.

The Internet of Things is used not only to transfer information but also in the management of remote devices, like when an automatic valve is implemented on a pipe. Now, this implementation is virtually represented on the cloud and any change on the valve is noted and transferred to the executable device at the end. The CPU receives this information as a tag and performs DAC, i.e. converts the received digital value to analogue value. The IoT system does not rely on the data channels. Retries can be made when data is not transmitted from the sensors to the cloud. Message brokers (Apache Qpid, RabbitMQ, and Apache ActiveMQ) are used for the exchange of the signals between the devices in the distributed system.

INTELLIGENT KNOWLEDGE AS A SERVICE SOFTWARE PLATFORM

Intelligent Knowledge as a Service Platform (iKaaS) is used to enable multi cloud-based services in a trouble-free manner. Service providers and consumers extend cloud capabilities and knowledge to empower services. IoT devices are installed in public administration, health support service providers, and town management services. Tools required for the interpretation and understanding of the data are not available so useful data is not known due to technological and privacy issues. The iKaaS software platform is shown in Figure 7.

iKaas securely provides useful data and performs analytics of the underlying platform. Technology providers can re-use or adopt and integrate the solutions offered using the iKaaS, which serves as the analytical and service management tools. The public can make use of the services provided by the iKaaS through public administrations.

Ubiquitous, heterogeneous sensing, Big Data cloud computing technologies have been combined by the iKaaS to enable the IoT to process data ingestion, data storage, analytics, and knowledge sharing phases.

There are two cloud ecosystems in the ideal platform. They are the local cloud and the global cloud.

- Local cloud: The local cloud provides users with their requested services. It provides storage access to the services. It compromises the computing storage and network capabilities. The local cloud can have multiple nodes, such as sensors, devices, and actuators. The resources have enough power and storage and serve the users in a particular area. Users can access different services from their devices directly to the local cloud.

Figure 7. iKaaS software platform

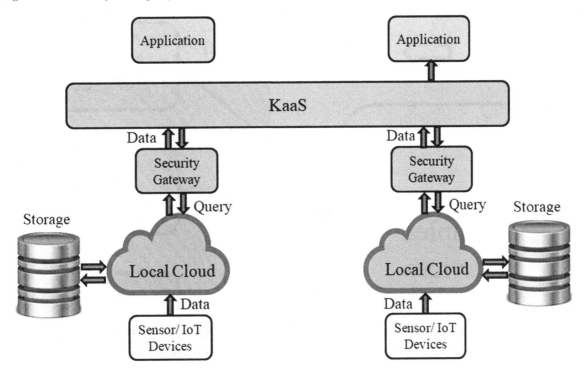

- Global cloud: It is the backbone infrastructure, improving business opportunities for service providers.

The functionalities of the iKaaS Cloud ecosystem include:

- The global cloud has a consolidated service-logic, description of the resources. The services can be re-used.
- The global cloud has autonomic service management and the local cloud also has the same autonomic service management. It can understand the requirements, find the service, process it, analyze the best service configuration pattern, and reconfigure the service while the execution of the service is done.
- The local and global cloud anticipates data storage and processing. A large set of data obtained from the IoT devices is effectively communicated, processed, and stored. It can also derive knowledge and information ensuring security and privacy.
- The primary part of the global cloud is iKaaS. It deals with device behavior aspects, the provided service, and user preferences.

The services offered to the user are determined by iKaas functionality. The IoT service depends on the local data collected from devices and on the service support functionality offered within the cloud.

Figure 8. Service composition and decomposition

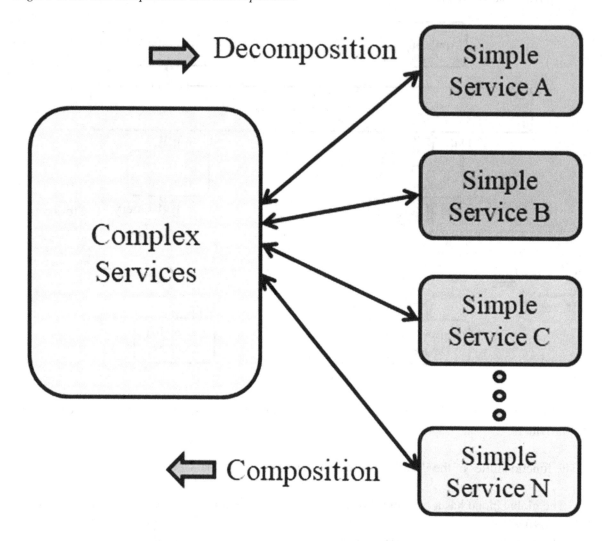

Advanced Data Processing and Analytics

The infrastructure's information is analyzed using the information stream processing algorithms. The hidden patterns and unknown correlations of data are unveiled by Big Data analytics. The knowledge acquisition and information stream processing about IoT and Big Data services are included in the iKaaS platform. The challenges and requirements of information stream processing over the cloud are analyzed.

The services are provided with processing capabilities and cover the knowledge acquisition life cycle. The heterogeneous data is collected with the help of information stream processing and virtualization services.

The existing approaches and design solutions explain the technical challenges such as:

- Using smart virtual objects as a multi cloud-based resource through information stream processing, information extraction, and virtualization.
- iKaaS local and global cloud environments allow services like decomposition, migration, and resource allocation that are supported by the storage mechanisms for smart virtual objects.
- The data collected from a large number of smart objects is processed by the analytics engine and mechanism.

The objective is to extract useful information and provide knowledge to face situation-aware applications. Processing and storage of data is done in a global or local cloud, or both, with the help of flexible service execution. Thus, the discovery of smart virtual objects and data storage is supported by the mechanisms in this task and provides an efficient and cost-effective service. The large volume of anonymized data aggregated slowly from the smart virtual devices is also managed dynamically.

Service Composition and Decomposition

A combination of a number of sources, functionalities, and functional services makes the IoT and Big data, a complex large scale application. For example, the application used for monitoring the healthy aged people includes services like measuring and monitoring the blood pressure, heart rate, weight of that person, and notification and remainders. It has also an application to home automation also. IoT and Big data play a vital role in this application as a service. So, the iKaaS services should be developed as small and autonomous for an easy approach with the known APIs for operating them. The decomposition of an application provides loose coupling and high cohesion of multiple services. The composition and decomposition logic is shown in Figure 8.

These multiple services have complex services for many applications. The simple service processes on its own and communicates with the small mechanisms. High-level services are divided into multiple services that are transferred as individual services at the run time. These are maintained and managed through the use of programming languages and data storage technologies.

Pattern of Service Composition

The composition and decomposition of services has a deep impact on the iKaas service design pattern. It is overcome by designing the service as independent. Single complex services are divided by the end-users. The dataset is designed independently using iKaas services. A single iKaaS service has multiple service instances at the runtime. The pattern for composition and decomposition is shown in Figure 9.

Figure 9. Pattern for composition and decomposition

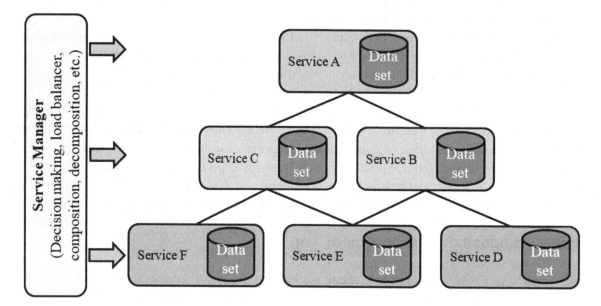

Migration and Portability in Multi Cloud Environment

Individuals or organization can shift the services with other cloud vendors without issues relating to implementation, integration, and compatibility. This is called service migration and is used in cloud computing implementation. This concept is defined as the process in which the application is implemented on the other cloud vendors or private cloud architecture. iKaas runtime services are portable among different platforms, desktop distribution, and clouds. The multi-cloud and distributed computing environments are supported by service migration. iKaas distributed with local and global cloud for service mitigation is shown in Figure 10.

The platform functionalities and capabilities of iKaaS services are distributed between the local and global cloud, thus making it a fully distributed architecture. The edge and fog computing use the concept of a local cloud in which the pre-processing is done at the lowest level. Fog computing reduces the network operation cost by making the data sources move to the pre-processing at the earlier stage. The disadvantage is that it is difficult to identify where the services are migrated with respect to users' mobility, circumstances, and environmental context.

The latency in the local cloud is overcome in edge computing which provides the resources to large-scale data processing systems.

The data are sent to the core network and the result is sent to the users after processing in the cloud paradigm. The big data acquisition, aggregation, preprocessing, and reduction of data storage are handled by the fog and the cloud.

Figure 10. Service mitigation of iKaaS distributed with local and global cloud

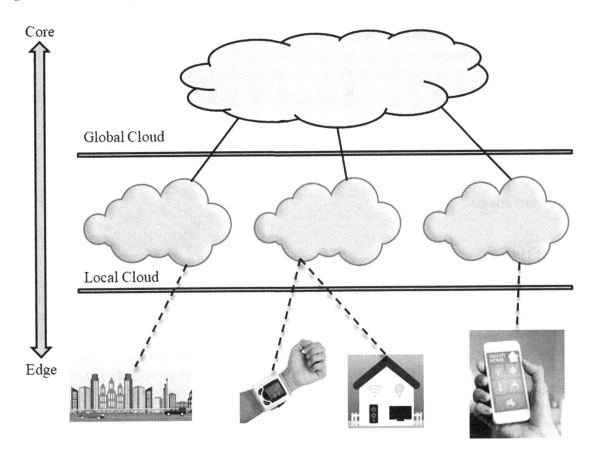

Cost Function of Service Migration

The strategy of service migration is difficult to define in service migration as there is a difference in the transmission and service migration costs between the cloud and user. The advantages of service migration are reduction in network overhead and less latency. The framework for dynamic, low-cost migration services has been developed and presented by iKaaS to the hybrid cloud infrastructure. An algorithm is developed for placing the services in different clouds to minimize cost. The service migration in the iKaaS cloud environment is based on the Markov-Decision Process.

Dynamic Selection of Devices in Smart Cities

In iKaaS, end services are more important as they provide the data needed for the optimization of iKaaS service providers. In the multi-cloud architecture, the end devices are considered as the endpoints in end to-end services. For example, if the end device is suitably attached to the local cloud, the other service functionalities at the local cloud are close to the data source.

The key factors defining device sustainability are:

- Location of the device: Defined as the location where the owner has placed devices for the better performance of service functions.
- Battery levels and evolution: it makes note to reduce whether the data processing and transferring depends on the device.
- Availability of sensors: the sensors are exposed by users for inclusion in the service.
- User away and reaction times: the devices can be used while the user travels and if they can see the alert and react accordingly.
- Data quality: it deals with the quality of data given as inputs.

The main objective of using iKaas is to produce and store the knowledge of the device in a suitable way for the functionalities at the end-to-end system while performing their joint services and cloud optimization process.

CONCLUSION

IoT and Big Data analytics for a smart city with cloud computing have been proposed in this chapter. Machine learning and Big Data analytics are used to drive IoT devices. These technologies can improve productivity, economy, environment, and quality of life when IoT and other ICT devices are properly implemented. These new and growing technologies help to meet the different challenges to develop and implement smart cities. The developer of such a platform must have a clear goal in selecting IoT platforms and use complex data analytic tools, IoT services, and data base management. This chapter has provided the fundamentals and anatomy of popular technologies of smart cities, integration of Big Data and the IoT cloud, and an intelligent knowledge-based service platform is described. Various challenges and benefits of IaaS, PaaS, and SaaS paradigm have been explained. The iKaaS software platform provides an opportunity for every citizen through public administrations service and management tools.

REFERENCES

Ahmed, M. (2019). A novel big data analytics framework for smart cities. *Future Generation Computer Systems*, *91*, 620–633. doi:10.1016/j.future.2018.06.046

Balaji, L., Dhanalakshmi, A., & Chellaswamy, C. (2017). A variance distortion rate control scheme for combined spatial-temporal scalable video coding. *Journal of Mobile Multimedia*, *13*, 277–290.

Bilal, K., & Erbad, A. (2017). Edge Computing for Interactive Media and Video Streaming. *IEEE International Conference on Fog and Mobile Edge Computing (FMEC)*,1-6. 10.1109/FMEC.2017.7946410

Chellaswamy, C., Chinnammal, V., Dhanalakshmi, A., & Malarvizhi, C. (2017). An IoT based frontal collision avoidance system for railways. *IEEE International Conference on Power, Control, Signals &Instrumentation Engineering (ICPCSI)*, 1082-1087. 10.1109/ICPCSI.2017.8391877

Chellaswamy, C., Famitha, H., Anusiya, T., & Amirthavarshini, S. B. (2018b). IoT based humps and pothole detection on roads and information sharing. *IEEE International Conference on Power Energy Information and Communication (ICCPEIC)*, 84-90. 10.1109/ICCPEIC.2018.8525196

Chellaswamy, C., Sivakumar, K., Nisha, J., & Kaviya, R. (2018a). An IoT based dam water management system for agriculture. *IEEE International Conference on Recent Trends in Electrical, Control and Communication (RTECC-18)*, 51-56. 10.1109/RTECC.2018.8625696

Datameer. (2016). *Big data analytics and the internet of things*. Author.

Datameer Inc. (2013). *The guide to big data analytics*. New York: Datameer.

Deloitte. (2015). *Smart cities big data*. Deloitte.

Dohler, M., Vilajosana, I., & Vilajosana, X., & Losa, J. (2011). Smart cities: An action plan. *Proceedings of Barcelona smart cities congress 2011*.

Enbysk, L. (2013). *Smart Cities Council.* https://smartcitiescouncil.com/article/smart-citiestechnology-market-top-20-billion-2020

Fady, A. M. I., & Elsayed, E. H. (2019). Trusted Cloud Computing Architectures for infrastructure as a service: Survey and systematic literature review. *Computers & Security*, *82*, 196–226. doi:10.1016/j.cose.2018.12.014

Gangid, N., & Sharma, B. (2016). Cloud Computing and Robotics for Disaster Management. *IEEE Inter. Conference on Intelligent Systems. Modelling and Simulation*, 1-6.

Gantz, J., & Reinsel, D. (2012). *The digital universe in 2020: Big data, bigger digital shadows, and biggest growth in the far east*. EMC Corporation.

He, H., Kamburugamuve, S., Fox, G. C., & Zhao, W. (2016). Cloud based Real-time Multi-Robot Collision Avoidance for Swarm Robotics. *International Journal of Grid and Distributed Computing*, *9*(6), 339–358. doi:10.14257/ijgdc.2016.9.6.30

Hollands, R. G. (2015). Critical Interventions into the Corporate Smart City. *Cambridge Journal of Regions, Economy and Society*, *8*(1), 61–77. doi:10.1093/cjres/rsu011

Jin, J., Gubbi, J., Marusic, S., & Palaniswami, M. (2014). An Information Framework for Creating a Smart City Through Internet of Things. *IEEE Internet of Things Journal*, *1*(2), 112–121. doi:10.1109/JIOT.2013.2296516

Jin, L., Xiao, Y., Zheng, X., Kim-Kwang, R. C., Liang, H., & Xiaohui, C. (2017). A cloud-based taxi trace mining framework for smart city. *Software, Practice & Experience*, *47*(8), 1081–1094.

Kamburugamuve, S., Christiansen, L., & Fox, G. (2015). A framework for real-time processing of sensor data in the cloud. *Journal of Sensors*, 1–12.

Kehoe, B., Patil, S., Abbeel, P., & Goldberg, K. (2015). A Survey of Research on Cloud Robotics and Automation. IEEE Trans. On Automation & Eng., 12(2), 398-409.

Kumar, B. (2016). Security threats and their mitigation in infrastructure as a service. *Perspectives in Science*, *8*, 462–464. doi:10.1016/j.pisc.2016.05.001

Mohammad, M. (2018). A hybrid algorithm using a genetic algorithm and multiagent reinforcement learning heuristic to solve the traveling salesman problem. *Neural Computing & Applications*, *30*(9), 2935–2951. doi:10.100700521-017-2880-4

Neirotti, P., Marco, A. D., Cagliano, A. C., Mangano, G., & Scorrano, F. (2014). Current Trends in Smart City Initiatives: Some Stylised Facts. *Cities (London, England)*, *38*(5), 25–36. doi:10.1016/j.cities.2013.12.010

Salim, F., & Haque, U. (2015). Urban Computing in the Wild: A Survey on Large Scale Participation and Citizen Engagement with Ubiquitous Computing, Cyber Physical Systems, and Internet of Things. *International Journal of Human-Computer Studies*, *8*(1), 31–48. doi:10.1016/j.ijhcs.2015.03.003

Sas. (2017). https://www.sas.com/en_us/insights/analytics/big-data-analytics.html

Satyanarayanan, M. (2017). Edge Computing for Situational Awareness. *IEEE International Symposium on Local and Metropolitan Area Networks (LANMAN)*, 1-6.

Stefania, C. (2017). Resource management in cloud platform as a service systems: Analysis and opportunities. *Journal of Systems and Software*, *132*, 98–118. doi:10.1016/j.jss.2017.05.035

Vanolo, A. (2014). Smart mentality: The Smart City as Disciplinary Strategy. *Urban Studies (Edinburgh, Scotland)*, *51*(5), 883–898. doi:10.1177/0042098013494427

Yunhe, P. (2016). Urban Big Data and the Development of City Intelligence. *Engineering*, *2*(2), 171–178. doi:10.1016/J.ENG.2016.02.003

Zheng, Y., Capra, L., Wolfson, O., & Yang, H. (2014). Urban Computing: Concepts, Methodologies, and Applications. *ACM Transactions on Intelligent Systems and Technology*, *5*(3), 1–55.

Zheng, Y., Wu, W., Chen, Y., Qu, H., & Ni, L. M. (2016). Visual Analytics in Urban Computing: An Overview. *IEEE Transactions on Big Data*, *2*(3), 276–296. doi:10.1109/TBDATA.2016.2586447

Chapter 8
Big Data Issues:
Gathering, Governance, GDPR, Security, and Privacy

Karthika K.
Adhiyamaan College of Engineering, Hosur, India

Devi Priya R.
Kongu Engineering College, Erode, India

Sathishkumar S.
iD https://orcid.org/0000-0003-3825-4148
Adhiyamaan College of Engineering, Hosur, India

ABSTRACT

Various unimaginable opportunities and applications can be attained by the development of internet-connected automation. The network system with numerous wired or wireless smart sensors is called as IoT. It is showing various enhancement for past few years. Without proper security protection, various attacks and threats like cyberattacks threat causes serious disaster to IoT from the day it was introduced. Hence, IoT security system is improvised by various security and the management techniques. There are six sections in security management of IoT works. IoT security requirement is described intensively. The proposed layered of security management architecture is being defined and explained. Thus, this proposed architecture shows the security management system for IoT network tight security management for a network of the IoT which is elaborately explained with examples and about GDPR. In information security, intrusion recognizable proof is the showing of placing exercises that attempt to deal the protection, respectability, or availability of a benefit.

I. INTRODUCTION

In this advanced period, web has transformed into an essential wellspring of correspondence in pretty much every calling. With the extended utilization of framework designing, its security has created to be

DOI: 10.4018/978-1-7998-3111-2.ch008

astoundingly segregating issue as the workstations in particular affiliation hold private information and delicate data. The framework used to screen the framework security is known as Network recognition. Interruption discovery is to get ambushes against a machine structure. It is a discriminating enhancement great to go part and additionally an element extent of examination.

According to a study by **Faizal M.A. et al. (2010)** a Static Threshold Based Method for Intrusion Detection System is proposed that works for detecting DDOS attacks. The threshold is formulated by set of features that are Timestamp, Duration, IP address of the host being monitored,connection pool,Source and Destination Services, Number of Connections and Status flag of connection. The results are validated by using Statistical Process Control Chart (Shewhart Chart). This intrusion detection system acts on network layer that considers the number of connections made by the attacker which is the main cause of Denial of Services. The TCPDump utility is used to capture the TCP traffic for analysis purposes.

Gupta et al. (2013) proposed Profile Based Intrusion Detection System in cloud. This work is based on signature cum behavior based algorithms. The algorithms run for each virtual machine profile and rank the dataset (TCPDump). The dataset is updated and synchronized for new attack patterns regularly for each profile. The use of IP filtering is also incorporated for insider, outsider and malicious intent users. The intrusion detection system implementation is cloud based and uses multiple thresholds to build signature description of each virtual machine. The thresholds are computed on the basis of frequency threshold historically. **François et.al.(2012)** the major work done by these researchers is on TCP Syn flooding attack and most of the features are network based indicators such as bandwidth utilization, packet loss rate, connection type and also include signatures of attacks. **Cepheli et al. (2016)** proposed the intrusion detection system to prevent DDos attacks. **Hwang et al. (2007)** introduced the hybrid intrusion detection with weighted signature. **Xiao et al. (2015)** proposed the approach to detect DDos attack against data center with correlation analysis but detailed mathematical background to compute threshold is neither mentioned, nor there any section in the paper giving details on the method used to validate the results. **Singh et al. (2015)** proposed a data streaming approach to defend against DDos Flooding attacks. **Faizal M.A. et al. (2009)** proposed a threshold based technique for network intrusion detection system. The detection of the intrusion from the normal situation suggested in this work is based on the static threshold. It is obtained from the outcome of observations and experiments. The upper limit and lower limit is calculated by using the sample statistics in which upper control line and lower control line equations are used along with the mean value.

Hai Ji et al. (2013) put forward virtual machine monitoring (VMM) based intrusion detection and prevention system named as VMFence. Its role is to monitor the network flow as well as of file integrity. The work states that a privileged VM is used as a centralized architecture to apply the security in the cloud environment. **Jun-Ho Lee et al. (2011)** elaborated a multilevel based DDOS attack detection system which considered the application level traffic only. The authors used anomaly detection management module named as AAA that refers to three keywords authentication, authorization and accounting.

Jisa David and Ciza Thomas (2015) introduced a DDOS approach to prevention of attacks on the basis of Current Mean Entropy which is applied on the flow of the network traffic. The approach used the adaptive threshold approach to track the network's activities and behavior of the users. **Praveen Kumar Rajendran, M. Rajesh and R. Abhilash (2015)** discussed the proposed hybrid intrusion detection system for private cloud which is based on empirical research. The authors tested the intrusion detection system on data which is collected by using the network speed. Jmeter is used to calculate the network speed.

Miao Du et al., (2020) proposed a training model to protect the big data in smart environment using various algorithms such as OPP and OJP .This paper assurance the perfection on datasets.

Shuang Wang et al. (2020) discussed the privacy of big data in medical field and also discussed about difference confidential preserving methodologies against various attacks in the medical field. And also reviewed about the current challenges in the research to enhance the privacy of data in medical field. **Rong Jiang et al.(2019)** analysed the privacy of data in medical field using analysis method in urban computing .

II. SYSTEM MODEL

A Network Intrusion Detection System examines the moving toward network traffic and differentiates the dubious activity on the framework. Organization Intrusion Detection is the most basic and most comprehensively used framework security methodology used to perceive the weak assaults by watching the framework conduct and subsequently taking essential developments against them. Organization Intrusion Detection frameworks are halves into host based and network based. This gathering depends on the data sources that are used. Host Based framework uses the accounts and data kept up by the working framework. By using these narratives, the framework can screen things like structure logs; customer's records and archive systems as shown in Figure 1.

Figure 1. a. Centralized attack detection architecture, b. Distributed attack detection architecture.

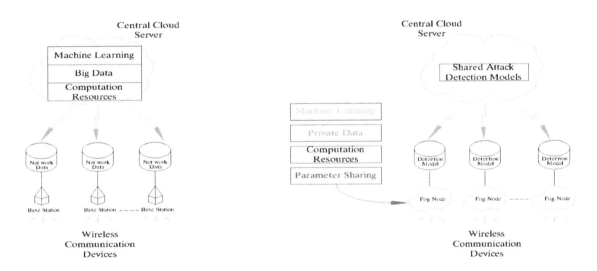

The central cloud repository collects all the large-scale big data from various IoT devices via base station to improve the efficiency of attack detection in the IoT network. Because of various problems occurring in the privacy of IoT devices the formation of large-scale big data is difficult and challenging. Potential data providers may not be encouraged to share their data due to the high potential for data loss. Massive communication bandwidth is required to accumulate a huge volume of data. Processing such a large volume of data that requires huge computing power storage.

2.1 Security Specifications

The IoT fundamental security issues require personality validation tools and ensuring data confidentiality. The three key areas are data confidentiality, data integrity and data availability. Breaking one of these three essential security zones can lead to security problems for the IoT system. In this way, every one of the four layers of the IoT network system should meet these base prerequisites. The Basic Security Requirements for IoT is shown in Figure 2.

2.2 Information Confidentiality

The target of information classification is to ensure the privacy of touchy information by utilizing a couple of instruments and by killing unapproved access. For IoT machines, for instance, Data Confidentiality is to protect the data from unauthorized access that has been collected from various sensors and nodes .It is guaranteed by Data Encryption. With a lot of effort only, unauthorized person can access the data due to the encrypted data is converted in to image content [5]. Other Techniques to provide the data confidentiality is Two-venure affirmation techniques. The client can legitimately pick up the information dependent on two ward verification checks.

Figure 2. IoT fundamental security detail

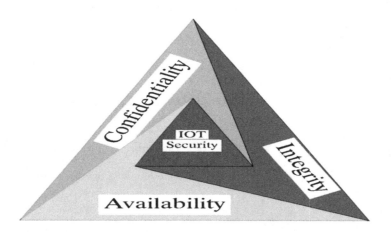

2.3 Integrity of Data

Respectability of Data shields significant information from the solidifying of cybercriminals during correspondence. There are assortments of cases, for instance, a server outage that can alter the data. To assure the integrity of information at the principal level is (CRC) Cyclic Redundancy Check (CRC). CRC method is a simple fault localization component for coding the message.

It includes detecting errors using a fixed length check value and guaranteed the integrity of data by checking the control value in IoT Communication Networks. It utilizes adaptation Control strategies to change and fortify information to hold report changes in the framework, at that point ensure information trustworthiness by reestablishing changing information in the event of cancellation or loss

2.4 Data Availability

The availability of data is important for IoT security, the availability of data ensures that consumers can access data assets in ordinary and horrible conditions, and the availability of data further impedes the flow of data from it. To guarantee the availability and reliability of data, the IoT needs reinforcement as well as excessive methods to permit significant information replication and foresee data loss in case of device failure or conflict. Denial of Service (DoS) and Distributed Denial of Service (DDoS) assaults cause information access security issues, filtering routers will mitigate the problem and ensure IoT system data availability.

III. GENERAL DATA PROTECTION REGULATION AND SECURITY GOVERNANCE

3.1 Data Privacy and Protection Rules Regulations

Data privacy and protection rules regulations still should be refreshed for the period of big data. Indeed, many existing regulations have not been checked on with regards to data warehousing (e.g., privacy laws covering just wiretapping). Additional consideration must be taken by associations and steady watchfulness is required in this regularly changing administrative scene. An association ought to along these lines be totally legit with people about the utilization of their own data. This may even mean clarifying at the beginning of an association with a person that the accurate motivations behind any data examination may not yet be characterized, yet that more data will be given when the reasons become obvious, in accordance with the graduated consent model. The General Data Protection Regulation (GDPR) is a legal framework that provides rules for the collection and storage of personal data from people living in the European Union (EU). The European Parliament adopted the GDPR in April 2016 to replace an obsolete 1995 law on data protection. It includes provisions requiring business to protect EU citizen's personal data and privacy for transactions taking place within EU Member States. The GDPR also controls the transfer of personal data outside the EU.

3.2 Security Governance

Security Governance is may be defined as the set of roles, responsibilities and practices exercised by executive management. The goals of security governance are providing strategic direction, verifying enterprise resources, ensuring that objectives are achieved and ascertaining that risks are managed appropriately. Many organizations are taking proactive steps to ensure their investments in security controls directly support their objectives for the business in the security governance and risk management. The combination of both security governance and risk management provides logical and physical security, organization gain an advantage for competing in the global economy through an optimized IT infrastructure and also better protection for their digital, physical and human assets.

IV. SECURITY MECHANISMS

For instance, Battery-Powered Network Devices and Low-Power Wireless Sensors depends on the IoT security mechanisms. Consequently, any proposal should consider effective security mechanisms for IoT security. Low-Power Consumption Devices and Low-Computing Capability Devices are nodes and sensors, IoT devices security techniques should be as lightweight as might be anticipated under the circumstances. The node gathers the data and gatecrashers captures the data or used to compress the network system without the proficient protection. Therefore, to ensure the system, a few essential security mechanisms should be included at all levels.

4.1 Threats and Attacks on Element Layer

Various hubs and sensors are available in the component layer so as to perform information assortment from associated network environment. The hubs and sensors can undergo different assaults like unapproved access, listening in, spoofing, and so forth.

Unapproved Access

RFID, labels, standardized tag names, actuators and canny discovery gadgets are the different hubs and sensors in the component layer to perform information assortment from the environment, due to the nonexistence of verification administrations, illicit gatherings may get to the information and cause changes in it to or even delete the information.

Eavesdropping Data collected by wireless components such as RFID and tags can be easily read by attackers, as noted by reference. Using all of this data, attackers can hack into any IoT system or sniff out important information such as the user's password or private details.

Spoofing

The spoofing is that the attackers send false information to nodes and sensors that claim to act like the original failure, and then the attackers can have full access to the system.

4.2 Security in Element Layer e The essential layer of an IoT framework environment is the most minimal layer of the four layers. Sensors and nodes are present in the elementary layer; these devices undergo attacks such as unauthorized access, eavesdropping and identity theft.

V. IOT SECURITY MANAGEMENT SYSTEM

As stated by the IoT Network System Architecture, the construction of the IoT security management system (IoTSMS) is carried out. Before building the security management system, five common security issues in the IoT network system need to be considered. Smart sensors can be threatened, so security management needs to deal with low-powered smart devices, privacy issues for basic layer devices, various layers facing the same attacks, and complication and compatibility issues of the system. A security management system is essential for such requirements in an IoT environment that counteracts all distinguish dangers and is well suited with IoT Network System Architecture. It can also be said that due to the construction of an IoT network environment with four layer system architecture, the management of network security will in fact be systematized in the same way as a layered architecture. To Protect IoT environment, four-layer protection management system is proposed for this implementation. The Security management system for IoT is shown in Figure 3.

The principles applied on four layers are outlined below:

(i)   A usefulness layer is made where an assortment of security functions are required at all levels.
(ii) A well-defined security function is performed by each layer.

Figure 3. Security management system for IoT

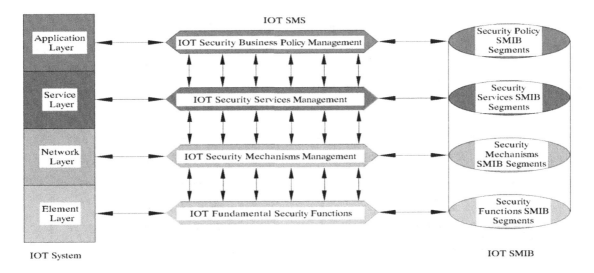

(iii) The selection of functionality of every layer is done by considering the existing methods.
(iv)   Standardized protocols.
(v)   Choosing layer boundaries to diminish the flow of information through device interfaces.
(vi)   The quantity of layers is steady with the layers of the IoT network similarly that there is no need to be different security functions via the same layer.
(vii) The three aspects of the security management system are: IoT network system architecture consisting of four layers on the left, IoT SMS in the middle part having four layers as IoT Basic Security Feature, Security Services Management, Security Mechanism Management and Security Business Policy Management.

To order to achieve data confidentiality, data integrity and data quality, the entire layer has its security management comparison features. SMIB IoT is in the right side of this graph, the SMIB conducts X.509 version 3 recommendation validation, which includes fragments of smart sensor IDs, client identities, overview review and security logs, given the appropriate data specifications.

Both physical device security and network security also includes in IoT security, including the processes, technologies, and measures necessary to fortify IoT devices as well as the networks. It compasses industrial machines, smart energy grids, Personal IoT devices and building automation system. IoT security is the technology that safeguards connected devices and networks. It involves adding internet connectivity to a system of interrelated computing devices.

A. Functional Layers of IoT Security Management

Thus, it is clear that Security management for IoT consists of four layers, which include the layer of management of commercial policies of security IoT, the layer of management of security services IoT, the layer of management of mechanisms IoT Security and the IoT Basic Security Function Layer. All of these layers have an individual function to protect the IoT safety management system.

B. Management of IoT Security Policy Specifications

The Management of IoT Security Policy layer is mainly focused on trade customer needs like detecting and preventing each and every attack from various points of attack, maintaining the safety of all smart devices and avoiding IoT network from threats, and predicting system failure. The administration of IoT security business policies is shown at comparatively less requirements in Figure 4.

Figure 4. IoT security business scheme administration prerequisites

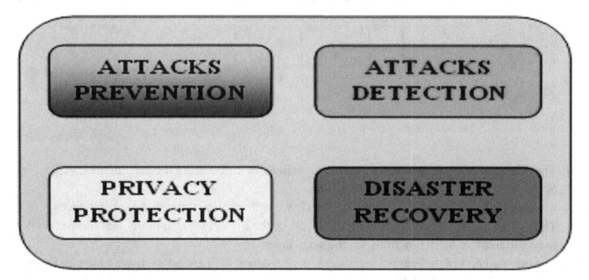

C. Security Services Function in IoT

The most well-known security services provided by the IoT Security Services Functional Layer, for instance, Authentication includes Peer Entity, Administration and Data Origin Privacy includes Connection, Connectionless, field and Traffic Flow are certainly the best known part of IoT security. The data in the IoT condition is still evolving. Integrity administration under this condition implies that changes must be made separately by approved substances and by approved instruments. Essential Security of the IoT framework integrity includes connection, connectionless, specific field, non-repudiation as well as the administration of entry control. The IoT Security Services functionality layer area is shown in Figure 5.

Figure 5. IoT security services functionality layer

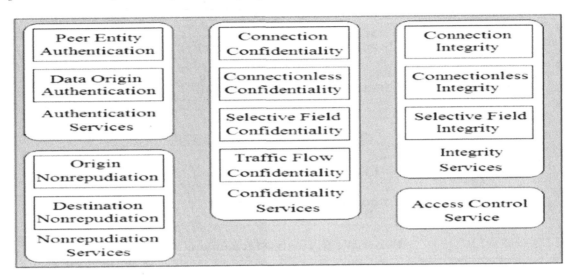

D. Role of IoT Security Mechanism

Security instruments provide methods, calculations, and plans to assist in determining security services characterized in the layer of security services. The functionality layer of the IoT security component gives the security systems as either explicit tools or as unavoidable tools. Security Techniques are Traffic Padding, Integrity of data, Trade in Authentication, Control Direction, Encipherment, Machine Signature, Access and Security that are legitimately authorized. Inevitable security tools embed confidentiality into features, security name, even identification, security review trail, Security Rehabilitation, Host IDS and Devices and against Infection Security components. The IoT Security mechanisms functionality layer is shown in Figure 6.

E. Fundamental Role of IoT Protection

As a comprehensive autonomous security server, an essential things of the IoT SMS is to be pre-owned as it can provide protect for multiple applications at the same time.

Thus, various generic arithmetic and encryption modules are considered to be the lowest layer of functionality. Message Digest, Secure Hash Algorithms and one-way hash are basic security functions given by the IoT fundamental security system. This layer provides key security communication functions such as RSA, Elliptic Curve and Diffie Hellman Algorithms. It incorporates time stamping, verify and validate the code and message, elliptic curve algorithm techniques, certificate including the standard X.509.This layer contains all the essential cryptographic functions necessary for the application of the IoT SMS.The IoT Fundamental security functionality layer is shown in Figure 7.

Figure 6. IoT security mechanisms functionality layer

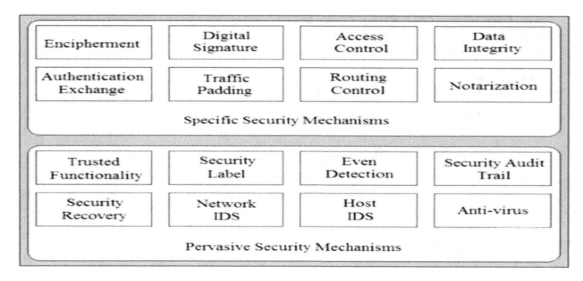

Figure 7. Iot fundamental security functionality layer

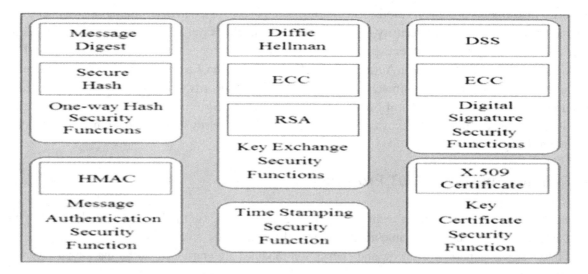

F. IoT Information Based on Security Management

An important component of IoT SMS is IoT SMIB. To facilitate the incorporation of all IoT security services in an IT or communications environment, this information database must be configured. The knowledge base for IoT security management consists of smart sensor Identification Conceptual Modules, Security Logs, Access Control List and User Profiles. For storing information, no material or method is implied by this definition. IoT system's normal operation needs IoT SMIB. It is a depository of all the application data and parameters.

PKI for the IoT Security

To provide a trustworthy model, IETF(Internet Engineering Task Force) has generated the PKI(Public Key Infrastrucutre).For protecting the IoT network, PKI's essential function to the degree is responsible for providing X.509 certificates, upgrading and key storage, conducting the number of protocol services, and enforcing access control.

The PKI forms a fundamental framework for security in data communications applying Encryption, Decryption Algorithms and Authentication. Due to the presence of PKI, the IoT device does not endangered to the trial and error and mischievous issues .PKI protects the data integrity measured by the smart devices, sensing also allows accessibility to the protocol and application configuration. It also ensures element layer's privacy.

Wireless Sensor Network (WSN) nodes are used to encrypt data in the IoT system, transmit data to an encryption gateway, and then encrypt data before communicating to the top layer. In accordance with conventional methods, a key is cut from each sensor when the data collected is subjected to encryption. If compromised a key then can compromised the entire system.

PKI supplies a set of mathematically linked public keys and private keys. If a key helps with data encryption, the associated key helps with data decryption. The information assembled by sensors and smart devices and it is encryption and decryption performed by the public and private keys if it is the component layer in the IoT framework.

5.1 Security Challenges in IoT

There are number of challenges in an IoT environment, it includes preventing the IoT devices and end-to-end security, a major issue in an IoT security is the use of default password, which can lead to security breaches. Even if passwords are changed, they are often not strong enough to prevent penetration.

5.2 Tools and Legislation in IoT Security

IoT security framework provides tools and checklists to assist companies creating and employing IoT devices.GSM Association, the IoT security foundation, the industrial internet consortium have been released the framework.

In September 2015, the FBI announced a public service announcement, which alert regarding the potential vulnerabilities of IoT devices and offered consumer protection and safeguarding recommendations.

In August 2017, Congress released the IoT CyberSecurity improvement Act.

5.3 IoT Modular Security Management Framework Benefits

The modular framework created by the IoT security management system offers a variety of security mechanism and a security services. Therefore, high protection will be given to vendors, network providers and device manufacturers that can protect their data and are always protected. The specific framework for security service management will invoke various module security mechanisms by executing the comprehensive critical security feature in order to fulfill the optimum IoT network device security and management needs.

In view of the security needs of every client, the modular security management system IoT SMS performs efficacious safety approaches in the IoT network framework. The introduced IoT SMS will be accompanied by new security in addition to new technologies. In an IoT system environment, a mutual security platform is provided.

Information Security describes three goals of security: Preserving Confidentiality, Integrity and Availability.

Data Confidentiality

Data confidentiality is one of the basic principles in words of security. It protects the data from exposure to prohibited person. Only an authorised person could obtain access to sensitive data. For instance, Bank Details .Only an authorised person and bank Employees are able to access the bank details, but no one else should. A defeat to maintain confidentiality means that is known as breach. Once the secret has been disclosure, there is no way to undiscovered it.

Data Integrity

To ensure that the legitimacy of data is refers to integrity – that data is not altered and that the source of the data is authentic. For instance, Creating Website for selling the products .It consists of products with prices, So that customers can buy anything for whatever cost they choose. If the defeat of integrity happens, the websites are directed to be not authentic because the cost of a product has been altered and didn't authorize this alteration.

Availability

To ensure that the data is accessed only by the authorised users is refers to Availability. If the malicious attacker is not accomplished to compromise the first two components of information security then the attacker may try to perform attacks such as DoS that would slow down the server, creating the website inaccessible to authorised users owing to insufficient of availability.

5.4 IoT Security Threats in Industries

So many industries are facing IoT security Threats, from smart appliances to manufacturing plant. For instance, Life-threatening in health device, smart door locks.

Protocols Used in the Scenario of IoT SMS

Through an experimental scenario of the smart home to show the entanglement of security administrations in the IoT system. Every single functions and data essential for each layer are described. The wireless communication c IEEE 802.15.4 is preferred mainly to improve the security service for confidentiality, authentication and integrity so that all low potential and low rate smart gadgets in the component layer can react to them.

The 6LoPWAN protocol is preferred in the network layer which can execute the routing mechanism of lossy networks and low power. The routing techniques accomplish electronic signature uses RSA with SHA-256 and for one-way and hash functions uses AES with 128-bit keys also supports to provide integrity and privacy security services.

CoAP is favored at the application layer because it runs on user datagram wipe out transfer speed necessities and is helpful for low power and storage capacity gadgets. This protocol sends a "Request and Response" communication model to the middle of the endpoints and accepts to accomplish the above security services by using AES as the encryption algorithm.

Table 1. Evaluation of existing security conventions with smart home application

Layers	Protocols	Security Services			
Application Layer	IETF CoAP	Data Confidentiality	Authentication	Data Integrity	Nonrepudiation
Service Layer	IEEE Routing	Data Confidentiality	Authentication	Data Integrity	Key Management
Network Layer	IETF 6LoWPAN	Data Confidentiality	Authentication	Data Integrity	Availability
Element Layer	IEEE 802.15.4	Data Confidentiality	Authentication	Data Integrity	Access Control

Table 1 indicates that most of the security guard needed at all layers is similar excluding for specific methods to be used in operation practice.

The Smart Home Scenario Flow of Data

For instance, in the Smart Home Security Management, given the Essential Basic Security task, Security System function and Equivalent Security Service function, can work out the progression of information. In security management system, smart property can compute the flow of data in, in the perspective of the Essential Basic Security Module, Security System Module and Equivalent Security Service Module.

(i)   Various sensors are used to monitor environmental data like Vapor Concentration, Light Intensity and Temperature. By using one-way hash function data processing is done, for the purpose of form a digital signature message and invoking such message with the authentication service management in the element layer. Symmetric key cryptography for AES technique for data encryption in CCM mode with a particular authentication code and 32-bit keys of message integrity code implement by the protocol IEEE 802.15.4.

(ii)   Symmetric Encryption Function is used to encode the data that is created in the Element Layer and it is summoned the symmetric encryption in the network layer by the data integrity service management function. The Routing Techniques for Low Power and Loss Networks is executed by the 6LoWPAN convention, which applies the 128-bit Keys in AES that can provide secrecy and security assets to privacy. To stave off the DoS Attack during the Internet, Wi-Fi or Cellular Network Transmission, the administration layer assembled the encrypted information and the Functionality Service Management function is invoked the NIDS Feature Module. The application layer validation administration the executive's module summons the critical module of accreditation power to confirm the client's personality by looking at the client profile. The client at that point decodes the message utilizing the PKI module's private key.

(iii) The user on the smartphone prefers the API for the measurement of temperature, humidity and illumination in the house remotely under the effective safety protection.

VI. BIG DATA AND PRIVACY

To reduce Threats and Preserve sensitive data in big data is by properly managing the big data. Owing to big data compasses large and complex data sets, Majority of conventional privacy procedure cannot operate the scale and velocity needed. To handle the volume, velocity, variety and value of big data as it is proceeded in the middle of surroundings, prepared, explored and splitted by creating a framework. It is to protect big data and make sure that it can be used for analytics. In present-days, the big data has only become feasible in gathering, repository also evaluation . Datafication is the procedure of reanalysing of information into usable sets. For instance, Gathering of data from Social Media, Financial, Medicine and so on.

6.1 Overview of Security in Big Data

In future, it is expected that the volume of data will arise elevated. These days, security is an important concern in the field of technologies. As compared with the security issues of big data with other areas security, each and every minute attacks are happening in big data, these attacks can be on various parts of big data such as storage, data source and so on.

To safe-guard data as well as analytics methods from various types of attacks, malicious activities, there are incorporated measures and techniques refer as big data security. There are various types of attacks originated from both online and offline in big data.

6.2 Statistics of Big Data

For instance, per day Over 1 Million PB in size and operates higher than 24 PB of data on Google. Each month, 32 billion browses are achieved on Twitter. Over 1 thousand million distinctive people look in on YouTube and More than 6 billion hours of video views on YouTube. In the past two years, 90% of the data has been created in the world today.

The volume of computerised data induced will greater than 40 Zettabytes which is equal to 5,200 gigabytes for each and every human being on planet earth.

1 GB is equal to around 1 digital movie;
1 PB is equal to 1 Million GB or a QB;
1 EB is equal to 1 Million GB;
1 ZB is equal to 1 Trillion GB or 1 Million Petabytes.

6.3 Privacy Threats in Big Data and Safeguard Against Them

Using Embed devices can monitor the patient health and inform to their doctor if anything is going wrong. It can also leads to enormous privacy issues. In every single day, Persons are sharing 1000's of data, their daily activities such as where they move, what they purchase, what they consume, what they peruse and write down, who they talk with, what they view, how much they snooze, what games they play and more but they are endangered to disclosure in ways unbelievable a generation ago. In every single day Persons are sharing thousands of data, their daily activities such as where they move, what they purchase, what they consume, what they peruse and write down, who they talk with, how much they sleep, what games they play and more. It also leads to enormous privacy issues.

Majority of security risks are due to lack of relevant measures. Relevant Measures refers to defence provided by enhanced software applications, Threats identification mechanisms, Patches of security. These tools need to prevent the system itself from any risk. In Big data, this threat enlarges many double up, because there are number of devices, platforms for retrieving the data. Hence it is the challenging task for providing security, when access the large quantity of data along with the system and it also requires tactics, measures and strategy.

6.4 Recent Challenges in Big Data

- Not follow up the system updates, patches and audits.
- Lacking of security procedures during transfer of automated data.
- Distributed Systems have limited levels of protection.
- Persons at risk if attack happens on system that carry sensitive data of the persons.
- Observing and keep an eye on is hard task in big data.

Certainly, just only talk up about the challenges is not the solution. Mostly, there aren't adequate resources to keep the system renovated at all times. For instance, some of the system used in the hospital affected by ransom ware. During the attack they were using Windows XP, for a period now a system that has not been supported by windows. A hospital has pivot point on saving lives of the patient so they may not always have the resources to keep the systems updated. Hence, it's not easy to blame the concern to keep the system updated and it's a challenging task to solve the issues in the big data application environment.

The challenges of big data are not only limited to single platform, also includes attack the mesh computing. The most familiar challenges of big data includes are distributed data, data mining and Endpoint vulnerabilities. There are various challenges to secure the big data are real-time protection of data, counterfeit data generation and protect the data in system.

Distributed Data is distributed the processing throughout various systems for analysis quicker. For instance, Hadoop. Cyber crooks pressure the map reducer to display the erroneous list of key-value pairs. Reduce the workload on a system in distributed processing it may leads to security issues. Distributed system may bring down the load, but in the end additional systems mean huge security problems. The information contains sensitive information such as personal and financial information.so it becomes the biggest security issues. Companies need to give protection against various types of threats. The attackers do manipulate the data on terminal devices and transmit the altered data to the receiver end is referred as endpoint vulnerabilities. For instance, cybercriminals obtain the access of manufacturing system that uses sensors to identify the vulnerabilities. After acquiring access, criminals make the sensors to display the untrue results. To solve the problem can use fraud identification technologies, analyse the logs and validate the authenticity of both the endpoints.

Every organization prefers limited access to confidential data such as medical records, personal information and so on. Medical researchers are requires the data to use, but they don't have rights to access the data. So many organizations provide solution for this problem is granular access to the data. It is refers that a person can able to view only the data what they want. Instead of designing big data using granular access, it provides alternation solution for accessing the data. Big data keeps individual redundant in data repository. For instance, Medical field Researchers can only access the medical related information excluding the patient details.

6.5 Opportunities in Big Data

Cyber security and big data have made an appearance in the today's business. It gives rise to both for company opportunities and threats. In the forthcoming days, big data has introduced latest opportunities to analysis and protect cyber-attacks. It's the important challenging task for number of companies to safeguard the information. Nevertheless, to predict the cyber-attacks over 3 Gigabits require to be analysed in each and every second. During the processing and analysing of data, the size of data needs to be considered. An organization needs to analyse how recent technologies safeguard the sensitive data. If this goal is attained, then the opportunities are vast in big data.

6.6 Big Data Advantages

The big data offers advantages includes identification of fraudulent, renewal of SIEM systems, Through Business intelligence, can maximize the sales and retail campaigns as there is plenty of data available.

Importance of big Data Security

Today, each and every organization using Hadoop to process the huge data sets for seeing the possible and make use of big data. Employees in the organization have to take concern about the data security. After the data is processed by hadoop, it saves a various kinds of data from different sources, so it requires protecting the confidential data such as person's credit card details and user's credentials. The important attributes of big data is size of the data. So to secure the data from unauthorised users, by using various techniques such as user authentication, firewalls and educate the users.

6.7 Improvement in Big Data Security

In the opinion of cloud computing professionals, the majority of appropriate techniques to improve big data security are by providing security enhanced and timely patches. The first concern to make security for systems and place extra view on the security. Various retailers providing different solutions to safeguard the big data applications from various security threats. Antivirus industries are freely exchange the appropriate information regarding big data security risks and upgrades. Industry heads provide important benefits for the security of big data by develop what can survive the up to date malicious malware and ransom ware attacks. It's not only up to the IT to retain the concern safe and secure. The persons acquiring the system need to be educated to identify malicious content to prevent the system. For instance, If an organization providing an access to the data by spell out roles and giving permission to the user. The user of that system can be guided on the threat and how to keep away from upcoming disclosure to that threat by renovating the system.

There are some suggestion to reinforce the security are confidential information should be retain separately in the devices and servers, give significance to application security rather than device security.

6.8 Security Practices in Big Data

In every organisation there are collection of huge data and stored so securing big data is not a simple task, there are some finest practices to make the big data secure. Flows of big data are entry, storage and exit. Some of the security practices in big data include use data encryption algorithms to safeguard the data, use only updated Antivirus protection and fulfil proper logging mechanism.

6.9 Security Tools in Big Data

There are four criteria in big data security are privacy in data, audit and reporting, authentication and authorization. The most important strategy to secure the big data includes encryption, Intrusion detection and prevention, user access control and centralised key management.

Encryption algorithms techniques are to protect the inactive and travel data across the huge capacity of big data. Every organization requires encrypting user data as well as simulated data by machine. There are so many encryption tools are there to operate on distributed file system and multiple big data storage such as NoSQL, Hadoop and so on.

Due to lack of proper access control measures leads to disclosure the big data system. The fundamental network security tool is user access control. By using access control can protect the big data system from internal threats.

To detect and prevent the big data from various types of attacks, intrusion detection is used. An intrusion detection system protects the big data from various vulnerabilities, threats and attacks by scanning the traffic. It is placed directly in back of firewall to protect the system before damage happens.Key Management plays a key role to protect the big data. By using key management focal point can audit logs, policies and secure keys. To handle confidential data every companies is an essential to use key management.

VII. CONCLUSION

An enlarging organization uses analytics of big data tools to enhanced business techniques. It will give opportunities to the hackers to attack big data and also increases the security issues. Big data platforms have so many privacy concerns and government regulations, but the organization does not know the processing happens and storage of data. Fortunately, latest security techniques uses smart big data analytics tools to know adequate information. For instance, security intelligent tools can reach an end to reinvent security. Tool is very important for protecting the network from various types of cyber-attacks. There are numerous patents on security systems and providing techniques for IoT security. Nevertheless, the full explanation is unfinished and non-comprehensive structure to the knowledge of the author. Most of the time our aim is to provide a specific concern and portion of the solution for a one section of the

IoT network. The steps for implementing services connecting the security management functions and a variety of mechanism proposed by IoT SMS. The functional security architecture presupposes four basic level layers, in the matching sense like the various leveled layer model of the IoT framework, and involving an IoT SMIB fragement based on the four functional security layers. The execution of this IoT SMS encourages the combination of imaginative strategies and innovations. The proposed SMS IoT model will not have a specific platform and associated platform functionalities. Overall, many services and network providers are responsible for running the IoT system. The best execution of IoT SMS or its appropriate deviations for various network platforms should be considered as future work in this area.

REFERENCES

Cepheli, Ö. (2016). Hybrid intrusion detection system for ddos attacks. *Journal of Electrical and Computer Engineering*.

David, J., & Thomas, C. (2015). DDoS attack detection using fast entropy approach on flow-based network traffic. *Procedia Computer Science*, *50*, 30–36.

Du, M., Wang, K., Xia, Z., & Zhang, Y. (2020). Differential Privacy Preserving of Training Model in Wireless Big Data with Edge Computing. *IEEE Transactions on Big Data, Volume*, *6*(2), 283–295.

Faizal, Zaki, Shahrin, Robiah, Rahayu, & Nazrulazhar. (2009). *Threshold verification technique for network intrusion detection system.* arXiv preprint arXiv:0906.3843

Faizal, M. A., Zaki, M. M., Shahrin, S., Robiah, Y., & Rahayu, S. S. (2010). Statistical Approach for Validating Static Threshold in Fast Attack Detection. *Journal of Advanced Manufacturing Technology*, *4*(1), 53–72.

François, J., Aib, I., & Boutaba, R. (2012). FireCol: A collaborative protection network for the detection of flooding DDoS attacks. *IEEE/ACM Transactions on Networking*, *20*(6), 1828–1841. doi:10.1109/TNET.2012.2194508

Gupta, S., Kumar, P., & Abraham, A. (2013). A profile based network intrusion detection and prevention system for securing cloud environment. *International Journal of Distributed Sensor Networks*, *9*(3), 364575. doi:10.1155/2013/364575

Hwang, K., Cai, M., Chen, Y., & Qin, M. (2007). Hybrid intrusion detection with weighted signature generation over anomalous internet episodes. *IEEE Transactions on Dependable and Secure Computing*, *4*(1), 41–55.

Jiang, Shi, & Zhou. (2019). A Privacy Security Risk Analysis Method for Medical Big Data in Urban Computing. *IEEE Access, 7*, 143841-143854.

Jin, H., Xiang, G., Zou, D., Wu, S., Zhao, F., Li, M., & Zheng, W. (2013). A VMM-based intrusion prevention system in cloud computing environment. *The Journal of Supercomputing*, *66*(3), 1133–1151.

Lee, J.-H., Park, M.-W., Eom, J.-H., & Chung, T.-M. (2011). Multi-level intrusion detection system and log management in cloud computing. In *13th International Conference on Advanced Communication Technology (ICACT2011)*, (pp. 552-555). IEEE.

Rajendran, P. K. (2015). Hybrid intrusion detection algorithm for private cloud. *Indian Journal of Science and Technology, 8*(35), 1–10.

Singh & Panda. (2015). Defending Against DDOS Flooding Attacks-A Data Streaming Approach. *International Journal of Computer & IT*, 38-44.

Tang, C., Tang, A., Lee, E., & Tao, L. (2015). Mitigating HTTP Flooding Attacks with Meta-data Analysis. In *2015 IEEE 17th International Conference on High Performance Computing and Communications, 2015 IEEE 7th International Symposium on Cyberspace Safety and Security, and 2015 IEEE 12th International Conference on Embedded Software and Systems*, (pp. 1406-1411). IEEE. 10.1109/HPCC-CSS-ICESS.2015.203

Wang, S., Bonomi, L., Dai, W., Chen, F., Cheung, C., Bloss, C. S., Cheng, S., & Jiang, X. (2020). Big Data Privacy in Biomedical Research. *IEEE Transactions on Big Data, Volume, 6*(2), 296–308.

Xiao, P., Qu, W., Qi, H., & Li, Z. (2015). Detecting DDoS attacks against data center with correlation analysis. *Computer Communications, 67*, 66–74.

Chapter 9
Big Data Analytics and Its Applications in IoT

Shaila S. G.
Dayananda Sagar University, India

Bhuvana D. S.
Dayananda Sagar University, India

Monish L.
Dayananda Sagar University, India

ABSTRACT

Big data and the internet of things (IoT) are two major ruling domains in today's world. It is observed that there are 2.5 quintillion bytes of data created each day. Big data defines a very huge amount of data in terms of both structured and unstructured formats. Business intelligence and other application domains that have high information density use big data analytics to make predictions and better decisions to improve the business. Big data analytics is used to analyze a high range of data at a time. In general, big data and IoT were built on different technologies; however, over a period of time, both of them are interlinked to build a better world. Companies are not able to achieve maximum benefit, just because the data produced by the applications are not utilized and analyzed effectively as there is a shortage of big data analysts. For real-time IoT applications, synchronization among hardware, programming, and interfacing is needed to the greater extent. The chapter discusses about IoT and big data, relation between them, importance of big data analytics in IoT applications.

OVERVIEW OF IOT:

Internet of Things (IoT) deals with global network of physical objects or things interconnected through the internet. These are embedded with electronics, software, sensors, and network connectivity. The major advantage here is the objects can be sensed and controlled remotely across the network. IoT is helping us in building the physical world based smart environment. In IoT applications, things or ob-

DOI: 10.4018/978-1-7998-3111-2.ch009

jects refers to a wide variety of devices. IoT concepts have made many contributions to society right from an automated lighting system until automated driving cars. The IoT is a new revolution that has low costs and high technology implementations. According to expert's analysis by 2020, there will be at least 50 billion devices/objects connected via the internet. IoT is just not concerned with connecting things, it also helps in information exchange which leads to knowledge development. IoT deals with a series of steps such as filtering, processing, categorizing, condensing and contextualizing the data into information. Further, this information is organized and structured to infer the knowledge. Thus knowledge is defined as information obtained from organizing and structuring and put into action to achieve the specific business objective.

IoT helps in handling the resources efficiently, support in minimizing the human effort, time, offers improved security, helps in automation using Artificial Intelligence. IoT devices connecting the real world use certain set of standards and protocols like Zigbee, Bluetooth, MQTT (Message Queue Telemetry Transport), CoAP (Constrained Application Protocol), NFC (Near Field Communication), AMQP (Advanced Message Queueing Protocol) to access the internet. The data generated by the IoT devices is huge in terms of Velocity, Volume and Variety and this huge data set is termed as Big Data.

OVERVIEW OF BIG DATA:

In general, the Big Data is defined using 3Vs such as Velocity, Volume and Variety. Velocity is the rate at which the data grows and how fast the data is gathered for analysis. Volume refers to the enormous data being generated, whereas Variety refers to the different types of data being generated like structured, semi- structured and unstructured data. There is a fourth V to describe the big data, it is referred as veracity, which includes availability and accountability. In general, data generated by sensors in IoT applications will be considered as raw data. This raw data need to be fine-tuned before it is used by the decision makers. In general, during data collection, it is noticed that data missing, data redundant, data in the wrong format, etc. Hence, preprocessing is needed to get the relevant data in required format to avoid erroneous and misleading outputs that reduce the efficiency. According to the B2B report of data quality index test, it was shown that every data repository has got 40% bad data in which 15% are duplicate, 8% are missing, 11% are invalid and 6% comes from malicious or unauthorized users. These data weaken the organization's marketing and financial automation, increase the resource consumption and cost and leads to lower customer satisfaction and invalid reports. Thus, there is a great need of data preprocessing. Apache Hadoop, Apache Spark, etc are used for this purpose. Hence, we use techniques such as data mining, analytical tools and machine learning to extract the useful information from the big data.

RELATION BETWEEN BIG DATA AND IOT

The real value of an IoT application is determined by creating smarter products, delivering new business outcomes, and also delivering the intelligent insights. As lots and lots of devices are interconnected in an IoT network massive amount of data inflow is encountered. Researchers have predicted that by 2020 1.7MB of data will be produced each second by a single person. Researchers have found that connected cars alone have the capability to send 25 gigabytes of data to the cloud every hour. In today's world, it is not possible to imagine a world without data and processing the data manually or using a traditional database system by Gani et al (2017). The challenge here is to visualize the heterogeneous data, dark data, unstructured data, images etc. Also what kind of data is difficult to process and how to know it in advance is the real challenge. Deriving intelligence from big data technology enables the IoT application to infer knowledge from raw data. Big Data analytics is commonly used with IoT devices to improve the energy efficiency in sensors, verification and assessment and to monitor accidents and environmental risks. However, the extraction of the valuable information from massive amount of data generated by sensors, RFID tags and other devices is still remained as a challenge. Here, the quantity is high, but the quality of data will be low. Some of the frameworks which are used in analyzing data generated through IoT device including Hadoop, Oozie, Spark and Storm to drive meaningful insights, which will help in strategic decision making. The main goal here is to discover the unseen patterns and co-relations among the data using big data analytics. Thus, for every IoT application if big data is added a better decision can be done. The company revenue, productivity, efficiency can be increased with cost effective solution. The combination of both technologies IoT and Big data can solve many real-time problems in more efficient way by Elragal & Elgendy (2014).

The following section discusses the case studies of IoT in big data domain

CASE STUDY 1: SMART HOME TECHNOLOGY

The advancement of the Internet of Things (IoT) and Big Data analytics have led to the insurgent growth in computer industry. With the prelation of automation, we have experienced improvement in the day to day life of people. Abdullah and Mitul (2013) has proposed IoT based home automation using micro web server, controlling devices, smart phones and application software. The architecture is divided into 3 parts, home environment, remote environment and gateway. Remote environment allows the remote users to monitor the home environment via the mobile phone using the network connection. The purpose of gateway is to perform data translation between internet, router and the Arduino server. Hardware interface module consist of hardware like sensors and actuators to monitor the home environment. Advancement in the home automation is done by implementing voice recognition-based control. The voice messages are converted to text and is transmitted to Arduino UNO via the Bluetooth model. Due to the limited range of Bluetooth model, it is better to prefer the GSM model. Home appliances are connected to the microcontroller, serial communication between the appliances and the microcontroller is enabled via the GSM model. Sending and receiving commands takes a time of 2 seconds. Due to the wide coverage of the GSM network, the users can access the home appliances from anywhere in the world.

Big Data Analytics in Establishing Smart Home

In the home automation technology IOT devices are remotely controlled. In addition, big data analytics focus on improving the safety and comfort of the consumers. Due to the complexity of the application, bulky data cannot be used directly by the decision-making algorithms. Updating the analytical tools and security system has led to the financial gains of the system. The number of processes on the data depends on the complexity of the home environment. Analytics can be involved in several stages of home automation from local analytics to offsite analytics. Example- Smart metering is a part of smart home automation environment. Big data analytics focus on the improving the customer interaction and also allowing inter device communication in the home automated environment.

Future Advancement in the Smart Home:

Image processing-based home automation must be developed. Where in the cameras will capture the gestures of the users inside the environment. Machine learning techniques will be used to make decisions from the gestures captured and will take appropriate actions to monitor the home environment. Another advancement is Electromyography(EMG) based home automation, biomedical signals are used to control the home environment.

Best Practices to Implement Smart Home Into a Reality:

Consumers must be positively affected by improving their revenues. Analytics market must be able to understand the requirements of the consumers and provide additional services to positively affect them. Data protection and security is the major concern of the system. Smart home consists of several interconnected devices, they must be self-operable and self-configurable.

CASE STUDY 2: SMART METERING

Smart metering is machinery implemented on tank levels, smart grids and stock calculations. Lengthy processing time is required to process this massive data. Even a committed or dominant system will not be able to achieve desired goals. Considering this catalyst, smart metering was produced. Elemental stride of smart metering is to collect the electricity consumption data and analyzing the data, aids the decision makers. Depending on the pre-historic electrical data and the observed electrical data, energy bill is predicted. Processing and managing the high volumes of data and advanced analytical tools are the demands. Data is transformed to information and gain better insights for decision making. With the improvement in digital machinery like cell phone, computers, tablets have made advancement in the smart metering system. Smart grids are the applications of smart metering, this embedded system will facilitate 2-way communication, logical actuators and central processing units. Cost efficiency is maintained while merging the layers, domains and zones. SCADA is the best way to control and monitor the smart grids. The goal of SCADA is to provide data presentation, acquisition and efficient communication.

Challenges to Overcome:

Data management: The cost of storing, processing the data is the companies expense. Availability of the bulk data makes it famished. Unavailability of storage structures and efficient decision makers makes the data undernourished, the unused data creates considerable loss. Customers must be given information about the usage of the grid system. Communication network is used for inter node communication, this leads to breach in the data security. Managing the network with high network, fault tolerance, low latency is a challenge.

Advisable Data Storage Systems for Smart Grid System:

The unwieldy data requires efficient analytical tools to speed up the input/output processing. Data storage plays a crucial role, collected data must be available to the analytical tools. Big data analytics plays a critical role in this case. Distributed file system is preferred that allows multiple users to access, share and communicate. Local copy of the data will be available to the users. Example- HDFS, Google GFS.

Data Analytics in Smart Grid Systems:

The grids collect data from various sources and feeds it to the analytical tools. Big data analytics can be done in two ways: batch processing, where the data is processed in periods of time. Stream processing is also used in the real time processing.

CASE STUDY 3: SMART TRANSPORTATION

Smart transportation is a footstep for implementing smart city. Smart transportation system earlier used image processing techniques. This system suffered from several drawbacks, quality and the weather conditions were triggering the system. This would affect the algorithm efficiency also. Later advancement moved towards RFID, which would increase the efficiency of the system. Traffic congestion management can be done with the help of IOT devices. Smart transportation would be a solution to the existing traffic condition to some extent. Location data of the vehicles is up to certain terabytes, storing this data is a great challenge.

Challenges of big Data Techniques in Smart Transportation:

Data may contain junk values and missing values. Challenge here is to use an efficient analytical tool to preprocess the data to eliminate the junk and missing values. Authorized access must be enabled to ensure data protection. Hyper computing makes the decision making faster and satisfy the time constrained. Smart transportation requires parallel computing and grid technology.

CASE STUDY 4: SMART SUPPLY CHAINS

The supply chain management deals with the conversion of raw materials into finished products. Supply chain management is used to improves the customer value and gains. Some examples of supply chain managements are transportation, accounting, maintenance, etc. Data captured must be maintained securely. Combination of big data and IoT have developed the automated system to take better decision. IoT enabled environment will communicate with the data sources to improve the efficiency. System must be able to cope up with the changing needs. Better tracking and flexible data storage system is supported by using RFID and cloud-based GPS. The data is gathered from production phase and consumers phase. Managers will be able to monitor the different phases. Big data analytics are required to make better and deeper insight from the bulky data generated from different phases of smart supply chain management.

Importance of Big Data in Supply Chain Management:

Big data analytics is the core of Supply chain management. Surplus data generated from different sources need to be fine-tuned to gain useful insight. Three levels of data analytics are available, namely descriptive analysis, predictive analysis, and perspective analysis. Descriptive analysis takes into consideration the number of processes in the system. It also summarizes the report of output, it makes it easier for the human to interpret. Predictive analysis finds it better in risk management and analysis. Perspective analysis finds it better in fields like transportation, manufacturing and other domains etc. based on these three analytics the return on investment is planned.

Opportunities for Big Data Analytics in Supply Chain:

The main goal of introducing big data analytics in supply chain management is to find feasible solutions. Traditional methods were not up to the mark. Data is evolving to multiply the complexity of the decision makers. Efficient algorithms are needed to predict the optimum supply chain patterns.

Key Characteristics of the Supply Chain Management:

Products or entities in demand, a region where the product must be sold, a mechanism to transport the products and minimum number of entities to maintain good data quality are the key characteristics of supply chain management. Supply chain partners like producers, consumers, and items must be dependent to overcome the complexity of the system

Applications of big Data Analytics in Supply Chain:

a. Predictions must be improved according to the customer needs: It is a damage to the system if it doesn't satisfy the customer needs. Customers fulfillment must be taken care for what they pay. Big data analytics plays a vital role as it gives a 360-degree view to satisfy the customer needs.
b. Improved efficiency of the system: cost efficiency and time constraints are maintained. New business priorities can be set to improve the business efficiency.
c. Reducing the Error: Error assessment must be done; necessary steps are taken to minimize the error.
d. Improving the traceability: Better tracking capabilities are required to trace the phases in the supply chain management. Flow of goods in both the direction can be traced.

Challenges of Supply Chain Management are:

a. Many organizations suffer to handle their bulk data. Data collection, analyzing and storage have become a milestone. The amount of data collected also matters to maintain the efficient predictive results.
b. Unstructured data collected from various resources is a major issue.
c. When large data is processed it is time consuming.
d. Focusing on the return of investment.

CASE STUDY 5: SMART AGRICULTURE

In developing countries like India where agriculture is backbone for the economic growth, science and technology plays a vital role to abolish the traditional and manual practices. In agriculture system which includes manual or physical work, implementation of technology is required which reduces the cost and energy. Technology will yield better results and will improve the lifestyle. Wastage of water is a major problem to farmers. Efficient IOT system like smart water system, will check the water level in the soil and will efficiently use the water by Xu and Lie (2017). Depending on the values like humidity and temperature collected from soil sensors, algorithms predict the amount of water to be used. According to the values collected the motor will turn on/off to supply or cutoff water to the plants. Disease detection and classification is another advancement in the field of agriculture. Leaf, root, fruit and stem disease detection is done. Classifying the diseases like fungal, bacterial, parasitic, etc. storing and processing this large data set available from the farm lands is a tedious job. Sorting the data and finding the efficient algorithms to process the data. Cloud platform comes into picture to handle this large data sets. With the large demand for food globally, there is a need for automation in the system. Managing the climatic changes, environmental changes is important as they cause a biggest threat to the agriculture. To overcome this several Machine learning algorithms are combined with the IOT environmental parameter sensors. To monitor the environmental changes several weather parameters are collected every day and preprocessed and are fed to the machine learning algorithms to predict the future of these weather parameters. Big data analytics are used to handle this large weather data. Farmer can take prior steps to overcome this weather conditions. Using big data analytics, it becomes easy for farmers to navigate shifts in environmental conditions. Big data analytics is used to monitor the crop health condition. Predictive analysis will priory predict the disease based on the historic data and the observed data. So, farmers can take appropriate actions to overcome the disease.

Advantages of Using Data Analytics in Agriculture:

Data analytics is helping farmers, seed companies and machine industries to improve their returns. Data analysts can help farmers to take better decisions. This reduces the burden on the farmer. Advantages of using smart agriculture is listed below:

a. New seed traits can be generated by genome mechanism.
b. More precise farming techniques will be used to increase the gains and profit to the farmers.
c. Water management, disease detection techniques are used to improve the yields.

CASE STUDY 6: SMART TRAFFIC LIGHT SYSTEM

Traffic management system is a hectic task in urban areas. Increasing vehicles in urban areas leads to accidents, congestion etc. An automated system which is much précised than before is required. A system consists of nodes that are locally connected through a network, these node interact with each other to predict if any pedestrian or bike or any other vehicle is present on road. The nodes keep track of its surroundings and they communicate with the nearest traffic light. There is an account made of distance and time at which the vehicle may come to the expected point and traffic signals are managed.

Changing the timing cycles according to traffic congestion rate, latency through which information to the neighboring node and detecting approaching vehicles are done using IoT networked sensors. Extra care should be taken not to remove ambiguity which might lead to accidents or collision. Many of the use cases in smart traffic system work on M2M architecture and they have very less human intervention. They use many decision algorithms to detect the presence of vehicles and approaching vehicles. In these techniques mostly textual data is produced. For these kind of textual analysis Hadoop environment is best to be used. Apache Hadoop is a framework where it allows large processing of data using distributed processing. Components of traffic control system includes a central control system, smart traffic controller nodes, cameras and queue detectors are required for general case. If any add-on functionality we need we can make the network flexible and expand it.

Internal Working of Smart Traffic and Signals:

Since we are concentrating on traffic jams most of the time, empty road insertions are also should be taken care. Series of phases which helps in building a smart traffic and signal lighting system is described as follows:

a.   Sensors and traffic light will collect the traffic data and communicates with the traffic light manager.
b.   Synchronizing the work of different traffic lights in the junction that helps them in interoperability.
c.   Timing in the traffic lights must be maintained. Time is predicted by the decision makers in real time.
d.   Informing and updating the drivers to cope up with the new changes.
e.   Prioritizing the transportation of the ambulance and vehicles of VVIPs will be done in real time and efficient decisions must be taken.

   Challenges in Smart Traffic Light System:

a.   Some regions lack infrastructural facility like roads, zoning, etc.
b.   These high-level applications require high speed internet 24/7.
c.   There are large number of peripherals connected in the system. As the number of peripherals increase, the system is more prone to attack.

CASE STUDY 7: HUMAN BEHAVIOUR PREDICTION

This application has to be deployed from a different branch of specialization called human dynamics. Here the main aim is to describe human behaviour in real-time. Ahmad and Mazhar (2016) explained the behavior system based on the quantity of data provided by smartphones, social networks, and smart cities. The interconnections of domains like networking, IoT, big data a Smart Buddy application was provided which was able to provide ecosystem, that focuses on the analysis, the ecosystem provided by smart cities, wearable devices (e.g., body area network), and big data to determine human behaviours as well as human dynamics. Human dynamics analysis has to be done on lots and lots of statistical data. The basic goal here is to analyse human behaviour and predict the future by using algorithms and techniques. Smart Buddy is a high-level architecture that is used for large scale data processing services.

Smart Buddy consists of three domains: the object domain, IoT server domain, and application domain. It provides intelligence to understand the behaviour and even actions based on the information revived, such as the web data. Social network data, body, and network data, etc. Data obtained is integrated with data collection. We assume that the objects have a lot of metadata, and they also generate heterogeneous types of data. Hence the data pre-processing step is required to eliminate redundant data and unnecessary metadata. Communication media such as IP, ZigBee, WiFi, etc are used to communicate·

Required big Data Ecosystem:

Human dynamics is majorly coming from large number of statistical measurements of the system. There are billions of human dynamics in everyday life such as social activities, decisions, interests, shopping sports etc. We need to analyse large number of data before analysing the future action of an individual (human behaviour). The large-scale data produced here needs to be processed in an efficient manner, to analyse and find human behavioural pattern. To process data in an efficient way we use Hadoop ecosystem. This high-level system architecture for large-scale data processing has made appreciable contribution in analysing data, processing them and finding human behaviours. The major challenge we face in this system is it's very difficult to analyse human behaviour. Sometime crucial steps are to be taken which does not depend on previous steps taken during the same situation.

CASE STUDY 8: BUILDING NATIONAL GEOSPATIAL BIG DATA PLATFORM

A considerably large amount of information is produced from national geospatial data from different sources. Special categories of special data are making big data analysis for geospatial data more complicated. To make developers and analysts make their work easy. Korean government launched a 5-year national project involving business and research community. The goal is to develop a platform for efficiently storing, extracting, processing and analysing geospatial big data. Various sensors are deployed which produces large amount of data, the data that is produced is also not kept at a constant phase it is increasing exponentially. It is widely agreed that 80% of data in the world has a geospatial component and is growing at an annual rate of 20%. In the US, the Federal Geographic Data Committee (FGDC) develops national geospatial standards to promote coordinated development, use and sharing of big spatial data on a national basis. This system is continuously checked and reviewed for up-gradation. The geospatial data collected using sensors are gathered for analysis. The capacity of these datasets has exceeded the capacity of current computing system, which indicates that there is a greater need to develop applications that can process geospatial data efficiently. The data collected is heterogeneous, inconsistent, has variable quality thus suffering from uncertainty, and incompleteness. Modern techniques such as big data analytics and machine learning algorithms have supported it to conclude a strong decision support value

Challenges of Spatial big Data:

a.   Volumes in which specio-temporal data is increasing. It is also observed that transactional data base structure needs constant upgradation to handle such huge volumes of data.

b.   There is a constant challenge in developing predictive algorithms to satisfy the velocity of real time data.

c.   Complex structures of data such as vector data, imagery data, map data, geo-tagged textual data make the predictive model deteriorate the efficiency.

d.   Visualisation of data is very difficult.

CASE STUDY 9: HOME INTRUSION DETECTION SYSTEM

The purpose of this application is to detect intrusions in the given environment using sensors. Ahmad & Mazhar (2016) proposed an approach to detect home intrusions in ultra-high-speeds is very necessary. This is to improve the security of a locality. In the increasing crime rate and theft rate, these kinds of applications are necessary. Regions are divided into sections, under each section PIR motion sensor is placed and each door has got a door sensor. The sensors on doors can detect the motion when doors are opened and closed. Each door sensor is reading is noted at regular intervals, and notified to the house owner. The method of HIVE is usually used for this goal to be achieved. HIVE has been developed by integrating a set of intrusion sensors and actuators and IoT technology. It utilizes sensors to detect the intruder actions and it will activate the alarm. House owners will be able to monitor the system via messages and notifications. Even in certain use cases HIVE is also beneficial in forwarding the messages to police officers via an android application. In any wireless home automation system, control unit like LINUS PCs are used, these PCs are interfaced with ZigBee and for controlling process, a remotely placed smartphone or tablets are used. ZigBee is best used when smartphones are using Wi-Fi to communicate with the control unit through UDP and TCP protocols, on top of that users can specify conditions of sensors to trigger actuators by themselves. The data in the intrusion system obtained is heterogeneous. Big data advent in the system can help in handling the load. The big data solutions have provided data security and data maintenance advantages to this system.

Big Data Solution:

We can use Hadoop ecosystem to overcome the challenges in intrusion detection system. The layered IDS architecture: Capture, Filter, Load Balance and Hadoop layers and finally decision-making layer helps in achieving the real time expected outputs. Expected accuracy was achieved by having true positive and true negative values. The efficiency was calculated based on comparing results with less time efficient traditional techniques and also considering the processing time using Hadoop eco-system. An accuracy level of 99% was achieved.

CASE STUDY 10: AIR POLLUTION MONITORING SYSTEM

By using empirical analysis the precision of conventional air automatic monitoring system is increased. This application highlights the concepts of air monitoring in real-time by using IoT networks and data analysis techniques applied to make them better. Chen Xiaojun et al (2015) have propsed in their work that the cost of the hardware is reducing day by day due to advancement in IoT techniques. There is a rise in pollution in nature and thus it as to be monitored. Thus, we require to develop a monitoring system to reduce pollution of air. A huge data is collected which cannot be handled by using laboratory experiments. The amount of polluted air can be known by using air quality valuation. Air pollution monitoring system was used in society with deployment of n number of sensors so that accuracy is improved within the system. The decision making is improved by using data analysis solutions.

Some of the Challenges Faced in air Pollution Monitoring Were:

a.   There is inter-relationship between different pollutants (like Nitrogen Dioxide and Ozone gases) in the environment, making analysis and fetching pattern is very difficult.
b.   Few of the weather factors such as intensity of sunlight, wind speeds, air pressure made an impact on various pollutants.
c.   An element of hysteresis, where pollutants build and their disseminations was very difficult to predict.
d.   Human activities such as peak hour traffic also affected the values.

Looking at the above challenges there was a necessary of building a data analysis model which can take all these factors into consideration and build its predictive model.

CASE STUDY 11: HEATH CARE MONITORIAL SYSTEM

Heath care in urban area is very easy, but the soldiers in dangerous places like borders need safety. So concentrating on how big data and IoT has made an advent in saving life's, one of the case study of heath care monitoring of soldiers. Having a look at how dangerous a soldier. According to Iyer and Patil(2015) proposed a technique and introduced where, the entire system can be mounted on the soldier's body to continuously monitor and keep a check on their health and monitor the location is in a GPS. All these data are sent to the control room where data monitoring and data maintenance are done. This equipment what soldiers are wearing are the tiny equipment which are space-efficient having sensors and transmission modules. In case of any danger, we can take immediate action on the person, if the person injured is found to be in unsecured places we can send defense vehicles and save him. In any defense system will be 100000000+ active troops and 900000+ reserved troops. So the health care for those people who are sacrificing their lives on as is equally important. Heartbeat sensors, temperature sensors, if panic found then buzzer sensors, grove gas sensors can be made use.

Another case study is to exhibit how big data and IoT domains are working together to bring better results is chronic disorders. Increase in the world population is leading to an increase in various chronic disorders (chronic disorders are those which last for more than 6 months). These chronic disorders take a long time to evolve from the initial stage to the final death stage. These, when detected at an early stage, can be blocked at that stage itself. So early assessment of these diseases is necessary. Technology development regarding the biomedical field can save a life. With technology help, we should be able to handle long term and short term medical records of patients. Highly sensitive data inputs are taken from various sensors. ECG sensors have been more famous these days since they have better conductivity, better electrical property, and reduced cost. ECG sensor readings are transmitted through communication protocols like ZigBee/ WiFi. Then the data can be sent either for storing or processing. The doctor remotely location can view patients' data and give suitable suggestions. This helps in dealing with an emergency. The first stage is data acquisition followed by data transmission, data pre-processing, data processing, decision making, if any emergency contact a doctor. Looking at the death stages due to chronic heart diseases is at its peak, considering this. The motivation for the project was established and developed. The project had remote patient monitoring in emergencies, where it is impossible to take an ambulance and rush towards hospital many deaths happen on the way to hospitals due to traffic or unavoidable circumstances. So, it has to be quick and efficient analysis that can be remotely monitored. That too having an android application can be more beneficial and easy to use. Big data and IoT together put in hand can produce powerful and efficient applications. IoT helping in monitoring and controlling signals while big data is helping in making better decisions. These techniques together solved the chronic heart disease issue with 97.01% accuracy.

CASE STUDY 12: WEATHER MONITORING SYSTEMS

The large amount of weather's data is collected day to day basis and reports are drawn. The challenging task of weather monitoring system is to keep all the records on report. IBMs Deep thunder is one of the application which can analyses the weather. It can predict the weather reports in a particular locations such as airport with decent accuracy. This type of monitoring is used in agriculture because the farming involves a various risk. These were able to alert farmers regarding floods, drought and rainfall. In traditional system weather conditions were monitored using embedded systems. They used to have a micro-processor and micro-controller for having a look at data collected from various sensors. Through serial communication, a LabView processing is done. Further weather controlling process done manually. An automated weather monitoring where the actions to be taken based on data analysed had to be automated. Predicting temperature and humidity in a particular region is both cost effective and energy effective. Home thermostats are used. Apache Spark is used to process high velocity inputs. High energy consumption is reduced by combining habits and weather forecasts. Temperature fluctuations are handled by Twing span. This approach attempted the distributed graph platform analytics of high velocity data. But when there is a change in occupant numbers more or less fluctuations are seen and more energy is consumed.

CASE STUDY 13: SMART PAYMENT

Smart payment application is not only used in online transactions but it is used from wholesales shops to retiles. There are few applications which is adopted slowly in daily life because of literacy rate. Security and accuracy plays a crucial role compared to time and spacing issuing or else the transactions will be corrupted in banks. If any applications are developed the users will have a lesser knowledge on interior working of the application and organizations have to develop trust over their products with their customers. As the complexity is increasing the more and more security needs to be added. The utility of data science and big data analytics in financial domain has become very common these days, more than how efficiently data is analysed, how, much security we are giving to data matters allot in smart finance. As user trust the software and keep all sensitive data in it, there should be enough security to address this. Some of the use cases in smart payment are digital banking, block chain and AI role in banking, chatbots, Robotics in banking and financing etc has been described in paper written by Khan et al(2017).

CONCLUSION:

Looking at the above-given examples we can make it clear that big data and IoT have interdependency on each other. When they come together to achieve a particular goal we are can able to provide a much more efficient and reliable application. Sensors that collect 1,000 readings per second, at 1KB of data per reading, grow to 1MB of data per second, per sensor. At 10,000 sensors, we are streaming a GB/second of data. Looking at these statistics we can easily understand what level of the advent of Big Data is making on IoT (and vise-Versa). The combination of IoT and Big Data is the perfect union for innovation to flourish, driving businesses. Big data is about large chunks of data assimilating in organizations. IoT is about interconnected devices. IoT and Big Data as a single unit have provided numerous benefits to both organizations and end-users.

REFERENCES

Abdullah, A. M. K., & Mitul, A. F. (2013). Design and Implementation of Touchscreen and Remote Control Based Home Automation System. *Proceedings of 2013 2nd International Conference on Advances in Electrical Engineering (ICAEE 2013)*, 347-352.

Ahmad & Mazhar Rathore. (2016). *Real time intrusion detection system for Ultra-high-speed big data environments*. Springer Science+Business Media.

Ahmad, A., & Mazhar Rathore, M. (2016). Defining Human Behaviors using Big Data Analytics In Social Internet of Things. *IEEE 30th International Conference on Advanced Information Networking and Applications*, 1102-1107. 10.1109/AINA.2016.104

Chen, X., Liu, X., & Peng, X. (2015). IoT- Based Air Pollution Monitoring and Forecasting System. *International Conference on Computer and Computational Sciences (ICCCS)*, 257-260.

Elragal & Elgendy. (2014). Big Data Analytics: A Literature Review Paper. *ICDM 2014: Advances in Data Mining. Applications and Theoretical Aspects*, 214-227.

Gani, Nasaruddin, & Marjani. (2017). Big IoT Data Analytics: Architecture, Opportunities, and Open Research Challenges. *IEEE Access, 5*, 5247-5260.

Iyer, B., & Patil, N. (2015). Health Monitoring and Tracking System For Soldiers Using Internet of Things (IoT). *International Conference on Computing, Communication and Automation (ICCCA2017)*.

Khan, M., Wu, X., Xu, X., & Dou, W. (2017). Big Data Challenges and Opportunities in the Hype of Industry 4.0. *IEEE ICC 2017 SAC Symposium Big Data Networking Track*. 10.1109/ICC.2017.7996801

Xu, X., Lie, Y., Zhang, Z., & Zhu, S. (2017). Study and Implementation on the Monitor of Liquid Level of Liquid Scintillator. *Second International Conference on Mechanical, Control and Computer Engineering*, 131-134.

Chapter 10
Big Data Analytics in Cloud Platform

Sathishkumar S.

ⓘD https://orcid.org/0000-0003-3825-4148

Adhiyamaan College of Engineering, Hosur, India

Devi Priya R.

Kongu Engineering College, Erode, India

Karthika K.

Adhiyamaan College of Engineering, Hosur, India

ABSTRACT

Big data computing in clouds is a new paradigm for next-generation analytics development. It enables large-scale data organizations to share and explore large quantities of ever-increasing data types using cloud computing technology as a back-end. Knowledge exploration and decision-making from this rapidly increasing volume of data encourage data organization, access, and timely processing, an evolving trend known as big data computing. This modern paradigm incorporates large-scale computing, new data-intensive techniques, and mathematical models to create data analytics for intrinsic information extraction. Cloud computing emerged as a service-oriented computing model to deliver infrastructure, platform, and applications as services from the providers to the consumers meeting the QoS parameters by enabling the archival and processing of large volumes of rapidly growing data faster economy models.

1. INTRODUCTION

Nowadays, most researchers focus on implementing machine learning, statistical, and other significant data optimization approaches for knowledge extraction and data mining. Data mining is one of the increasing computing paradigms in every data-generating industry day by day. Data mining is used to mine user-required data patterns using various algorithms, methods, and techniques from a large volume of data. Furthermore, the data format, quantity, forms, and veracity are different, and the mining pro-

DOI: 10.4018/978-1-7998-3111-2.ch010

cess's efficiency is reduced. The data pattern is essential to study these parameters input data, discover information, and extract it. The Integration of Knowledge Discovery and Knowledge Extraction is the primary process in big data analytics. Knowledge provides the learned input data with physical and logical information. The information derived from the broad dataset helps to mine the query pattern accurately.

In various real-time applications, Big data analytics use to analyze the data to enhance mining accuracy. Big data management becomes a crucial job as the significant data behavior is continuously changing in terms of volume and variety, degrading the data mining process efficiency. Information extraction is used as a pre-processing function to generate knowledge from structured and unstructured data to deliver the data in a machine-comprehensible, readable, and interpretable format, thereby enhancing the data mining process.

Currently, people are sharing and communicating over the internet without face-to-face interactions. They post and share their knowledge, opinion, and experience on social media sites massively. Twitter, Facebook, WhatsApp, LinkedIn, and Instagram are the popular social networks through which users post their opinions, experiences, marketing, education, and business information. Different types of data have been shared on social websites over the past 15 years, including travel and tourism. People who travel worldwide share their experiences through comments, pictures, location, merits, demerits, etc. Using the site, distance, path, famousness, and others allows other people to travel better. It increases the travelers' happiness and makes them happy, which raises a country's money flow. Therefore, big data analytics is applied to the big data concept to provide useful new traveler information.

The work's main objectives are to design and implement a novel framework by integrating knowledge discovery, data analytics, knowledge extraction, and data mining for one of the world-connecting applications as Travel big data analytics. It is one of the socio-economic fields affecting the economic status of the Government. Therefore, by providing useful guidance to tourists abroad, all countries focus on improving the tourism industry. This study analyzes the data from the social network and offers better online advice over the internet. They use portable devices such as mobile devices, tabs, laptops, and other gadgets to reach and support travelers.

This section presents various earlier research methods and algorithms used for knowledge discovery, knowledge extraction, and big data analytics with pros and cons. It uses to obtain the research problem and arrive at an idea to design and implement the research methodology. For example,

1.1 BACKGROUND DETAILS

AmirGandomi and MurtazaHaider (2015) present detailed information about big data analytics, and it collects from various developers and industry practitioners. The main objective was to discuss big data analytics over structured and unstructured data. The discussion shows that the heterogeneity of data, extensive and noise, needs to be handled before data processing.

Artola et al. (2015) designed and experimented with a structured search engine to extract user-required patterns from big tourism data. Based on the user query input, the real-time data is collected and integrated for big data analytics.

Nguyen et al. (2016) Proposed using knowledge-based locations to acquire knowledge by searching and browsing extensive collections of general and cultural heritage databases using user interaction through SNS. Researchers have shown that given particular geolocation, current social media data combined with technology, Researchers can find interesting information for visitors, providing dynamic information in favor of any travel agent.

Zhao et al. (2016) stated that big data analytics is essential for maintaining big data since it is too dynamic and increasing daily. Significant data sources are also increasing, and it delivers the data with more variations in terms of type, size, behaviour, and attributes. So, managing big data in recent days is not as easy as using a simple software tool. Different industries need different learning methods, analyses, and predicting big data according to their business data.

Huang et al. (2017) Proposed smart tourism as an individual tourism support system in the context of information services and all-encompassing technology. This paper compares the characteristics of both traditional tourist information services and smart tourism services.

Karampatsou Maria (2018) presented his research work for examining the performance of the significant data phenomenon in the travel industry. The author proposed a method by combining quantitative and qualitative analysis.

Qi Ouyang et al. (2018) proposed a trip-reconstruction plan using a density-based spatial clustering method (DBSCM). It uses to extract the travel patterns from smart card users. The DBSC method analyses the location, crowd in the area, links among sites, and travel mode from the data. Anyway, it is insufficient data for traveling throughout the country or world, and it needs improvements.

Visuwasamand Raj (2018) The main objective of this paper is to design and implement a Novel Approach for travelers from different countries. It is a system that provides a set of graphical data from big data analytics on tourism. It also refers to various social media websites to the target location. They need to go to extract the relevant information according to the user's current location.

Deng and Cai (2019) proposed that the spatial and temporal distribution characteristics of tourism flows would play an essential role in the tourism economy's efficient growth. To minimize the negative effect of the unequal spatial and temporal distribution of tourism flows on the tourism industry and tourism destination stakeholders. Taking as an example the number of visitors at the Guiyang Long mountain scenic spot, the DA-HKRVM algorithm is used in this paper to estimate the number of visitors.

Siyang Qin et al. (2019) Proposed a Big data method for monitoring tourist flow location information to analyze the travel behaviour in rigid areas. The data used in the experiment is the mobile phone call-detail record (CDR). By collecting data from the CDR, the proposed method will analyze the tourist locations, sources, movements, resident information, etc. The information obtained from the data analysis is used to develop a "smart tourism" model in real-time operations. Still, the information is not sufficient for new data when traveling to a new location.

Zhang et al. (2019) Proposed data nodes classified using the Bayesian Decision Tree (BDT). An analysis model of tourism visitors is then constructed. Finally, the smart estimation model of the tourist traveler is designed by the implemented differential operator according to the Autoregressive Integrated Moving Average model.

Proposed the use of location-aware for acquiring knowledge from searching and browsing extensive collections of general and cultural heritage information repositories using user's interaction through SNS. Researchers showed that given particular geolocation, current social media data combined with technology, researchers can find interesting information for tourists, providing dynamic information in favor of travel agents.

The above survey shows that various methods developed to provide the travel and tourism industry with a better solution. But the information needs to be fine-grained to support travelers. Big-data analytics variety is the gap in the methods of data delivery. This process could provide a fine-grained dataset for the extraction of knowledge. Thus, this work explains the difference between different Big Data deployments such as mobile, internet, cloud, and distributed cloud. In terms of application, this study pompously offers a Mobile Application that uses information exploration, information extraction, and data mining.

The application is also fully supportive of both national and international data. Hybrid CNN-RNN with Novel GNSS Application and Spatio-Temporal Dependence Approach suggested by and wide provides new thoughts for forecasting the daily stream. This strategy has good prospects in developing tourism management, creating a stable tourism industry with sustainable growth.

2. PROBLEM STATEMENT

A semi-automatic web application to guide data has been proposed in the existing system for the statically and offline-based data aggregation to create a travel sequence and research works, but customer satisfaction is not reasonable. This recommendation for data processing series does not cost- and time-efficient. Significant data usage is developed hurriedly in different everyday uses such as medical, health care, education, finance, and travel. People information's to all of the other destinations on the world map from some source locations. Since the sector influences the financial status, this study aimed to develop and implement a new mobile application that can be used as an "electronic guide" by any national and international data without manual assistance. It decreases the traveler's cost and increases a country's financial profits. Describes the effect that creative approaches like this can have on managers of natural resources and authorities, especially when identifying, evaluating, and eventually reducing crowding.

3. Generally Big Data: Intro

Technology advances have enabled businesses to receive the benefits of simplified processes and cost-effective projects. But the availability of data from any possible source-social media, sensors, business applications, and also more-is one thing that has become a massive success for companies across the globe.

These vast information stores that bomb company's day in and day out are collectively referred to as big data. Many entrepreneurs have heard about this, and many seek to develop their ability to move their business forward, but only a majority have succeeded in doing so.

For the very same moment, the enterprise space is now cloud computing to improve its operations and development software.

Big data with cloud computing is a versatile mixture that can transform a company. Researchers will analyze the primary properties of big data in this article and create a case for keeping the cloud resources.

Gardner considers big data as high-volume, high-speed or high-speed data assets providing low-cost, creative processing of information that allows extensive knowledge, decision-making, and process automation.

With **Five Vs,** gardner's description, the idea of big data, and what it includes can be well understood.

Volume - The data amount that private corporations, public companies, and other companies obtain regularly is large. For extensive data, this provides a defining attribute size.

Velocity- It will very quickly accumulate data. But what is essential is the speed at which this information can be analyzed in order so that it becomes relevant data.

Variety- The types of knowledge collected are very distinct. Structured data can be used and exchanged globally in databases and non-structured data such as tweets, emails, images, videos, etc.

Veracity- There will be more noise in big data due to its scale and versatility. Variety contributes to data stability and how poor-quality data derived from one of the most useful to the business through the big data tools and research strategies.

Value- The correct reality is gathered and examined to provide a detailed understanding.

Figure 1. Big data's 5 V's

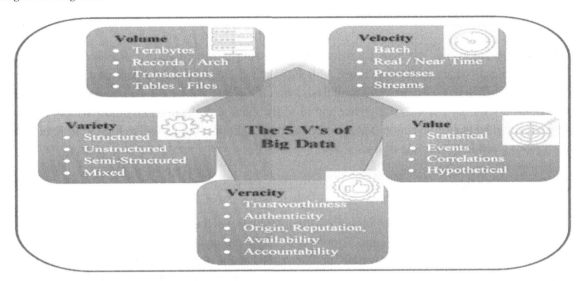

3.1 Techniques Including Big Data

Many methods and techniques have developed and adapted to integrate, maintain, interpret, and interpret extensive data. These practices and statistics are drawn from various mathematics and economics fields, computer science, and technology. It means that a business would like to adopt a versatile, diversified approach to the value generated from big data. In a world of factor is known, some strategies and techniques are required.

Several layers as well as data have been updated successfully. Others have recently developed others to capture value from big data, generated by some academics and others entities businesses, particular those with online business models and predicted for large-scale data processing.

This research focuses on updating the potential benefit of data collection by being huge. Tasks requiring unique customization of a market setting, strategy, and skills are not standardized instruction manuals on capturing value. However, Researchers decided to look at some essential techniques and technologies to use big data to analyze how the levers would work to use the big data describe. The big data report has already been written; novel strategy; these are not comprehensive lists.

3.2 Techniques Including Big Data Analyzing

Cash technologies run a discipline that personal trainers can set up to examine, Statistics and computer programming, for example (especially machine learning).

Researchers have such a list of specific methodological approaches that apply in the range

. Improvement of new and established techniques, especially in response to needs. Researchers / Developers / Authors and all note that many of these are not procedures are specific. It takes the use of big data.

Any of these are (e.g., Classification, Data Mining) can be used well for small databases. However, it is possible to provide all the techniques researchers list here for extensive data. It is possible to use large and diverse datasets to analyze original and brilliant outcomes rather than small, less varied matters.

3.2.1 Association Rule Learning

Collection of Relationships methods for discovering exciting information, i.e. "Rules of association" between variables in wide ranging databases. Although their strategies that have several ways of creating and checking feasible laws. Market basket analysis, which can be calculated by a company, is an application. Items are mostly purchased together and used for marketing details. (The most widely opinion expressed would be that of invention that many supermarket shoppers only tend to buying milk in order to buy bread) Used in the mining of data.

3.2.2 Classification

Based on such a training data set containing existing data points Classified, a collection of techniques for recognizing types in new data points is owned. An application Activity (e.g., purchase decisions, consumption rate) in one position is section-specific A reasonable expectation or objective potential effect of customer service forecasting. Such Approaches are methods almost always defined as supervised learning since a training package exists; In addition, they vary with respect to supervised learning for Cluster Analysis.

3.2.3 Cluster Analysis

A Statistical Approach for grouping objects into various categories Groups into small groups of similar items whose properties are pre-specific to Unknown. Statistical Approach for Classifying Objects into Different Categories Groups into small groups of identical objects whose properties are specified in advance to Unknown. An instance of studying clusters splits Self-similar members attract customers. In this approach there has been no use of training data. This methodology is inconsistent with the classification of a form of supervised learning.

3.2.4 Data Fusion and Data Integration

A selection of methods to incorporate and analyze information to generate the most efficient and insightful from multiple sources through considering a single information source, is more precise than they were generated. For processing Signal processing methods is used for such types of information fusion. Internet of Things Integrated sensor networks is indeed an example of an application to gain an advanced perspective on such a dynamic and distributed performance evaluation system along with an oil refinery. By default, social networking data is analyzed. Information analysis are being connected to value propositions in actual environments to be analyzed.

Figure 2. Big data analyzing techniques

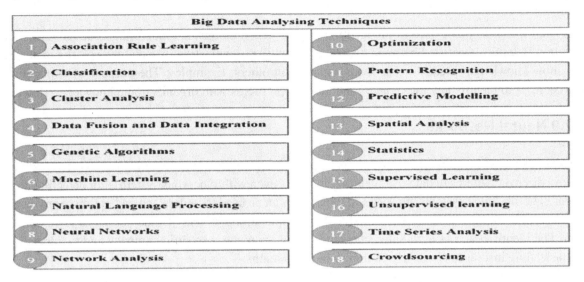

3.2.5 Genetic Algorithms

A tool used for the optimization of "optimal survival" or natural evolution. Solutions may be coded as "chromosomes" in this process, which can be shared. There are individual chromosomes chosen to live in the "world" model. It determines each person's fitness or success in the population. These algorithms are often defined as a type of "evolutionary algorithm" and are the most appropriate solution to non-linear issues. Examples of applications include updating the work schedule to create and improve the investment portfolio's performance.

3.2.6 Machine Learning

Computer science subdivision (historically an area known as "artificial intelligence") interacts with algorithms for development and design which require computers to process activities based on empirical data. Learning to identify autonomy Making right decisions based on intricate patterns and data is the critical focus of machine learning science - An demonstration of machine learning in the NLP.

3.2.7 Natural Language Processing (NLP)

Technology of computing (a discipline traditionally known as 'artificial intelligence') and linguistics are a series of sub-specialized techniques that use computational methods to interpret (natural) human language. So many NLP approaches are kinds of machine learning. Uses a social media integration of the NLP Emotion analysis to Assess whether prospective buyers are reacting to something like a trade proposal.

3.2.8 Network Analysis

The suite which methods used in the identification of interrelationships Individual nodes in a map or network. Relations identified between people in a group or organization in social networking analysis, e.g., how knowledge spreads or has more impact than others. Examples: The purpose of application marketing is to identify key idea leaders and identify problems with organizational knowledge flow.

3.2.9 Neural Networks

Algorithmic models, design, even functions inspire Biological Systems, neurological structures which always discover patterns in data (i.e., neurons and links even within nervous system). For detecting non-linear patterns, linear systems are very suitable. They can be used to understand and optimize practices. Supervised learning contains some neural network applications; others include non-supervised education. The identification of high-value clients at risk of dropping a specific company and the detection of misleading insurance claims are examples of applications.

3.2.10 The Optimization

A collection of predictive strategies which used optimize the efficiency of complex overhaul systems and Procedures in accordance with one or more quantifiable metrics (such as speed, cost and reliability). Examples of applications include enhancing operational activities such as Planning, Reconfiguring for forwarding and floor plan and overall strategy such as model range policy, related profit planning and Research & development portfolio strategy. - An instance of a technique for optimization for genetic algorithms.

3.2.11 Pattern Recognition

Desired output (or attribute) for an input value (or explanation) algorithm for the given stage. The group of assignable machine learning techniques. An example of techniques through classification.

3.2.12 Predictive Modelling

A massive techniques Used to construct a statistical method or allowed to select to help predict the probability of something like a result. Excellent demonstration of a proposal using predictive models for customer relationship management The customer would either "regret" (i.e., alter service provider) either have each ability to do so that one customer will sell to another product. Examples of regression A lot of predictive modeling techniques.

3.2.13 Spatial Analysis

The collection of methodologies which are used in some statistics to evaluate topographic, Digitized architectural or geographical features in something like a collected data. Geographic Information Systems (GIS) Capturing information collected provides a thorough understanding of spatial analysis data, containing location data, e.g. identifies or axes for coordinate latitude / longitude. Linking remotely sensed data to geographic regression are examples of applications (Example: how does a customer want to purchase an item? Linked with the place?) or simulations (Example: how production will be distributed. Does the chain network operate for locations in different locations?)

3.2.14 Statistics

Data collection, arrangement and interpretation sciences, along with creation of studies & tests. To make conclusions as to what relationships might be among parameters, statistical methods are also used. The occurrence ('null hypothesis') and the relationship between variables might be the product of some fundamental positive association (i.e., 'statistically significant'). Inferential statistics Type I is often used for mitigating (False Positive) and errors in Type II (False Negative). For example, an A / B test to decide the most useful type of marketing material to improve profit.

Figure 3. Supervised and unsupervised learning

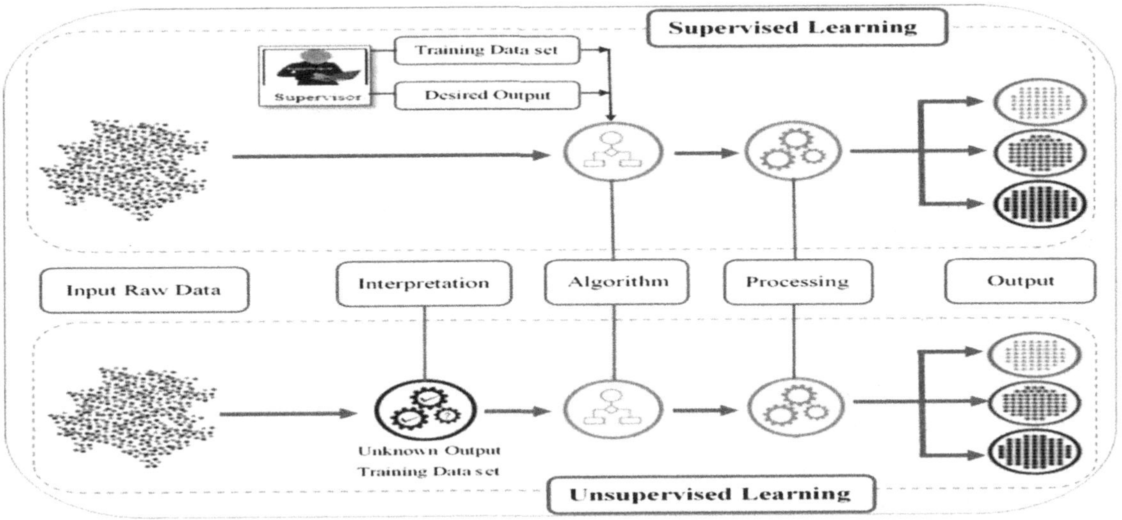

3.2.15 Supervised Learning

A collection of techniques for machine learning that predict the task or relationship of a training and testing data sets. The concept and support of machine learning algorithms provide examples. It's different from studying under supervision.

3.2.16 Unsupervised learning

A collection of techniques for machine learning that expose the invisible structure within unnamed results. An example of unsupervised learning (as opposed to training data) is cluster analysis.

3.2.17 Time Series Analysis

Collecting mathematical and communication systems techniques to analyses set of data rows and mark scores simultaneously removes relevant attributes through records. Instances of time series forecasting Include the monthly expense of the stock market indices or even the percentage of customers identified with such a specific condition each day.

Demand forecasting uses a model Predicting future time - series data values based on known previous data with the same or other sequence. There are a few of these approaches in use. For example, structural modelling distorts the Trend sequence, seasonal and rest components that are useful for identifying data cycle patterns. Predicting sales statistics for software examples, or showing the number of customers dealing with normal level.

3.2.18 Crowdsourcing

A suite with methods used to identify interrelationships Individual nodes in a map or network.

3.3 A Perfect Pair: Big Data and Cloud Computing

As Researchers can see, the possibilities even before researchers combine large amounts of data with cloud computing, researchers are infinite. Researchers are going to have massive data bundles lying around if researchers have big data. It would be impractical or unworkable to use our machines for research.

Cloud computing allows us to use advanced technology and pay only for the time and power researchers use! Big Data also power the creation of cloud software. Without big data, cloud-based services would be small since there would be no real need for them. Bear in mind that cloud-based applications also obtain big data.

In general, cloud computing services are primarily attributable with large datasets. In like, the one and only way researchers gather large amounts of data is that researchers had services that are interested in the possibility of processing and understanding it, sometimes within seconds. They're both perfect matches since one cannot be without the other.

3.4 Advantages of big Data With Cloud Computing

Big Data with Cloud platform has become a natural match because it offers a flexible and sensitive solution for big data and business analytics. Large data projects generally start with data storage and simple analysis modules, which may not be sufficient to extract rapidly process, and analyze large data volumes.

It requires infrastructure upgrades, which can be implemented by adding additional servers to your pre-built infrastructure. However, the data growth rate cannot change even this new infrastructure very quickly enough. Placing big data in the cloud offers many benefits, including scaling up.

These are other benefits of moving extensive data to the cloud.

Figure 4. Benefit of cloud computing

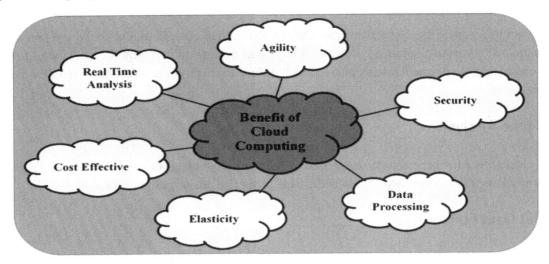

Agility:

It takes days or weeks to install and run a server to work on campus. Cloud vendors immediately provide an infrastructure with the necessary resources. Moreover, all analytical requirements are under one roof.

Security

Most major cloud vendors offer sophisticated security solutions to protect data, detect and protect their customers' data using threat intelligence. The cloud is considered the most secure because it does not carry the risk of physical attack, and it generally offers many local storage solutions.

Data Processing

Large databases enable large-scale processing of un-configured data, taking a few minutes to sort and sort. A cloud site integrates unstructured data from social media, such as data structured in the consumer profile database. Transferring data to the cloud is easy and fast, with most cloud providers providing support for migrating to the shadow of large databases.

Elasticity

Unlike the on premise solution, the cloud operating system expands automatically, adding storage as data increases. Also, the site reduces or increases the warehouse according to the data requirements. All significant vendors offer backup systems such as AWS Backup, and many third-party solutions provide managed cloud backup services.

Cost-effective

Companies that want to use sophisticated technology to run their operations, but are budget conscious, can find cloud computing solutions. Running a large data center can be costly for an IT budget. With cloud computing, the payment pricing plan allows the company to pay only for the savings and computer service it uses.

Real-time Analysis

It also makes sense for the analysis to be carried out immediately as it is obtained in real-time. The cloud platform allows users to use current data and enable predictive analytics in real-time.

3.5 Big Data Functions

Big Data offers researchers fresh perspectives that which keep open new business models & opportunities. The beginning consists of three key acts that involve the following:

a). Integrate

Big Data compiles information from a variety of sources and applications. Traditional approaches to data integration, including ETL (Extraction, Transformation, then Load), typically do not work. New techniques and technologies are expected for the analysis of massive terabyte or petabyte data sets.

b). Manage

Large data backup. The fix for storage would be in the clouds, onto campus, or even both. On every format researcher want, researcher can save having a great data and carry the suitable processing requirements and features vector to the historical data as required. Based on where certain data resides, many individuals determine their cloud service. This same clouds are now becoming famous although it meets clients' current needs for storage as well as allows you to rotate assets as needed.

c). Analyze

As researchers explore and act on our results, researchers invest in big data. Get new clarification by visually comparing our various data sets. Explore the data to make new findings. Report the results with others. Establish machine learning and artificial intelligence data models. Keep our data up to speed.

3.6 Stands to Benefit From Big Data and Data Analyzation:

- Big data makes it possible to get a full response because you have more knowledge.
- More complete answers suggest a heavy focus on data-i.e. a very different approach to coping with stress.

3.7 Is big Data Going?

Discover how the cloud concept requires the flexibility to modify:

- Building benefits by investing in data and research.
- Use of the web to accelerate closed-loop data science, data exploration, and intelligence systems.
- Providing the lowest possible cost by embracing ' platform-as-a-service'.

Cloud-based management-a-service enables companies to master big data, integrating data, operations, and analytics. It provides cloud computing companies a low-cost way to access and manage vast amounts of information from different sources. The unique properties of the cloud provide agility and scaling and real-time processing.

Advantage of cloud is it balances the sector for smaller companies. Before the cloud was widely accepted, only large companies had the infrastructure and resources to analyze and use big data. Cloud computing sites allow small companies to store and manage their data without much investment in infrastructure.

4 CLOUD COMPUTING BUILDING BLOCKS

The structure squares of distributed computing worldview establish three administration models and four arrangement models. These can be delineated as underneath:

4.1 Cloud Computing Service Delivery Models

These are isolated into three fundamental classes, which are:

- Software as a Service (SaaS)
- Platform as a Service (PaaS)
- Infrastructure as a Service (IaaS)

4.1.1 Software as a Service (SaaS)

In this, the provider gives the client administration to get to the product to create an application where programming given on month to month lease premise. The more the client uses it, the more will be claimed. Figure 5 representing to Software as a Service (SAAS) model is demonstrated as follows:

Low Initial Setup Cost:

Programming as administration applications is offered on a membership-based model. Subsequently, there is no compelling reason to buy a permit key. It reduces the underlying arrangement costs for the product, equipment, and even the required labor.

Figure 5. The layered architecture of cloud services

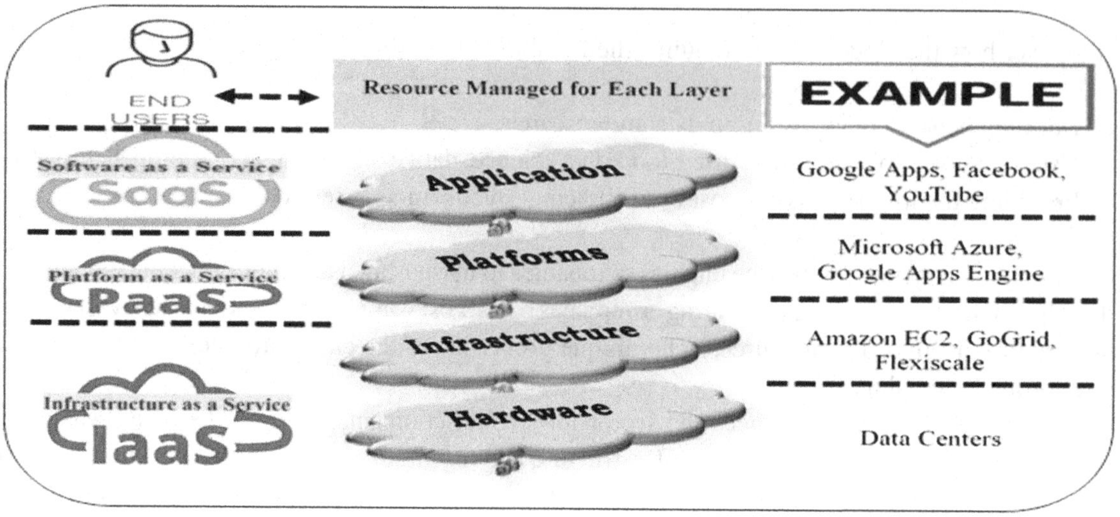

No Requirement for Updates by the Customer:

Generally, a business wanted IT overhauls on a promising premise to stay aware of the most recent up and coming advancements. It was an unavoidable use until the beginning of the administrations researchers are examining. In the SaaS model, the SaaS gives deals with every one of the updates. The client does not have to get into problems with downloading and introducing any patches.

4.1.2 Platform as a Service (PaaS)

Platform as a Service provides runtime environment. Platform as a Service provides platform for programmers to create, test, run, and deploy applications. This platform provides pay-as-per use basis service to the customer. In Platform as a Service, back end scalability is managed by the cloud service provider and thus end user need not to worry about managing the infrastructure.

4.1.3 Infrastructure as a Service (IaaS)

IaaS offers a custom framework. It enables clients to get to servers, stockpiling, data transmission, and other essential registering assets. For instance, Amazon EC2 enables people and organizations to lease pre-designed machines through foundation highlights, such as service providers.

Although dependent on a scope of major highlights, IaaS savvy offers exceptional highlights that client projects will encounter when its accessibility can extraordinarily influence the relationship's cloud.

The most pertinent highlights are:

- As the geographic conveyance focuses
- User Interfaces and APIs utilize an alternate framework.

- Unique segments and administrations that endorse explicit applications (e.g., load balancing firewalls) Virtualization stage and working system selection.
- An assortment of charging strategies and time (e.g., paid ahead of time versus post-paid, hourly versus monthly) selected working frameworks to run their very own applications. Figure 5 representing the Platform as a Service (PAAS) model is demonstrated as follows:

Compared with the various conventional service hosting environments like dedicated server farms, it has found that the architecture of cloud computing is more customizable. The layers are loosely coupled with the layers present above and below. Figure 5 shows all the above cloud providers (SaaS, PaaS, and IaaS) in different layers with the resources are managed. Each layer has its importance in the cloud environment.

4.2 CLOUD COMPUTING DEVELOPMENT MODELS

Cloud services can be deployed in many ways, depending on the organizational structure and the provisioning location. The models deployed are:

4.2.1 Public Cloud

As evident from the name, a public cloud is available to the end-users – public or large organizations for use while a third party organization owns the infrastructure.

Figure 6. Public cloud architecture

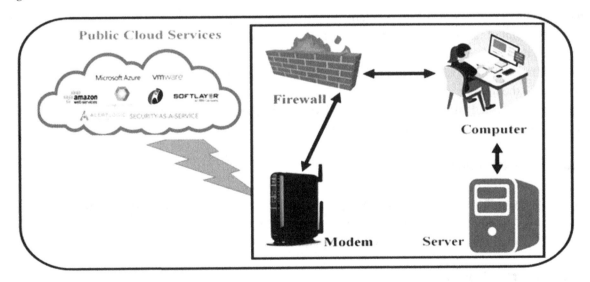

It is hosted on the internet and can be used by anyone who has access to the internet and pays for the services. The main advantages of public cloud include the availability of resources anytime anywhere, continuous uptime, on-demand access, scalability, 24/7 support, easy setup, and inexpensiveness. However, two significant drawbacks compel serious users to avoid public clouds - data privacy and security. Figure 6 represents a public cloud architecture.

Figure 7. Hybrid cloud architecture

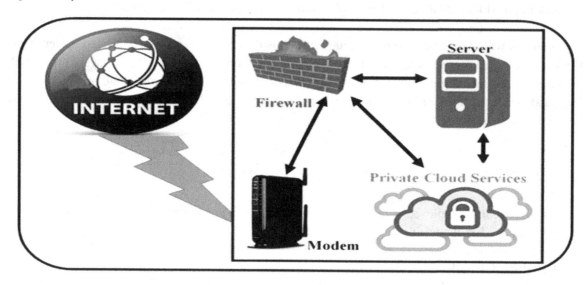

Public cloud computing offers various advantages like greater scalability. Cost-effective is one feature which makes it pocket friendly and saves money.

Services like SaaS, PaaS, IaaS are readily available on the Public Cloud platform, making them easily accessible from anywhere through any internet-enabled devices. Location plays no hurdle as it is location independent, and the services are available to the client. Above all, it ensures reliability, which means no single point of failure will interrupt your service reliability. Apart from the various advantages, there are some disadvantages of Public Cloud Computing.

The first and foremost drawback is no control over privacy or security. Secondly, a setback cannot be applied for the use of sensitive applications. A significant issue is that it lacks complete flexibility, and the reason is as the Platform depends on the platform provider. The data management protocols need to revised as at present protocols are not stringent.

4.2.2 Private Cloud

As compared to the public cloud, the private cloud is more secure. That is the only significant advantage a private cloud environment has over public clouds. However, this add-on comes with a higher cost, making it an unpopular choice amongst small-scale users working on a tight budget.

4.2.3 Hybrid Cloud:

As evident from the name, a hybrid cloud is a mix of private and public clouds.

In the said composition, at least once private and public clouds must exist. Such a formation leads to reduced capital expenses, improvement in resource allocation, and overall agility. The drawbacks of such a system include a wider surface area for attackers to work. Privacy and integrity are significant causes of concern in such an environment. Figure 7 represents a community cloud architecture.

4.2.4 Community Model

A people group cloud is a shared framework among a few associations from a particular group with primary processing concerns (i.e., banks or heads of exchanging firms). It is identified with administrative compliances, such as review prerequisites, or it might be identified with execution necessities, such as facilitating applications requiring a brisk reaction time. The arranging standard for the network cloud may fluctuate, yet the individuals from the network by and large share comparative security, protection, execution, and consistent prerequisites.

A people group cloud model is a community-oriented exertion where the foundation is shared and conjointly gotten to by a few associations from a particular gathering that offer explicit registering concerns, for example, security, consistency, or purview contemplations. The people group cloud can be either on-premises or off-premises and can be administered by the Participants. A people group cloud model helps counterbalance fundamental difficulties crosswise over colleges, government organizations, and undertakings, for example, cost weights, innovation intricacy, and spending prerequisites, security concerns, and an absence of area explicit Providers.

Network mists are a crossover type of private mists fabricated and worked explicitly for a focused on gathering. These people group have comparative cloud necessities, and their definitive objective is to cooperate to accomplish their business goals. Network mists are frequently intended for organizations and associations taking a shot at common tasks, applications, or research, which requires a focal distributed computing office for structure, overseeing and executing such extends, paying little heed to the arrangement leased.

4.3 CLOUD COMPUTING VENDORS

A portion of the organizations examining the cloud worldview field is enormous names in the IT or PC industry. Picking the correct open cloud supplier is vital because the end client doesn't know about physical assets and gadgets. The rundown for huge cloud players in the market holds the names of Google Cloud Platform, IBM Cloud and Microsoft Azure, and so forth.

Be that as it may, picking among them thoroughly relies upon the undertaking's needs. In the electronic application, Google is viewed as the pioneer among the other merchants, so there is no uncertainty that the organization offers magnificent cloud client backing and adequately managing the difficulties being confronted. The utilization of distributed computing is on a fundamental level interminable. Microsoft, IBM, and Google contribute an immense measure of cash fluctuating from a large number of dollars into the exploration. Here are a few instances of distributed computing administrations given by regular cloud specialist organizations:

- **Cloud Computing Services by Google:** Google recognized for the reconciliation of numerous applications and subsequently gave various cloud administrations to buyers. Such abnormal state joining makes Google a top CSP. It enables the purchasers to get their assignments achieved every day. It also encourages shoppers to set aside significant cash measurements as creating and keeping up programming for such administrations and applications can be tedious and over the top expensive. Here are probably the most mainstream cloud administrations offered by Google:

(a) **Gmail**: Gmail is an email service that provides users with about 15GB of storage. Apart from the storage, Gmail effectively fights off spam and allows mobile access too. It also has a chat applet called Hangouts that can store conversations in the form of an email. Google also offers business packages for services like Gmail under Gsuite, allowing many small and big enterprises to optimize their business communications via email.

(b) **Google Docs**: Google Docs is developing as the most significant contender for work area applications like MS Excel, MS Word, and MS PowerPoint. Google has propelled their partner under Google Docs so clients can make spreadsheets, introductions, and specialty word archives, all on the web, and store them in the cloud administrations. In this manner, such reports are constantly accessible on the web and can be gotten to from any place and whenever. It is profoundly helpful for colleagues that are working remotely. They can co-work and work on a similar archive immediately because of the separation. Such records are very secure also because the documents are scrambled utilizing a significantly propelled encryption innovation. They can be gotten to just by the approved clients.

(c) **Google Analytics:** Google Analytics is an administration that screens a Website, traffic. By making a one-time arrangement, all guests that please a site can be followed. It is an exceptionally nitty gritty following enabling you to see traffic socioeconomics and sources. Likewise, there is the best-in-class online business following for web-based business organizations where objectives can be arranged and broke down to monitor deals and the site's execution.

(d) **Google Ad words and Google Ad-sense:** Both of the previously mentioned Google Ad words and Ad-sense are promoting devices. Organizations can utilize promotion words to run a few advertisements like hunt crusades, show battles, and dynamic remarketing efforts. Promotion sense is an administration used by bloggers and sites to show advertisements on their site. Google shares a piece of their promoting income with such Ad-sense distributors. Both are exceptionally mainstream items by the organization.

(e) **Picasa:** It had been one of the most well-known items by the organization; however, Google has now ceased this administration.

It is anything but a total rundown of cloud administrations offered by Google as the organization continues propelling more items from time to time. The previously mentioned are anyway the most broadly utilized and effective ones by the organization.

- **Cloud Computing Services by Microsoft:** The cloud stage offered by Microsoft is likewise called Windows Azure. It contains a lot of cloud benefits that are provided generally to application engineers and clients. Every one of the administrations kept running in the Microsoft Data focuses that have arrangements worldwide. These administrations include:
  (a) **Windows Azure:** Windows sky blue is a windows situation that can store information and run cloud applications.
  (b) **Windows Azure App Fabric:** This application gives foundation to the applications that keep running in the cloud or inside n association.

(c) **Windows Azure Marketplace:** Windows Azure Marketplace is an online market managing application programming and information.

(d) **SQL Azure:** SQL Azure comprises of social database benefits that convey a particular variant of Microsoft SQL administration for its operation.

- **Amazon Web Services:** Amazon Web Services offers an answer to the business of all sizes. Thanks to AWS, organizations' arrangement is financially savvy, adaptable, and versatile IT framework and administrations. The administrations can be downsized at whatever point is required. AWS enables organizations to choose a stage that would be reasonable for their particular needs and organizations, remaining consistent with the distributed computing model, pay for just what they use. What's more, AWS likewise guarantees top-level security by utilizing propelled information protection and physical security systems to ensure client information. The extensive AWS stage offers the accompanying administrations:

  (a) Amazon Simple Storage Services (Amazon S3): Amazon S3 offers secure, stable, and versatile stockpiling for the web. It very well may be utilized to store and recover information of any size on the web.

  (b) Amazon Route S3: Amazon Route S3 is a versatile and dependable DNS administration.

  (c) Amazon Simple DB: the Amazon Simple DB offers center database functions.

  (d) Amazon Virtual Private Cloud (VPC): Amazon Virtual Private Cloud (VPC) interfaces the current IT framework of an organization to the Amazon Web Services cloud through a Virtual Private Network (VPN).

  (e) Amazon Elastic Compute Cloud (EC2): Amazon EC2 offers configurable distributed computing resources.

  (f) Amazon Cloud Front: Content delivery offered by the web service Amazon Cloud Front can move client information with short and insignificant postponement by utilizing its worldwide system.

  (g) Amazon Relational database services (RDS): The web server, Amazon RDS, oversees a social database in the cloud.

  (h) Amazon Simple Queue Service (SQS): Amazon SQS is a reliable, scaled, and facilitated line to store messages.

Distributed computing Services by Salesforce.com: Salesforce.com has effectively made a noteworthy imprint in distributed computing advancement. It is presumably best known for its business the executive's SaaS, in reality, driving in this area. The profoundly wanted and request the administration stage running over the internet. Deals power gives its own Force.com.

Application Programming Interface (API) and designer toolbox valuing are on for every sign in the premise. Designers can have numerous advantages like utilizing App Exchange applications transferred by others, sharing their applications in the registry, or distributing private applications open by approved organizations or customers.

5. CONCLUSION

This section also gives the nitty-gritty perspective on Cloud Computing features, and unmistakable structures obstruct the cloud, and Technical parts of cloud conditions are described. Further, the examination challenges about the Cloud and IoT are reviewed. Essential Optimization strategies are additionally clarified.

Finally, in our modern world, either Big Data & cloud services play a very important role. Combining the two sets it difficult for those with better ideas, but limited resources make it more difficult for a business plan. They often allow small firms to use the data they collect, but they do not have a way to assess their daily schedule.

Modern elements of the conventional model 'software as a service' of cloud computing, along with Artificial Intelligence, allow companies to gain insights based on the extensive data they collect. In a well-planned scheme, companies all these would be used for small payments, leaving rivals who fail to use these emerging developments in the dust.

Cloud-based management-a-service enables companies to master big data, integrating data, operations, and analytics. Advantages of the cloud is that it balances the sector for smaller companies. Small companies can purchase a subscription to their preferred vendor and store and analyze data instantly.

REFERENCES

Amir Gandomi, A. (2015). Beyond the hype: Big data concepts, methods, and analytics. *International Journal of Information Management, 35*(2), 137–144. doi:10.1016/j.ijinfomgt.2014.10.007

Artola, C., Pinto, F., & Pedraza, P. D. (2015). Can internet searches forecast tourism inflows? *International Journal of Manpower, 36*(1), 103–116. doi:10.1108/IJM-12-2014-0259

Li, Y. (2016). The concept of smart tourism in the context of tourism information services. *Tourism Management*, 1–8. doi:10.1016/j.tourman.2016.03.014

Li, Deng, & Cai. (2019). Statistical analysis of tourist flow in tourist spots based on big data platform and DA-HKRVM algorithms. In *Personal and Ubiquitous Computing*. Springer.

Maria, K. (2018). *Big Data in Tourism*. Semantic Scholar.

Nguyen, T. T., Camacho, D., & Jung, J. E. (2016). Identifying and ranking cultural heritage resources on geotagged social media for smart cultural tourism services. *Personal and Ubiquitous Computing*. Advance online publication. doi:10.100700779-016-0992-y

Qi, . (2018). Passenger travel regularity analysis based on a large scale smart card data. *Journal of Advanced Transportation, 2018*, 1–11.

Qin, S., Man, J., Wang, X., Li, C., Dong, H., & Ge, X. (2019). Applying big data analytics to monitor tourist flow for the scenic area operation management. *Discrete Dynamics in Nature and Society*, 1-11. doi:10.1155/2019/8239047

Visuwasam & Raj. (2018). NMA: integrating big data into a novel mobile application using knowledge extraction for big data analytics. In *Cluster Computing*. Springer Nature.

Zhang & Li. (2019). Intelligent Travelling Visitor Estimation Model with Big Data Mining. *Enterprise Information Systems*, 1–14. doi:10.1080/17517575.2019.1590860

Zhao, L., Chen, L., Ranjan, R., Choo, K. R., & He, J. (2016). Geographical information system parallelization for spatial big data processing: a review. *Cluster Computing*, *19*(1), 139–152.

Chapter 11

Convergence of AI, ML, and DL for Enabling Smart Intelligence:
Artificial Intelligence, Machine Learning, Deep Learning, Internet of Things

Revathi Rajendran

SRM Valliammai Engineering College, India

Arthi Kalidasan

SRM Valliammai Engineering College, India

Chidhambara Rajan B.

SRM Valliammai Engineering College, India

ABSTRACT

The evolution of digital era and improvements in technology have enabled the growth of a number of devices and web applications leading to the unprecedented generation of huge data on a day-to-day basis from many applications such as industrial automation, social networking cites, healthcare units, smart grids, etc. Artificial intelligence acts as a viable solution for the efficient collection and analyses of the heterogeneous data in large volumes with reduced human effort at low time. Machine learning and deep learning subspaces of artificial intelligence are used for the achievement of smart intelligence in machines to make them intelligent based on learning from experience automatically. Machine learning and deep learning have become two of the most trending, groundbreaking technologies that enable autonomous operations and provide decision making support for data processing systems. The chapter investigates the importance of machine learning and deep learning algorithms in instilling intelligence and providing an overview of machine learning, deep learning platforms.

DOI: 10.4018/978-1-7998-3111-2.ch011

INTRODUCTION

Rapid human growth has created an imperative need of smart technology for effective enhancement of every aspect of urban living in daily life. A lot of data is being generated by smart devices and sensors connected to the internet requiring skills for the analyses and management. Traditional techniques on large datasets can take a considerable amount of time creating an urge to develop an artificial intelligent system to perceive data from the environment and turn into action without any human intervention with optimal precision. In 1950s, Alan Turing, British polymath explored the mathematical possibility of artificial intelligence. Humans use all available information and reason for solving problems and making decisions. A question arises about why machines cannot do the same thing as humans? In seminal paper Computing Machinery and Intelligence, Turing discussed how to build intelligent machines and how to test their intelligence which leads to the evolution of AI and further Machine learning and deep learning as shown in Figure 1.

Artificial intelligence (AI), a mimic of human intelligence, attempts at simulation of human intelligence and produces a new intelligent machine that would have the ability to process information with human consciousness, behavior, and thinking integrated with appropriate algorithms. AI has been applied in many fields, such as Image Analysis, Natural Language Processing (NLP), Robotics, interactive computer games, multiuser virtual environments and Expert Systems. AI can be classified as Narrow AI and Strong AI. Narrow AI is an AI system that is intended for a particular task and a Strong AI with generalized human cognitive abilities, is capable of providing solution to any problem without human intervention even for an unfamiliar task.

Figure 1. Evolution of Smart Intelligence

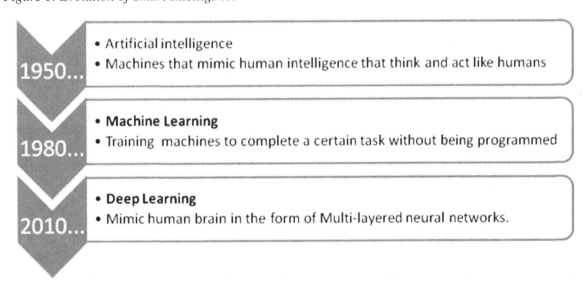

Artificial intelligence brings welcome changes in automation of the tasks in all the processes and systems, by making them faster. AI technology enables machines to have cognitive functions for making devices smart and autonomous by learning and adaptation based on the data acquired. Instilling intelligence to make smart machines greatly reduces human efforts and time complexity.ML platforms

Figure 2. Classification of Machine Learning

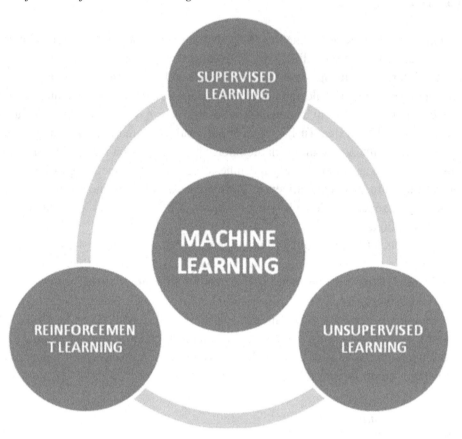

are used for the achievement of smart intelligence in machines to learn and modify the parameters to improve their performance. ML is excellent for predictive analytics whereas AI prescribes suggestions or decision for reality.

Machine learning (ML) is the core of artificial intelligence and the fundamental approach toward designing intelligent computers. Deep learning (DL) is a subclass of machine learning. In machine learning, the features to be analyzed have to be included by the user, whereas, in deep learning, the system learns to take features of its own based on the application to be performed. Deep learning is time consuming more than machine learning since it has to be accomplished using large data.

MACHINE LEARNING

Machine learning is the core of artificial intelligence and the fundamental approach toward designing intelligent computers. The main goal is to reflect human learning activities by machines to discover and acquire knowledge automatically. Machine learning involves a number of disciplines such as the probability theory, statistics, approximation theory and algorithm complexity theory. ML process follows the concepts of training and inference i.e. iterative learning and extraction of input from output. The applications of machine learning span the entire field of artificial intelligence. DL is a machine-learning method based on characterization of data learning and brings machine learning closer to artificial intelligence.

Learning algorithms vary based on the nature of the feedback available to a learning system (Lina Zhou, Shimei Pan, Jianwu Wang Athanasios and V.Vasilakos, 2017), ML can be classified into three main types (as shown in Figure 2) as supervised learning, unsupervised learning, and reinforcement learning. Learning models solve different machine learning problems from classification to clustering and regression analysis. Global intelligence can be achieved by deploying learning models using centralized infrastructure whereas local intelligence can be achieved by a decentralized infrastructure in modern AI systems (Giang Nguyen et al, 2019).

In supervised learning, the learning system is presented with examples of input-output pairs, and the goal is to learn a function that maps inputs to outputs. In unsupervised learning, the system is not provided feedback or output, and the goal is to uncover patterns in the input. As in unsupervised learning, a reinforcement learning system is not presented with input-output pairs. In other words system models use training samples with no prior knowledge of data. Reinforcement learning operates with limited knowledge of the environment and takes superior decisions from the feedback based on its previous experiences. It is different from above two models and follows trial and error behavior strategy.OpenSpiel is a collection of environments and algorithms for reinforcement learning and search/planning in games. It includes tools for the analysis of learning methods and other common evaluation metrics.

Figure 3. Types of Machine Learning

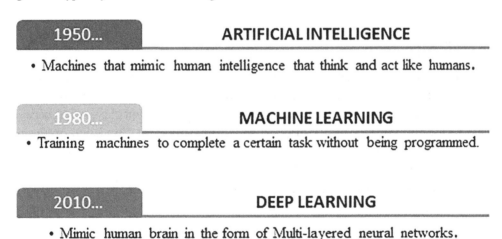

Supervised learning algorithm takes input data from a training set and known responses to the data as output and trains a model for the generation of reasonable predictions for the response to new input data. It is a predictive mechanism in which a portion of data can be training data, some for the validation of model and the others for the determination of accuracy. The two main learning tasks in supervised learning are classification and regression. Supervised learning problems can be grouped into regression and classification problems. In classification, the output of the learning tasks will take the form of binary class classification or multi-class classification. In regression, the output has one or more continuous-valued numbers where each item of a set are expressed in terms of probability. A classification problem arises when the output variable is a category while a regression problem arises when the output variable is a real value.

Unsupervised learning is useful when there is no specific goal or is not sure of what information the data contains. It concretes a good way to reduce the dimensionality of data. Unsupervised learning problems can be grouped into clustering and association problems. A clustering problem discovers the inherent groupings in the data based on the features. An association rule learning problem discovers rules that describe large portions of data. Clustering algorithms fall into two broad groups, namely hard clustering and soft clustering based on the data points on a single group or multiple groups.

MACHINE LEARNING ALGORITHMS

Machine learning functionalities include Wind and solar Energy Forecasting, Cyber Security in Smart Grid(Dongxia Zhang, Xiaoqing Han, & Chunyu Deng,2018),Object Detection and Recognition(X. Zhou, W. Gong, W. Fu & F. Du, 2017), power generation, Big Data Analytics, fault detection, adaptive control, sizing,malware detection, automatic driving and detection of network intruders. Some of the prevalent algorithms of machine learning (Ahmed K. Abbas, Najim A. Al-haideri & Ali A. Bashikh, 2019) are listed as follows:

(i) Support Vector Machine

Support Vector Machine (SVM) are among the most robust and accurate methods in all machine-learning algorithms and supports both binary and multi-class classifications. It is based on the concept of decision boundaries. A decision boundary separates a set of instances having different class values between two groups. Support vector machines found use in many applications like lost circulation occurrence in drilling operations (Ahmed K. et al., 2019), classification of (EEG) signals for the diagnosis of neurological disorders such as epilepsy and sleep disorders (B. Richhariya &M. Tanveer, 2018).SVM has proven its efficiency in Breast Cancer prediction and diagnosis and achieves the best performance in terms of precision and low error rate.

(ii) Naïve Bayes

A Naive Bayes Classifier which is a Bayesian network that uses the Bayes Theorem assumes that features are statistically independent. It is a supervised machine-learning algorithm that has proved to be a classifier with good results. Naive Bayes are easy to apply on a wide range of tasks as there is no need to set the free parameters like SVM and Neural Networks. Naïve Bayes are used to determine early gesture recognition (Hugo Jair Escalante, Eduardo F. Morales & L. Enrique Sucar, 2016) and Big Data Classifications (Nanfei Sun, Bingjun Sun, Jian (Denny) Lin, Michael Yu-Chi Wu, 2018).

(iii) Decision Trees

Decision tree approach is a supervised learning algorithm in which the entire dataset is labeled. It sorts out the classes based on parameter values. ID3, C4.5, CHAID and CART are some of the frequent decision tree algorithms. Though the computation time is less there is considerable building time. They are widely used in medical image classification, data modeling.

(iv) K-means Clustering

It is an unsupervised learning approach in which test dataset are not labeled. In K-means clustering, the dataset is a partitioned into a set of K-small clusters in which each is represented through its cluster mean. Agglomerative Clustering pairs up to create big clusters in the bottom-up manner. In contrast, Divisive Clustering uses broken parts of a big cluster dividing them into the small clusters in a top-down manner. K-means Clustering are prominently used for detection of thermal infrared images (M. R. S. Mohd, S. H. Herman & Z. Sharif, 2017), Intrusion Detection (M. Jianliang, S. Haikun & B. Ling, 2009).

(v) Neural Networks (NN)

A neural network is also referred to as an artificial neural network (ANN) if originated from the biological theory of neurons. Single layer perceptron is the basic form of NN that consists of a single neuron with adjustable weights and used for the classification of linearly separable classes. A Multilayer perceptron (MLP) is an efficient and robust algorithm used for modeling non-linear and complex problems. A series of algorithms based on R-CNN such as Regions with ConvolutionalNeural Network (R-CNN), SPP-Net (spatial pyramid pooling), Fast R-CNN and Faster R-CNN are used in object detection (Xinyi Zhou, Wei Gong, WenLong Fu, Fengtong Du, 2017).

(vi) Logistic Regression

Logistic regression models the probabilities for classification problems with two possible outcomes 0 and 1. It is an extension of the linear regression model for classification problems. It fits in a model that can predict the probability of a binary response belonging to one class or the other. It is commonly used a starting point for binary classification problems. Logistic regression models (LRMs) used for creating a predictive model for recovery form hemorrhagic shock (A. Lucas, A. T. Williams & P. Cabrales, 2019) and Multiple Sclerosis Detection (S.Wang et al,2016).

DEEP LEARNING

Deep learning is a subcategory of machine learning that uses multi-layer neural networks in which a model learns to perform classification tasks directly from images, text, or sound. Deep learning is realized using neural network architecture. Features that are invisible to human view can be extracted easily by DL. DL models bring two significant improvements over the machine learning approaches in the two phases, namely training and prediction. In deep learning, classification, regression, dimensionality reduction, clustering, and density estimation are the outputs of the learning tasks. Deep learning

Algorithms (D. Zhang, X. Han & C. Deng, 2018) are well-suited for the identification of applications such as face recognition, text translation, voice recognition, and ATM services, cyber physical systems and internet of things.

(i) Restricted Boltzmann Machine (RBM)

Restricted Boltzmann Machines (RBMs) were originally designed for unsupervised learning purposes from unlabeled data. RBM contains a visible layer for input and hidden layers with latent variables. RBMs are the building blocks of deep belief networks and combined together to form deep neural networks (M. Mohammadi, A. Al-Fuqaha, S. Sorour & M. Guizani, 2018). The training procedure uses back propagation and gradient descent algorithms for training the data. They belong essentially a type of energy-based undirected graphical models, and include a visible layer and a hidden layer, and where each unit can only assume binary values (i.e., 0 and 1).The goal is to train the network to increase a product or the log of the probability of vector in the visible units to enable probabilistic reconstruction of the output. A stack of RBMs, is called a Deep Belief Network (DBN), performs layer-wise training and achieves superior performance (Chaoyun Zhang, Paul Patras& Hamed Haddadi, 2019). RBM are used in many applications such as indoor localization, prediction of energy consumption and posture study for the extraction of component features from available data.RBM are used for Prognostics and Health Assessment, Intrusion detection in smart cities (Asmaa Elsaeidy, Kumudu S. Munasinghe, Dharmendra Sharma & Abbas Jamalipour, 2019).

(ii) Auto-Encoders

Auto-Encoders (AEs) are also designed for unsupervised learning and attempt to copy inputs to outputs. Each AE consists of an input layer and an output layer that are linked through one or more hidden layers. AE reconstructs the input at output layer in simplest way without any distortion. AEs are frequently used for learning compact representation of data for dimension reduction and the recreation of the original dataset. There are a number of extensions of Auto-Encoder (AE) like denoising AE, contractive AE, stacked AE, sparse AE, and Variational AE (VAE). VAE is a semi-supervised learning method that works for applications that work with diverse data and less availability of labeled data. The learning algorithm is based on the implementation of the back propagation (D. Zhang et al., 2018).Deep auto encoder models are used for structural condition monitoring and Fault Diagnosis applications.

(iii) Convolutional Neural Network

CNN is based on the human visual cortex and is the neural network of choice for computer vision (image recognition) and video recognition. CNN consists of a series of convolution and sub-sampling layers followed by a fully connected layer and a normalizing layer (D. Zhang et al., 2018). Convolution Neural Networks (CNNs or ConvNets) employ a set of locally connected kernels (filters) for capturing the correlations between different data regions. Deep convolution network results in hierarchical extraction of features. Convolution Neural Networks are used for Image Classification (Z. Lin et al., 2019), Wireless Network Intrusion Detection (H. Yang & F. Wang, 2019)

(iv) Recurrent Neural Network

Recurrent Neural Networks (RNNs) are powerful dynamic systems designed for modeling sequential data, where sequential correlations exist between samples. The RNN is trained via a Back Propagation Through Time (BPTT) algorithm, unrolling the RNN center of BPTT algorithm to come up with a feed-forward network over time spans. Several approaches are followed for making Recursive Neural Network deeper through the addition of layers between the input and hidden layers. Hidden layers stack the addition of the layers between hidden layers and the output layer. The problem associated with the (RNNs) is long term dependence on the storage of past information for a long duration. A combination of Convolution Neural Network along with Recursive Neural Network is used for Blood Cell Image Classification (GaoboLiang, Huichao Hong, WeifangXie, &Lixin Zheng, 2018) and Internet of Things (Manuel Lopez-Martin, Antonio Sanchez-Esguevillas& Jaime Lloret, 2017).

AI, ML, DL FRAMEWORKS AND LIBRARIES

Artificial intelligence platforms simulation of the cognitive function performed by human mind such as learning, reasoning and intelligence to complete tasks. The most widely used AI platforms are Infosys Nia for automation and innovation, Wipro Holmes for virtual agents and robotics, API.AI, Rainbird for Business operations, Ayasdi, Mindmeld for voice and chat assistants, Vital A.I for intelligent automation of business processes, KAI for Wearable and Receptiviti for Emotional Intelligence etc...Various AI Powered testing tools are Applitools, Testim, Sealights, Test.AI, Mabl, Retest, ReportPortal, Functionlize to perform automation.

Many ML tools have been developed to facilitate the complicated data analysis process and to propose integrated environments on top of standard programming languages. Tools such as Shogun, Rapid Miner, Weka3, Scikit-Learn, LibLinear, VowpalWabbit and XGBoost are designed for various purposes as analytics platforms, predictive systems, recommender systems, processors. A number of them are oriented to fast processing and streaming of large-scale data, while others specialized in implementing ML algorithms including NNs and DL. GitHub has open source tool maintaining information about software development, automated code reviews and code analytics.

Advancements in Deep learning usage in different domains, has assisted support from the introduction of a number of DL frameworks (Giang Nguyenet al., 2019) in recent years. DL frameworks such as TensorFlow, Caffe, Keras, PyTorch, Caffe2, CNTK, MXNet, and Deeplearning4j (DL4J) support Python, Java, and C++ as the programming languages of choice. Each framework has its own strength for building solutions based on supported DL architectures, algorithms, and ease of development. The obvious factors to consider in the choice of the framework are open source, licensing, open source, active community, Interface, programming language, modularity, ease of use, and performance.

Advancements of Deep learning usage in different domains, has gained support from several DL frameworks introduced in recent years. Each framework has its own strength based on its supported DL architectures, algorithms, and ease of development. Deep Learning libraries and tools (Bradley J. Erickson, PanagiotisKorfiatis, ZeynettinAkkus, Timothy Kline, & Kenneth Philbrick, 2017) are evaluated based on development environment, execution speed, training speed and GPU. Programmer selects the toolkit based on the development environment as some toolkits possess graphical integrated development environment, some with dedicated editor and visualization tools to monitor. Computational resources availability and GPUs also play a major role in the selection of a toolkit. Special libraries like cuDNN are used for the special type of calculations required for deep learning. Support to more than one GPU helps a substantial improvement to performance while storage with processing has a large impact on performance.

Table 1. Machine Learning frameworks and libraries

Tool	License	Written in	Interface	Library / Framework	Algorithms
Shogun	Open source GNU GPLv3 license	C++	Python, Octave, R, Java/ Scala, Lua, C#, Ruby	ML library	• Regression and Classification methods • Hidden Markov models • Clustering
RapidMiner	Business source	Java	Python, R, GUI, API	ML/NN/DL framework	• Naive Bayes • Linear Regression • Logistic Regression • SVM • Decision tree
Wekab	Open source, GNU GPLv3	Java	Java, GUI, API	ML/DL framework	• Feature selection • Clustering • Classification • Regression • Visualization.
Scikit-Learn	Open source, BSD	Python, C++	Python, API	ML/NN library	• Classification • Regression • Clustering • Dimensionality Reduction
LibSVM	Open source, BSD 3-clause	C/C++	Python, R, MatLab, Perl, Ruby, Weka, Lisp, Haskell, OCaml, Lab View, PHP Reused in DM tools like Weka, RapidMiner, and KNIME.	ML library	• Support Vector Classification for Binary and Multi-Class • Support Vector Regression (SVR)
LibLinear	Open source, BSD 3-clause	C/C++	MatLab, Octave, Java, Python, Ruby	ML library	• Logistic Regression • Linear SVM • L2-regularized logistic regression, L2-loss and L1-loss linear SVMs.
VowpalWabbit	Open source, BSD 3-clause	C++, own MPI library All Reduce	API	ML library	• Different Loss Functions Optimization Algorithms
XGBoost	Open source, Apache 2.0	C++	C++, Java, Python, R, Julia	ML boosting, ensemble	• Gradient Boosting Decision tree algorithm

Table 2. Deep learning frameworks and libraries

Tool	License	Written in	Interface	Library /Framework
H2O	Open source, Apache 2.0	Java	R, Python, Scala, REST API	Framework
TensorFlow	Open source, Apache 2.0	C++, Python	Python, C++a, Javaa, Goa	Numerical framework
Keras	Open source, MIT	Python	Python Wrapper for TensorFlow, CNTK, DL4J, MXNet, Theano	Library
CNTK	Open source, Microsoft permissive license	C++	Python, C++, BrainScript, ONNX	Framework
Caffe	Open source, BSD 2-clause	C++	C++, Python, MatLab	Framework
Caffe2	Open source, Apache 2.0	C++	C++, Python, ONNX	Framework
Torch	Open source, BSD	C++, Lua	C, C++, LuaJIT, Lua, OpenCL	Framework
PyTorch	Open source, BSD	Python, C	Python, ONNX	Library
MXNet	Open source, Apache 2.0	C++	C++, Python, Julia, MatLab, Go, R, Scala, Perl, ONNX	Framework
Chainer	Open source, Owners permissive license	Python	Python	Framework
Theano	Open source, BSD	Python	Python	Numerical framework

DIFFERENCES BETWEEN ML AND DL

Machine Learning is a methodology for the achievement of Artificial Intelligence whereas deep learning for application of Machine Learning. Traditional Machine learning tools heavily hinge on the features defined by the domain professionals. The benefit of deep learning lies in its ability to do automatic extraction of extract high-level features from data that has a complex structure and inner correlations. The focus of ML is on classification and regression based on known features previously learned from the training data. Deep learning enables an algorithm to make predictions, classifications, or decisions based on data, without being explicitly programmed.

Similar to ML methods, DL methods also have supervised learning and unsupervised learning. Learning models built under different learning frameworks are quite different. ML requires the storage of all the data in memory, which is computationally infeasible under big data scenarios. Deep learning algorithms require a large amount of data for perfect understanding of data. Its contribution to performance is rather small when data volumes are small. The performance of ML does not grow significantly with large volumes of data. In problem solving, Machine learning decomposes the problem into multiple sub-problems and solves the sub-problems, ultimately obtaining the final result whereas deep learning advocates direct end-to-end problem solving.

Deep learning has the added value of the ability to take decision with a smaller contribution from human trainers. Machine learning needs a programmer for the identification of the correctness or otherwise of a conclusion. Deep learning can help measurement of the accuracy of its answers on its own due to the nature of its multi-layered structure. The multi-layered approach of deep learning aims to complete classification tasks such as detecting abnormalities in medical images, clustering patients with similar characteristics into risk-based units, or highlight relationships between symptoms and outcomes within vast quantities of unstructured data.

FOCUS ON AI

AI promises to provide the autonomous and centralized systems being designed to benefit the human society in carrying out the tasks in an intelligent manner.AI operates on specifically designed GPU and processing devices as hardware for the execution of AI based tasks. AI has the potential to get better utilization in various fields like robotics, forecasting weather, Medical Diagnostics, face recognition, Speech recognition, autonomous vehicles and big data analytics, etc… As per (A. Adadi & M. Berrada, 2018) International Data Corporation (IDC) estimates the rise in total global investment in AI will be from 12 billion U.S. dollars in 2017 to 52.2 billion U.S. dollars by 2021.

A Few emerging trends in AI applications are explainable AI, block chain technologies, digital twins, automated machine learning and deep learning models. These include Machine learning and deep learning methods of AI form a centralized model for running special algorithms for training and validating datasets whereas combination of AI and block chain form decentralized models for making trusted platforms and enable accurate secured decision outcomes which cannot be tampered.

Companies like Google, tesla and uber test the driverless cars on the road through the use of artificial intelligence. AI enhances autonomous vehicles in terms of in-vehicle experiences, such as personalization, virtual assistants, Traffic Congestion, and intelligent driving systems. Facebook deep program and iPhone X assess facial recognition AI to tag the person in the photos and using a digital password. Explainable Artificial Intelligence (XAI) (A. Adadi et al., 2018) creates a set of techniques for getting an insight into the Black box problem and finding solutions. Personal devices have digital assistants such as Apple's virtual assistant Siri, Amazon's Alexa and Google home that rely on natural language processing (NLP) algorithms for application of AI. Many business organizations and social communities manage the data of huge dimensions for making well-versed decisions using AI.

AI techniques, Image classification and accurate assessment of complex images can now be used for detection of tumors at earlier stages with the same accuracy as medical experts. According to IBM's Watson, the AI medical diagnosis system has been used for detecting a reach nearly 90% of the consistency with the top medical experts to improve accuracy and efficiency of diagnosis and treatment. Deep learning histopathology identifies the automated recognition of metastatic breast cancer similar to experts. Smartphone apps like Skin, Vision and AI are used for skin cancer classification with huge datasets and the model is trained on millions of images.

CONTRIBUTION OF INTELLIGENCE TOWARDS SOCIETY

(i) AI in Healthcare: Artificial Intelligence in healthcare is now available for the detection of diseases at earlier stage to prevent mortality and reduce harm to patients. But the limits to which AI come into the present is based on how it presents risks and benefits to patients. As Siri and Alexa were using in the home as virtual assistants, there might be a chance in the future that bring virtual assistance to assist clinicians for providing immediate service to patients. Application of AI in healthcare has started from identification of minor problems and going up to chronic complications. AI diagnosis tools, doctors have the ability to identify unidentifiable and rare diseases and find the correct solution in duration of seconds. Deep learning convolutional neural networks is well suitable for analyzing medical images such as MRI and X-rays.

Google's DeepMind has taught machines the prediction of acute kidney injury at earlier stages with improved accuracy and read retinal scans with at least good accuracy seen in experienced junior doctors. Recently Google sister company Verily united with Pampers to develop "smart diapers" that auto-track sleep as well as bodily functions. Babylon the healthapp chatbot has the capability to clear GP exam conducted by Royal College of General Practitioners.AXA PPP company created two cradlesongs one by AI and another by humans. By using AI with deep learning AI system creates a new composition which was then converted into a song with the aid of a human to help in sleep better. Genomic combined with AI is possible to spot cancer, vascular diseases initial stage and predicts the health issues of the patients based on their genes.

(ii) Enabling Intelligence in IoT Systems

IoT offers a seamless platform to connect things anytime to achieve anything at any place to shape the existing systems by making use of smart Technologies and making them intelligent IoT restructures as smart devices by offering intelligence targets and all-in-one connectivity to complete the tasks at any place at any time. IoT systems facilitate various utilities in the system such as sensing identification, actuation, communication, and management. IoT along with AI would automate nearly all activities around us by making them smart and eases human life. Smarter IoT systems have AI and aims to achieve the automation and adaptation as goals according to the environment.AI, ML and DL algorithms enable computational processes to discover patterns in large datasets. Intelligence algorithms are used to extract information from raw data generated by billions of devices connected to the internet.

The two technologies, DL and IoT, become very familiar and get placed among the Gartner Symposium/ITxpo 2016 announcement in top three strategic technology trends for 2017 to meet analytic needs of IoT systems. Incorporation of ML and DL learning algorithms requires a large real time datasets for the achievement of higher accuracy. The main tools to achieve intelligence in IoT systems are ML and DL. ML makes the physical objects smart and facilitates learning in devices for making autonomous and more effective. In addition data analysis module is included for the evaluation of the data that is generated from devices.

(iii) AI Enabled Robots and Chatbots

Robots are assumed to be IoT devices since they contain multiple sensors and actuators to sense and act with AI (A. Ghosh, D. Chakraborty & A. Law, 2018) to help them in continuous learning and adaptation accordingly. Pepper from SoftBank Robotics is the world's first human-shaped robot with an emotion engine for understanding human emotions, namely joy, anger, sadness and surprise. Pepper is an assistant capable of recognizing faces interacting with humans through expression of emotions including movement, touch and words which can be displayed on the screen. It is used for commercial applications in various areas for interaction with customers. Sophia from Hanson Robotics is a social humanoid robot developed by Hanson Robotics, a Hong Kong based firm.it is the world's first robot citizen which has the ability to display more than 62 facial expressions and maintaining eye contact with humans. Moley Robotics from Robotic Kitchen is an advanced fully functional robot integrated into a kitchen.It has robotic arms, oven, hob, and a touchscreen unit for human interaction to imitate the entire role of human hands with the same speed, sensitivity and movement to prepare food like expert from its recipe library. ZEN Robotics, European based company has built an intelligent system known as SITA Finland, which is an automated system that categories construction and destruction debris intelligently by utilizing AI that could can take decisions of its own and predict the right course of action for the given task.

A Chatbot embedded with intelligence depends on the type of task or application it has to perform. Chatbot can be considered as a helper or collector depending on its assistance or collection of the information from the user. The helper chatbot is acknowledged by its natural language processing and learning from pre-defined models. It is not smart enough to respond when a user raises an enquiry whereas collector chatbot becomes intelligent when it responds by collecting information from the user and presenting it in a correct manner to serve the user's purpose. The best chatbot has been discussed by (Clifford Chi, 2019) with Watson Assistant, an advanced AI-powered chatbot acting as a platform to understand historical chat or call logs to provide recommendations for conversational abilities. Bold360's conversational AI analyses the context of an entire conversation and reply to customers with natural responses. Ruali, an AI chatbot powered with DL, predicts user next action from the context of conversation for taking action and asking customers for additional interpretation. It integrates with the most messaging channels, cloud storage platforms, customer service and enterprise business software. LivePerson an AI-powered chatbot collects over 20 years of messaging record data and can automate almost every industry's messaging through messaging channels like website, text messaging, Facebook Messenger and WhatsApp. Inbenta's chatbot powered by machine learning and NLP engine to detect the context of each customer conversation and accurately answer their questions.

(iv) Block Chain for AI

Block chain is a distributed, open source, decentralized technology to automate payments, trace and track transactions without third party. Data tampering and hacking of data possibility arise due to the centralized nature of AI as it is managed and warehoused in a centralized fashion (K. Salah, M. H. U. Rehman, N. Nizamuddin and A. Al-Fuqaha, 2019). Hence the concept of decentralized AI has been emerging as a combination of AI and blockchain technologies. Blockchain has now been foreseen as a trusted platform for storage of data in blocks. Each block contains the information relating to transactions and asset exchanges known as Ether or Bitcoin that take place among the users. Ethereum is an open source distributed platform that uses ether as a currency for making payments for making transactions. The Blockchain technologies for AI applications are categorized as permissioned and permission less systems based on the access of authorized users and publicly accessible.

CONCLUSION

Artificial intelligence helps building a smarter world when the intelligence of man is imitated by machines in an optimistic manner. Upcoming generations will lie under the shadow of smart technology and automation for the rapid development of a nation. Though these systems bring countless benefits, they also contain inherent risks, such as privacy, failure or bugs in the software or hardware arising due to various causes. A thorough knowledge of embedding intelligence by the humans should have the ability to prevent and fix problems by showing supreme power in the manmade systems.

ACKNOWLEDGMENT

This research received no specific grant from any funding agency in the public, commercial, or not-for-profit sectors.

REFERENCES

Adadi, A., & Berrada, M. (2018). Peeking Inside the Black-Box: A Survey on Explainable Artificial Intelligence (XAI). *IEEE Access: Practical Innovations, Open Solutions*, 6, 52138–52160. doi:10.1109/ACCESS.2018.2870052

Ahmed, K., Abbas, N. A., Al-haideri, & Bashikh, A.A. (2019). Implementing artificial neural networks and support vector machines to predict lost circulation. *Egyptian Journal of Petroleum.* doi:10.1016/j.ejpe.2019.06.006

Bradley, J. E., Korfiatis, P., Akkus, Z., Kline, T., & Philbrick, K. (2017). *Toolkits and Libraries for Deep Learning.* Retrieved from https://www.ncbi.nlm.nih.gov/pmc/articles/PMC5537091/

Chi, C. (2019). *Best AI Chatbots for 2019.* Retrieved from https://blog.hubspot.com/marketing/best-ai-chatbot

Elsaeidy, A., & Kumudu, S. (2019). Intrusion detection in smart cities using Restricted Boltzmann Machines. *Journal of Network and Computer Applications*, 135, 76–83. doi:10.1016/j.jnca.2019.02.026

Ghosh, A., Chakraborty, D., & Law, A. (2018). Artificial intelligence in Internet of things. *CAAI Transactions on Intelligence Technology*, 3(4), 208–218. doi:10.1049/trit.2018.1008

Hugo, J. E., Morales, E. F., & Sucar, L. E. (2016). A naïve Bayes baseline for early gesture recognition. *Pattern Recognition Letters*, 73, 91–99. doi:10.1016/j.patrec.2016.01.013

Jianliang, M., Haikun, S., & Ling, B. (2009). The Application on Intrusion Detection Based on K-means Cluster Algorithm. *International Forum on Information Technology and Applications*, 150-152.

Liang, G., Hong, H., Xie, W., & Zheng, L. (2019). Combining Convolutional Neural Network With Recursive Neural Network for Blood Cell Image Classification. *IEEE Access: Practical Innovations, Open Solutions*, 6, 36188–36197. doi:10.1109/ACCESS.2018.2846685

Lin, Z., Mu, S., Huang, F., Mateen, K. A., Wang, M., Gao, W., & Jia, J. (2019). A Unified Matrix-Based Convolutional Neural Network for Fine-Grained Image Classification of Wheat Leaf Diseases. *IEEE Access: Practical Innovations, Open Solutions*, 7, 11570–11590. doi:10.1109/ACCESS.2019.2891739

Lopez-Martin, M., Carro, B., Sanchez-Esguevillas, A., & Lloret, J. (2019). Network Traffic Classifier With Convolutional and Recurrent Neural Networks for Internet of Things. *IEEE Access: Practical Innovations, Open Solutions*, 5, 18042–18050. doi:10.1109/ACCESS.2017.2747560

Lucas, A., Williams, A. T., & Cabrales, P. (2019). Prediction of Recovery From Severe Hemorrhagic Shock Using Logistic Regression. *IEEE Journal of Translational Engineering in Health and Medicine*, 7, 1–9. doi:10.1109/JTEHM.2019.2924011 PMID:31367491

Mohammadi, A., Al-Fuqaha, M., Sorour, S., & Guizani, M. (2018). Deep Learning for IoT Big Data and Streaming Analytics: A Survey. *IEEE Communications Surveys and Tutorials, 20*(4), 2923–2960. doi:10.1109/COMST.2018.2844341

Mohd, M. R. S., Herman, S. H., & Sharif, Z. (2017). Application of K-Means clustering in hot spot detection for thermal infrared images. *2017 IEEE Symposium on Computer Applications & Industrial Electronics (ISCAIE),* 107-110. 10.1109/ISCAIE.2017.8074959

Nguyen, G., Dlugolinsky, S., Bobák, M., Tran, V., López García, Á., Heredia, I., Malík, P., & Hluchý, L. (2019). Machine Learning and Deep Learning frameworks and libraries for large-scale data mining: A survey. *Artificial Intelligence Review, 52*(1), 77–124. doi:10.100710462-018-09679-z

Richhariya, B., & Tanveer, M. (2018). EEG signal classification using universum support vector machine. *Expert Systems with Applications, 106,* 169–182. doi:10.1016/j.eswa.2018.03.053

Salah, K., Rehman, M. H. U., Nizamuddin, N., & Al-Fuqaha, A. (2019). Blockchain for AI: Review and Open Research Challenges. *IEEE Access: Practical Innovations, Open Solutions, 7,* 10127–10149. doi:10.1109/ACCESS.2018.2890507

Sun, N., Sun, B., Lin, J., & Wu, M. (2018). Lossless Pruned Naive Bayes for Big Data Classifications. *Big Data Research, 14,* 27–36. doi:10.1016/j.bdr.2018.05.007

Wang, S., Zhan, T.-M., Chen, Y., Zhang, Y., Yang, M., Lu, H.-M., Wang, H.-N., Liu, B., & Phillips, P. (2016). Multiple Sclerosis Detection Based on Biorthogonal Wavelet Transform, RBF Kernel Principal Component Analysis, and Logistic Regression. *IEEE Access: Practical Innovations, Open Solutions, 4,* 7567–7576. doi:10.1109/ACCESS.2016.2620996

Yang, H., & Wang, F. (2019). Wireless Network Intrusion Detection Based on Improved Convolutional Neural Network. *IEEE Access: Practical Innovations, Open Solutions, 7,* 64366–64374. doi:10.1109/ACCESS.2019.2917299

Zhang, C., Patras, P., & Haddadi, H. (2019). Deep Learning in Mobile and Wireless Networking: A Survey. *IEEE Communications Surveys and Tutorials, 21*(3), 2224–2287. doi:10.1109/COMST.2019.2904897

Zhang, D., Han, X., & Deng, C. (2018). Review on the research and practice of deep learning and reinforcement learning in smart grids. *CSEE Journal of Power and Energy Systems, 4*(3), 362–370. doi:10.17775/CSEEJPES.2018.00520

Zhou, L., Pan, S., Wang, J., & Vasilakos, A. V. (2017). Machine Learning on Big Data: Opportunities and Challenges. *Neurocomputing, 237,* 350-361.

Zhou, X., Gong, W., Fu, W., & Du, F. (2017). Application of deep learning in object detection. *2017 IEEE/ACIS 16th International Conference on Computer and Information Science (ICIS),* 631-634.

ADDITIONAL READING

Cyolakovic, A., & Hadzÿialic, M. (2018). Internet of Things (IoT): A Review of Enabling Technologies, Challenges, and Open Research Issues. *Computer Networks*. https://cloud.google.com/ml-engine/ https://medicalfuturist.com/top-ai-algorithms-healthcare https://www.predictiveanalyticstoday.com/artificial-intelligence-platforms/

L'Heureux, A., Grolinger, K., Elyamany, H. F., & Capretz, M. A. M. (2017). Machine Learning With Big Data: Challenges and Approaches. *IEEE Access: Practical Innovations, Open Solutions, 5,* 7776–7797. doi:10.1109/ACCESS.2017.2696365

Mathur, S., & Modani, U. S. (2016). Smart City- a gateway for artificial intelligence in India. *IEEE Students' Conference on Electrical, Electronics and Computer Science (SCEECS),* 1-3. https://www.softbankrobotics.com/corp/robots/

Wan, J., Yang, J., Wang, Z., & Hua, Q. (2018). Artificial Intelligence for Cloud-Assisted Smart Factory. *IEEE Access: Practical Innovations, Open Solutions, 6,* 55419–55430. doi:10.1109/ACCESS.2018.2871724

KEY TERMS AND DEFINITIONS

Artificial Intelligence: Science of simulating intelligence in machines and program them to mimic human actions.

Deep Learning: Application of multi neuron, multi-layer neural networks to perform learning tasks.

IoT (Internet of Things): Integration of various processes such as identifying, sensing, networking, and computation.

Machine Learning: To build a machine that improves automatically through experience.

Chapter 12
IoT Device Onboarding, Monitoring, and Management:
Approaches, Challenges, and Future

Selvaraj Kesavan
DXC Technology, India

Senthilkumar J.
Sona College of Technology, India

Suresh Y.
Sona College of Technology, India

Mohanraj V.
Sona College of Technology, India

ABSTRACT

In establishing a healthy environment for connectivity devices, it is essential to ensure that privacy and security of connectivity devices are well protected. The modern world lives on data, information, and connectivity. Various kinds of sensors and edge devices stream large volumes of data to the cloud platform for storing, processing, and deriving insights. An internet of things (IoT) system poses certain difficulties in discretely identifying, remotely configuring, and controlling the devices, and in the safe transmission of data. Mutual authentication of devices and networks is crucial to initiate secure communication. It is important to keep the data in a secure manner during transmission and in store. Remotely operated devices help to monitor, control, and manage the IoT system efficiently. This chapter presents a review of the approaches and methodologies employed for certificate provisioning, device onboarding, monitoring, managing, and configuring of IoT systems. It also examines the real time challenges and limitations in and future scope for IoT systems.

DOI: 10.4018/978-1-7998-3111-2.ch012

INTRODUCTION

Emergence of sound technologies in connectivity has transformed the conventional consumer practices, industrial processes, and applications of information technology to new standards. With a significant drop in the price of sensors, rapid growth in connectivity field and service computing models have boosted the flourishing of associated industries. Internet of Things (IoT) is an important emerging transformational technology. By and large, IoT systems have developed in a fast manner which made a tangible impact on all verticals of industrial sectors, on an individual's regular operations, and on global businesses. Many organizations have realized the financial benefits gained by employing IoT and its companion technologies. Internet of Things, along with its other supporting communication technologies, aims to connect millions of both passive and active devices.

Industrial Internet of Things (IIoT) is a remarkable revolution in IoT science and technology. It makes use of smart sensors and actuators to conduct the industrial manufacturing processes in a perfect manner. IIoT systems support multiple segments of industries like energy production, manufacturing, automotive, and healthcare. This system leverages the power of smart machines and real-time analytics. It organizes the age-old data that have been produced by poorly performing machines in the industries. IIoT is an intelligent asset that can sense, communicate, and store information (Sheng et al., 2015).

Intel and McKinsey predict that there would be 2000 billion connectivity devices in 2020 and the economic impact of IoT would be around $11.1 trillion per year by 2025. IoT is one of the key transformational technologies that determine winners in many industries. It is essential to implement measures to realize secure IoT and to scale up security so as to cope with the exponential growth of connectivity devices (Ha & Lindh, 2018).

It is foreseen that the growth of installed IoT devices would be tremendous in the coming years. Numerous passive and active sensors are employed in the connectivity domain to send data on events incessantly to the gateway and processing system. Connectivity technologies enable the devices to be smart and intelligent in analyzing the data and help the IoT system to make automatic provision, monitor, and control devices in real-time. The devices and sensors can be connected either directly to the cloud platform services or via a location gateway system. The crucial phase in the IoT process involves device enumeration and management, smart planning, and efforts to initiate the roll-on in a smooth manner. Sometimes, it may become necessary to deploy IoT sensors and devices in a hostile and restricted environment. In such instances, it is essential to provide the security to the devices and the IoT architecture. It is mandatory that the IoT system shall have updated firmware and software so that the devices can perform connectivity and transfer data without any security breach. The device could be decommissioned when its service is no longer required. Bringing devices into a connected environment and managing the IoT/IIoT systems pose certain difficulties and challenges.

IOT ECOSYSTEM

The Internet stands as a platform for devices to communicate. Billions of connectivity devices endorse the brilliance of IoT. Though connectivity is an enabler, its true value lies in data transmission, business insight, and data-driven economy.

Devices that establish connectivity on the Internet provide a range of advantages – for example, we can remotely control, monitor, fault diagnose, and collect data for analysis. Devices used for making connectivity are equipped with modern microcontrollers. Data transmission may seem to be a minor task in today's Internet protocols, but this is not true. Though in many instances, pure data transmission is set to be the goal of hackathons and other hands-on IoT workshops, it is the only part objective of the IoT system.

While the manufacturer-credentials are perpetual, the operational credentials are typically short-lived for use with designated communicating members. IoT devices differ from other kinds of computing device like a smart phone by having only a small number of communicating parties, restricting the number of operational credentials to be stored by the IoT system, and providing certain ease of operation.

The framework of IoT ecosystem is illustrated in Figure 1. The topmost layer outlines the industry verticals in IoT. The applications of IoT are spread over many sectors like agriculture, manufacturing, resources, retail, transportation, finance, home, healthcare, etc. The inner layer describes the IoT components and their functionalities. The core IoT components comprise minute sensors, actuators, and devices that are connected to nearby device gateway assigned with data communication protocols. The edge device gateway acts as a sensor agent. It collects information from a multitude of sensors, compiles and filters the data, and carries out edge analysis for real-time pattern matching and detection. The streaming data are organized and continuously forwarded to the platform for storage, processing, analysis, and visualization. IoT streaming data are also used for real-time analysis, event triggers, and notifications

Figure 1. IoT Ecosystem

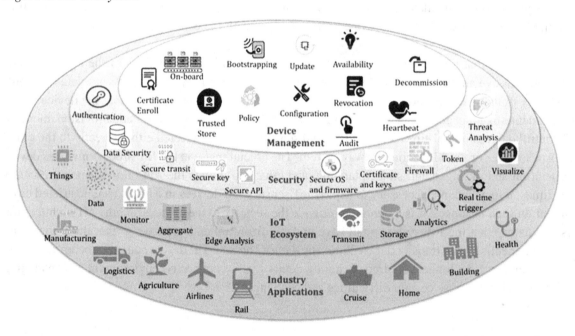

The end-to-end security is of utmost importance for realizing the true potential of the IoT. It protects the IoT components from attacks, provides data privacy, maintains data integrity, and builds customer confidence. Strong security policies and practices should be enforced to prevent attacks on sensors, devices, and data. Aspects like secure device firmware, good operating system, an appropriate certificate for the sensor, proper device identification, standard keys, token for data encryption at rest and transit, provision of firewall, and making the system capable of analyzing data pattern for security violations help in establishing a secure IoT system.

Device management is one of the key essentials in IoT system. It helps in device onboarding, organizing, monitoring, and remotely managing in a large scale and provides a seamless experience to the organization and the users. The innermost layer of the IoT layout summarizes various functionalities of device management. The prime functionalities of device management include device onboard, certificate enroll, update, revoke, device heartbeat monitoring, device availability, remote configuration, policy enforcement, decommission, etc. The following section explains device management and its working nature in detail.

IoT Device Life Cycle

It is important to have a defined life cycle for IoT devices. Six common device management stages are prescribed and the device manufacturers adopt these stages for providing complete end-to-end IoT solutions. A schematic showing the IoT life cycle appears in Figure 2.

Figure 2. IoT Device life cycle

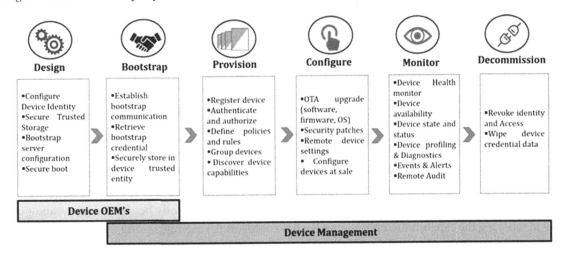

Design: Device-manufacturers produce devices and configure the devices in such a way as to onboard the metadata during manufacturing itself. Designing of a device includes configuring, assigning unique device identity, provisioning secure storage with options to store keys and certificates, onboarding bootstrap server credentials, and making allowance for secure boot options. A device built with adequate design helps the operators and the platform to query and get details for device onboard and management options.

Bootstrap: Bootstrapping is a process by which an IoT device is brought about and provided with a digital certificate (Sarikaya et al., 2018). IoT devices may or may not have an enabled IP address. Bootstrapping involves the incorporation of many tiny sensors. These tiny sensors do not have the capability of running complex software so as to handle requests from multiple entities such as gateway, authentication system, and data processing platform. It is important to get secure onboard communication, provide the platform, and set up environment credentials to the devices before commissioning. These tasks include the establishment of communication with the bootstrap server, retrieving bootstrap credentials, and securely storing the credentials in the device trusted entity (Pritikin et al., 2018).

1. Strategies at manufacturer level

Manufacturers configure the devices in abeyance to essential parameters such as device unique ID, serial number token, and certificate. Metadata are incorporated in the device's secure storage component. Minimal information in the device is used to establish basic connectivity between the device and platform. It is also possible to provide an authorized certificate with the device. Providing certificates during manufacturing itself helps to bring about direct authorization with the platform. It is necessary to make the platform be known to a list of devices in advance.

2. Strategies at deployment stage

An IoT device can be designed to suit with different platforms and applications. It is essential to configure the IoT devices in such a manner as to validate and securely send the data to an authorized platform. After manufacturing, the devices are deployed. During placement, it is desirable to confirm that the devices have a mechanism to receive details of certificate, token, and platform. The IoT devices are built either via wired or wireless using appropriate protocols. Such an arrangement helps to plug the device dynamically to any customer applications (Kesavan & Kalambettu, 2018).

3. Strategies during operation

The configuration and update should be dynamic while the devices are being operated. It becomes necessary to change the credentials and connection information when users change the platform or application. It is also important to change the security credential or token during operation in order to prevent attacks by man-in-the-middle and avoid compromising the security. Dynamic configuration meant for operation can be implemented using OMA LWM2M interfaces (Open Mobile Alliance, 2019),(Antonia et al., 2015).

Provision: Device should have the ability to establish mutual trust firmly between devices and platform by identifying the capabilities, exchanging the trust credentials, and registering the device identities in the platform registry.

Configuration: For maintaining device security, it is fundamental to update the device firmware and security patches without interrupting device operation. A good configuration provides the device the ability to make changes in current setup and update software and firmware. The agent at device receives command, data, and configuration details.

Monitoring: Monitoring of device availability and regularly checking its health are important measures to establish a sound IoT system. Details on device availability, its condition and operation status, and power usage pattern can be periodically sent to the monitoring and management platform.

Decommissioning: It is process of replacing the devices after failure or end of service life period of the devices. The device receives proper instructions and removes the bootstrap information, device's unique identity, and security credentials.

IOT DEVICE MANAGEMENT

Conventional device management is widely practiced with respect of mobile devices by mobile system operators and enterprises to remotely monitor, track, and update the software. Most of the handset device management practices are founded on OMA DM. Other standards that provide similar functionality are TR 69 and IEEE 802.1 AR. The advent of IoT has provided benefits to individual consumers and organizations and has improved the quality of life and businesses (Silva et al., 2019),(Umar et al., 2018). An IoT system consists of millions of sensors and devices which are put in action every day. Hence it is imperative to manage and operate the system in an efficient manner. Device management skills should be developed in order to handle the devices perfectly. Device management keeps the devices intact, provides long life to the devices, and leverages PKI for providing security and onboarding the devices into the IoT ecosystem (Skytta, 2017). The layout of device management is shown in Figure 3.

Primarily there are two ways to implement device management:

1. Platform dependent device management (In-band device management)
2. Platform independent device management (Out-of-band device management)

In-Band Device Management

Platform dependent device management provides vertically integrated device management service within the platform. Device provisioning, onboarding, and management are components of the platform. The vertically integrated setup makes device management simple and cost-effective, besides a seamless arrangement of multiple dynamic devices. However, as the devices are locked to a specific platform, it is not possible to stream the data to any other platform. Device management service is closely coupled with the platform. Amazon Web Services and Azure Cloud provide integrated device management as part of their IoT platform capabilities; this kind of management supports the provisioning of devices in single, just-in-time, and bulk fashions.

Figure 3. IoT Device Management

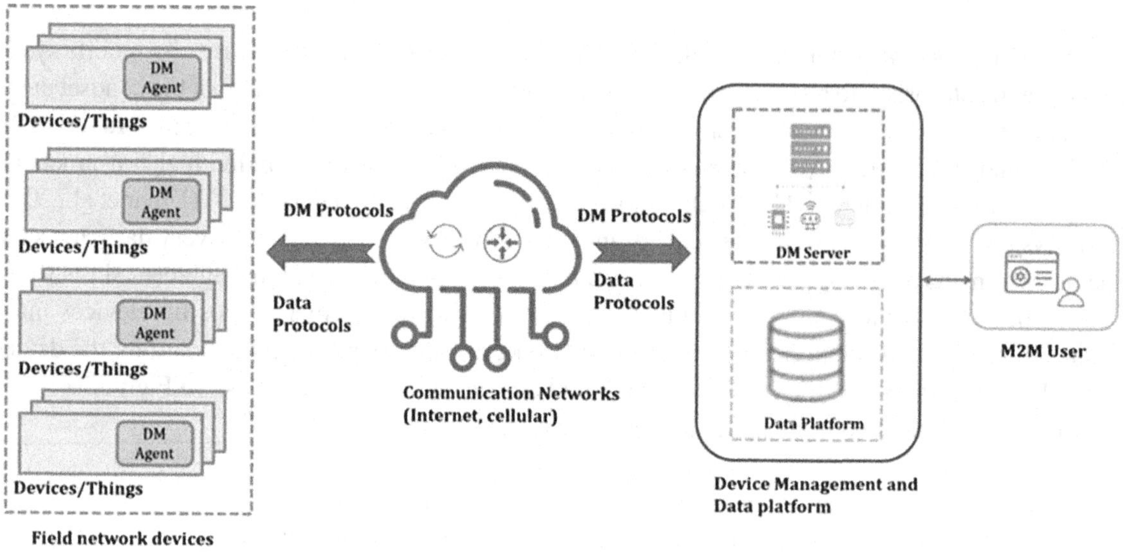

Out-of-Band Device Management

Platform independent device management enables carrying out device management outside the IoT platform and it can horizontally connect to multiple IoT platforms for data streaming. It makes the device ecosystem independent of a specific IoT platform and capable of changing the platform if required. It maintains loosely coupled platforms, avoiding the instances of the customer being locked to any specific platform. It also helps the device to stream the data to a hybrid IoT cloud environment. However, it needs the customer to select, host, and maintain the device management service in a separate environment.

Device Management Functionalities

The fundamental functions of device management are:

1. Device provisioning and onboarding
   a. Device bootstrapping
   b. Secure certificate transfer
   c. Certificate enrollment, update, and reconfiguration
   d. Automatic device onboarding - Create, Remove, Update, and Delete devices
2. Continuous device monitoring and diagnostics
   a. Remote monitor of devices condition, state, profiling, catalog, reboot, and reset of devices
   b. Maintain software catalog
   c. Remotely enabling policies
   d. Device availability and tracking
   e. Auditing – monitor remotely creating event alerts, fetching event logs and analyze
   f. Connection management - keep alive, reestablish state

3. Remote configuration and upgrade
    a. Over-the-Air (OTA) Update – Software, Firmware, Application, and Configuration
    b. Security patches
4. Decommissioning
    a. Device decommission and replacement of devices after service life period
    b. Certificate revocation

Device Provisioning and Onboarding

The conventional method of device provisioning and onboarding consumes a lot of time and involves great efforts; this is because of the manual processes carried out and the large participation of stakeholders in the complete process. It requires coordination among installation engineers, network operators, operational teams, and platform providers. It is essential to have a good management platform to make happen provisioning and onboarding as an automation process. This strategy helps to connect any number of devices dynamically and onboard to customer choice of platform in seconds. Automatic deployment provides solutions to problems and facilitates scaling up during production (Watsen et al., 2018).

Device provisioning is the process of configuring and setting up the devices and establishing a connection with the device management server. The device should be programmed to use certificates along with encryption keys to realize device and server authentication. The processes involved in device provisioning and onboarding are outlined in Figure 4. Device provisioning and onboarding system involve the device manufacturer, certificate authority (CA), device manager, bootstrap, and the IoT platform. Certificate authority needs to be set up or provisioned. Furthermore, communication between CA and bootstrap and device management service should be established. CA is required to sign device keys. Also, devices bootstrap, and device management services that have certificates and keys can initiate communication.

Figure 4. Device provisioning and onboarding

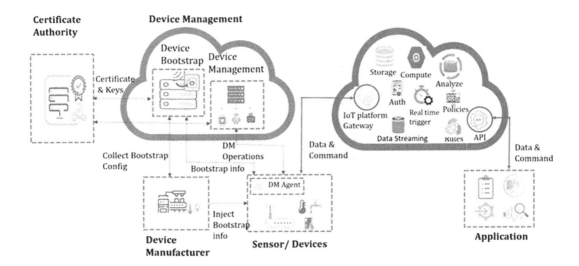

The measures involved in end-to-end provisioning are represented in Figure 5. The first step to be carried out in setting up bootstrap and device management service is to begin an account with the appropriate provider or customer service. During the manufacturing of the IoT devices, the device manufacturer identifies and enables the connection credentials in the devices. The bootstrap information includes the following:

- Device connection end point and the method adopted
- Device unique identity parameters that help the server to identify the device
- Identification of platform for streaming the data

Figure 5. Measures involved in end-to-end provisioning

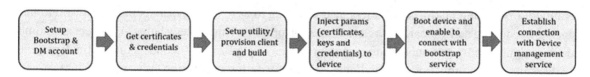

During manufacturing, the device manufacturer uses the software utility or device management client to feed the bootstrap information in the devices. The initial certificates and credentials required to connect with the bootstrap server are also fetched and stored in the devices. During device boot, the device management agent retrieves and parses the bootstrap configuration and establishes secure communication with the bootstrap service. Bootstrap service provides the bootstrap package whose URL is known to the device a priori and device able to install. After the bootstrap package gets installed successfully, the DM Client attempts to initiate a management session with the DM Server. Using bootstrap information, the device connects to the device management server and retrieves all the required credentials to establish communication with the data management platform. The certificates are shared securely between the device and device management server to protect the integrity and confidentiality of the information. Each device must have the respective pre-configured trusted CA certificates in order to authenticate device identity during initiation with the platform. The credentials are stored in the Hardware Secure Module (HSM) or secured local certification store or secure element of the devices. The downloaded certificates and keys are preloaded in the HSM. As soon as the device boots, it can access and verify using defined API's. In local file system-based storage, the device accesses the certificates internally and validate. The device management along with PKI maintains the certificate validity and permissions. The certificate can be made valid for either a long time or a short time. It also helps the device management to remotely revoke the permissions and decommission if required. Two common approaches, namely single-device provisioning and bulk provisioning, are commonly adopted in the industries for device provisioning.

- *Single-device provisioning*

In single-device provisioning, a single device is used at a time and the required credentials are provisioned. The device management server registers and provisions the device when it tries to connect for the first time with the required credentials. The device should get all the relevant certificates and keys from the device management server, authenticate, and connect to the data platform before ingesting the data. When the business need does not arise to provision multiple devices simultaneously, single-device provisioning method can be preferred as it helps to provision the devices and things one by one.

- *Bulk provisioning*

Bulk provisioning enables multiple devices to be registered and on boarded at one shot. The credentials and characteristics of the devices/things are collected and provisioned with device management. This strategy facilitates the devices to connect, authenticate, and stream the data. The bulk provisioning approach is more suitable if the properties of a large number of devices are known in advance.

Few challenges are foreseen in certificate generation, and provisioning and onboarding the devices. The following strategies are recommended to overcome the challenges:

1. The PKI and Device Management should support certification generation at IoT scale and speed.
2. The IoT ecosystem should support secure protocol to establish communication between IoT remote devices and platform. IoT devices should be protected from man-in-the-middle attack.
3. The certificate should have individual IoT device unique credentials to bind and enforce the rules and policies.

Continuous Device Monitoring and Diagnostics

Since the deployment of IoT devices has scaled to billions, centralized management of network is not viable to manage IoT devices. Continuous remote device monitoring is a crucial aspect of IoT device deployment but it helps to carry out diagnosis, take remedial measures in advance, minimizes downtime, avoids unplanned downtime, and improves the operation efficiency. IoT devices and sensors are deployed in the industrial environment and remote areas. It is difficult to manually track, monitor, check and diagnose the issues. Monitoring and implementing corrections on remote IoT devices differ from monitoring conventional network and endpoint devices.

Access to administrative audit logs, device profiling information, network connectivity diagnostic logs, and software catalogs is important for effectively locating and troubleshooting the issues. The device management server can query the individual devices about the present device condition, state, and device profile information. The device management server keeps track of the device counts and the working state of the individual devices and sensors. Queries are sent to the underlying devices/sensors via supporting protocols. Also the server can enable/disable and enforce specific policies to the devices remotely. Information on configuration and capabilities of the devices is kept as device profiling metrics and stored in data fields in the end devices. Device monitoring and diagnostics are explained through a graphic in Figure 6.

It may be required to audit the devices periodically in order to maintain security and compliance. Device management server retrieves the information periodically from devices or device pushes on event basis. The following information is generally retrieved from the devices:

- Device type
- Device unique identity/Serial number
- Operating system and applications version information
- Device hardware/software/communication capabilities

- List of installed applications, libraries
- Connectivity/application configuration
- Event/performance logs
- Power usage statistics
- Memory/processing capabilities of the device
- Hardware/software stack capabilities

Figure 6. Device Monitoring and Diagnostics

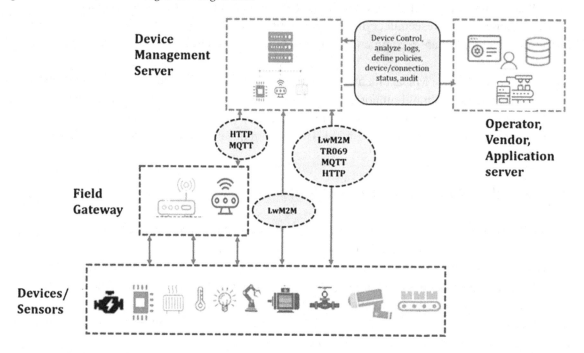

The auditing information is fetched by device management application or third-party system for visualization and analysis. In the case of IoT devices deployed in factories and remote environments, event/performance logs help the device managers/vendors to remotely diagnose the issues with the devices and act accordingly. It leads to maximize device uptime, quickly fix the unhealthy devices and reduce operational expenses. Device management also monitors the network connectivity out-of-the-box and the status and switches to different connectivity channels as and when required. It maps appropriate Personal/Wide Area Network and based on the network availabilities manages required credentials and monitors the key network parameters for connection status.

Remote Configuration and Upgrade

Remote configuration is one of the key functionalities of the device management system. It largely helps the device operators and vendors to configure software, libraries, and applications. The devices are deployed across the globe and sometimes in remote factory environments. Deployed devices need to run with updated, secured, latest software/firmware to keep pace with the environment. The layout of the software update and upgrade is presented in Figure 7.

Figure 7. Software update and upgrade

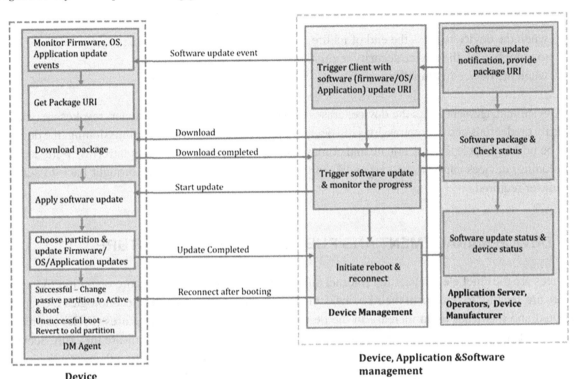

New configurations, software updates and upgrades are applied to IoT devices either directly or broadcasting the configuration link to the devices in bulk. The activity 'software update and upgrade' includes heartbeat interval configuration, authentication/authorization parameter definitions, data platform URL's, and framing new rules and policies. It also continuously monitors the latest version of the software from the server and updates in the device node. Device management seamlessly updates remotely placed device peripherals firmware, operating system secure patches, application updates, big fixes, and new features over the air without any manual intervention. Dynamic rollouts need to be staged across a device group to ensure high reliability irrespective of connectivity issues. Devices with similar properties need to be grouped to automate the tasks. In IoT deployments, it is inevitable to apply software configurations at scale to reduce operational burden and security vulnerability. The updates could be applied using appropriate management protocols.

Decommissioning

Decommissioning is part of IoT device life cycle to unbind the devices from the service. Device management helps to revoke the credentials from the remotely located devices and detach the devices from the platform. Device decommissioning is implemented

a. when the device reaches the end of its life
b. to comply with the device security regulations
c. when the device malfunctions

Device management locks the device, erases sensitive data in a secured manner, revokes associated security credentials and decommissions the device from its service. After decommissioning, the devices will be no longer able to authenticate and communicate with peer devices and platforms. With decommissioning, devices can also be suspended for specific periods of time and brought back to service whenever required.

IoT DEVICE MANAGEMENT AND PUBLIC KEY INFRASTRUCTURE

Devices are the chief elements of the Internet and need digital identities for secure operation. As enterprises are seeking to transform their business models to stay competitive, IoT technologies are rapidly adopted and this leads to an increase in the demand for Public Key Infrastructures (PKIs) to provide digital certificates for the growing number of devices and the software and firmware they run. Security credentials for authentication, authorization, and encryption are essential to ensure the protection of the devices and security of the data at transit and rest (Bertino & Islam, 2017).

IoT devices are globally distributed and deployed in remote locations. It is highly critical to ensure that certificates are provisioned securely, periodically refreshed with updated policies, and revoked based on needs. The management of signed credentials and keys are taken care of by the public key infrastructure environment. After IoT deployment, large infrastructure is required to manage certificates over a long period. IoT **ecosystem** leverages standards-based PKI to authenticate and establish trust between devices and services (e.g., cloud platforms), and ensure the integrity, source and encryption of all data transmitted within the IoT ecosystem. PKI facilitates the secure transfer of information across networks and makes it a clear solution for IoT service providers to ensure proper data security, authentication, and mutual trust (Slovetskiy et al., 2018).

When a device connects to the network, it must authenticate to establish trust between other devices, services and users. Once trust is established, devices, users and services can securely communicate the information. The functions of Public Key Infrastructure (PKI) in IoT system are listed below:

- Embeds the certificates to identify devices and make secure connections by establishing a strong trust among devices, services and users.
- Uses short-lived certificates in case there is a compromise.
- Provides strong authentication between users and devices in IoT.
- A strong cryptographic encryption mechanism tied to a device identity ensures that data is encrypted and authentic, and communications are secure.

- Provides the essential methods for strong cryptographic encryption and ensures private communication.
- Provides support for a wide variety of devices, sensors, and things in IoT ecosystem.
- Provides assurance that data have not been altered during transit.
- Provides authorization and digital integrity by digitally signing documents, emails, and various other types of data.
- Increases trust in the data being received from devices and in the results of data analysis.

DEVICE MANAGEMENT AND SECURITY

Security is a vital aspect of Internet of Things (IoT) ecosystem. IoT deals with millions of devices, a multitude of platforms, and a variety of streaming and stored data. Securing billions of devices and huge data in IoT is really a challenge and many technologies are in place to keep in secure the IoT system in every layer. IoT endpoints need to be protected to prevent hackers from gaining entry. Security breaches at device level are more challenging in situations where the end devices and sensors are installed in remote locations and it leads to severe consequences including business loss and losing customer confidence. Certificates from PKI are used for device identity, authentication, and registration. Data security at transit and rest helps to achieve end-to-end data confidentiality and integrity. IoT devices leverage private and public keys for encrypting data.

Device manufacturers and system developers must ensure that relevant certificates and keys are retrieved and stored securely in the device. In respect of static/fixed credentials, the manufacturers can embed or provision them during manufacturing or deployment respectively. However, in most of the cases, the devices are heterogeneous in nature and require ad-hoc certificate installation and configuration. It is not financially viable and cost-effective to update and configure credentials individually while devices are installed and operating in a remote environment.

Best Security Practices

Best security practices are prescribed below:

- Rolling the certificates
- Keeping proper public key infrastructure for key generation, management, and revocation

DEVICE MANAGEMENT STANDARDS AND PROTOCOLS

Device management for constrained IoT devices is still evolving. Open Mobile Alliance is developing LwM2M for constrained remote device management. Defined, standardized industry norms are available for device management in fixed network broadband devices, enterprise IP networks, mobile phones, and gateways. TR-069 is widely used for managing devices in the broadband category, SNMP is used for IP network devices and OMA-DM is employed for mobile phones and gateways. However, the standards are not fully suitable for IoT device management as most of the IoT devices are constrained in terms of power, memory, processing, and network capabilities. OMA LwM2M (Chang & Lin, 2016) is a prime, evolving device management standard for making interoperable IoT devices. LWM2M holds key interoperability standards in its specifications as compared to MQTT which lacks application layer inter-operability (Rao et al., n.d.). The LWM2M client specifications come with few already defined objects and resources along with the provision of defining specific objects after registering with Open Mobile Naming Authority (OMNA). It is based on the Constrained Application Protocol (CoAP) and utilizes Datagram Transport Layer Security (DTLS) as its main security mechanism.

1. TR- 069

TR-069 is a Wide Area Network device management protocol for the Customer premise equipment (CPE) defined by the Broadband Forum. TR-069 helps the Automated Configuration Server (ACS) to initiate the connection and understand the device parameters such as device type, manufacturer information, unique identification number and capabilities. It also tracks the real-time status of the device by monitoring the heartbeat. Bidirectional SOAP/HTTP is used for remote management of remote devices. TR-69 Meets the device management needs of internet access devices, Media & communication devices that are installed on a customer premise (Routers, IPTV STBs, ATA, IP Phones, femtocells, small cells, dongles, storage devices, mobile hotspots).

TR-69 provides the device management functionalities includes

- Remote configuration of devices
- Dynamic service provisioning
- Firmware image management
- Software module management
- Remote performance monitoring and diagnostics.

TR-69 protocol implementation leverages Remote Procedure call (RPC) on devices through of HTTP (S) and SOAP.

2. OMA -DM

OMA-DM (Device Management) standard was developed by the Open Mobile Alliance to ideally manage mobile devices (Vermillard, 2015). It also suits to manage IoT devices which are IP enabled. Technical specifications defined by OMA basically for the remote device management operations for high-end devices like consumer electronics, Automobile etc. mostly used for initial device provisioning, service provisioning, processing events and alarms apart from other trivial device management operations. OMA uses the protocol to define the device provisioning objects is referred to as SyncML(Synchronization Markup Language). SyncML is the platform-independent data synchronization and device management standard. Post device provisioning, the device can be monitored, tracked and configured remotely by the OMA-DM server. OMA-DM is transport agnostic – transport can be HTTP(s), WAP, SMS. OMA-DM is not optimized to address the IoT node's device management challenges.

3. OMA – LWM2M

OMA Lightweight M2M (LwM2M), the standard developed by Open Mobile Alliance (OMA), is a light, fast and structured protocol, ideal for low-capacity devices. The standard basically developed to address the IoT M2M device management challenges by extending the OMA-DM beyond the gateway to reach the sensor level (IoT Device Management Protocols, 2019). LwM2M created to serve the IoT market with a focus on lightweight nature. LWM2M is applicable to various radio technologies with IP and non-IP devices. LwM2M extensible object model and registry open to the whole industry and enables both management and application data handling with the same solution. It addresses the security need for software updates and device re-configuration.

It supports different bootstrap modes such as

- Factory bootstrap
- Bootstrap from smartcard
- Client initiated bootstrap
- Server initiated bootstrap

LwM2M was designed especially for resource-constrained devices (although basically any device can be managed via LwM2M). The standard is also quite effective over unstable connections and low bandwidth networks such as sensor or cellular networks. The communication between the client and the server is based on User Datagram Protocol (UDP) working over the Constrained Application Protocol (CoAP) with the support of data formats such as Type-Length-Value (TLV) which enable fast parsing and small data size.

LwM2M utilizes Datagram Transport Layer Security (DTLS) as its security protocol to ensure authentication, confidentiality and data integrity. The big role in security mechanisms in LwM2M plays the bootstrapping interface which offers bootstrap modes responsible for provisioning devices with essential information that would later on enable the client (device) to perform registration with the server and start the communication flow between them. Technical specification defined by OMA for Internet of 'Things'. i.e., Constrained IoT devices with a low foot print of memory and limited processing power. It has low client footprint and consume less power. It is also suitable for both fixed and mobile devices. The expected growth of IoT device deployment will go around 22 billion by 2024. It is highly critical to have end to end security embedded along with device management. LwM2M uses OSCORE (Object Security for Constrained RESTful Environments), new lightweight IoT security protocol specifically designed to address constrained nodes.

4. CoAP (Constrained Application Protocol):

CoAP is a one-to-one protocol uses UDP as underlying transport protocol helps event-based data transfer with high reliable, low overhead (Shelby et al., 2014). CoAP provides a request and response communications model and supports seamless end-to-end communication at the application level between constrained IoT devices and peer devices/Gateways. It works like HTTP in order to benefit from existing web-based technologies using the same methods (GET, PUT, POST, and DELETE) as HTTP, but with an additional ability for resource discovery and observation (Bormann et al., 2015).

The Connect service communicates with devices over CoAP, a specialized communication protocol for use with constrained nodes and constrained networks in the Internet of Things. Through the service, the Device management can communicate with the device, register and deregister devices and subscribe to resources to receive notifications. The service supports both real-time and proxied communication with devices and uses LwM2M resources to organize the communications.

5. Custom Device Management

In order to benefit from device management, devices need to be managed devices. An unmanaged device is configured to purely send the uplink data to the platform whereas a managed device has a piece of code called a device management agent which exchanges special device management messages between the IoT platform and the device over MQTT (Message Queueing Telemetry Transport) and HTTP (Hyper Text Transfer Protocol). MQTT is a highly reliable transport, uses TCP/IP, specifically designed for low power, constrained devices telemetry data transfer best suited for sensor data communication. MQTT is an ideal messaging protocol for IoT and M2M communications.

In custom device management a template is defined by the platform vendor/DM server and the platform vendor expects the device maker to embed an agent/jobs based on that template in the device. In this way the platform/DM server can remotely invoke the jobs from the platform (DM server) -the device receives the commands through the platform defined agent/job. The Jobs in turn call the native APIs in the device to do the device management operation. So, in custom device management, the device is deeply coupled with the platform. This is a model that can be adopted only in B2B business (enterprise IoT) where the platform vendor may enter into a partnership with an enterprise (and devices/things in the enterprise are connected to platform). Many platforms (like Watson, AWS) that are primarily designed for enterprise business (Uplink data collection, provide value add through analytics, then provide cognitive applications based on the data collected etc.) don't align with device management standards and don't support Device management natively.

In the IoT, a standard that is often mentioned alongside LwM2M is the Message Queuing Telemetry Transport (MQTT). MQTT has also been created with resource-constrained devices in mind. It is a publish /subscribe messaging protocol suited for low-bandwidth and unreliable networks. Unlike LwM2M, it has continuous session awareness due to the use of the Transmission Control Protocol (TCP) as a delivery protocol. TCP is generally considered to be a more reliable way of communication. In some IoT deployments, especially ones that involve resource-constrained devices, UDP is valued more due to its light weightiness and faster transmission of packets. What is worth mentioning is that the data model in MQTT is undefined and is usually specific to project or vendor requirements. Due to such flexibility, for example in the choice of payload, MQTT can be quite lightweight. It must be noted, however, that LwM2M is still going to have a smaller payload thanks to data types like TLV and the use of User Datagram Protocol (UDP) as a transport layer.

Despite being a very light and compact protocol with link consumption smaller than MQTT, LwM2M offers much stronger security mechanisms determined by very strict requirements. Although in MQTT it is recommended to use encryption and authentication via Transport Layer Security (TLS), this has a considerable impact on the link consumption and client's performance. Finally, it is important to note that MQTT is an M2M connectivity protocol rather than a device management standard. Due to its undefined semantics, MQTT, similarly to proprietary solutions such as Amazon Web Services (AWS), has mechanisms that ensure successful implementations but lead to proprietary lock-in situation where customers are dependent on vendor-specific products and services.

Table 1. Differences among different device management protocols

Protocol	OMA DM	TR 69	OMA LwM2M	MQTT
Architecture	Heavier	Heavier	Lighter	Lighter
Intend	Device management for consumer devices	Device management for broadband devices	Device management for telemetry devices	Telemetry data payload
Data model	Well Defined	Well defined	Well defined (OMNA, IPSO, GSMA)	Not defined. vendor and platform specific
Data model complexity	Complex Management Objects	Complex Management Objects	Simple, flat objects with uniform URI	No standardized data model
Data transfer velocity	slow	slow	Fast	real time
Message overhead	100s of bytes		10s of bytes	2 bytes
Message format	XML	XML	TLV, JSON	JSON, XML, encrypted binary, Base64
Transport	HTTP, WSP and OBEX bindings over TCP/UDP	SOAP/HTTP over TCP	CoAP over UDP and SMS bindings	MQTT Over TCP/UDP
Suitability	High end consumer devices	Broadband devices, Gateways	resource-constrained devices, sensors & powerful devices	Low power, constrained devices, Sensors
Response time	slow	slow	Fast	real time
Security	Native support to certificate & key based authentication	Native support to certificate & key based authentication	Native support to certificate & key based authentication	No native support. Enabling TLS adds network overhead and poor performance
Application layer security for constrain node	Not available	Not available	Support using OSCORE	Not available
Use case verticals	Mobile & consumer devices, Gateways	Customer Premises Equipment's, IoT gateways	Complex, large scale, heterogenous, long term IoT deployments	Simple, low variability without auto discovery IoT deployments
Interoperability support	Yes	Yes	Yes	No
Device management operation	Platform independent	Platform independent	Platform independent	Platform dependent (Vendor lock-in)
Lock &wipe	Yes	No	Yes	No
Memory footprint	High	High	Low	Low
Standard object for Bootstrap, Firmware update	Yes	Yes	Yes	No

Device Management Protocols Comparison

The following Table 1 outlines the differences among different device management protocols.

Device Management Standards and IoT Industry Verticals:

Sensors and devices used in numerous industry verticals. IoT enabled real time connectivity between sensors/devices to the gateway to the platform. Multitude of communication, transport protocols, standards used in IoT ecosystem to satisfy the real requirements of industries such as manufacturing, transport, building, utility, smart home, healthcare, agriculture etc. Table 2 provides the different industrial applications and its support to the standard device management capabilities.

Table 2. Different industrial applications and device management capabilities

Industry	Device OEM's DM agent (Industry standards)	Industry Interop	Mode of Transport	Device Management server	Native support Watson	Native support AWS	Native support Azure
All verticals that uses Constrained Devices	OMA LWM2M	Yes	IP, SMS, non-IP (LoRa, NB-IoT)	OMA LWM2M Server	No	No	Yes (through Adapter)
Consumer Electronics	OMA DM, OMA LWM2M	Yes	IP	OMA DM server, OMA LWM2M server	No	No	Yes
Automobiles/ Connected vehicles	OMA DM, OMA LWM2M	Yes	IP	OMA DM server, OMA LWM2M server	No	No	Yes
Media & communication	TR-69	Yes	IP	TR-69 server/ACS server	No	No	No
Industrial & Manufacturing	OPC UA agent (OPC server)	Yes	IP	DM server (OPC client)	No	Yes	Yes
Building &facilities	Bacnet agent (backnet server)	Yes		DM server (bacnet client)	No	No	No
Energy & Utilities	DLSM cosem agent, WI-SUN alliance/ LWM2M	Yes	IP	DLSM COSEM server	No	No	No

DEVICE MANAGEMENT IN ENTERPRISE (ENTERPRISE MOBILITY MANAGEMENT & BYOD)

Device Management Tools

Multiple systems in business add complexity in maintaining and managing the systems. Managing end devices in a separate environment requires individual administration, policy management and high cost. The organization needs consolidated management of devices and platforms using a single solution. Endpoints are desktop computers, laptops, tablets, smartphones, ruggedized devices, wearables and the Internet of Things (IoT)

This section briefs the widely used device and application management platform/tools for managing the proliferation of devices and sensors. There are many platforms available in the market for the efficient management of devices and applications. The leading platforms, tools, compliance and relevant deployment supports are captured.

IBM MaaS360

IBM MaaS360 is a comprehensive unified endpoint management framework and it is an opt fit for enterprises that want to maintain end to end device management and security. MaaS360 also provides application management and software distribution capabilities across the deployments. It is one of the most feature rich client management solutions, able to integrate with security platform like BigFix. It offers functionalities such as

- Management of BYOD and enterprise-issued devices
- Device state, compliance, audit, standard enforcement, violation detection and action
- Decommission of devices
- Handle lost, stolen and compromised devices
- Over the Air (OTA) update
- Application deployment, monitor and policy compliance
- Security and document management capabilities
- Advanced mobile threat detection and remediation capabilities
- Lock & Wipe
- Content access restriction and life cycle management

VMWare Airwatch

VMWare's Airwatch is one of the leading device management solutions available in the market. It manages devices across all the operating systems, seamless management of device operations, secure access to application portfolios and enforces policy, compliance. It streamlines the application deployment, configuration and patching. It clearly draws a boundary between privileged applications, data from personal applications. The ability of Airwatch platform to automate the device enrollment, monitoring and update reduces the manual task and improves operational efficiency.

Cisco Meraki

Cisco Meraki is a cloud-based management solution that aims to manage unified endpoint devices across different operating systems. It manages the life cycle of the devices including policy enforcement, remotely deploying software, applications, remote configuration, troubleshooting over the network without affecting the normal data flow. It realizes with detection of threat visibility and control, granular access control and analyzes the network activity.

Leshan:

Leshan is a simple, set of modular java libraries to implement OMA LwM2M server and client functionalities. Leshan has standalone LwM2M and LwM2M bootstrap servers. The CoAP and DTLS implementation are based on Californium and Scandium respectively. It provides IPSO based object support. The implementation can run on java supported devices and servers. The supported functionalities include

- Bootstrap - Create, read, update and delete client configurations
- Client
- Read& Write object, object instance information
- Read, write, and execute resources
- Start object, object instance and resource observations
- Event
- Server triggered event notification for registration, update and notifications
- Security Credentials
- Create, read, update, revoke and delete client credentials

Wakaama

Wakaama is C implementation of LwM2M server and Client. It is embedded friendly, designed for POSIX compliant systems. It can run on constrained devices to OS enabled devices. It built top of CoAP, allows to plugin 3rd party IP and DLTS stack. The basic functionalities of Wakaama include

- LWM2M Server
- Access Control
- Device, Connectivity
- Firmware Update
- Location update
- Connectivity Statistics

ARM Pelion

Arm Pelion is an IoT platform for managing connectivity, devices and data. The solution is compliant with OMA LwM2M specification and mange devices across all ranges including ultra-constrained, constrained, mainstream and rich processing devices like gateways. It provides

- Secure onboarding
- Device Provisioning
- over-the-air updates
- Device lifecycle management
- Support for ARM embed and 3rd party OS
- Deployment options including on-premise, public and private cloud, and hybrid environments

IoT PLATFORMS DEVICE MANAGEMENT SUPPORT

IoT Device Management in AWS

In AWS there is native support for a custom device management service. AWS device a management supports MQTT as device management protocol between devices and platforms (AWS Device Management, 2019). Device management is tightly coupled with the AWS platform. It helps to securely onboard, organize, monitor and real-time tracking of tiny sensors to rich processing IoT devices at scale. The devices are dynamically registered in bulk or one at a time, provisioned and organize the devices into a group based on properties. It continuously monitors and updates the firmware/software over-the-air (OTA). Device Agnostic AWS IoT device management manages a fleet of ultra-constrained devices to rich IoT devices such as connected cars.

AWS device management service provides

- Device onboarding – Register & onboard bulk devices, enable, assign credentials to the devices
- Device organization - Organize devices into groups and manage access policies.
- Remote device management - Remote monitoring, update firmware/software, patching and reboot on the deployed devices
- Search & Find - Search and find deployed IoT device using attributes or device availability in near real-time.

IoT Device Management in Azure

IoT device landscape consists of heterogeneous devices with a multitude of communication technologies, diversity of hardware options, environments, operating systems and programming languages. Cloud and IoT platform should be able to connect, monitor millions of devices without compromising security and privacy. The device management protocols enable seamless management of devices by abstracting the underlying complexity and ensure collecting and controlling the devices. Azure IoT platform offers device management as a service for provisioning and common device management operations (Azure IoT Device Management, 2019).

Microsoft Azure provides numerous services to onboard, connect and control a multitude of IoT devices, data ingestion and analysis. The device management platform is fully aligned with device management standards as it is working multiple OEMs as the OS vendor and hence interoperability is the key in their DNA. Azure provides IoT service to register, onboard, maintain a list of devices and provides access to a device. It supports IoT device-to-cloud, cloud-to-device communication using AMQP, HTTP and MQTT protocols. The device management uses customized, vendor-specific options using MQTT/AMQP.

Azure IoT natively supports MQTT, AMQP and HTTPS protocol for data communication and device management. It also supports LwM2M for device management through an adapter. A protocol translator acts in between the deployed LwM2M server and IoT hub for conversion and it helps to smooth message passing between LwM2M client and Azure IoT. Azure IoT leverage LwM2M standardized device management and community support to manage the growing number of IoT fleet of devices.

The key device management functionalities supported by azure are

- Zero touch device registration and rapid provisioning of devices rapidly (single, fleet of devices)

- Device authentication, authorization and policies
- Device configuration and update
- Containerized software update

IoT Device Management in Google Cloud Platform

Google Cloud Platform supports device-to-cloud messaging using Publish/Subscribe method (MQTT), large scale message ingestion using REST over HTTP. Google platform provides managed services for IoT device connectivity, control and data ingestion. Device management functionalities such as device registration, maintain device metadata, authentication, authorization, policies, device grouping, and remote configuration are taken care of by the device manager. The device communicates with device manager using standardized REST interfaces or gCloud commands. Device Manager can be accessed as part of IoT device management, Google Cloud Platform also provides service to monitor the devices, collects the logs of different events, analyze and derive the metrics from the collected data which helps for diagnosis and provide fixes. It also supports OTA update to the scale of deployed IoT devices with various options including inbuilt Android things-based OTA or custom Debian package or container-based image update.

IBM Watson Device Management

IBM Watch manages a fleet of devices and gateways by categorizing them into two device classes. The devices classified either managed or unmanaged devices. The device with a running device management agent is defined as managed devices. The agent recognizes the commands from Watson IoT device management server, sends and receives device capabilities for seamless enrollment. Managed devices perform the device management operations between platform and agent using MQTT as a device management protocol with custom, vendor specific operations. Watson IoT platform creates device model and stores the basic device instance metadata and properties. It updates the database based on the status, events, updates received from the end device. The stored details in the database can be retrieved by the application. The supported operations are

- Device enrollment
- Firmware update
- Remote device configuration
- Remote device reboot & reset
- Event notification
- Location update
- Device decommissioning

The devices can join device management activities with Watson IoT platform by sending a request to the platform. It can also send a message to the platform when it no longer needs to be managed and to become an unmanaged device. The device model in the database cannot be updated by the unmanaged device cannot directly update its device model in the database

Table 3. Different Device management tools

Tool	Device Management Agent	Device Management Server	Deployment
IBM MaaS360	OMA DM complaint	OMA DM complaint	Digital work place management, Enterprise Mobility Management/BYOD, Laptops, Tablets, Mobile phones
VMWARE Airwatch	OMA DM complaint	OMA DM complaint	Digital workplace management, Enterprise Mobility Management/BYOD, laptops, tablets, mobile phones
Cisco Meraki	OMA DM complaint	OMA DM complaint	Digital workplace management, Enterprise Mobility Management/BYOD, laptops, tablets, mobile phones
Leshan	OMA LWM2M	OMA LWM2M	IoT end point Device
Wakaama	OMA LwM2M	OMA LwM2M	IoT end point constrained devices
ARM Pelion	LWM2M, TR-69	LWM2M, TR-69	
Azure Device management	MQTT, OMA LWM2M	MQTT, OMA LWM2M	IoT end point devices, Gateways
AWS Device Management	MQTT	MQTT	Telemetry devices, Gateways
Google IoT Device Management	HTTPS	HTTPS	Telemetry devices, Gateways
Watson IoT Device Management	MQTT	MQTT	Telemetry devices, Gateways
IMPACT Device Server (Nokia)	OMA DM, OMA LWM2M, TR-69	OMA DM, OMA LWM2M, TR-69	Telco IoT platform to support multiple devices connected to a telecom operator

IMPACT Device Server (Nokia)

Nokia's intelligent management platform for all connected things (IMPACT) is a comprehensive IoT platform for connection, data and device management. IMPACT Device Manager (IDM) is a device manager for managing mobile, IoT and home gateway devices. It has vast support over 80 thousand diverse device models over different manufacturers and on the top, it supports to able to add/onboard new device models. In compliance with Lightweight M2M (LWM2M), OMA-DM and TR-069 are the industry standards for device management. The key features of the solution include

- Device Provisioning & Management:
  ○ Device discovery
  ○ Firmware & software update,
  ○ Device reset/reboot
  ○ Remote control & configuration
- Multiple Deployment Models: Cloud/SaaS, On-premise
- Rich APIs for integration (northbound & southbound)
- Industry leading Device certification

The Table 3 lists the different Device management tools in the market to manage enterprise device management and its standard compatibility.

IoT DEVICE MANAGEMENT CHALLENGES

Device Heterogeneity

IoT ecosystem comprises billions of tiny sensors, things, devices, gateways with different hardware, software, network and connectivity protocols. It is a huge challenge to monitor the remote, distributed devices with a multitude of capabilities. Interoperability between devices and protocols is difficult especially the devices using vendor-specific or custom protocols. The key challenges are

- Devices with multiple firmware and software versions
- Deployment of software, dependencies required for edge processing
- Interoperability among constrained, IP based and non-IP based devices
- Tracking device status and ensuring security at the IoT edge node/sensors

Lack of standards and Interoperability, multiple hardware vendors, industry service providers and agencies are deploying billions of sensors to innovate, automate the process and improve business efficiency. However, there is no common standard and interoperability across systems leads to difficulties in device management and communication. Even though LwM2M is evolving as a suitable device management standard for IoT, it is not completely adopted by the industry players. Most of the players still use customized, vendor-specific device management to manage IoT device ecosystem which leads to a lack of interoperability across the ecosystem and lock-in to the specific vendor and platforms.

Deployment at Large Scale

IoT deployment is kept growing exponentially and reaches around 20 billion connected devices by 2020. IoT will become a major factor contributing to the economy by transforming a conventional business into digital-enabled business models. Managing devices at a very large scale are really complex and challenging, considering the diverse communication technologies, multiple vendors, service providers and different standards. The device management and standards should support to manage and dynamically scale when IoT device deployment grows.

Security

Security is a vital aspect of IoT, and device management helps to secure communication between the device and the platform. The device hardware and software stack should capable of supporting adequate security measures. IoT devices are often constrained and have limited memory, processing power and connectivity which limits their security capabilities. It is important to choose sensors, devices capable of storing credentials securely and able to update firmware, software periodically. Also, device management must check the vulnerability to a security breach and revoke, decommission if the devices are compromised.

Selection of Proper Tool/Framework

It is highly important to select the appropriate device management tools/framework based on the device diversity, capability, protocol support, power constrain, tool, services capabilities and business need. The service providers can analyze their specific needs and choose out-band or in-band management options. Out-band management helps to seamlessly switch the device connectivity with multiple platforms, however in-bank management lock-in to the platform. The tool/service should have the capability to support feature demands such as on-boarding device dynamically, bulk onboard and horizontal scalability.

Issue With IP and Non-IP Sensors

IoT ecosystem consists of different capability devices and sensors. It is really hard to manage IoT devices, sensors of IP enabled and non-IP sensors. The tool and framework should be able to manage devices in public, private networks with and without IP. Most of the time, the non-IP devices depend on the edge gateway for connectivity and management. Service providers should choose a comprehensive framework to manage devices based on the sensor's capabilities and deployment scenarios.

Context Awareness

Near real-time detection of security threats and breaches helps to avoid downtime and critical business operations. At large scale deployment, the devices and device management service should aware of the context and act accordingly. However, it becomes tough for the device management to monitor all the remotely deployed devices in near real-time and act on the events. The device should keep informing about device state, device geolocation, network and power states. Many times, the devices are not aware of the context and still operating without informing/posting the event at the right time.

Protocol Support

With lack of standardization among hardware vendors, OEM's and service providers, the common protocol for device management is not streamlined. The service providers find a hard time in selecting appropriate devices with device management protocol support for their business need. Most of the time, the custom configuration, programming and flashing required to onboard the new devices to the fleet.

Constrained Device Capabilities

Monitoring and managing constrained device IoT devices are really a challenge. The device management is depending on the device's ability to run a device management agent, protocol support, remote connectivity event triggering and log storage feasibility. Because of low processing ability, footprint and power capability, the devices may not support complete life cycle of the device management features. The device credentials at the device should be stored securely and ensure that the device is not compromised at any cost.

FUTURE DIRECTION

In today's IoT ecosystem, there is no standard followed in device management implementation. Many IoT device vendors and solution provides implement closed device management solution and few others implement loosely coupled device management approach. Closed device management helps to increase vendor market presence and business potential. However tightly coupled device management created customers are being locked to the same vendor and create customers inertia. It is difficult to choose different applications or service providers.

Loosely coupled device management allows customers to use multi-vendor devices for the ecosystem. The consumer can make use of devices from heterogeneous suppliers, vendors and seamlessly onboard the new devices in the ecosystem. There is no standard between device ecosystem and software platform, which may have incompatibility while changing one platform to another platform.

As IoT ecosystem grows exponentially, it is very essential to have a common standard in device management for efficient onboarding from a multitude of devices and better interoperability across devices, software platforms and applications. The standard should make different IoT Devices firmware, software; operating systems are managed with the help of standardized methods. It should make sure the entire device vendor supports a common interface for the device management system.

Open Mobile Alliance's Device Management (OMA-DM) and Lightweight Machine-to-Machine (OMA LWM2M) attempt to create an open device management ecosystem for IoT. The device manufacturers, service, network and application providers need to adopt the standards and collaborate closely with each other's. It eliminates the consumer is being tightly coupled with specific vendors and service providers (Open Mobile Alliance, 2016).

Another important aspect is to have a device management agent to be run in devices which consume device memory, compute and power. Also, device management is mostly designed to deal with IP enabled devices. In the IoT world lot of non-IP devices present which are difficult in enrolling in open device management. Also, power management is very crucial in few IoT applications and adapting to the normal device management consumes a lot of power which leads to device failure.

CONCLUSION

It is very critical for enterprises and service providers to select feasibly, optimum device management platform at the start of their journey to an onboard fleet of devices and management. The platform should be capable of supporting heterogeneity, diversity of devices, protocols to the entire life cycle and cope up with the evolving IoT landscape. In this chapter, we have elaborately discussed the importance of IoT device management, device management functionalities, protocols, standards and challenges. We also discussed the predominately used device management protocols in IoT device landscape and outlined differences. More specifically, we have elaborately discussed widely used device and application management platforms/tools for managing the proliferation of devices, sensors. As per our interpretation, IoT device management is continuing to evolve, OEM's service and platform provides to move towards adapting LwM2M standards in the future to support interoperability across IoT systems.

REFERENCES

Antonia, C., Putera, L., & Lin, F. J. (2015). Incorporating OMA Lightweight M2M protocol in IoT/M2M standard architecture. *IEEE 2nd World Forum on Internet of Things (WF-IoT)*, 559–564.

AWS Device Management. (2019). Retrieved from https://aws.amazon.com/iot-device-management/

Azure IoT Device Management. (2019). Retrieved from https://docs.microsoft.com/en-us/azure/iot-hub/iot-hub-device-management-overview

Bertino, E., & Islam, N. (2017). Botnets and Internet of Things Security. *Computer, IEEE, 50*(2), 76–79. doi:10.1109/MC.2017.62

Bormann, C., Hartke, K., & Shelby, Z. (2015). *The Constrained Application Protocol (CoAP)*. RFC 7252. https://www.rfc-editor.org/rfc/rfc7252.txt

Chang, W.-G., & Lin, F. J. (2016). Challenges of incorporating OMA LWM2M gateway in M2M standard architecture. *IEEE Conference on Standards for Communications and Networking (CSCN)*, 1–6. 10.1109/CSCN.2016.7785166

Ha, M., & Lindh, T. (2018). Enabling Dynamic and Lightweight Management of Distributed Bluetooth Low Energy Devices. *International Conference on Computing, Networking and Communications (ICNC): Wireless Ad hoc and Sensor Networks*, 615-619. 10.1109/ICCNC.2018.8390355

IoT Device Management Protocols: LwM2M, OMA-DM and TR-069. (2019). https://www.muutech.com/en/iot-device-management-protocols-lwm2m-oma-dm-and-tr-069

Kesavan, S., & Kalambettu, G. K. (2018). IOT enabled comprehensive, plug and play gateway framework for smart health. *International Conference on Advances in Electronics, Computers and Communications (ICAECC)*, 1-5. 10.1109/ICAECC.2018.8479431

Open Mobile Alliance. (2016). *OMA Device Management Protocol*. http://www.openmobilealliance.org/release/DM/V2_0-20160209-A/OMA-TS-DM_Protocol-V2_0-20160209-A.pdf

Open Mobile Alliance. (2019). *Lightweight Machine to Machine Technical Specification*. http://www.openmobilealliance.org/release/LightweightM2M/Lightweight_Machine_to_Machine-v1_1-OMASpecworks.pdf

Pritikin, M., Richardson, M., Behringer, M., Bjarnason, S., & Watsen, K. (2018). *Bootstrapping Remote Secure Key Infrastructures (BRSKI)*. Internet-Draft draft-ietf-anima-bootstrapping-keyinfra-16.

Rao, S., Chendanda, D., Deshpande, C., & Lakkundi, V. (n.d.). Implementing LWM2M in Constrained IoT Devices. *IEEE Conference on Wireless Sensors (ICWiSe)*, 52–57. 10.1109/ICWISE.2015.7380353

Sarikaya, B., Sethi, M., & Garcia-Carillo, D. (2018). *Secure IoT Bootstrapping: A Survey* https://tools.ietf.org/id/draft-sarikaya-t2trg-sbootstrapping-05.html

Shelby, Z., Hartke, K., & Bormann, C. (2014). *The Constrained Application Protocol (CoAP)*. RFC 7252.

Sheng, Z., Mahapatra, C., Zhu, C., & Leung, V. C. M. (2015). Recent Advances in Industrial Wireless Sensor Networks toward Efficient Management in IoT. *IEEE Access: Practical Innovations, Open Solutions, 3*, 622–637. doi:10.1109/ACCESS.2015.2435000

Silva, Rodrigues, Saleem, Kozlov, & Rabêlo. (2019). M4DN.IoT - A Networks and Devices Management Platform for Internet of Things. *IEEE Access, 7*, 53305-53313.

Skytta, V. (2017). Lightweight Machine to Machine Protocol as Part of Multiprotocol Device Management System. Communication and Information Sciences, Aalto University.

Slovetskiy, S., Magadevan, P., Zhang, Y., & Akhouri, S. (2018). *Managing Non-IP Devices in Cellular IoT Networks*. https://www.omaspecworks.org/wp-content/uploads/2018/10/Whitepaper-11.1.18.pdf

Umar, B., Hejazi, H., Lengyel, L., & Farkas, K. (2018). *Evaluation of IoT Device Management Tools*. The Third International Conference on Advances in Computation, Communications and Services, Barcelona, Spain.

Vermillard, J. (2015). *Bootstrapping device security with lightweight M2M*. https://medium.com/@vrmvrm/device-key-distribution-with-lightweight-m2m-36cdc12e5711

Watsen, K., Abrahamsson, M., & Farrer, I. (2018). *Zero Touch Provisioning for Networking Devices*. Internet-Draft draft-ietf-netconf-zerotouch-25.

Chapter 13
Machine and Deep Learning Techniques in IoT and Cloud

J. Fenila Naomi
Sri Krishna College of Engineering and Technology, India

Kavitha M.
Sri Krishna College of Engineering and Technology, India

Sathiyamoorthi V.
iD https://orcid.org/0000-0002-7012-3941
Sona College of Technology, India

ABSTRACT

For centuries, the concept of a smart, autonomous learning machine has fascinated people. The machine learning philosophy is to automate the development of analytical models so that algorithms can learn continually with the assistance of accessible information. Machine learning (ML) and deep learning (DL) methods are implemented to further improve an application's intelligence and capacities as the quantity of the gathered information rises. Because IoT will be one of the main sources of information, data science will make a significant contribution to making IoT apps smarter. There is a rapid development of both technologies, cloud computing and the internet of things, considering the field of wireless communication. This chapter answers the questions: How can IoT intelligent information be applied to ML and DL algorithms? What is the taxonomy of IoT's ML and DL and profound learning algorithms? And what are real-world IoT data features that require data analytics?

INTRODUCTION

Machine learning is a technique of data analysis that automates analytical model construction(Smola & Vishwanathan, 2008). It is a crucial sub-area of artificial intelligence, allowing machines without specific programming to enter a self-learning mode. When exposed to new knowledge, these computer

DOI: 10.4018/978-1-7998-3111-2.ch013

programmers are allowed to learn, evolve, develop and alter on their own. Identify trends and make decisions based on the idea that systems can learn from knowledge with limited human intervention.

The significance of machine learning is that data processing has always historically been characterized by trial and error, an approach that becomes difficult when information sets are broad and heterogeneous. By providing intelligent solutions to analyze massive amounts of knowledge, machine learning emerges as a solution to all of this. By developing fast and efficient algorithms and data-driven models for real-time data processing(Mahdavinejad et al., 2018; Tanskanen, n.d.), machine learning is able to produce accurate results and analysis.

Rapid advances in hardware, software and communication techniques have facilitated the development of sensory instruments connected to the Internet that provide physical world observations and information measurements. Internet-connected device technology, known as the Internet of Things (IoT), continues to expand the existing Internet by offering connectivity and interactions between physical and cyber worlds. The key to developing intelligent IoT apps is intelligent processing and evaluation of big data. The key contribution is the taxonomy of machine learning algorithms explaining how different techniques are applied to the data in order to extract higher level information.

To understand which machine learning algorithm is more appropriate for processing and decision making on smart data generated from the things in IoT, it is essential to consider the following three concepts. First is the IoT application, second is the IoT data characteristic and third is the data-driven vision of machine learning algorithms. These machine learning algorithms are categorized according to their structural similarities, types of data that can handle, and the amount of data that can process in a reasonable time.

Machine learning becomes more affordable through the use of cloud platforms(Katzir, 2019; Michalski, n.d.), is that the technology will be misapplied. Cloud providers promote machine learning is having a wide value. Many open-source and proprietary machine-learning systems support the types of predictions. Cloud-based machine learning solutions(Bankole & Ajila, n.d.; Jamshidi et al., 2014) from the three public cloud providers: Google, AWS, and Microsoft which are very different from each other. Public clouds also provide cheap data storage. Finally, they all provide software developer kits (SDK) and API that allow embedded machine-learning functionality directly into applications and they support most programming languages. The real value of machine learning technology is the use from within applications because the types of predictions that are made are operational and transaction focused.

Popular methods of machine learning are supervised learning, unsupervised learning, semi - supervised learning and reinforcement learning. Supervised learning maps an input to an output pairs are known as labelled data. Supervised Learning has two sub classes: Classification and Regression. A task is considered as a classification task if the output is categorical and a regression task if the output is a continuous value. A data that does not have a label then it comes under unsupervised learning which is mostly used for finding relationships in datasets, reducing dimensionality or identifying anomalies. Semi-supervised learning is a mixture of supervised and unsupervised learning which typically works with a small amount of labelled data and a large amount of unlabelled data. Reinforcement Learning deals with how an agent takes actions in an environment to maximize a reward.

A wider family of machine learning strategies focused on artificial neural networks is deep learning. In deep learning, a computer model learns directly from images, text, or sound to perform classification tasks. Deep learning models, may achieve state-of-the-art precision, often exceeding human-level efficiency. By using a wide collection of labeled data and neural network architectures that include several layers, models are trained. On the other hand, uses advanced computing power and special types of neural networks can be applied to large amounts of data to learn, understand, and identify complicated patterns. Automatic language translation and medical diagnoses are examples of deep learning.

Deep Learning models fall into three groups in a broad categorization: generative, discriminatory and hybrid models. Discriminative models generally include supervised learning, while for unsupervised learning, generative models are used. The advantages of both discriminative and generative models are incorporated into hybrid models.

The idea of intelligent, independent machine learning has fascinated humans for decades. The important aspect of deep learning with cloud provides security and preserves privacy. The overall goal of the machine learning and deep learning techniques with IoT and cloud are to remove technological market entry barriers of service and application providers of the Internet of Things by exploiting the capabilities of smart object platforms establishing through syntactic and semantic interoperability.

BACKGROUND

Machine learning(Smola & Vishwanathan, 2008) in conjunction with IoT will play an increasingly important role in our lives as the days go by, as both are fields of computer science that are currently in a rapid state of development. Users are undoubtedly becoming 'smarter' in various aspects of our daily life, with machine learning and deep learning playing a crucial role in this. Well known thought leaders like Bill Gates and Dr Judith Dayhoff say that the IoT has given our physical inanimate world a digital nervous system. IoT has really exploded over the past three years, demonstrating its potential in applications ranging from wearable and automated cars to smart homes and smart cities, creating an impact everywhere.

According to recent research by Gartner, there are around 16 billion devices connected to the IoT now and this is expected to rise to 25 billion by 2020. All such connected devices generate a deluge of information that needs to be monitored and analyzed, so that they learn continuously from the available sets of data and improve themselves without any manual intervention. That's how IoT devices are becoming smarter. So how will such a large ocean of data get analyzed and monitored? This is where the role of machine learning and deep learning comes in. There are different Machine learning and Deep learning algorithms and techniques that are implemented to easily analyze massive amounts of data in a short span of time, increasing the efficiency of the IoT. Also, different Machine learning and Deep learning techniques such as decision trees, clustering, neural and Bayesian networks, help the devices to identify patterns in different types of data sets coming from diverse sources, and take appropriate decisions on the basis of their analysis. Such challenges are faced especially in the case of embedded systems. The most important thing is that there is no programming or coding support given to these devices all through this process. Hence, it would not be wrong to say that if the IoT is the digital nervous system, and then machine learning acts as its medulla oblongata. Without implementing machine learning and deep learning, it would really be difficult for smart devices and the IoT to make smart decisions in real-time, severely limiting their capabilities.

The IoT helps in the inter-networking of different physical structures and hardware devices like buildings, vehicles, electronic gadgets and other devices that are embedded with the actuators, sensors and software, so that they can collect and exchange data between each other. While the Internet of Things is still in its infancy, it has become very clear that it will soon be a part of everyone's life, if that is not already the case. As different companies realize the revolutionary potential of the IoT, they have started finding a number of obstacles they need to address to leverage it efficiently. Many businesses and industries use machine learning and, more specifically, the ML-as-a-Service (MLaaS) to exploit the IoT's potential.

Machine learning is basically a part of computer science that makes any system smart enough to learn on its own without actually being programmed for that task. It helps a system or device learn in the same way as humans learn by themselves. As we learn any type of system on the basis of our experience and the knowledge that is gained after analyzing it, machines too can analyze and study the behavior of a system or its output data and then learn how to take different decisions on that basis. Recently, there have been many factors that have come together to make ML a reality large data sources, the increased computational power required for processing the information in split seconds, and different algorithms that have become more reliable. In different cases, machine learning can be used, such as when the appropriate outcome is known (supervised learning), when data is not originally known (unsupervised learning), or when learning depends on the outcome of the interaction between any particular model and the environment (reinforcement learning).

The primary aim behind ML is to automate the implementation of various analytical models so that, with the aid of available data, algorithms can learn continuously. Google's self-driving vehicle is one such development that uses different ML techniques with IoT to create a completely autonomous vehicle. It combines the advanced features of different modern cars (like speech recognition, lane assistance, adaptive cruise control, parking assistants and navigators).

R Ravinder Reddy, et al(Far, 2019) tells how Internet of Things (IoT) offers engineering teams an innovative way to collect data and observe the status of their products, services and equipment in the field. Machine learning techniques are used to learn from these data to make the device or thing intelligent. For example, using the machine learning identifying the abnormalities from our wearable and taking necessary actions like calling doctor and ambulance automatically when it necessary. Mehdi Mohammadi, et al(Tanskanen, n.d.) discusses why DL is a potential approach to achieve the desired analytics in various types of data and applications. It then addresses the feasibility of using new DL techniques for IoT data analytics, and presents its promises and challenges. On various DL architectures and algorithms, they present a detailed background. They also review and summaries important research attempts identified in the IoT domain that leveraged DL and also addresses the smart IoT devices that have integrated DL into their intelligence background. DL implementation approaches on the fog and cloud centers in support of IoT applications are also surveyed.

In the edge computing world(Li et al., 2018), He Li, Kaoru Ota, et al implement deep learning for IoTs. As current edge nodes have limited processing resources, they are also developing a novel offloading strategy to improve the efficiency of edge computing IoT deep learning applications. They measure the efficiency of performing multiple deep learning tasks in an edge computing environment with our strategy in the performance assessment. The findings of the assessment indicate that our approach outperforms other deep learning optimization methods for IoT. Jie Tang, et al(McDonald, 2019) investigates two ways to combine deep learning with low-power IoT products successfully. Omid Ameri Sianaki, et al presents a review of the applications of the Internet of Everything and the machine learning techniques in the fields of health, smart electrical grid, and supply chain management. A review of the literature has been conducted to demonstrate the future issues and challenges that researchers will face.

MAIN FOCUS OF THE CHAPTER

Internet of Things (IoT)

In IoT terms, every connected device is considered a thing. Things usually consist of physical sensors, actuators, and an embedded system with a microprocessor. Things need to communicate with each other, creating the need for Machine-to-Machine (M2M) communication. Using wireless technology such as Wi-Fi, Bluetooth, and ZigBee, connectivity can be short-range or wide-range using mobile networks such as WiMAX, LoRa, Sigfox, CAT M1, NB-IoT, GSM, GPRS, 3 G, 4 G, LTE, and 5G. It is important to keep the cost of IoT devices low because of the vast use of IoT devices in all kinds of daily life applications.

Depending on the application, IoT devices should be able to handle simple tasks such as data collection, M2 M communication and even some pre-processing of data. Thus, when designing or selecting an IoT system, it is mandatory to find a balance between cost, processing power, and energy consumption. Since IoT devices constantly collect and share a vast volume of data, IoT is also strongly bound to "big data". Therefore, an IoT infrastructure generally introduces techniques to manage, store, and analyze big data. Using an IoT platform such as Kaa, Thingsboard, DeviceHive, Thingspeak, or Mainflux to support M2 M communication, using protocols such as MQTT, AMQP, STOMP, CoAP, XMPP, and HTTP, has become a standard practice for IoT infrastructures.

IoT systems have monitoring capabilities, management of nodes, storing and analyzing data, configurable data based laws, etc. It is often important that any data processing takes place in the IoT computers, depending on the application, instead of some centralized node as it happens in the "cloud computing" infrastructure. So, as the processing partially moves to an aspect of the end network, a new computing paradigm, called "edge computing," is implemented. However, because these devices are low-end devices most of the time, they may not be ideal for performing severe processing tasks. As a result, an intermediate node with adequate resources is required to manage advanced processing tasks, physically located close to the end network components, in order to reduce the overload caused by large data transmission to some central cloud nodes. "The solution came with the" Fog nodes" introduction by providing storage, computing, and networking facilities, fog nodes support IoT devices with Big Data handling.

IoT is an advanced automation and analytics system that offers complete service or product solutions dealing with artificial intelligence, sensors, networking, electronics, cloud messaging, etc. There is greater clarity, power, and efficiency in the framework generated by IoT. A cloud-like network contains all information from which all the things around us are related. For instance: a house, where we can link our home appliances via each other such as air conditioner, lamp, etc. and all these items are managed on the same platform. We can connect our car, track its fuel meter, speed level, and also track the position of the car because we have a platform. If there is a shared forum where all of these items can communicate with one another, it will be awesome so we can set the room temperature depending on our choice. This can be done through the Internet of Things (IoT).

Features of IoT

The most important features of IoT on which it works are connectivity, analyzing, integrating, active engagement, and many more. Some of them are listed below:

- **Connectivity:** Connectivity refers to creating a proper link between all items that could be server or cloud from the IoT to the IoT network. It requires high-speed messaging between the devices and the cloud after connecting the IoT devices to allow for efficient, secure and bi-directional communication.

- **Analyzing:** After linking all the related objects, the collected data is analyzed in real time and used to create powerful business intelligence. If we have a good understanding of knowledge obtained from all of these things, then we call our system a smart system.

- **Integrating:** To enhance the user experience as well, IoT incorporates the different models.

- **Artificial Intelligence:** IoT, through the use of data, makes things smart and improves life. For example, if we have a coffee machine whose beans are going to end, then the coffee machine that we order from the manufacturer will order the coffee beans of our choice.

- **Sensing:** The sensor devices that are used in IoT technologies detect and quantify any environmental changes and report on their status. IoT technology adds passive networks to networks that are involved. There couldn't be a productive or true IoT world without sensors.

- **Active adherence:** IoT offers the relevant technology, service, or resources for active interaction between each other.

- **Endpoint Management:** It is necessary to be the endpoint management of the entire IoT system, otherwise the system will fail completely. For instance, if a coffee machine itself orders the coffee beans when it finishes, but what happens when it orders the beans from a supplier and for a few days we are not present at home, leads to the IoT device failure. So, there has to be a need for control of endpoints.

IoT and Cloud Architecture

Typical IoT system architectures as shown in Figure 1 include devices (or nodes) which are deployed in physical spaces and usually include one or more sensors, hubs (or gateways or edge) bridge between communication protocols and are located relatively close to the devices. A centralized cloud environment which stores and processes the data, and front-end devices which users can interact with, explore the data and get notifications. Obviously, there are scenarios where the devices communicate directly with the cloud environment and scenarios where the devices act as the frontend device, but logically, this architecture describes the common roles in the setup.

Figure 1. IoT Architecture

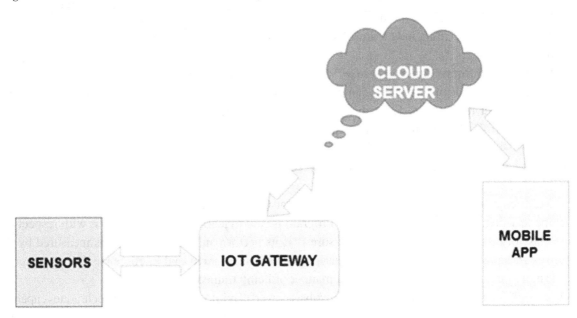

Finally, the data is stored on cloud servers, where it is available for advanced processing using a range of ML techniques and sharing between other devices, leading to the development of smart apps with modern added value. The so-called smart city has already appeared in several respects with IoT apps. The most important applications could be grouped into the following categories:

- **Smart Homes:** This category includes typical home appliances such as refrigerators, washing machines or light bulbs that have been built and are capable of interacting through the internet with each other or with approved users, providing better system control and management, as well as maximizing energy usage. New innovations are spreading, providing smart home assistants, smart door locks, etc., in comparison to basic devices.
- **Health-care assistance:** In order to enhance the well-being of a patient, new devices have been developed. Without the need for their physical presence, plasters with wireless sensors will track the condition of a wound and report the data to the doctor. Other sensors can monitor and record a wide range of measurements, such as heart rate, blood oxygen level, blood sugar level, or temperature, in the form of wearable devices or small implants.
- **Smart Transportation:** Optimized route recommendations, simple parking reservations, economical street lighting, and telemetry for public transit, accident prevention, and autonomous driving can be offered using sensors embedded in cars, or mobile devices and devices mounted in the area.
- **Environmental Conditions Monitoring:** Wireless sensors distributed throughout the city build the ideal infrastructure for tracking a wide range of environmental conditions. In order to build advanced weather stations, barometers, humidity sensors, or ultrasonic wind sensors may aid. In addition, smart sensors will track the city-wide levels of air quality and water pollution.

- **Logistics and Supply Chain Management:** A product can be easily monitored from production to the store with the use of smart RFID tags, dramatically reducing cost and time. Furthermore, smart packaging can include features such as brand security, quality assurance, and personalization of customers.
- **Security and Surveillance Systems:** Video input can be collected around the streets from smart cameras. Smart security systems can detect criminals or avoid dangerous situations with real-time visual object recognition. Even though there is a lot to do in terms of standardization when it comes to IoT infrastructure and innovations, as discussed so far.

Machine Learning and Deep Learning Techniques

Tom M.Mitchell is the chair of Machine Learning at Carnegie Mellon University. His definition of Machine learning is quoted as: A Computer Program is said to learn from experience E with respect to some class of tasks T and performance measure P, if its performance at tasks in T, as measured by P, improves with the experience E. Machine Learning is a branch of Artificial Intelligence. Using computing, design systems can learn from data in a manner of being trained.

The word Deep Learning(Tang et al., n.d.) involves powerful reinforcement learning techniques capable of processing a vast volume of unstructured knowledge. Deep learning methods are ideal for the handling of large data and computer-intensive procedures such as recognition of image patterns, recognition of speech and synthesis, etc. As CPU power requirements grow, powerful GPUs are commonly used to perform deep learning tasks. Like ANNs, deep neural networks are built with deep learning. The term 'deep' refers to the vast number of layers that make up the neural network that are hidden. The number of layers is similar to the number of measured features in a deep learning technique. The features are automatically calculated in deep learning, and before implementing such a method, there is no need for feature estimation and extraction. In addition, the development of deep learning has implemented a wide range of network architectures.

Deep learning(Wang et al., 2018) is a machine learning technique that teaches computers to do what comes naturally to humans: learn by example. Deep learning is a key technology behind driverless cars, enabling them to recognize a stop sign, or to distinguish a pedestrian from a lamppost. It is the key to voice control in consumer devices like phones, tablets, TVs, and hands-free speakers. Deep learning is getting lots of attention lately and for good reason. It's achieving results that were not possible before. In deep learning, a computer model learns to perform classification tasks directly from images, text, or sound. Deep learning models can achieve state-of-the-art accuracy, sometimes exceeding human-level performance. Models are trained by using a large set of labeled data and neural network architectures that contain many layers.

The systems might learn and improve with experience and with time, refine a model that can be used to predict outcomes of questions based on the previous learning(Berral-García, 2016).

- **Algorithm Learning Types:** There are number of different algorithms that can employ in machine learning and deep learning. The required output decides which to use. It falls under following learning types:

  - **Supervised Learning:** Supervised learning as the name indicates the presence of a supervisor as a teacher. Basically, supervised learning which trains the machine using data which is well labeled. A **supervised learning algorithm** analyzes the training data that will allow the algorithm to correctly determine the class labels for **unseen instances(Drotar & Smeakal, n.d.).**

Example: A Robotics - A highly developed AI(McDonald, 2019) that serves as a housekeeping robot. In case of Supervised Learning, A robot is learning to sort garbage using visual identification. It sits all day picking out recyclable items from garbage as it passes on a Conveyor belt. Each item is labeled with an identification number on a sticker. It places items such as glass, plastic and metal into different bins.

- **Un-Supervised Learning:** The problem of an unsupervised learning is trying to find hidden structure in unlabeled data. With Unsupervised learning, there is no right or wrong answer, it's just a case of running machine learning algorithm and seeing what pattern and outcomes occur.

Example: A Robotics - A highly developed AI that serves as a housekeeping robot. In case of Unsupervised Learning, Robot develops a theory that there is usually dust under a sofa. Each week, the theory is confirmed as the robot often finds dust under sofas. Nobody explicitly tells the robot the theory is correct but it is able to develop confidence.

- **Semi-supervised Learning**: This is a blend of the two previous classifications. It uses both labelled data and unlabeled data. It mostly operates like unsupervised learning with the changes that a portion of the labelled data that creates.
- **Reinforcement Learning**: The algorithms try to forecast the output for a problem based on a collection of tuning parameters in this learning style. The estimated output then becomes an input parameter, and once the optimum output is found, the new output is estimated. This learning style is used by Artificial Neural Networks (ANN) and Deep Learning, which will be discussed later. For applications like AI gaming, skill acquisition, robot navigation, and real-time decisions, reinforcement learning is primarily used.

Selecting the right Machine learning and Deep Learning techniques [16] are a key part because there are dozens to choose from by understanding their strengths and weaknesses in various applications are essential. The most common Machine Learning and Deep Learning techniques in Internet of Things (IoT) and Cloud are tabulated in Table1.

Table 1. Machine Learning(ML) and Deep Learning(DL) techniques in Internet of Things (IoT) and Cloud

ML and DL Techniques	Learning Types	Algorithm Types
AdaBoost	Supervised	Ensemble
Autoencoder		
Bayesian Network Seasonal Autoregressive Integrated Moving Average (BN-SARIMA)	Supervised	Bayesian
Convolutional Neural Network (CNN) and Deep CNN (DCNN)	Supervised / Reinforcement	Deep Learning
Coupled Hidden Markov Model (CHMM)	Reinforcement	Markov Mod
Decision Tree	Supervised	Decision Trees
Deep Belief Networks (DBN)	Unsupervised / Reinforcement	Deep Learning
Deep Recurrent Attention Model (DRAM)	Reinforcement	Deep Learning
Fuzzy C-Means (FCM)	Unsupervised	Clustering
Feed Forward Neural Networks (FF-NN)	Supervised	Artificial Neural Networks
Fully Convolutional Networks (FCN)	Reinforcement	Deep Learning
Inception Neural Networks	Reinforcement	Deep Learning
K-Means	Unsupervised	Clustering
k-Nearest Neighbor (k-NN)	Supervised	Instance Based
Logistic Regression	Supervised	Regression
Markov Decision Process (MDP)	Reinforcement	Discrete Time Stochastic Control
Markov Random Field (MRF)	Unsupervised	Markov Model
Nonlinear Auto Regressive eXogenous model (NARX)	Reinforcement	Deep Learning
Q-Learning	Reinforcement	Stochastic Control-Markov Model
Random Forest (RF)	Supervised	Ensemble
Recurrent Neural Network – Long Short Term Memory (RNN – LSTM)	Supervised / Reinforcement	Deep Learning
Regression Tree	Supervised	Decision Trees
Restricted Boltzmann machines (RBMs)	Unsupervised	Deep Learning
Support-Vector Machine (SVM)	Supervised	Non-probabilistic Linear Classification

In the following subsections, the aforementioned ML and DL techniques are briefly analyzed(Far, 2019; Gupta et al., 2015; Ravinder Reddy et al., 2018):

• AdaBoost

The first practical boosting algorithm proposed by Freund and Schapire in 1996 is AdaBoost, short for "Adaptive Boosting". It's an ensemble algorithm which is used to form a strong classifier along with other weak classifiers. It focuses on problems with classification and aims to turn a collection of weak classifiers into a powerful one. It is possible to describe the final equation for classification as $F(x) = \text{sign} \left(\sum_{m=1}^{M} \left(\theta_m f_m(x) \right) \right)$, where f_m stands for the weak m^{th} classifier and the corresponding weight is θ_m . It is precisely the weighted mix of weak M classifiers. In real time, a large number of features need to be processed and AdaBoost demonstrates a great advantage in that aspect. It can set the strong classifiers in a cascading order, where each classifier is fed with the characteristics processed from the previous one, to further enhance the AdaBoost results in terms of speed.

Figure 2. (a) the general structure of the autoencoder, and (b) a specific diagram of the structure of the autoencoder containing 6 input data

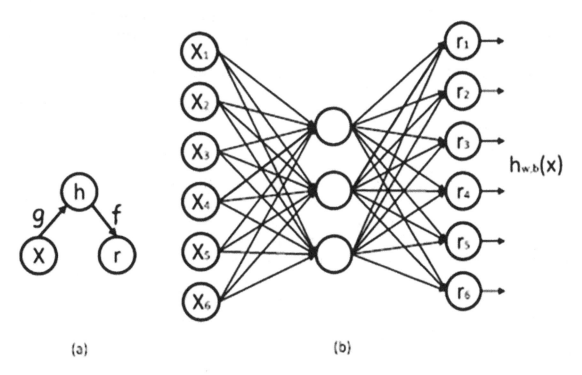

• Autoencoder

A neural network trained to copy its input into its output is an autoencoder. Three layers, including an input layer, a hidden layer, and an output layer, consist of an autoencoder. A code used to represent the input is represented by the hidden layer, and its output is an input reconstruction. The network consists essentially of two key components: an encoder function f, which extracts the input dependencies, and a decoder function g, which generates a reconstruction. By minimising the error between input and output, the autoencoder is trained. Figure 2 illustrates a brief architecture and a basic example of an autoencoder. It contains a deep model that can be built in a layer-by - layer manner through a stack of autoencoders. As the input layer of another autoencoder, the hidden layer of a well-trained autoencoder is fed, and a multi-layer model is built iteratively. Sparse autoencoder, denoising autoencoder and contractive auto-encoder are included in the autoencoder variants.

• Bayesian Network Seasonal Autoregressive Integrated Moving Average (BN-SARIMA)

A Directed Acyclic Graph (DAG), which implements a probability distribution for a given set of random variables, is represented by a Bayesian network(Rish, n.d.). The model can be inferred, provided a training set as variables, and can be used later to assign labels to new data. A Bayesian network is a model which describes all the variables and their relationship. Thus, in a Bayesian network, the observation of some variables can provide information about the state of another set of variables in the network. To achieve short-term forecasting, the Bayesian Network Seasonal Autoregressive Integrated Moving Average (BN-SARIMA) can be used. A combination of Bayesian Network and ARIMA model acts as an estimator. An ARIMA model is a type of regression analysis, widely used for the analysis and forecasting of time series. In ARIMA model, one dependent variable regresses on the previous values of the same variable (AR). The forecasts are based on the difference between the present and past values of variables in a time series (I). Furthermore, the Moving Average (MA) implies that the regression error is a linear combination of errors previously measured. The methods can be evaluated against the RMSE, MAE, and MAPE metrics. This technique is used for short term forecasting.

• Convolutional Neural Network (CNN) and Deep CNN (DCNN)

A deep learning approach based on Convolutional Neural Networks (CNN) is widely used for image recognition. A CNN is a type of ANN because it consists of an input, a layer of output, and some layers that are hidden. Pooling, convolutional, non-linear, subsampling, or fully connected (FC) layers can be the hidden layers in a CNN architecture. Features are learned from the input data in convolutional layer. Weight and bias values are comprised of the features or filters. A significant feature of CNN is that the same philtres are used by various neurons. Neurons are units that apply a transfer function to the sum of their input signals, which is weighted. Non-linear layers are accompanied by convolutional layers, which transform all negative values to zeros. Then, with sub-sampling layers, dimensionality reduction is applied. Finally, the classification of the input data is carried out by the FC layer, which is essentially a Multi-Layer Perceptron. A deep convolutional neural network (DCNN) consists of many neural network layers. Usually, two distinct layers forms, convolutional and pooling, are alternated. Any filter's depth increases in the network from left to right. Usually, the last stage is made of one or more layers that are completely connected as shown in the Figure 3. For instance, in a wide range of image datasets, such as Google Street View images, mobile images, and 3D images constructed with advanced hardware (e.g., a Ground Penetrating Radar (GPR)), CNN and DCNN techniques are used. The CNN and DCNN combinations work very well in the image classification.

• Coupled Hidden Markov Model (CHMM)

Markov Models are stochastic models of sequences based on the distribution of probability. A Markov chain is the simplest Markov model. The distribution of a variable that adjusts its value randomly over time in a Markov chain depends only on the distribution of the preceding state. A Hidden Markov Model is similar to a Markov chain; except for fine tuning it uses hidden states. A probabilistic function of a state represents each state. Perhaps the most effective framework for modelling and classifying dynamic behaviours in perceptual computing, HMMs are common because they provide dynamic time warping, a training algorithm, and simple Bayesian semantics. The Markovian structure, however, makes strong limiting assumptions that the signal-generating system is a single process with a small number of states and an extremely restricted state memory. For vision (and speech) applications, the single-process model is often inappropriate, resulting in low ceilings on model efficiency. Coupled HMMs provide an effective way to address many of these issues and deliver initial conditions with superior training speeds, model likelihoods, and robustness.

Figure 3. CNN and DCNN Framework

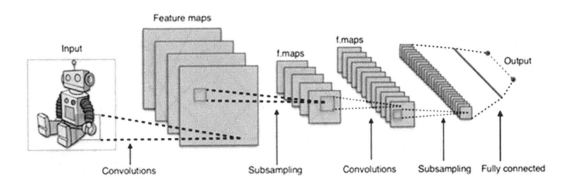

• Decision Tree

Decision trees are structures that deal with the tasks of classification and are a decision process with many possible results. A decision tree is constructed from top to bottom and consists of multiple nodes, where each node may be either a class or a condition that pushes a test item to a class. It is a simplistic solution to problems of classification. At any stage of a decision tree, a new classification sub-process takes place, breaking down the main task to smaller sub-tasks. Decision tree can be used to predict traffic congestion.

• Deep Belief Networks (DBN)

Deep belief networks as shown in Figure 4 are deep leaning technique that generate outputs using probabilities and unsupervised learning.(Han et al., 2015) They are composed of binary latent variables and both undirected and directed layers are used. The whole input is learned by each layer in deep belief networks. Networks of deep belief operate globally and enforce each layer in order. Inside their layer, nodes in a deep belief network do not interact laterally. Different layers are connected by a network of symmetrical weights. The connexions in the top layers are undirected and the connexions between them form associative memory. The connections are guided at the lower levels. Two tasks are performed by the nodes in the hidden layer, which serve as a hidden layer to the preceding nodes and as visible layers to the active nodes. The correlations in the data are identified by these nodes. Deep belief networks can be used in image recognition, Video recognition, etc. Motion capture data involves tracking the movement of objects or people and also uses deep belief networks.

Figure 4. Deep belief networks

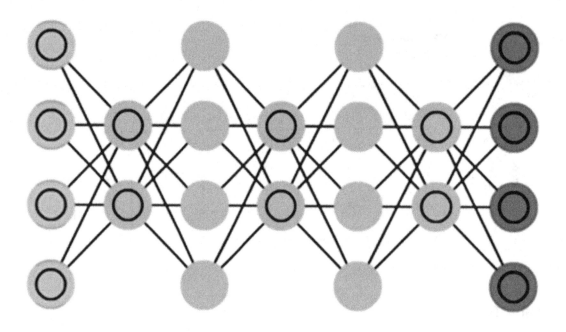

• Deep Recurrent Attention Model (DRAM)

A deep learning approach from an image input called the Deep Recurrent Attention Model (DRAM) for sequential classification of multiple objects implies that the model prevails on multiple digit recognition over CNNs. The following five network structures or interconnected hidden layers are composed of DRAM architecture: (a) A glimpse network consisting of three convolution layer and a fully connected layer, and its function is to extract important features from an input image chunk. (b) A recurrent network, which incorporates the performance of glimpse networks that retain spatial information. (c) An emission network that predicts the next position of the image chunk to feed the glimpse network. (d) A context network that uses a low-resolution version of the initial image to help the broadcast network identify important objects in the image. (e) A classification network that carries out a classification of the object based on the final vector of the function.

• Fuzzy C-Means (FCM)

Fuzzy clustering is a type of clustering where more than one cluster may belong to each data point. Clustering or cluster analysis involves assigning cluster data points in such a way that the objects in the same cluster are as similar as possible, while the objects belonging to the various clusters are as different as possible(Ba et al., 2014). Through similarity steps, clusters are identified. Such measurements of similarity include distance, connectivity, and strength. Different measures of similarity can be selected based on the data or application. In the field of bioinformatics, image processing, clustering is used for a number of applications.

• Feed Forward Neural Networks (FF-NN)

The structure of the neural network and the learning method are mostly identified by Artificial Neural Networks. By creating weighted neural connections, a neural network is created. There is an input layer in a neural network where the input variables are inserted into the network, and each neuron represents a variable, and there is an output layer where the labels are distributed and a label is represented by each neuron. One or more hidden layers are located between those layers. The network is called the Feed Forward Neural Network (FF-NN) as shown in Figure 5, which is the simplest type of an ANN, since there is no loop in the neuron connections.

Figure 5. Feed Forward Neural Network (FF-NN)

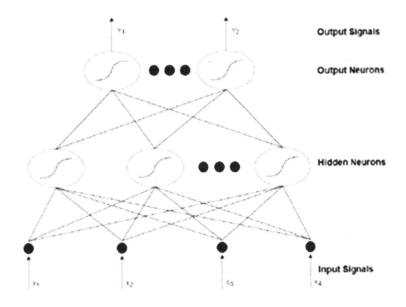

• Fully Connected Networks (FCN)

Fully Convolutional Networks (FCNs) as shown in Figure 6, is built from layers that are locally related, such as convolution, pooling and upsampling. In FCN, no dense layer is used. It decreases the number of parameters and the time of computation. The network can also work without requiring any fixed number of units at any point, regardless of the original image size, provided that all connections are local. Segmentation networks typically have 2 components to obtain a segmentation map (output), which is Downsampling and Upsampling paths. Downsampling path captures semantic/contextual information and Upsampling path recovers spatial information.

Figure 6. Convolutional Networks (FCNs)

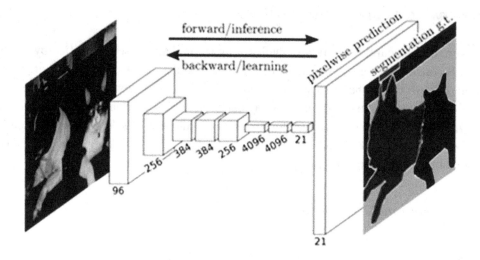

• Inception Neural Networks

The inception network is more robust than a CNN and is meant to be a method that is less computationally intensive. The concept is to use various filters to perform the input data convolution. In addition, maximum pooling is carried out as well. Outputs are concatenated and sent to the next layer of inception. Inception layers stacked form an Inception Network. There are also several auxiliary classifiers in the initial network structure. These are structures used to compute an auxiliary loss on the inception layers and support the training phase. Inception Neural Network used for image classification.

• K-Means

K-Means is one of the most common clustering algorithms. K-means Clustering is a method of unsupervised learning that is used when you have unlabeled information (i.e. data without specified groups or categories). The objective of this algorithm is to find groups, with the number of groups represented by the K variable, in the data. Based on the characteristics given, the algorithm operates iteratively to assign each data point to one of the K groups. The aim of the K-Means algorithm is to divide data into a number of clusters, so that the data given and the mean value of their cluster have a minimum square error. To explore the Internet of things logistics system application, an Internet of things big data clustering analysis algorithm is based on K-means.

• k-Nearest Neighbour (k-NN)

Instance-Based algorithms perform data classification directly to the training instances based on the comparison of new test data. The comparison based on a function of similarity and its output is fed into a function of classification. Instance-based algorithms store training instances in their memory, but as the information is increased, they can be memory-consuming. The instance-based algorithm k-Nearest Neighbour (k-NN) is used as stated in k-NN, an algorithm used for supervised classification and regression, to make real-time autonomous detections(Kwon et al., 2018). The key principle of k-NN is that there is a minimum gap between similar data. In order to select the ideal k factor that minimizes errors when classifying data, k-NN can run several times on the testing data.

• Logistic Regression

Methods in the category of regression analysis try to create mathematical models capable of explaining the relationship between two or more variables or defining them. The dependent or response variable is the performance of the scheme. The relations between the dependent variable and the independent ones (repressors') can be discovered by fitting a regression model to the scheme. Logistic regression is a method of regression analysis used to establish a dependent variable's relationship with one or more independent variables. When the dependent variable has binary values, logistical regression is applicable. Since it is a regression analysis, logistic regression is sufficient in ML for prediction tasks.

• Markov Decision Process (MDP)

Another implementation of the Markov Model is the Markov Decision Process (MDP). The MDP is a model that is suitable for problems of optimization and decision making. It is comparable to the chains of Markov, but adds two new components. There are a variety of acts in the MDP that can lead to a certain condition. MDP rewards promote the selection of the most appropriate actions.

• Markov Random Field (MRF)

The MRF is an undirected graph representing the Markov property of a number of random variables. In a number of areas, Markov random fields are used, ranging from computer graphics to computer vision, machine learning or computational biology. MRFs are used to create textures in image processing as they can be used to generate versatile and stochastic image models.

• Nonlinear Auto Regressive eXogenous model (NARX)

A nonlinear autoregressive exogenous model (NARX) in time series modelling is a nonlinear autoregressive model that has exogenous inputs. This means that the model applies both past values of the same series and current and past values of the driving (exogenous) series, that is, of the externally defined series that affects the series of interest, to the current value of a time series.

• Q-Learning

Q-Learning is a model-free method of reinforcement learning that provides the opportunity to estimate the reward or punishment in a Markovian domain for an action. The algorithm learns by repeatedly performing all the behaviour possible and estimating the resulting state.

• Random Forest (RF)

An additional common ensemble algorithm is Random Forest (RF). Using a proliferation of decision trees as weak learners, RF is used for regression and classification tasks while obtaining their mean value or the most sampled values as an output. RF is generally less susceptible than single decision trees to the over-fitting effect. Random-Forest (RF) as the machine learning platform used for rules discovery and real-time anomaly detection.

• Recurrent Neural Network – Long Short Term Memory (RNN – LSTM)

A recurrent neural network (RNN)(Gers et al., n.d.) is a type of artificial neural network and another most common deep neural network styles in which a directed cycle forms connections between units. This creates an internal state of the network that enables complex temporal behavior to be exhibited. RNNs may use their internal memory to process arbitrary sequences of inputs, in contrast to feed forward neural networks. This function of using internal memory to process arbitrary input sequences makes RNNs applicable for tasks such as un-segmented recognition of related handwriting, where the best known results have been achieved. The Recurrent Neural Network (RNN)'s fundamental feature is that the network includes at least one feedback connection, so that the activations can flow in a loop around it. This helps the networks, for example, to do sequence recognition / reproduction or temporal association / prediction to do temporal processing and learn sequences. RNNs are used to model the time series since a 'memory' is created by the feedback mechanism, i.e. an ability to process the time dimension. Memory is important because a long-term / historical modeling of time values is needed for many time series problems (such as traffic modeling). Long Short Term Memory Networks (LSTMs) are a specific type of RNN that is capable of learning long-term dependencies, especially because they are capable of remembering long-term data.

• Regression Tree

Regression trees are similar to decision trees, but instead of a binary class, a numeric value is the response variable of the tree. The independent variables are used in a regression tree to fit a regression to a response variable. Then, a binary recursive partitioning takes place, where the squared regression error is calculated. The branch is selected with the variables holding the smallest number of square errors. The regression tree technique is used for traffic predictions.

• Restricted Boltzmann machines (RBMs)

Restricted Boltzmann machines (RBMs) are probabilistic graphical models that can be interpreted as stochastic neural networks. RBMs consist of m visible units to represent observable data and n hidden units to capture collections between observed variables, providing us a stochastic representation of the output. Figure 7 shows a two-level RBM with *m* visible variables and *n* hidden variables. RBMs are successful in dimensionality reduction and collaborative filtering. A Deep Belief Network (DBN) forms a deep learning model by stacking RBMs, which is trained in a layer-by-layer manner using a greedy learning algorithm, and the contrastive divergence (CD) method is applied to update the weights. Neural networks are prone to trap in the local optima of a non-convex function, resulting in poor performance. DBN incorporates both unsupervised pre training and supervised *fine*-tuning methods to construct the models: the former intends to learn data distributions with unlabeled data and the latter aims to obtain an optimal solution through fine tuning with labeled data.

Figure 7. An RBM with m visible and n hidden variables

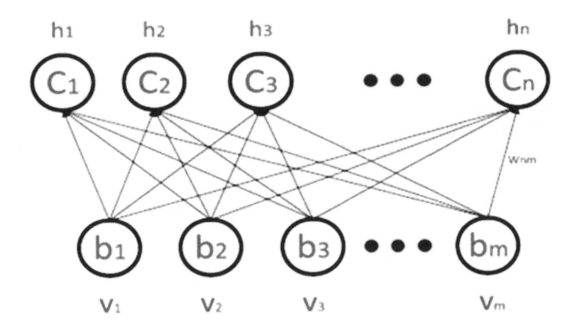

• Support-Vector Machine (SVM)

A support vector machine (SVM)(Cortes & Vapnik, 1995) is a type of algorithm for deep learning that performs supervised learning for data group classification or regression. In machine learning, supervised learning systems, which are labelled for classification, provide both input and desired output data. For potential data analysis, the classification offers a learning basis. They are used to sort two classes of information by grouping. To divide the groups according to pattern(Bishop, n.d.; Fusco et al., 2015), the algorithms draw lines (hyperplanes). An SVM generates a learning model that assigns one category or another to new examples. Via these functions, a non-probabilistic, binary linear classifier is called SVMs. SVMs can use methods such as Platt Scaling in probabilistic classification settings.

An SVM(Cristianini, n.d.) needs labelled data to be educated, like other supervised learning machines. For classification, classes of materials are numbered. SVM training materials are individually categorised at various points in space and grouped into clearly separated classes. SVMs may perform unsupervised learning after processing various training examples. With the boundary around the hyperplane being maximised and also between both sides, the algorithms will attempt to achieve the best separation of data.

In 1963, Vladimir N. Vapnik and Alexey Ya Chervonenkis invented SVMs. Since then, systems have been used in the classification of text, hypertext and images. With handwritten characters, SVMs will function and the algorithms have been used to perform tasks such as sorting proteins in biology laboratories. In chatbots, self-driving vehicles, facial recognition applications, expert systems and robotics, among other things, supervised and unsupervised learning systems SVMs(Steinwart & Christmann, 2008; Vapnik, n.d.) are used.

Significance of Machine Learning and Deep Learning in IoT and Cloud

With IoT, devices connected to each other, interact with each other and gather a massive amount of data every day. IoT devices may also be configured in many applications to activate certain behaviour based either on certain predefined conditions or on some input from the data collected. However, human involvement is required in order to evaluate the data collected and extract valuable information and develop smart applications. IoT devices not only need to collect data and communicate with other devices, but they also need to be independent. They need to be able to take decisions based on context and learn from their collected knowledge. The development of the word "Cognitive IoT" (CIoT) contributed to this need. Intelligent IoT devices are also expected to build automated smart applications with automated resource allocation, communication and operation of the network(Sianaki et al., 2018).

The implementation of ML algorithms(Szegedy et al., 2015) in an IoT infrastructure will bring about major changes in the applications or the infrastructure itself. ML can be used for network management, congestion reduction, and management of resource utilisation, but also for data analysing and decision-making in real time or offline. In addition, the quantity of collected data often increases as the number of devices increases. Having to deal with "big data" is very common in IoT applications. With traditional databases, big data cannot be adequately handled. To handle the large volume of structured and unstructured data and special techniques for analysing them, special infrastructure is required. There are several ML algorithms that can help deal effectively with big data, including "Ensemble" or Artificial Neural Networks (ANN)(Marsland, n.d.).

For a wide range of applications such as smart home, smart healthcare, smart manufacturing, smart transportation, smart grid, smart agriculture etc., the vast number of sensors deployed in IoT produces enormous data volumes. Analyzing such data in order to promote better decision-making, increase efficiency and precision, improving revenue is a crucial mechanism that makes IoT a powerful concept for corporations and a paradigm that enhances the quality of life. Although it is promising to improve the quality of our lives to extract concealed knowledge and inferences from IoT data, it is a complicated task that traditional paradigms cannot achieve. In the development of smarter IoT, deep learning could play a very important role as it has shown remarkable results in various fields, including image recognition, data retrieval, speech recognition, natural language processing, indoor localization, physiological and psychological state detection, etc., and these form the foundation services for IoT applications.

FUTURE RESEARCH DIRECTIONS

The future Internet of Things (IoT) will have a profound economic, commercial, and social effect on our lives. Participating nodes are typically resource-constrained in IoT networks, making them draw cyber attack objectives. Comprehensive attempts have been made in this regard, primarily through conventional cryptographic techniques, to resolve information security problems in IoT networks. However, the distinctive characteristics of IoT nodes make existing solutions insufficient to cover the whole security spectrum of the IoT network. This is, at least in part, due to the resource constraints, heterogeneity, the IoT devices' vast real-time data generated, and the networks' extensively dynamic conduct. Therefore, Machine Learning (ML) and Deep Learning (DL) techniques that are capable of providing IoT devices and networks with embedded knowledge are leveraged to cope with various technologies.

CONCLUSION

The Internet of Things technology is being increasingly used mainly with the advent of smart. Due to the rapid evolution of System-on-a-Chip, there is a big marathon for developing intelligent systems where small devices process their own data and take decisions to improve user experiences. This novel paradigm, known as Edge or Fog Computing, will allow the Internet to grow even more, improve the user experience and reduce the dependency on Cloud infrastructures. This study highlighted the fact that a wide variety of Machine Learning and Deep learning algorithms has been proposed and evaluated for various applications, indicating that the type and scale of IoT data in these applications is ideal for Machine learning and deep learning exploitation. As the number of IoT devices rises, the data diversity and volume scale up, therefore, Machine learning and deep learning can create many meaningful applications.

REFERENCES

Ba, J., Mnih, V., & Kavukcuoglu, K. (2014). *Multiple object recognition with visual attention.* arXiv:1412.7755

Bankole, A., & Ajila, S. (n.d.). Predicting cloud resource provisioning using machine learning techniques. *26th Annual IEEE Canadian Conference on Electrical and Computer Engineering*, 1–4. 10.1109/CCECE.2013.6567848

Berral-García, J. L. (2016). *A quick view on current techniques and machine learning algorithms for big data analytics.* ICTON Trento. doi:10.1109/ICTON.2016.7550517

Bishop. (n.d.). *Pattern recognition and machine learning (information science and statistics).* New York: Springer-Verlag.

Cortes, C., & Vapnik, V. (1995, September). Support-vector networks. *Machine Learning, 20*(3), 273–297. doi:10.1007/BF00994018

Cristianini. (n.d.). *An introduction to support vector machines: And the kernel-based learning methods.* Cambridge University Press.

Drotar & Smeakal. (n.d.). Comparative Study of Machine Learning Techniques for Supervised classification of Biomedical Data. *Acta Electrotechnica et Informatica, 14*, 5–10.

Far. (2019). *IoT and Machine Learning/Deep Learning.* Retrieved from https://medium.com/datadriven-investor/iot-and-machine-learning-deep-learning-f102bf578c99

Fusco, G., Colombaroni, C., Comelli, L., & Isaenko, N. (2015). Short-term traffic predictions on large urban traffic networks: Applications of network-based machine learning models and dynamic traffic assignment models. *Proceedings of the 2015 IEEE International Conference on Models and Technologies for Intelligent Transportation Systems (MT-ITS)*, 93–101. 10.1109/MTITS.2015.7223242

Gers, F.A., Schraudolph, N.N., & Schmidhuber, J. (n.d.). Learning precise timing with LSTM recurrent networks. *Journal of Machine Learning Research*, 115-143.

Gupta, S., Agrawal, A., Gopalakrishnan, K., & Narayanan, P. (2015). Deep learning with limited numerical precision. *International Conference on Machine Learning*.

Han, Mao, & Dally. (2015). *Deep compression: Compressing deep neural networks with pruning, trained quantization and Huffman coding.* Academic Press.

Jamshidi, P., Ahmad, A., & Pahl, C. (2014) Autonomic resource provisioning for cloud-based software. *Proceedings of the 9th international symposium on software engineering for adaptive and self-managing systems*, 95-104.

Katzir, R. (2019). *Distributing a machine learning algorithm across IoT devices, edge and cloud.* Retrieved from https://medium.com/digital-catapult/distributing-a-machine-learning-algorithm-across-iot-device-edge-and-cloud-731480bfcceb

Kwon, D., Park, S., Baek, S., Malaiya, R. K., Yoon, G., & Ryu, J. T. (2018). A study on development of the blind spot detection system for the IoT-based smart connected car. *Proceedings of the 2018 IEEE International Conference on Consumer Electronics (ICCE)*, 1–4. 10.1109/ICCE.2018.8326077

Li, H., Ota, K., & Dong, M. (2018). Learning IoT in Edge: Deep Learning for the Internet of Things with Edge Computing. *IEEE Network, 32*(1), 96–101. doi:10.1109/MNET.2018.1700202

Mahdavinejad, Rezvan, Barekatain, Adibi, Barnaghi, & Sheth. (2018). Machine learning for internet of things data analysis: a survey. *Digital Communications and Networks*, 161-175.

Marsland. (n.d.). *Machine learning: An algorithmic perspective.* Boca Raton: Chapman & Hall/CRC.

McDonald. (2019). *The Internet of Things requires machine learning and AI.* Retrieved from https://www.ibm.com/blogs/internet-of-things/iot-the-internet-of-things-requires-machine-learning/

Michalski. (n.d.). *Machine learning an artificial intelligence approach.* Springer.

Mohammadi, M., Al-Fuqaha, A., Sorour, S., & Guizani, M. (2018). Deep Learning for IoT Big Data and Streaming Analytics: A Survey. *IEEE Communications Surveys and Tutorials, 20*(4), 2923–2960. doi:10.1109/COMST.2018.2844341

Ravinder Reddy, R., Mamatha, Ch., & Govardhan Reddy, R. (2018). A Review on Machine Learning Trends, Application and Challenges in Internet of Things. *International Conference on Advances in Computing, Communications and Informatics (ICACCI)*.

Rish, I. (n.d.). An empirical study of the naive Bayes classifier. *IJCAI Workshop on Empirical Methods in AI*.

Sianaki, O. A., Yousefi, A., Tabesh, A. R., & Mahdavi, M. (2018). Internet of Everything and Machine Learning Applications: Issues and Challenges. *2018 32nd International Conference on Advanced Information Networking and Applications Workshops (WAINA)*.

Smola, & Vishwanathan. (2008). *Introduction to Machine Learning*. Cambridge University Press.

Steinwart, & Christmann. (2008). *Support vector machines*. Springer-Verlag.

Szegedy, C., Liu, W., Jia, Y., Sermanet, P., Reed, S., Anguelov, D., Erhan, D., Vanhoucke, V., & Rabinovich, A. (2015) Going deeper with convolutions. *Proceedings of the IEEE Conference on Computer Vision and Pattern Recognition*, 1–9.

Tang, Sun, Liu, & Gaudiot. (n.d.). Enabling Deep Learning on IoT Devices. *Computer*, 92 – 96.

Tanskanen, M. (n.d.). *Applying machine learning to IoT data*. Retrieved from https://www.sas.com/en_us/ insights/articles/big-data/machine-learning-brings-concrete-aspect-to-iot.html

Vapnik, V. (n.d.). Support vector clustering. *Journal of Machine Learning Research*, 2, 125–137.

Wang, Ma, Zhang, Gao, & Wu. (2018). Deep learning for smart manufacturing: Methods and applications. *J. Manuf. Syst.*, 48, 144-156.

Chapter 14

Perspectives of Machine Learning and Deep Learning in Internet of Things and Cloud:
Artificial Intelligence–Based Internet of Things System

Preethi Sambandam Raju
https://orcid.org/0000-0002-3541-0830
SRM Valliammai Engineering College, India

Revathi Arumugam Rajendran
SRM Valliammai Engineering College, India

Murugan Mahalingam
https://orcid.org/0000-0001-9100-8523
SRM Valliammai Engineering College, India

ABSTRACT

This chapter brings out the perspective outcomes of combining three terminologies: artificial intelligence, cloud, and internet of things. The relation between artificial intelligence, machine learning, and deep learning is also emphasized. Intelligence, which is the capability to attain and apply knowledge in addition to skills, is analysed in the following sections of the chapter along with its categories that include natural intelligence, artificial intelligence, and hybrid intelligence. Analysis of artificial intelligence-based internet of things system is deliberated on two approaches, namely criterion-based analysis and elemental analysis. Criterion-based analysis covers the parameter-based investigation to highlight the relation between machine learning and deep learning. Elemental analysis involves four main components of artificial intelligence-based internet of things system, such as device, data, algorithm, and computation. Research works done using deep learning and internet of things are also discussed.

DOI: 10.4018/978-1-7998-3111-2.ch014

INTRODUCTION

Artificial intelligence is a part of computer science that deals with empowering skills and knowledge to the inhuman things in the world. It mainly encompasses two noteworthy thrill terms, namely, machine learning and deep learning. A profound scrutiny of three reckoning terms such as Artificial intelligence, machine learning and deep learning are laid out. A streamlined implementation of deep learning algorithm in Raspberry Pi with Beings classification algorithm of accuracy 98% is achieved.

Machine learning is an outlet of artificial intelligence that enables prediction of the actions and enrich the learning capability of a physical system. It depends on formerly educated features from the training data (Xin et al., 2018). Multi layered function in machine learning is achieved with the help of deep learning; which is a novel machine learning technique; which works with neural networks that are similar to the neuron structures of the human brain. The alliance between three terms, namely, Artificial Intelligence, Machine learning and Deep Learning indicates the benefit that deep learning has use of unsupervised or semi-supervised feature learning and hierarchical feature extraction for automatic and resourceful swapping of features (Deng et al., 2014). The relationship and differences between three terms artificial intelligence, machine learning and deep learning is put up in Figure 1.

Figure 1. Relation and Differences among Artificial Intelligence, Machine Learning and Deep Learning

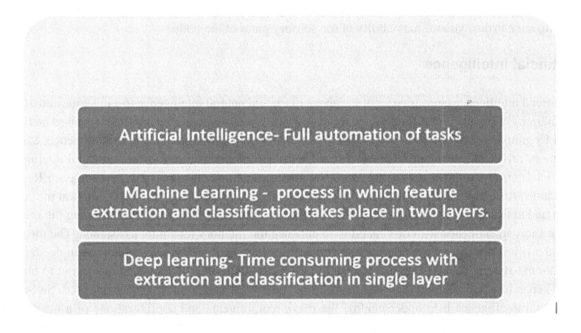

INTELLIGENCE

Intelligence is the most fascinating factor for a human as well as a machine in the present state. It can be described as the capability to estimate, reason, distinguish relations and analogies, study from practice, store and retrieve information from memory, resolve difficulties, comprehend multifaceted ideas, practice natural language effortlessly, categorize, simplify, and adapt to new situations. This intelligence can be demarcated into three varied types, such as, natural, artificial and hybrid. Intelligence along with its detailed subtypes is shown as taxonomy in Figure 2.

Natural Intelligence

Natural intelligence is generally present in humans and animals. It can be the extraordinary smelling power of a dog or the capability to have clear view in night for some animals. It can be categorized into nine types, namely, linguistic natural intelligence, melodic natural intelligence, logical and mathematical natural intelligence, spatial natural intelligence, kinaesthetic' natural intelligence, intrapersonal natural intelligence, interpersonal natural intelligence, memory natural intelligence and sensory natural intelligence (Wang et al., 2009) (Gardner et al., 1983). Linguistic natural intelligence is the ability to speak with the use of phonology and semantics. Melodic natural intelligence is the capability to create communication with a variety of sounds, pitch and rhythm. Logical and mathematical natural intelligence involves the creation of relationships between various factors. Spatial natural intelligence refers to the perception of visual information and reconstruction of visual images. Kinaesthetic' natural intelligence refers to the use of the body parts to solve problems along with the use of motor skills of the body. Intrapersonal natural intelligence denotes to influence on others feelings, motivations and decisions. Interpersonal natural intelligence is used in the identification and making judgements on other persons' decisions. Memory natural intelligence relates to remembering of facts, figures over a long time. Sensory natural intelligence is the extraordinary ability of the sensory parts of the body.

Artificial Intelligence

Artificial intelligence helps transfer of the above discussed natural intelligence to a machine and making it smarter. Based on the assistance of the smart working machines, artificial intelligence based on Forbes and Cognitive world can be of seven types, namely, Reactive machine artificial intelligence, Limited memory artificial intelligence, theory of mind artificial intelligence, self-aware artificial intelligence, artificial narrow intelligence, artificial general intelligence and artificial super human intelligence. Reactive machine artificial intelligence does not help storage of the old memories, but simply looks at the current part and assists in taking decisions. Limited memory artificial intelligence helps retaining the memory for a short span of time with no capability to enhance the memory for future assistance. The theory of mind artificial intelligence is related to an very advanced type of intelligence which can understand the emotional state of things. This is expected to be like the mind like intelligence transferred to humans and hence like human mind that sets the machine mind state that could also be monitored. Self-aware artificial intelligence help understanding the need, requirements and configurations of a machine by itself. A fully aware conscious system is the ultimate goal for many artificial intelligence researchers. Artificial narrow intelligence (Page et al., 2018) is the present small intelligence used today in an initial state without being in the form expected to be. This is also known as weak artificial intelligence. Artificial general intelligence is advanced machine intelligence where the device is fully responsible for the decisions and actions of only one operational case. Artificial super human intelligence is just a replica of humanoid robot, where it can do all actions of a human.

Figure 2. Intelligence Taxonomy

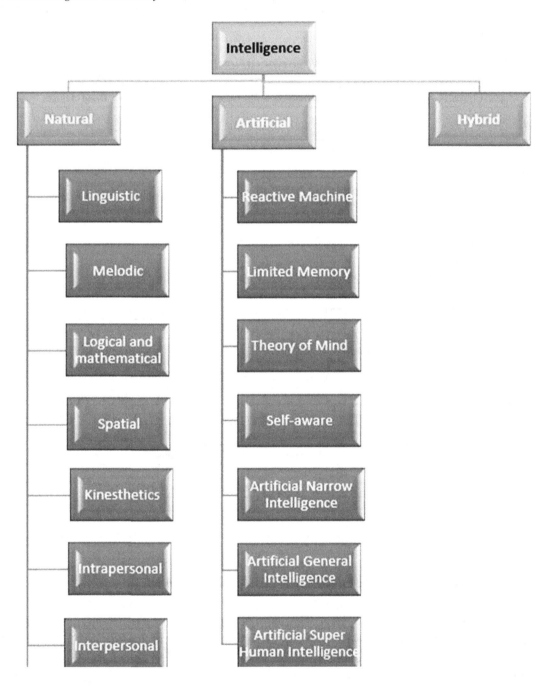

Hybrid Intelligence

Hybrid intelligence offloads some of the artificial intelligence work to the humans. At times, two different techniques could also be combined (Huang et al., 2008). This is mainly done to overcome the short comings of the artificial intelligence and to enhance natural intelligence. Table 1, shows the advantages and disadvantages of three types of intelligence and Table 2 shows the examples of various types of intelligence.

Table 1. Advantages and disadvantages of three types of intelligence

Intelligence types	Advantages	Disadvantages
Natural	God given specific ability	Can be lost due to some accidents and cannot be retained for a long period.
Artificial	Expected result can be obtained. Retention and replication is possible	Can show minimal cruelty.
Hybrid	Combines the advantages of both types and overcomes the disadvantages of both	Coordination between natural and artificial intelligence types must be effective and meaningful.

Table 2. Examples of types of intelligence

Intelligence Types	Examples	Intelligence Types	Examples
Linguistic Natural	Orators	Reactive Machine Artificial	Chess playing system
Melodic Natural	Singers, Musical instrument specialists	Limited Memory Artificial	Self driving cars
Logical and mathematical Natural	Mathematicians, Scientists	Theory of mind Artificial	Robots with emotional intelligence
kinesthetics' Natural	Players, Dancers	Self-aware Artificial	Self driven reacting machine
Spatial Natural	Astronauts, Map readers	Artificial narrow intelligence	Smart phone, siri
Intrapersonal Natural	Motivational speakers, monks	Artificial general intelligence	Pillo healthcare robot
Interpersonal Natural	Media communicators,	Artificial Super human intelligence	Alpha 2 humanoid robot
Memory Natural	Eidetic people	Hybrid Intelligence	Cindicator
Sensory Natural	Assistance dog		

ARTIFICIAL INTELLIGENCE BASED INTERNET OF THINGS

Smart automation is enhanced development of human machine interaction which helps many applications of smart automation involving the use of artificial intelligence along with Internet of Things (IoT). Successful automated artificial implementation requires a combination of three major techniques which are deep Learning or Machine Learning, IoT and Cloud computing. Some set of challenges are encountered in the case of such automated implementation (Yao et al., 2018), (Tang et al., 2017). IoT application depend on multiple sensors. Hence a combination with artificial intelligence requires the design of a novel neural network structures for multisensory data fusion. IoT devices are restricted systems with limited computational, energy and memory resources. This creates a barrier in deploying deep neural networks on IoT devices. Dependability assurance is important in IoT applications. Accurate results ae needed for achievement of high prediction. In data analytics, which is a base for machine learning, labelling of data is an important step. Data labelling for learning and training purposes is time-consuming. Overcoming this problem requires the teaching of recognition of objects and concepts for the sensing devices without (numerous) examples, where ground truth values are provided. Deep learning is known for high performance computing and gulps high power. So, the steps to reduce the power consumption or steps to handle this high power by IoT device must be worked upon. Machine learning libraries usually call on many third-party libraries, which can be difficult to migrate for IoT devices. Sometimes it hangs on to the IoT device when there is a problem in third party libraries. Machine Learning is quite easily deployable for IoT devices operating with low data sets. It has problems faced by deep learning. There are some additional difficulties seen in defining the features of interest and splitting the problem into various subsets using techniques like the correlation based feature, statically resampling and the decision tree. In machine learning, operation is not as complex as deep learning. Hence edge processing can yield good results (Yazici et al., 2018).

Researchers concerned in implementing the Internet of Things with artificial intelligence have come up with,

- DeepSense (Yao et al., 2017) a framework that provides a unified yet customizable solution only for certain combinations of deep neural network topologies that are particularly well-suited for learning from sensor data.
- Deep Internet of Things (Yao et al., 2017), an algorithm that can directly compress the structures of commonly used deep neural networks. The compressed model can be deployed on commodity devices. This helps reduction in execution time, energy and memory to great extent. But still the effect on the final prediction accuracy is not much to speak of.
- RDeepSense (Yao et al., 2018) meant to achieve accurate and well-calibrated estimations through changes in the objective function for faithful reflection of prediction accuracy.
- Generative Adversarial Networks (GAN) (Goodfellow et al., 2014) are used overcoming the main problem seen in deep learning – labelling enormous data.
- To support high power consuming and high power computing deep learning incorporated in Internet of Things devices. Offloading to cloud is performed (Yao et al., 2018); it also helps to calling the third party libraries. Cloud computation reduces power consumption with a considerable latency.
- Deep learning integrated with Internet of Things and Cloud cannot meet real-time requirements as computation depends upon on network connectivity and other network parameters. Only single task performing Internet of Things devices with deep learning are verified. With future researches enabling multi-tasking low power Internet of Things devices with deep learning. Artificial intelligence based internet of things is undergone two types – criterion analysis and elemental analysis.

CRITERION ANALYSIS

Analysis of parameters such as data dependence, processors support, extracted feature dependence, problem solving method, execution time, interpretability, processing steps, computing and algorithmic analysis is carried out for getting a clear understanding of the clear cut relationship between machine learning and deep learning. Data dependence deals with the nature and volume of data needed for improved processing (LeCun et al., 2015). Data dependency can be functional or conceptual and can be considerably supportive in reverse engineering. Processors points out to the minimum requirement for processing unit (Coelho et al., 2017). Graphical processing unit (GPU) is the best solution for rapid processing. At contemporary the exploration is poignant in the track of optimizing a central processing unit to assist in learning algorithms. This optimization helps overcoming the problem of the reliance on GPU and its high cost. Dependency on extracted features refers to the processing dependency on these features of interest (Deng et al., 2017). Feature engineering that involves the creation of feature extractors, diminishes data complexity and makes outline more noticeable to learning algorithms. Problem solving method is the overview of achieving the final solution. Machine learning on overview involves two steps, namely, detection and recognition. Deep learning follows the end to end method. Execution time is the time taken for learning algorithms to be implemented in physical device with training and testing phases. Hence it involves two time periods, namely, training period and testing period. Interpretability refers to the ability to do good prediction with the help of known steps. This parameter is the main reason for putting deep learning down as it does not reveal the process of prediction. Processing steps involve step by step mechanism of achieving the final output. Computing involves storage and space where operation is involved. (Louridas et al., 2016). Computing term is considered both in the criterion and elemental analysis, as it depends on operational methods and hardware components for processing. The layout explaining the clear cut deviations of deep learning from machine learning based on the certain parameters is represented in Table 3.

ELEMENTAL ANALYSIS

Four elements are involved in building artificial intelligence based Internet of Things system. They are device, data, algorithm and computation as shown in Figure 3. Physical device is needed for sensing, recording and storage the parameters from the environment. Data is the input to the Artificial Intelligence based Internet of Things system, the device works on this input to take a feasible solution. The algorithm runs on the device which performs the analytics of the input data. Computation is the processing of incoming data using algorithm on the device. The factors influencing the three elements are discussed below.

Table 3. Machine Learning Vs Deep Learning

References	Parameters		Machine Learning	Deep Learning
[Deng, L., et al., 2014]	Data dependence		Works well even with small data sets	Performance improves with increase in data sets.
[LeCun, Y et al., 2015]	Processors support		Can operate with CPU. GPU is not mandatory	GPU is required for the performance of complex operations
[Coelho, I. M., 2017]	Dependency on extracted feature		Process is based on the precision of features extracted.	No burden of designing a feature extractor.
[Xin, Y. et al.,2018]	Problem-solving method		Splits a problem into various subsets; finds a result for each subset and finally combines to conclude a solution for the problem.	Follows from start to finish of problem solving technique
	Execution time	Training time	Takes less when compared to Deep Learning	Gulps a longer time
		Test time	Is depending on data volume. Consumes large time for bulky data.	Is quick and easy
[LeCun, Y et al., 2015]	Interpretability		Easy to predict and understand the algorithm flow to the result	The working of neurons cannot be predicted
[Louridas, P. et al, 2016]	Steps involved		Feature engineering, apply machine learning algorithm, train and evaluate ML. Finally usage of the ML model	Similar to ML but feature engineering is done automatically
[Li. H. et al., 2018]	Computing		Can be Edge, Fog or Cloud	Mostly relies on cloud because of its complex nature. But parts of layers can be offloaded to edge.
[Xin, Y. et al.,2018]	Example algorithms		e-KNN, SVM, Decision Tree, and Bayes	DBM, CNN, and LSTM.
[Nabipor, M. et al., 2020]			SVC, Naïve Bayes, KNN, Logistic regression	ANN, RNN, LSTM
[Maqsood, H. et al., 2020] [Nabipor, M. et al., 2020]	Prediction		A decent prediction is only achieved	As it does a deep analysis accurate prediction is possible
[H.Gunduz, 2019] [Lahmiri, H. et al., 2019] [Wang, W. et al., 2020]	Detection		A remarkable detection is not achieved	Due to the ability to learn linear and nonlinear features without need for features extraction

Device Characteristics

Device plays an important role in realizing a smart environment (Asano et al., 2016), (Xiao et al., 2014). Devices can be Arduino, Raspberry Pi, Jetson, Beagle bone (Sambandam Raju et al., 2019), (Geng et al., 2019). The operation of the device is influenced by five characteristics that include scalability, diversity, interoperability, management and resource constraint. Scalability involves increase or decrease in the number of physical devices that have influence on the performance of Artificial Intelligence based Internet of Things systems. It has an impact not only on accuracy but also on computational resources. Diversity of different devices should not interrupt the process of machine and deep learning algorithms.

Figure 3. Elements of Artificial Intelligence of Internet of Things

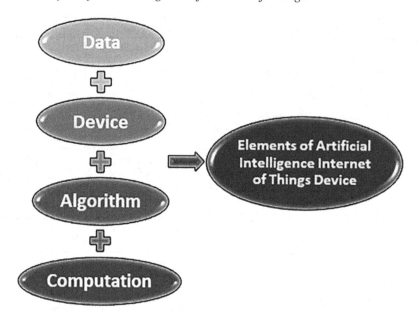

A Devices are capable of generating diverse formats of data. Internet of Things random devices leads to interoperability issues which face difficulty in establishing meaningful connection in spite of different operating systems, connector types, versions and protocol standards. Management of the device between various states and modes for smooth functioning with the prescribed artificial intelligent algorithm is the main challenge in Artificial Intelligence based Internet of Things deployment. Internet of Things devices in current stage of development has constraints especially in the areas of energy and processing power. So direct deployment of machine and deep learning algorithms leads to resource constraint problems.

Data

Learning algorithms works on many types of data that include those relating to health, motion, environmental, biological, traffic and generalized image for processing (Zhang et al., 2019), (Mahmud et al., 2018), (Liang et al., 2015). Data can be of two types, Internet of Things data and Big data. Generally big data have characteristics of six V's- Variety, Volume, Veracity, Velocity, Veracity and Value. The characteristics that distinguish Internet of Things data from big data are large scale streaming data, heterogeneity, time correlation, space correlation and high noise (Ghosh et al., 2018). Therefore, Artificial Intelligence based Internet of Things devices involves mostly Internet of Things data (IoT data) influenced by factors such as data volume, data integration, data traffic, data management, data labelling, minimum labelled data, data preprocessing, real time data and data analytics. Internet of Things devices are capable of producing millions of data in nano seconds, hence the volume of IoT data requires efficient handling. Data integration deals with different formats of data generated by interoperable and diverse Internet of Things device. Internet of Things traffic are mainly due to volume, diversity, speed and uncertainty of produced IoT data. Generally, IoT data are heterogeneous in nature. This heterogeneity can be of two types, namely, syntactic and semantic. Syntactic heterogeneity is of different data types, formats and models. Semantic heterogeneity is the difference in the data meanings and interpretations.

This type of heterogeneity leads to efficiency and generalization problems. So data management of these heterogeneous data is critical for artificial intelligence algorithms. Data labelling is an important part of preparing training data for artificial intelligence based algorithms. Data labelling is very difficult in data produced by Internet of Things devices. Choice of some crucial data can help overcoming the tedious part of data labelling. They can be labelled minimally. But the constraint lies in the part of choosing the crucial minimum data for labelling. Generally machine learning or deep learning algorithm data requires preprocessing in Artificial Intelligence based Internet of Things. Devices generate real time data which are fast streaming and hence the smart algorithm should have ability to comply with real time generated data without waiting for preprocessing. Data analytics involves the issue of real time data and should overcome latency arising as a result of analytics. Hence artificial intelligence based internet of things lead to a new branch of data analytics and to large steaming data analytics. Though this new branch of analytics is in the budding stage, this analytic technique helps to overcome the issues faced in the implementation of artificial intelligence algorithms.

Algorithm

Artificial intelligence systems generally use training algorithms such as gradient, stochastic gradient descent, momentum, Levenberg -marquardt, back propagation (Shrestha et al., 2019) and machine learning techniques such as k-means, K- nearest, decision tree, random forest, bayes theory, hidden markov model (Xie et al., 2019). Implementation of these learning algorithm faces issues that include performance, precise processing, critical infrastructure, butterfly effect and noise effect. Performance of artificial intelligence algorithm involves latency, speed and effectiveness of algorithm. The issue of the critical infrastructure is the result of the presence of prototype versions of internet of things devices alone. Hence, a full fetched model considering all factors of smart automation is needed. In deep learning and machine learning algorithms, a small noise in the input layers changes the prediction level and accuracy to a great extent. In contrast to this, noise effect also relies on the butterfly effect, in which a small variation in initial state results in huge variations at a later state.

Computation

Computation plays an important role in Artificial Intelligence based Internet of Things. Computation can be cloud, fog and edge. In cloud computing latency is the main issue but it supports storage and fast computation. So, in order to reduce latency, some important computation can be pushed to lower levels and can be done in edge and fog (Muhammed et al., 2019). Therefore a hybrid computation to poise all shortcomings requires consideration.

On the overview of criterion based and elemental analysis and in implementation of machine learning algorithms for artificial intelligence based internet of things system, precise algorithm, data preprocessing and data labelling are the three foremost challenges. Similarly, for deep learning techniques enactment huge data set, requirement of CPU and GPU for huge data set training, overfitting issues, noise and butterfly effect are five significant challenges.

Implementation of Raspberry Pi Based Beings Classification

Numerous Internet of Things project when clubbed with artificial intelligence thrive to become super auto computing models. IoT based light automation (Preethi et al., 2019), video surveillance (Preethi et al., 2020) can be clubbed with artificial intelligence. Let IoT based light automation (Preethi et al., 2019) be considered. This Arduino based framework is capable of controlling light bulbs based on motion. A streamlined deep learning to detect the motion is caused by living and non-living thing enhances IoT automation to turn into intelligent automation. A Raspberry Pi is connected to PiR sensor, Pi Cam, light bulbs and a streamlined deep learning algorithm is uploaded as portrayed in figure 4. A Beings Categorization (BC) algorithm is built for enhanced human intervention algorithm. Beings Categorization (BC) algorithm is a machine learning algorithms as a service (MLAS). Beings Categorization- Machine Learning As a Service (BCMLAS) is deployed using Nanonets bearing the model id c4067ff5-78f9-4e14-954d-9de2d5690c3c which uses all the available images in the web for data set creation. This algorithm has four main layers mainly input, pretrained, hidden and output layer. The training of the algorithm nearly took 27 minutes and yielded an accuracy of 97%. BCMLAS is capable of categorizing the images fed into three categories – human beings, Living beings excluding human and non-living beings. So on the PiR sensor detection the camera is triggered to capture a picture. This captured image is fed to BCMLAS for categorization. On successful detection of human, the lights and fans are operated. On condition of some pet animals' interventions BCMLAS classifies to living beings excluding human and hence the home appliances are not powered. In case of flinging a ball to diverse places in home BCMLAS sorts to third category - non-living beings and the basic gadgets are not operated. Thus, redundant switching is evaded, intelligence is added.

Figure 4. Raspberry Pi implemented with Beings Classification algorithm

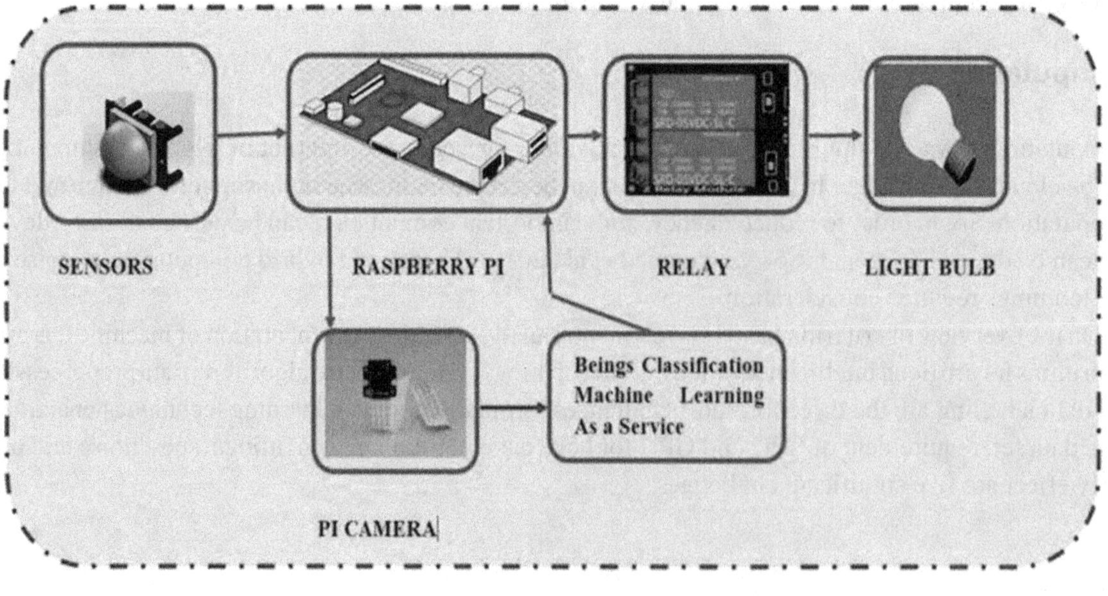

Figure 5. Accuracy Vs Number of Images for Being Classification model

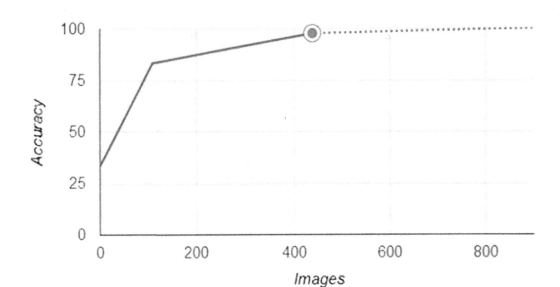

Accuracy is considered to ratio of successful correct predictions made to total number of predictions of the algorithm. In Figure 5 accuracy is marked in Y axis and number of images predicted in X axis. It is found to rise as the image set surges and have reached 97.6% at 438 training image data set that includes 149 animal, 146 human and 143 non-living beings images.

Figure 6. Confusion matrix for Beings classification model

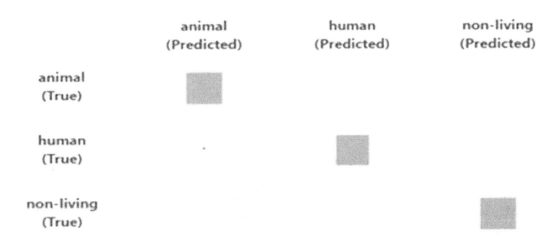

Table 4. Description of probability and Categorization of Beings Classification

Image	Probability of animal	Probability of human being	Probability of non-living being	Algorithm categorization	Categorization
1	0.0143	0.2499	0.7358	Human Being	Human Being (adult)
2	0.2079	0.6760	0.1159	Human Being	Human Being(child)
3	0.1136	0.2451	0.6411	Animal	Non-Living Being (ball)
4	0.0057	0.1196	0.8746	Non-Living Being	Non-Living Being(toy car)
5	0.9347	0.0284	0.0368	Animal	Animal (dog -pet)

Confusion matrix or error matrix helps to visualize the algorithm performance. Figure 6 expresses a confusion matrix plotted for three categories of Being Classification. Then the algorithm is tested for set of various images, description about five tested images tabled and the probability values is given in table 4.The red highlighted text in table indicates the wrong prediction made by the algorithm.

CONCLUSION

In this chapter the challenges facing coalescing artificial intelligence and Internet of Things have been portrayed in detail. The role of intelligence, natural intelligence, artificial intelligence and hybrid intelligence are dimensioned in all aspects. The encounters of artificial intelligence based internet of things is conversed and many research outcomes of such devices is deliberated. Further criterion based approach and elemental approach for analysis of artificial intelligence based Internet of things have been elucidated. An approach to make IoT automation to intelligent automation is achieved by streamlined deep learning implementation in Raspberry Pi. The working of Beings classification algorithm which is based on machine learning as a service is tested. Accuracy and confusion matrix for the algorithm is discussed.

ACKNOWLEDGMENT

This research received no specific grant from any funding agency in the public, commercial, or not-for-profit sectors.

REFERENCES

Asano, S., Yashiro, T., & Sakamura, K. (2016). Device collaboration framework in IoT-aggregator for realizing smart environment. *TRON Symposium (TRONSHOW)*, 1-9.10.1109/TRONSHOW.2016.7842886

Coelho, I. M., Coelho, V. N., Luz, E. J. S., Ochi, L. S., Guimarães, F. G., & Rios, E. (2017). A GPU deep learning metaheuristic based model for time series forecasting. *Applied Energy*, *201*(1), 412–418. doi:10.1016/j.apenergy.2017.01.003

Deng, L., & Yu, D. (2014). Deep learning: Methods and applications. *Found. Trends Signal Process.*, 7(3–4), 197–387. doi:10.1561/2000000039

Gardner, H. (1983). *Frames of Mind: The Theory of Multiple Intelligences.* Basic Books.

Geng, X., Zhang, Q., Wei, Q., Zhang, T., Cai, Y., Liang, Y., & Sun, X. (2019). *A Mobile Greenhouse Environment Monitoring System Based on the Internet of Things.* IEEE. doi:10.1109/ACCESS.2019.2941521

Ghosh, A., Chakraborty, D., & Law, A. (2018). Artificial Intelligence in Internet of Things. *CAAI Transactions on Intelligence Technology*, 3(4), 208–218. doi:10.1049/trit.2018.1008

Goodfellow, I., Abadie, J. P., Mirza, M., Xu, B., Farley, D. W., Ozair, S., . . . Bengio, Y. (2014). Generative Adversarial Nets. https:// arxiv.org/abs/1406.2661

Gunduz, H. (2019). Deep learning-based Parkinson's disease classification using vocal feature sets. *IEEE Access: Practical Innovations, Open Solutions*, 7, 115540–115551. doi:10.1109/ACCESS.2019.2936564

Huang, F., Xu, J., Gu, J., & Lou, Y. (2008). Optimum Design of Network Structures Based on Hybrid Intelligence of Genetic - Ant Colonies Algorithm. *International Conference on Intelligent Computation Technology and Automation (ICICTA)*, 116-120. 10.1109/ICICTA.2008.205

Lahmiri, S., & Shmuel, A. (2019). Detection of Parkinson's disease based on voice patterns ranking and optimized support vector machine. *Biomedical Signal Processing and Control*, 49, 427–433. doi:10.1016/j.bspc.2018.08.029

LeCun, Y., Bengio, Y., & Hinton, G. (2015). Deep learning. *Nature*, 521(7553), 436–444. doi:10.1038/nature14539 PMID:26017442

Li, H., Ota, K., & Dong, M. (2018). Learning IoT in Edge: Deep Learning for the Internet of Things with Edge Computing. *IEEE Network*, 32(1), 96–101. doi:10.1109/MNET.2018.1700202

Liang, M., Li, Z., Chen, T., & Zeng, J. (2015). Integrative Data Analysis of Multi-Platform Cancer Data with a Multimodal Deep Learning Approach. *IEEE/ACM Transactions on Computational Biology and Bioinformatics*, 12(4), 928–937. doi:10.1109/TCBB.2014.2377729 PMID:26357333

Louridas, P., & Ebert, C. (2016). Machine learning. *IEEE Software*, 33(5), 110–115. doi:10.1109/MS.2016.114

Mahmud, M., Kaiser, M. S., Hussain, A., & Vassanelli, S. (2018). Applications of Deep Learning and Reinforcement Learning to Biological Data. *IEEE Transactions on Neural Networks and Learning Systems*, 29(6), 2063–2079. doi:10.1109/TNNLS.2018.2790388 PMID:29771663

Maqsood, H., Mehmood, I., Maqsood, M., Yasir, M., Afzal, S., Aadil, F., Selim, M. M., & Muhammad, K. (2020). A local and global event sentiment based efficient stock exchange forecasting using deep learning. *International Journal of Information Management*, 50, 432–451. doi:10.1016/j.ijinfomgt.2019.07.011

Muhammad, K., Khan, S., Palade, V., Mehmood, V., & De Albuquerque, V. H. C. (2019). Edge Intelligence-Assisted Smoke Detection in Foggy Surveillance Environments. *IEEE Transactions on Industrial Informatics*. . doi:10.1109/TII.2019.2915592

Nabipour, M., Nayyeri, P., Jabani, H., & Mosavi, A. (2020). Predicting Stock Market Trends Using Machine Learning and Deep Learning Algorithms Via Continuous and Binary Data; a Comparative Analysis. *IEEE Access: Practical Innovations, Open Solutions*, 8, 150199–150212. doi:10.1109/ACCESS.2020.3015966

Page, J., Bain, M., & Mukhlish, F. (2018). The Risks of Low Level Narrow Artificial Intelligence. *IEEE International Conference on Intelligence and Safety for Robotics (ISR)*, 1-6. 10.1109/IISR.2018.8535903

Raju, P. S., Mahalingam, M., & Rajendran, R. A. (2020). Review of Intellectual Video Surveillance through Internet of Things. In *The Cognitive Approach in Cloud Computing and Internet of Things Technologies for Surveillance Tracking Systems* (pp. 141–155). Academic Press. doi:10.1016/B978-0-12-816385-6.00010-6

Sambandam Raju, P., Mahalingam, M., & Arumugam Rajendran, R. (2019). Design, Implementation and Power Analysis of Pervasive Adaptive Resourceful Smart Lighting and Alerting Devices in Developing Countries Supporting Incandescent and LED Light Bulbs. *Sensors (Basel)*, 19(9), 2032. doi:10.339019092032 PMID:31052250

Shrestha, A., & Mahmood, A. (2019). Review of Deep Learning Algorithms and Architectures. *IEEE Access: Practical Innovations, Open Solutions*, 7, 53040–53065. doi:10.1109/ACCESS.2019.2912200

Tang, J., Sun, D., Liu, S., & Gaudiot, J. (2017). Enabling Deep Learning on IoT Devices. *Computer*, 50(10), 92–96. doi:10.1109/MC.2017.3641648

Wang, W., Lee, J., Harrou, F., & Sun, Y. (2020). Early Detection of Parkinson's Disease Using Deep Learning and Machine Learning. *IEEE Access: Practical Innovations, Open Solutions*, 8, 147635–147646. doi:10.1109/ACCESS.2020.3016062

Wang, Y., Kinsner, W., & Zhang, D. (2009). Contemporary Cybernetics and Its Facets of Cognitive Informatics and Computational Intelligence. *IEEE Transactions on Systems, Man, and Cybernetics. Part B, Cybernetics*, 39(4), 823–833. doi:10.1109/TSMCB.2009.2013721 PMID:19349246

Xiao, G., Guo, J., Xu, L. D., & Gong, Z. (2014). User Interoperability with Heterogeneous IoT Devices through Transformation. *IEEE Transactions on Industrial Informatics*, 10(2), 1486–1496. doi:10.1109/TII.2014.2306772

Xie, J., Yu, F. R., Huang, T., Xie, R., Liu, J., Wang, C., & Liu, Y. (2019). A Survey of Machine Learning Techniques Applied to Software Defined Networking (SDN): Research Issues and Challenges. *IEEE Communications Surveys and Tutorials*, 21(1), 393–430. doi:10.1109/COMST.2018.2866942

Xin, Y., Kong, L., Liu, Z., Chen, Y., Li, Y., Zhu, H., Gao, M., Hou, H., & Wang, C. (2018). Machine Learning and Deep Learning Methods for Cyber security. *IEEE Access: Practical Innovations, Open Solutions*, 6, 35365–35381. doi:10.1109/ACCESS.2018.2836950

Yao, S., Hu, S., Zhao, Y., Zhang, A., & Abdelzhar, T. (2017). DeepSense: A Unified Deep Learning Framework for Time-Series Mobile Sensing Data Processing. *Proc. 26th Int'l Conf. World Wide Web*, 351–360. 10.1145/3038912.3052577

Yao, S., Zhao, Y., Shao, H., Zhang, A., Zhang, C., Li, S., & Abdelzhar, T. (2018). RDeepSense: Reliable Deep Mobile Computing Models with Uncertainty Estimations. *Proceedings of the ACM on Interactive, Mobile, Wearable and Ubiquitous Technologies, 1*(4), 173. doi:10.1145/3161181

Yao, S., Zhao, Y., Zhang, A., Hu, S., Shao, H., Zhang, C., Su, L., & Abdelzhar, T. (2018). Deep Learning for the Internet of Things. *Computer, 51*(5), 32–41. doi:10.1109/MC.2018.2381131

Yao, S., Zhao, Y., Zhang, A., Su, L., & Abdelzhar, T. (2017). DeepIoT: Compressing Deep Neural Network Structures for Sensing Systems with a Compressor Critic Framework. *Proc. 15th ACM Conf. Embedded Network Sensor System.* 10.1145/3131672.3131675

Yazici, M. T., Basurra, S., & Gaber, M. M. (2018). Edge Machine Learning: Enabling Smart Internet of Things Applications. *Big Data Cognitive Computing, 2*(3), 26. doi:10.3390/bdcc2030026

Zhang, C., Zhang, H., Qiao, J., Yuan, D., & Zhang, M. (2019). Deep Transfer Learning for Intelligent Cellular Traffic Prediction Based on Cross-Domain Big Data. *IEEE Journal on Selected Areas in Communications, 37*(6), 1389–1401. doi:10.1109/JSAC.2019.2904363

ADDITIONAL READING

Ferrero Bermejo, J., Gómez Fernández, J. F., Olivencia Polo, F., & Crespo Márquez, A. (2019). A Review of the Use of Artificial Neural Network Models for Energy and Reliability Prediction. A Study of the Solar PV, Hydraulic and Wind Energy Sources. *Applied Sciences (Basel, Switzerland), 9*(9), 1844. doi:10.3390/app9091844

Kaplan, D. Y. (2019). *The. Usage Analysis of Machine Learning Methods for Intrusion Detection in Software-Defined. Networks Artificial Intelligence and Security Challenges in Emerging Networks.* IGI Global publishers.

Khaliq, K. A., Chughtai, O., Shahwani, A., Qayyum, A., & Pannek, J. (2019). Road Accidents Detection, Data Collection and Data Analysis Using V2X Communication and Edge/Cloud Computing. *Electronics (Basel), 8*(8), 896. doi:10.3390/electronics8080896

Lima, Z., García-Vázquez, H., Rodríguez, R., Khemchandani, S., Dualibe, F., & del Pino, J. (2018). A System for Controlling and Monitoring IoT Applications. *Applied System Innovation, 1*(3), 26. doi:10.3390/asi1030026

Oliveira, L., Rodrigues, J., Kozlov, S., Rabêlo, R., & Albuquerque, V. (2019). MAC Layer Protocols for Internet of Things: A Survey. *Future Internet, 11*(1), 16. doi:10.3390/fi11010016

Silva, J., Rodrigues, J., Al-Muhtadi, J., Rabêlo, R., & Furtado, V. (2019). Management Platforms and Protocols for Internet of Things: A Survey. *Sensors (Basel), 19*(3), 676. doi:10.339019030676 PMID:30736424

Véstias, M. P. (2019). A Survey of Convolutional Neural Networks on Edge with Reconfigurable Computing. *Algorithms, 12*(8), 154. doi:10.3390/a12080154

Yiner, Z., Sertbas, N., Odabasi, S. D., & Kaplan, D. Y. (2019). *Attack Detection in Cloud Networks Based on Artificial Intelligence Approaches, Artificial Intelligence and Security Challenges in Emerging Networks*. IGI Global publishers.

KEY TERMS AND DEFINITIONS

Big Data: Indicates the huge volume of data sets used computationally to expose beneficial patterns or trends.

Cloud: Is a computing technique which provides on- demand services to store, process and compute databases.

Data Dependency: The level of dependency on the input data.

Execution Time: The time taken for effecting an algorithm for production.

Extracted Feature Dependence: The level of dependency on the specific feature obtained from the data through feature engineering.

Feature Engineering: The study which involves obtaining precise features from huge data sets.

Intelligence: Is the capability to attain and apply knowledge in addition skills.

Interpretability: The ability to detect future aspects with available input parameters.

IoT: Internet of things is grid of internet linked objects with capability to analyse, gather and exchange data.

Problem Solving Method: The way of dealing with a problem for obtaining the best outcome.

Chapter 15

Real–Time Problems to Be Solved by the Combination of IoT, Big Data, and Cloud Technologies

Shaila S. G.
Dayananda Sagar University, India

Monish L.
Dayananda Sagar University, India

Rajlaxmi Patil
Dayananda Sagar University, India

ABSTRACT

With the advancement of computation power and internet revolution, IoT, big data, and cloud computing have become the most prevalent technologies in present time. Convergence of these three technologies has led to the development of new opportunities and applications which solve the real time problems in the most efficient way. Though cloud computing and big data have an inherent connection between them, IoT plays a major role of a data source unit. With the explosion of data, cloud computing is playing a significant role in the storage and management. However, the main concern that accompanies IoT are the issues related to privacy, security, power efficiency, computational complexities, etc. Misinterpretation of data and security limitations are the bottlenecks of big data whereas the limitations of cloud computing involve network connection dependency, limited features, technical issues, and security. The chapter considers use cases to address their real time problems and discusses about how to solve these issues by combining these technologies.

DOI: 10.4018/978-1-7998-3111-2.ch015

INTRODUCTION

Nowadays, people are into IoT era, wherein, things around us generates data. The increase in the usage of IoT devices have proportionally increased the generation of data. As a solution to support the storage and processing of this data, cloud has been chosen. IoT, turns out to be a network of things also referred to as physical objects that are embedded with electronics, sensors and software. It involves network connectivity for receiving and transmitting the data from one node to other node or to the controller. In the IoT network, every node will have a unique identifier, embedded system and the ability to transfer data over the network. On the other side, the data collected from IoT components will be voluminous and referred as Big Data. Data sets grow rapidly due to the availability of large number of less expensive IoT devices such as mobile devices, software logs, RFID and sensors. Day to day the velocity at which data is created, collected and analysed is increasing. It is related to three key words: volume, variety and velocity. The generated data can be structured or unstructured or semi-structured. Structured and unstructured data require advanced analytical techniques to be processed. Storing and processing such a huge data is not an easy task. Thus, Cloud has emerged as a supporting platform that stores and provides access to the shared pool of resources based on the users demand and convenience. Cloud provides services in three major categories such as Infrastructure-as-a-Service (IaaS), Platform-as-a-Service (PaaS), and Software-as-a-Service (SaaS). At the base of the stack, IaaS provides virtual hardware, networking and storage to the end users. PaaS is the core that acts as a middleware by providing abstract environment where applications are deployed. SaaS provides on demand services to the users and also the applications.

Combining these technologies together will securely connect and retrieve data from any device around us. This supports leading technologies like Wireless Sensor Networks (WSN) and Radio Frequency Devices (RFID). Wireless sensor protocols and RFID integrate IoT data into the enterprise applications which create a platform for Big Data analytics in the cloud which is cost effective and scalable. Automatic lifecycle management that involve day to day life activities involve a wide variety of data. The convergence of these three technologies gives the convenience platform for storing and analysing. The intermediate layer between the IoT and its applications is cloud, cloud hides all the necessary functionalities and complexity to implement it. Data analysis, data integration and data sharing is made easier after the convergence of these technologies. Cloud APIs can be used to access the data stored in the cloud from anywhere. Secured access and protected storage are guaranteed by the cloud.

LITERATURE SURVEY

Yu Liu et al (2015), proposed an approach in medical monitoring system to deliver an application that runs based on the IoT and Cloud Computing technology based on the hospital information system. Zainab Alansari et al (2018) faced lots of Challenges during IoT and Big Data Integration. Different data analysis, Business intelligence and analytical applications that are emerging today help the industries and organizations in transforming their business to improve their quality and scale their productivity. Real-time processing of the data from multiple sources are used collectively to enhance the intelligence of the smart things by Priya et al. IoT and Bigdata can be integrated to provide service to the organizations and individuals, it facilitates the organization by providing a better business model to compete in the real world. An IoT-Cloud Based Solution for Real-Time and Batch Processing of Big Data is proposed by Nada Chendeb Taher et al, considering Healthcare application. Here, healthcare management is built on IoT, Big Data Analytics and Cloud Computing. Authors collects the data from the different medical IoT devices and storing this bulk data on the cloud like Amazon Web services and process the real time and long-term data. It is observed that Cloud, Big Data, IoT based application for healthcare deals very well with response time and allowed cost model to facilitate the health care. Related work by Oracle in Driving Real -Time Insight (2016) proposed that Oracle IoT Cloud Service and Oracle Big Data Cloud Service are ready to work with an organization to connect, analyse, and integrate the data collected from different IoT devices, collected data is in large scale. This bulk data need to be transmitted to the other connected devices or to the application controlling the environment. The complexities involved in IoT, Cloud Computing and Big Data are handled by Oracle. The complexities exist from devices to applications, data to analytics and security to scalability.

CONVERGENCE OF THREE TECHNOLOGIES

1. Convergence of IoT and Big Data Technologies:

IoT devices connects the virtual and real world by connecting set of devices on internet. This devices on the internet use a set of IoT standards, Protocols and technologies like Bluetooth, Cellular, Wi-Fi, ZigBee, MQTT (Message Queue Telemetry Transport), CoAP (Constrained Application Protocol), NFC (Near Field Communication), AMQP (Advanced Message Queueing Protocol), Zwave and many more. The data generated by these connected IoT devices is huge in terms of volume, velocity and variety. The traditional database and analytical tools cannot store, process and analyse this structured or unstructured format of data. The data generated from these devices need to be analysed. Though, applying Big Data analytics on IoT device can improve the energy efficiency of sensors, verification and assessment is possible and can monitor accidents and environmental risks, but the challenges is to extract the valuable information from massive volumes of data generated by sensors, RFID tags and other devices. Here, the quantity is high, but the quality of data will be low. Thus, the data is proceeded to analyse using analytical tools like Hadoop Map Reduce and Apache spark to drive meaningful insights, which will help in strategic decision making. Some of the frameworks which are used in analysing data generated through IoT device including Hadoop, Oozie, Spark and Storm.

Mathew and Al Hajj,(March 2017) in their related work propose that hadoop can handle different types of structured and unstructured data generated by devices. It supports data processing and storage for Big Data applications in scalable clusters. Data mining, Predictive analysis and Machine learning can also be done. Apache Hadoop consists of two sub-projects. They are MapReduce and Hadoop distributed File system. Hadoop is mainly used for parallel processing. Hadoop computes and stores terabytes of data. Map Reduce is another widely used computational framework which processes data parallelly across a large set of clusters by applying independent map and reduce operations. While performing map operation set of data is taken and broken into tuples, which constitute another set. Then these tuples are sent as input to reduce task and combines them. The sequence of operation is map followed by reduce. The advantage of MapReduce is that it can scale over multiple computing nodes. Next is Hadoop Distributed File system (HDFS) which accounts for storage part of Hadoop applications. HDFS provides data for map-reduce model. It is fault tolerant and built using low cost hardware. These systems are fault tolerant as data is stored across multiple systems creating redundant copies of it. Network traffic is reduced and throughput is increased. Through command line interface one can interact with HDFS. It follows master-slave architecture. It checks the status of cluster nodes in distributed storage and processing environment. Name nodes and Data nodes are used. Name node hardware contains operating system Linux and name node software. Master server is name node and manages file system namespaces, provides access to files and supports file operations such as open, close and rename files or directory. Similar to Name node, data node is commodity hardware having operating system Linux and data node software. Every node in a cluster will have a data node. On client request it performs read operation on file systems. Apart from this on name node instructions they perform operations like block creation, replication and deletion. Another storage and processing system is Google File System which is scalable and fault tolerant distributed file system, built by google. It accommodates different data generated by google. The asset of using google file system is it exploits the strength of shelf-servers while minimizing hardware weakness. Google file system works on the principle of autonomic computing, the computers are able to diagnose and solve problems in real-time without human intervention. Google File system are highly fault tolerant, supports critical data replication, high throughput, automatic and efficient data recovery, high availability, namespace management and locking and reduced interaction between client and master because of large chunk of server. Apache Oozie is a workflow scheduler for Hadoop. Ozie is a web-application which triggers workflow actions. In case, the Big Data that is collected has discrepancies and inconsistency in data fields and content then, data cleaning has to be done and to be loaded into downstream for operations. IoT devices data which is collected is refined using this Big Data analytics framework. Another tool used as stream processing engine for contemporary IoT applications is Apache Spark. It offers a rich set of APIs in the areas of ingestion, data cleansing, cloud integration, multi-source joins, static data streams, time-window aggregations, transformations, and gives strong support for machine learning and predictive analytics. Apache spark uses Directed Acyclic Graph (DAG) scheduler, a query optimizer and physical execution engine, it gives high performance for batch and streaming data. Many coding languages like SQL, Python, R, Java, Scala are supported. Parallel apps can be built efficiently. SQL and Data Frames, Machine learning library (MLiB), Graph X and spark streaming all these libraries are combined in application. Apache spark runs everywhere using its standalone cluster mode. Another tool which supports processing vast amounts of data in an immune and horizontal scalable method in a distributed real-time system is Apache Storm. It supports micro-level batch processing. Big data uses RDBMS (Relational Database Management System) for database management system that uses relational model for denoting real-world entities or relationship. It uses table to represent a collection of related data values. SQL should be able to digest the data generated by IoT devices and analyse rapidly for decision making, from a business point of view. NoSQL can also be used for storage and retrieval of data. NoSQL supports non-relational, schema-free, supports simple API, distributed features. NoSQL is most widely used in Big Data applications due to its high availability and high scalability.

2. Convergence of Big Data and Cloud Computing:

The enormous amount of data which is generated by devices, are stored in cloud infrastructure. Cloud offers on demand pay-per-use services by using underlying distributed computing environment. Usually these services are rendered as PaaS (Platform as a Service), SaaS (Software as a service), IaaS (Infrastructure as service) in cloud. Apart from this AaaS (Application as Service) and DaaS (Database as a Service) are becoming popular for applications in implementation environment. On demand, the cloud provides resources and uninterrupted services across the diverse locations and it provide security to data by using simple software interface, which makes the cloud ideal partner for Big Data. IaaS offers services such as data centre space, servers, storage space and cloud networking components connected through the internet. The services are offered similar to on-premises infrastructure. IaaS are widely used in website hosting and monitoring, backup, recovery, inter networking and clustering etc. It is the responsibility of the service provider to maintain the physical data centre, servers, storage and security. IaaS is provided by Microsoft Azure, Amazon EC2, Google cloud platform(GCP), Digital Ocean and many others. PaaS is built on IaaS. Computing resources are delivered by vendor like cloud software and hardware infrastructure like restful API's and operating systems that are required to develop and test the applications. Cloud users can build and maintain the hardware and also support installing and hosting data sets, development tools and analytical applications. These features are provided by platform as a service layer. PaaS is offered by Salesforce.com, Microsoft Azure, Google App Engine, Oracle Cloud, SAP and OpenShift, Heroku, AWS. SaaS is built on IaaS and PaaS. Cloud provide services to the users on a pay per use basis. Third party providers can host applications and make them available to the cloud users on subscription basis. Software as a service is provided by Dropbox, Forse.com, Microsoft Office 360, AppDynamics, Adobe Creative Cloud, Google G Suite, Zoho, Salesforce, Marketo, and SAP Business by Design, Oracle CRM, Pardot Marketing Automation.

Based on an organization's ability to manage and secure assets as well as business needs. Cloud deployment can be classified as Public, Private and Hybrid clouds. Public cloud is a SaaS platform to provide services to the consumers. Service providers bears the cost of bandwidth and infrastructure. It is the most economical option for consumers. It has limited configurations allowing multiple users to share the same cloud, and the cost is determined based on pay-per-use basis and a subscription basis. Public cloud lack in terms of Service-Level-Agreement (SLA) specifications and security. Advantages of using public cloud is high reliability, zero maintenance, lower costs and on-demand scalability. Certain organizations working with sensitive information cannot use public cloud. Due to the security issues public clouds are not widely used. Private cloud is popular among large and medium-scale financial enterprises and government agencies to build their own data centres for IT needs and specific business/ operations. Private cloud provides better security of assets and business operations. The main advantage of private cloud is more scalable, flexible and customizable. Private cloud can be built on a third-party service provider or can be built on premises. Hardware and software environment can be maintained solely by the users in the private cloud. Hybrid cloud is a combination of a public and private cloud. Hybrid cloud provides combined features of both public and private cloud, apart from providing more control over critical operations and assets, they are very flexible and cost efficient. Hybrid cloud acts as a public cloud whenever required, for instance, business applications can use the public cloud for hosting high-volume applications like web sites, emails etc., For sensitive and confidential data storage and processing like finance, government records, data recovery hybrid cloud can also act as private cloud.

Lidong Wang and Alexander, (2016) proposed that most popular cloud service providers in the industry are Amazon Web Services (AWS) Cloud, Microsoft Azure, Google Cloud Platform (GCP), IBM Cloud and Oracle Cloud. AWS Cloud Computing provides the solution for IaaS, PaaS and SaaS cloud deployment models. It is one of the leading cloud service providers. Amazon elastic computing is designed for web scale computing. It provides secure and resizable Cloud Computing capacity. The user has complete control over the instance and it provides flexible cloud hosting services. Amazon Simple Storage Service (S3) is primarily built for object storage and retrieval of data from anywhere with ease. Any amount of data for any kind of use cases, like archives, backup, web applications, enterprise applications, Big Data analytics, IoT devices. For managing database over cloud, amazon web service provides amazon relational database service. This service makes it easy to set up a scalable relational database in the cloud. It is important to note that basic operations like database setup, backups, modification and hardware provisioning are automated. Users can keep track of migration across multiple AWS solutions by using amazon migration hub. They provide visibility into status of migration by providing key metrics for individual applications. To support networking, AWS provides some solutions like Amazon Virtual Private Cloud (VPC) and Amazon Direct connect. By using Amazon VPC, virtual network can be launched in isolated AWS section by having complete control over IP address range, route tables, creation of subnets and network gateways. Amazon Direct connect helps to build a dedication connection between users network and AWS direct connect locations. Many app development tools are provided like AWS Command Line Interface, Amazon API Gateway, AWS Code Commit, Amazon Elastic Transcoder, AWS Step Functions. To manage the AWS Infrastructure on cloud many tools and services are provided like Amazon CloudWatch, AWS OpsWorks, AWS CloudFormation, AWS Trusted Advisor, AWS Configuration. To perform analytics, operations tools and services like Amazon Quick Sight, Amazon EMR, Amazon Kinesis are provided. The vast amount of different data can be processed and analysed. For Governance and Security purpose amazon cloud offers AWS CloudTrail, AWS Organizations, Amazon Inspector, Amazon iam. AI and Machine learning services are provided through Alexa Skills Kit, Alexa Voice Services (AVS), Amazon Lex, AWS DeepLens, Amazon Sage Maker. To manage widely dispersed IoT devices, users can make use of AWS IoT that provides deep and wide functionality to collect, store and analyse data from IoT devices and helps to build virtual solutions for any use case and spans them to cloud. It can also help users to build smart IoT devices by integrating with AI services and without internet connectivity. Amazon app stream 2.0 can deploy desktop applications to any computer securely. To develop mobile apps on cloud, AWS provides services like Amazon mobile hub, amazon Cognito and Amazon pinpoint. Next popular cloud service provider is Microsoft Azure. This offers several tools like DevOps and provides serverless computing support and integrated tools to allow IT professionals to obtain solutions by enabling them to manage both web and mobile applications. It is configured to develop mobile platforms, open source software, programming languages, multiple operating systems and managing devices, databases, and frameworks. Advantage of Azure cloud is that it can provide maximum data security and on premises management of application development is done with ease. And inbuilt AI is used efficiently to develop data-driven, intelligent apps and creating new user experiences based on real-time IoT analytics. Next is Google Cloud Platform (GCP) which provides modular services and set of tools for app development, networking, machine learning, Big Data analytics, storage, security. Apart from this, it offers various computational infrastructure services such as Cloud engine- as an IaaS, Google App Engine- as PaaS, for storage- Google cloud storage and Google Container Engine like Dockers, kubernetes. For Big Data processing, Google Cloud Dataproc service helps to run apache Hadoop and apache spark clusters in a simple and efficient way. Google Cloud IoT Core is a service provided for IoT devices to collect, manage and store information on them and build applications. To build and deploy AI and machine learning use cases, Google AI Cloud serves the purpose. Oracle Cloud is offered by Oracle company. It provides service in all three major categories of infrastructure, platform and software through its data centres. It supports a wide range of integrated digital solutions including intelligent business applications, platforms, storage networks, servers and data offered as a service.

3. Convergence of IoT and Cloud Computing:

IoT and Cloud have complementary relationship which serves to increase the efficiency in everyday tasks. IoT generates massive amount of data and cloud provides the resources, services and storage option. On cloud, data can be stored remotely and accessed easily. Message queueing telemetry transport is a light weight messaging protocol that is used to exchange data between IoT devices and cloud. IoT devices provide utility-based service in cloud such as tracing as a service through RFID and sensing as service through sensors. Zainab Alansari, et al (2018) in their related work proposed that storing and processing these heterogeneous data generated by these devices will be the challenge. Machine learning and Artificial Intelligence (AI) techniques and methodologies are used to logically take the decisions in the real time environment. Artificial Intelligence system comprises of machine learning and deep learning to create a sophisticated environment to perform jobs given by the human in a much better way. Machine learning, an application of AI, learns from the environment to make better decisions. Variety of algorithms are available to iteratively learn and to perform the actions. Deep learning uses artificial neural network which is inspired by the human brain. Since IoT generates large amount of data that is stored in the cloud, this data is chosen as input to the models to perform actions on the environment.

The following protocols are used in Cloud Computing for Internet of Things: Web Application Messaging Protocol (WAMP) – AutoBahn for IoT is a sub-protocol of web socket which provides publish-subscribe and remote procedure call (RPC) messaging patterns. Application components distributed on multiple nodes communicate with each other using WAMP. WAMP supports connecting a sensor or actor to other application components over an efficient protocol and by using the same protocol user can connect to the front end like web browser. Another protocol is Xively's Cloud for IoT. Xively is an IoT cloud platform, which act as platform-as-a-service for creating solutions on cloud. It provides cloud based API that simplifies the development process. It supports various platforms such as Android, Arduino, Armemd, C, Java. The various services provided by Xively are real-time messaging based on MQTT protocol, supports business logic with connected product management, security by using device-user relationship and integration with back-end servers. Next one is Amazon Web Services that provides a wide range of services like device software, which can connect IoT devices and operate them. The data which is collected can be securely transferred, controlled and managed by using control services. Analytics can be applied on this data using Data services provided by Amazon. By using IoT and cloud together there are multiple benefits such as faster application processing and analysing can be achieved. Data can be stored and accessed remotely. Security can be enhanced by using cloud API's and back-end infrastructure tools. If any security breach happens then it will be reported instantly. Some of the other technologies used with IoT, Big Data and Cloud to derive meaningful insights into decision making are: Artificial Intelligence (AI) that provide intelligence to machines to do work, which normally requires human intelligence. AI leads to wisdom. Machine Learning (ML), subset of AI that learns from data and act without human intervention or being explicitly programmed and improve based on experience. ML leads to knowledge. Deep Learning, implemented through Neural networks, motivation behind neural networks is biological neurons (brain cells). It overcomes the limitation of ML. They extract features much more efficiently than ML and overcome dimensionality problem as well. Edge computing, performing the computation on the source devices such as IoT devices, laptops and edge server. To minimize the long-distance communication between the server and client in order to reduce latency and bandwidth.

ISSUES IN THE CONVERGENCE OF IoT, BIG DATA AND CLOUD COMPUTING:

IoT, Big Data and Cloud have complementary relationship, though they are different technologies at the core. Cloud provides the common platform for IoT and Big Data. IoT is data generation source and Big Data is used for analysis of the data generated. Convergence of these technologies provides information-based outcomes rather than product as a solution.

Despite the numerous advantages which can be achieved by combining these three technologies there are certain setbacks which need to be considered. The secure transfer of data is of at most importance. The data which is sent from IoT devices should be unaltered and secured it should not be prone to denial of service attack, packet sniffing, spoofing, hijacking and clickjacking by Far and Rad. The asset of IoT devices is data, and that data should always be accessible to authorized users. Data authentication needs to be performed at both source and destination ends. Data encryption must be performed on the data collected, so that no attack can performed on stored data. One must use SSL (Secure Socket Layer) protocol to transfer data. If transmission of data is happening through wireless transmission medium then it must be secured using public and private keys. Side channel attacks like power monitoring attack, timing attack, electromagnetic attack, acoustic cryptanalysis, etc. should be prevented so that adversaries will not learn about critical details of program on running on IoT devices. The stored data is an asset to Big Data. Hence, data cannot be compromised under any circumstances. Data source should be known and transaction logs should be maintained as data passes through various channels. K. Subrahmanya and Raghupathi, (2018), proposed that only authenticated users should be allowed access. Cryptography techniques should be applied on data, validation and filtration of end input points should be done. Platform heterogeneity also leads to data security vulnerability. So, while deploying Big Data in cloud if any of the existing security tools won't work, then new security tools should be built for this platform. After analysis is done using Big Data analytics tool, the data is stored in cloud-based infrastructure. About the data stored in cloud, the top most customer concern is data breach, errors due to customer fault (Human error), data loss due to accidents like natural calamities with no backup. Insider threats, DDoS(Distributed Denial of Service) attacks in which multiple machines send packets with huge overhead, Insecure API's, shared memory and resource could provide new bench for exploits, Account hijacking, Advanced persistent attacks, meltdown etc. should be taken care in the cloud.

REAL-TIME PROBLEMS

Related work by Oracle in Driving Real -Time Insight (2016) proposed that real time problems solved using integrating Big Data, Cloud Computing and IoT are smart cities, industry revolution 4.0, healthcare, supply chain management, Agriculture, Smart waste management, Transportation and Logistics etc. Google uses an approach in Big Query, it consists of Big Data warehouse for enterprise management. Here, the data varies in petabyte scale for low-cost business analytics. Big Query is a server less theme, so do not need a database administrator to manage the infrastructure. Google uses NoSQL Big Data database service, which is referred as Bigtable. It handles massive datasets that is supporting Google Search, Gmail and Maps, among many more services. Hadoop provides the Big Data computation power required for processing large parallel data sets. Cloud provides a flexible and agile platform for computing the Big Data, as the data is scalable it allows massive amounts of computation, and Hadoop distributed file system is flexible for structured and unstructured workloads.

1. **Retail Management Use case** -- retail shops are the ways in which people satisfy their day to day needs. Analysing customers order and invoice details and their behaviour generate huge data. The Data can be collected from various sources such as social media websites, product sales histories, GPS histories, etc., is stored on cloud that is accessed by different gadgets to gain useful information. The main aim is to understand the customer's behaviour to provide him attractive offers. This also helps to improve the customer relationship. Depending on the location of the customer, offers are computed to satisfy him. Amazon Go store is an example of this. Here sensors and cameras are used to track the customers in the shop, adding the elements into the cart is also tracked. Amazon Go app need to be installed in the smart phones, a QR code is scanned while entering the shop, this helps to detect the customer presence in the shop. While leaving the shop again the QR code is scanned, this even allows the customers to do online payments. This also reduces the involvement of shopkeepers and cashiers. Amazon Go mirrors are also available which allows the users to try any variety of dresses virtually. Wasting time in changing their dress for each try is reduced. Changing the backgrounds in the mirror, and capturing screenshots are also possible. These images will be available to the users in their mobile phones via the Amazon Go app.

2. **Insurance IoT Use case** - Several different IoT sensors are present to gather the weather data. Insurance companies use this weather data to prepare for disasters and to take subsequent actions in prior and to determine the value of the insurance amount. Insurance companies can take steps to cope up with the future environmental disasters. Risk profiles can be obtained by analysing the real time weather inputs from the different IoT sources and long run prehistoric weather data. This historic data is stored in cloud for future use. To obtain the driver and the vehicle behaviour and the condition, several IoT sensors are used. Damage based policies can be generated by the Insurance companies.

3. **Automobile Engineering**- Engine performance, fuel efficiency, and tyre air pressure and break pressure information are gathered using connected sensors. Sensors throughout the vehicle monitors and collects the different data from different parts. Flash lights will appear on the dashboard when an adverse condition occurred in engine. It also sends message directly to the manufacturer when an error occurred. It also helps the manufacturer in trouble shooting and control management. Break pressure sensors are widely used to know the pressure of the pumps when brakes are applied. When brakes are applied tires stop motion and start to skid, this may lead to accidents when the vehicle is not able to stop suddenly. Presence of the brake sensors will check the pressure applied by the brakes, when the pressure is high, automatically the pressure is reduced to avoid skidding and hence we can avoid accidents. Automobile dealers can use the information collected from different sensor sources to schedule the services to the vehicles. Accordingly, they can order spare parts. Additional historic information like GPS location, last service details and preventive maintenance are considered before scheduling the service of the vehicle. This also allows pay per use model to support the customer.

4. **Industry 4.0 IoT** - To satisfy the needs of the user several products are manufactured in the industries. A decade ago, these industries were human controlled. Human involvement was seen in each step of production and was prone to failure also. Now, industry is merged with technology to improve the production and perfection. In nuclear power plants and chemical reactors every second is important. Sensors are present to sense the temperature periodically and perform cooling when the temperature exceeds the safe limit. Fire accidents are also avoided by installing fire sensors, which automatically sense the fire in the building or industry and will turn on the extinguishers to

turn of the fire. Automated equipment is used that are network controlled to improve the production. If any failure occurred in the production mechanism the system can reconfigure itself to restart the production process.

5. **Agriculture IoT**- Technology, agriculture suppliers and farmers are related to each other with the help of IoT, Cloud Computing and Big Data. Sensors are installed on farming equipment, shipping containers, and delivery vehicles to communicate valuable information for tracking, like to improve their production process, improve their yield forecasting and to accelerate the delivery process. In the field of agriculture several advancements have been done already done, there are drone cameras and sensors, etc to detect the diseases in leaves, roots, fruits of the plant. Even advancements have been made to improve the security of the farmland by identifying the intrusion of pests, animals, etc into the farm land and taking security measures to avoid crop loss due to theft. Smart cows are in boom now. It is easy to understand the behaviour of the cow using this application. Usually the mood of the cow is determined by the movements of the ears. Sensors are placed on the ears. Timely information is collected from the ear movements to judge the mood of the cow. This application is useful to determine the health conditions of the cow. Even in bulls it is useful as most of the Indian farmers still rely on bulls for rowing their farmlands. It is necessary to monitor the health of the bulls periodically. If technology is successfully indulged with agriculture, it will be a great help to the Indian farmers. They can improve their yields, reduce their crop losses hence leading to the economic growth of India.

6. **Smart cities**- Cloud-based Hub is used for developing smart city. Basically, the infrastructure is focused on the IoT components used in the smart city architecture. IoT hub is cloned with the platform as a service layer of the cloud. Examples of this implementation is seen in Canada, US and France. As it is known that the data hub is connected to PAAS layer, bulk data collected will be stored in the cloud. Multiple hubs in the ecosystem can be connected. Several smart homes can be connected with the traffic hub, medical emergency hub, disaster hub, parking hub etc. Since, it is an interconnection of several hubs, large data collected can only be handled by cloud. Smart cities, monitoring the status of streetlights, parking, and field equipment to reduce the traffic and to support the public transports, metropolitan cities use these services to monitor the cities. For instance, street light management system in the smart cities provides a unique ID to each street light. If the street light goes off, it must have the capability to reconfigure otherwise an alert message will be sent to the technician, so that he can fix with faster actions. The City of San Francisco provides real-time information about available parking spaces by sending updates to the user's mobile phones via the parking application. In this city several sensors are already installed in the public areas like parking, garage gates and on street, continuously the real-time data stream are collected to adjust the price of parking in relation to demand.

7. **Military application**- Wireless Sensor Networks (WSN) are present in certain military bases and hostile environments, which are not accessible by the human. It is easy to monitor the environment via the WSN. Self-configuration, power management and security are the major concerns of WSN in military applications. Cluster-tree based multi-hop model with optimized cluster model is used to design the WSN which makes it easily design the sensor network for military usage in remote large-scale environments.

8. **Smart Dustbin with IoT**- Clean environment leads to healthy living. The main objective is to maintain the level of cleanliness in the city for better living. For the disposal of garbage municipal services have provided public dustbins in the localities. But the garbage collectors will not frequently

collect the garbage from the dustbins and this leads to unhealthy environment causing illness in the locality. Smart dustbin is a solution to this problem. The level of the garbage in the dustbin is monitored. These dustbins are located in several distinct locations in the city. Depending on the levels of the garbage in the dustbin, alert messages are sent to the garbage collectors and to the municipal department monitoring the garbage collectors. Municipal department can also monitor the garbage collectors on their work. RFID and GSM modules are used to track the garbage collector vehicles, if the vehicle passes nearby and does not collect the garbage, an automatic message will be sent to the members of the locality and municipal department also. Accordingly, actions can be taken on the garbage collector for not doing the job. The garbage collectors, municipal service and members of the locality can check the status of the dustbin on their mobile phone via the application.

SOLUTION TO THESE ISSUES

To safeguard the interest of users, devices, and companies, the whole process from collection of data by IoT devices to deploying them in cloud. The whole path should be secured, protected and reliable. Proper protection measures should be taken to authorize the users, restrict access to devices, data which is sent should be encrypted, access to cloud resources should be restricted. For IoT devices, tools should be used to audits and monitor fleets and sends alerts if there are deviations from what have defined as normal behaviour for each device in IoT. With the evolution of these technologies, security has become a major concern with increasing threats like ransomware, malware etc. It can be addressed only by building the tools and technologies that are structured to grow along with it. Prevention should be taken by applying advanced algorithms, artificial intelligence and tools which can predict and prevent the attack before occurrence by studying the previous mechanism and data behaviour.

CONCLUSION

The chapter discusses the convergence of IoT, Big Data and Cloud. More opportunities are created with advanced applications which improve the human day to day life activities. IoT devices generate the huge amount of data from billions of devices. Big Data analysing the data and Cloud is used for storage purpose. Various tools and services are used by converging all these technologies, Artificial intelligence and Machine learning are also applied with these technologies to leverage the solution they offer. These technologies used in convergence with each other can be discussed by considering various use cases such as smart homes, industry revolution 4.0, Health care, automobiles, etc., Few concerns are discussed which needs to be addressed before reaping the benefits of it like successful integration of these three technologies to leverage the benefits of each other. Also security concerns should be addressed efficiently.

REFERENCES

Alansari, Z., Anuar, N. B., Kamsin, A., Soomro, S., Belgaum, M. R., Mira, M. H., & Alshaer, J. (2018). Challenges of Internet of Things and Big Data Integration. *International Conference on International Conference on Emerging Technologies in Computing.* 10.1007/978-3-319-95450-9_4

Far, S. B., & Rad, A. I. (2018). *Security Analysis of Big Data on Internet Things* (https://arxiv.org/abs/1808.09491).

Liu, Y., Dong, B., Guo, B., Yang, J., & Peng, W. (2015). Combination of Cloud Computing and Internet of Things (IoT) in Medical Monitoring Systems. *International Journal of Hybrid Information Technology, 8*(12), 367–376. doi:10.14257/ijhit.2015.8.12.28

Mathew, A. R., & Al Hajj, A. (2017). Secure Communications on IoT and Big Data. *in Indian Journal of Science and Technology, 10*(11).

Priya, I. P., & Tripathi, A. (n.d.). *Big Data, Cloud and IoT: An Assimilation* (Unpublished doctoral dissertation).

Subrahmanya Sarma & Raghupathi. (2018). Security Issues Of Big Data In IoT Based Applications. *International Journal of Pure and Applied Mathematics, 118*(14).

Taher, N. C., Mallat, I., Agoulmine, N., & El-Mawass, N. (2019). An IoT-Cloud Based Solution for Real-Time and Batch Processing of Big Data: Application in Healthcare. *3rd International Conference on Bio-engineering for Smart Technologies.*

Wang, L., & Alexander, C. A. (2016). Big Data Analytics and Cloud Computing in Internet of Things. *American Journal of Information Science and Computer Engineering, 2*(6), 70–78.

Chapter 16
Survelliance of Type I and II Diabetic Subjects on Physical Characteristics:
IoT and Big Data Perspective in Healthcare@NCR, India

Rohit Rastogi
https://orcid.org/0000-0002-6402-7638
ABES Engineering College, Ghaziabad, India

Devendra Chaturvedi
https://orcid.org/0000-0002-4837-2570
Dayalbagh Educational Institute, India

Parul Singhal
ABES Engineering College, Ghaziabad, India

ABSTRACT

The Delhi and NCR healthcare systems are rapidly registering electronic health records and diagnostic information available electronically. Furthermore, clinical analysis is rapidly advancing, and large quantities of information are examined and new insights are part of the analysis of this technology experienced as big data. It provides tools for storing, managing, studying, and assimilating large amounts of robust, structured, and unstructured data generated by existing medical organizations. Recently, data analysis data have been used to help provide care. The present study aimed to analyse diabetes with the latest IoT and big data analysis techniques and its correlation with stress (TTH) on human health. The authors have tried to include age, gender, and insulin factor and its correlation with diabetes. Overall, in conclusion, TTH cases increasing with age in case of males and not following the pattern of diabetes variation with age, while in the case of females, TTH pattern variation is the same as diabetes (i.e., increasing trend up to age of 60 then decreasing).

DOI: 10.4018/978-1-7998-3111-2.ch016

INTRODUCTION

It is a technology that has made the non-connectivity appliance a connectivity appliance. The appliances that contain technology that helps us to communicate us with human and technology. Let us take some example the GPS is a latest technology that are inbuilt in car help the driver to make it easy to travel within the road, i.e. it is that technology in which we require internet base technique.(Rastogi, Chaturvedi, Satya, Arora, Yadav et al, 2018)

HISTORY OF IOT

IoT has evolved when the major language that are not famous on that days such as machine language, commodity analysis etc. Now a days Automation, control system, wireless sensor networks that are connect to internet and helps us to make us easier to do work.

Kevin Ashton in 1999 was first who coined the term IoT i.e. "Internet of Things". But in earlier the concept of IoT was purposed in Carnegie Mellon University in 1982 that work on the concept of Network smart devices.

Now a days the technology is increasing day by day is increasing day by day like CISCO is introducing a new technology and in future the technology will replace every human work with this technology. (Rastogi, Chaturvedi, Satya, Arora, Yadav et al, 2018)

IoT AS MEDICAL HEALTH CARE

IoT helps in medical field to make our future bright such as, major technology has being evolved in this field such as pacemaker. With the help of IoT we can create digitalized health care facilities; we can connect to medical resources easily and can get medical facilities easier.

Devices enabled with IoT services are applicable for remote health monitoring and especially in emergency notification facilities. They may help us in from blood pressure and heart rate monitors and latestgadgets like pacemakers to monitor specialized implants.

Now a days "smart beds" can be seen in the medical facilities that is a another a feature of IoT. Doctor can interrogate their patient with the help of video call from far away from the place, even the nurses can be appointed through internet facilities. A 2015 Goldman Sachs reported that by increasing revenue and decreasing cost, gadgets being used for health care devices in USA are helping to save nearly $300 billion in annual expenditures in health sector.

FUTURE PERSPECTIVE OF IOT

With the base of IoT wireless design has been made which can enhance our technology and made our work easier.Much wireless technology has been developed and these technology has been categorized in three ways i.e. short, medium and long range wireless.

- Short Range Wireless-With short frequency and applied for home purpose.

- Bluetooth Mesh Networking– Applied with large no. of nodes and using BLE, it is used in application layer.
- Light-Fidelity (Li-Fi)–Same as wi-fi, uses visible light communication for high bandwidth.
- Near-Field Communication (NFC)–Protocols making capable communication of 2 devices in four centimetre range.
- Radio-Frequency Identification (RFID)–Tags are embedded in items, appliesEM fields to retrieve big data.

BIG DATA CHARACTERISTICS

There are major four characteristics of Big data, namely volume, variety, velocity and veracity. Volume is the quantity of the data which is to be stored and which determines whether a data set is large enough to be considered big data or not. The nature and type of generated data is known as variety whereas the processing speed of data and its generation to handle a specific need is called velocity. Veracity characterizes the quality and value of the available data. (Gautam, 2016)

APPLICATIONS OF BIG DATA

Healthcare

Big data finds a major application in the healthcare industry. Nowadays, in major hospitals and large healthcare centers, there is a huge influx of patients suffering from a wide variety of ailments. Thus, the doctors rely more on the patient's clinical health record which means gathering huge amount of data and that too for different patients. This is not possible with the help of traditional data processing and storing software. Hence, big data comes into the picture.

Predictive analysis is an important result of big data which ensures the patient's quality care and safety. It helps the doctors to give the right prescriptions to their patients keeping their medical histories in mind.

ROLE OF BIG DATA IN IoT

In big data system, heavy quantity of unorganized data is generated by IoT devices and stored. Then this data can be processed or organized accordingly. Analysis of this data can be done using tools like Spark or Hadoop, Map-Reduce. This data needs light fastening speed of analysis as it is collected through the internet.

BIG DATA TOOLS

For storage and analysis of the Big data, the main tools are:

a- Apache Hadoop: Java based free software framework to store a heavy amount of data effectively in the form of a cluster, Runs in parallel on a cluster toenable the user to process data across all the nodes.

b- Microsoft HDInsight:Big Data solution by Microsoft, using Azure Blob storage as the default file system, provides high availability with low cost.

c- Big Data in Excel: MS Excel can be used to access Big Data. MS Excel 2013 has a feature which allows the user to access the stored data in a Hadoop platform.

BIG DATA SECURITY

It is a term used for all measures and techniques to secure the data and all the data analysis processes. The threats to data can include information thefts which can endanger critical and confidential information stored online. There are several ways to implement data security. One simple way is encryption. Encrypted data is useless to any third party as long as it does not have the key to access it. Data stays protected during both input and output processes. Another way of securing the data is by building a strong firewall, which act as strong data filters and avoid any external sources or third parties.(Satya et al., 2019)

TTH (TENSION TYPE HEADACHE)

TTH stand for tension type headache. It is a condition of body in which one experiences ache/ pain like a physical weight or a tight band around your head. It can generally last for some days or can even continue long. TTH is different from migraine as it can be affected due to everyday activities, which is not in the case of TTH.

Tension type headache arises due to

- Constant stress
- Incomplete sleep
- Anxiety
- Depression
- Emotional Disturbance

More than half of the world experiences TTH in one form or the other. It has been called by different names over the years for example: tension headache, muscle contraction etc.(Chauhan et al., 2018)

It is not accompanied by nausea or vomiting and is also not affected by physical factors. Thus one will continue to do his daily task without even knowing if he is suffering from such headache or not. It also does not have any visual disturbances. The pain in TTH spreads all over the head unlike migraine which pains only on a particular side of your head.

Symptoms of TTH include:

- Feeling of pressure across the forehead
- Aching head all over the area
- Tenderness of head and neck muscles etc.(Chauhan et al., 2018)

TTH can be divided into two main types: Chronic and Episodic

WHEN TO SEEK MEDICAL EMERGENCY?

One must seek medical emergency if

- Loss of balance, vision, speech, etc. occurs
- Headache starts suddenly and becomes uncontrollable
- Headache accompanied with high fever
- Headache pattern changes
- Medicines fail
- One has side effects from medicines such as pale skin, rashes, depression, nausea, vomiting, cramps, dry mouth etc.
- One is pregnant

One needs to learn to keep balance among alternative therapy with no-drug consumption, using right and necessary medications only and nurturing healthy habits. It is not necessary that one is having TTH only whenever headache happens. There may be sufficient chances of brain tumor or rupture of a weakened blood vessel also known as aneurysm in heavy TTH cases. One might also face headaches after a severe head injury. Protecting your head from such injuries is very important. Tension headaches are very common and it mars the QoL and efficiency and productivity in job along with life satisfaction. Such kind of aches checks an individual from active participation in different activities. One may need to take a break from job and be at home or even if one goes to work it may make your work impaired. (Arora et al., 2019; Mullaly et al., 2009)

PREVENTIONS

Biofeedback Training: It is used to check some predefined body responses in constrained environment to decrease the pain. Some important body indications are used as parameters like muscle tension, heart rate and blood pressure.

Cognitive Behavioral Therapy: The method supports individual to learn how to handle stress and helps to shorten the frequency and severity of one's headaches.

TENSION TYPE HEADACHE, STRESS & IT'S CAUSES

Tension headache is a widespread are found in people with about 90% of headaches It comes under several names and Includes headaches, tension, muscle contractions, stress, headaches, normal headaches and essential headaches. Pain levels are usually in the range of suppression to moderate. It is accompanied by vomiting and nausea. Most types of headaches found in people with about 90% of headaches under different names like headache, muscle contraction, stress, headache, headache, essential headache etc. Pain levels are usually in the range of suppression to moderate with vomiting and nausea (Chaturvedi et al., 2018; Chauhan et al., 2018; Chobanian et al., 2003; Rastogi, Chaturvedi, Satya, Arora, Yadav et al, 2018; Satya et al., 2019).

Tension headache caused due to contraction of muscles in the neck or head regions. The major cause of contraction is due to variation of food, activities and stressors. This tension also occurs because of prolonged working on computer screen and driving for a long time. Heavy loads of work in the office, college or other departments can cause tension. Sometimes temperature variation may affect body muscles especially cold temperature

Others causes of tension headache are Smoking, poor posture, fatigue, alcohol, stress, caffeine, eye strain or other drugs (Arora et al., 2019; Rastogi, Chaturvedi, Satya, Arora, & Chauhan, 2018; Saini et al., 2018; Vyas et al., 2018).

Stress may be due to good and bad experiences. When the individual emphasizes what is happening around them, both bodies of these individuals bring more energy and strength to the bloodstream, and any stress from physical hazards may then be good. Emotionally replied: if it does not have certain strength, it may be bad again (Gautam, 2017).

The health problems associated with chronic stress include:

- Depression Health problem
- Digestive system
- Nervous system
- Skin condition
- Sleep problem(Chaturvedi, 2013a; Chaturvedi, 2012)

TYPES OF STRESS

- Survival stress (Rastogi, Chaturvedi, Satya, Arora, & Chauhan, 2018)
- Internal Stress
- Environmental stress
- Fatigue or overwork(Chobanian et al., 2003)

There are many things that can cause stress such as tension and emotional stress (Rastogi, Chaturvedi, Satya, Arora, & Chauhan, 2018). For example, when you work in the office and have an important deadline for completing a job, stress is caused due to time pressure.

The major reason of stress is:

- Retirement
- Wife's death
- Divorce
- Separation of marriage (Chobanian et al., 2003; Yadav et al., 2018).

STRESS SYMPTOMS

Stress affects many aspects of life, including behavior, emotions, thinking and physical health. It may be dangerous if you do not consult a doctor.

EMOTIONAL STRESS IS AS FOLLOWS

- I feel sick, annoyed, feel sick
- With control management, you have lost control or need control.
- Relax and quiet
- Don't worry (low self-esteem), alone, worthless, depressed
- Avoid others (Chaturvedi et al., 2017; Chobanian et al., 2003)

THE PHYSICAL SYMPOTMS OF STRESS INCLUDE

- Low energy
  - headache- Abdominal discomfort such as diarrhea, constipation, nausea
- Pain, pain, muscle tension (Maser et al., 2000; Satya et al., 2019)

COGNITIVE SYMPOTOMS STRESS INCLUDE

- Always worry
- Race ideas
- Forgetfulness and confusion (Chauhan et al., 2018; Reddy, 2004)

THE BEHAVIOURAL SYMPTOMS STRESS INCLUDE

- Change in appetite-don't eat too much or eat too much.

LONG TERM STRESS EFFECT

- Mental health problems such as depression, anxiety, personality disorder
- Obesity and other eating disorders
- Gastrointestinal disorders such as GERD, gastritis, ulcer colitis, irritable bowel (Arora et al., 2019; Low et al., 2009).

HANDLING OF STRESS

- Get moving
- Interaction with the people

- Engage yourself
- Eat healthy(Gautam et al., 2018)

MAIGRANE vs. TTH

Tension headaches can be detected from migraines. It can also uses migraine headaches if you have frequent tension headaches.

Unlike some types of migraine, headaches are not usually associated with damage, nausea, or vomiting. Physical activity usually causes migraine pain but does not aggravate headache pain. Increased sensitivity to light and sound may be due to headache, but these symptoms are not common.

The pain may be mild or severe. The symptoms of tension headache are as follows:

- Unpleasant pain, painful pain.(Chaturvedi, 2013b; Chaturvedi, 2004)
- Feel tightness or pressure on the forehead or side of the body or behind the head.

Tension headaches and occasional headaches may be chronic (Bansal et al., 2018; Mullaly et al., 2009).

CHRONIC HEADACHE

This type of headache lasts for several hours and may be continuous. If the headaches last for at least 3 months in more than 15 days, they are chronic.

In severe cases, doctors may find other problems like brain tumors. He may require you to do a CT scan, MRI or X-ray to check internal organs and tissues. (Chaturvedi et al., 2018)

Headaches may indicate serious medical conditions such as brain tumors or blood vessel ruptures (aneurysms)(Chaturvedi et al., 2018; Cryer, 2001).

HYPERTENSION

High blood pressure (or HTN) or high blood pressure is defined as abnormally high arterial blood pressure. Agreeing to the Joint National Committee 7 (JNC7), the normotensive pressure is systolic blood pressure <120 mm Hg and diastolic blood pressure <80 mm Hg. High blood pressure is defined as systolic blood pressure level 140 140 mmHg and / or diastolic blood pressure level 90 mmHg. The gray area between systolic blood pressure 120-139 mmHg and diastolic blood pressure 80-89 mmHg is defined as "prehypertensive" .Although prehypertension is not a medical condition by itself, prehypertensive subjects are at a higher danger of developing HTN (Chobanian et al., 2003)[12].

Figure 1. Complications on human due to diabetes (NPTEL, n.d.)

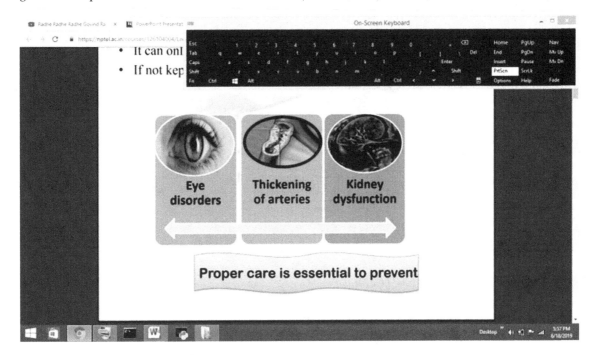

MENTAL HEALTH

Mental wellness is frequently interpreted as a concept related to mental disorders. Yet, mental health can be defined from a more universal point of thought, including the positive aspects of the concept (World Health Organization, 2003). In this report, mental health is defined as "a state of happiness in which souls are able to realize their abilities, cope with normal life stress, work productive and productive, and chip in to the community. The concept of mental health can be applied to the power of individuals to originate them, To cope with the conditions of life and to participate in society by contributing themselves. In addition, mental health is an important concept included in the definition of health by the World Health Organization (2014) and is presented as "a nation of perfect physical, mental and social wellbeing, simply in the absence of sickness or weakness, it is staged as "not".(Chatruvedi, 2014a; Chaturvedi, 2014b; Chaturvedi, 2013c)

DIABETES MELLITUS & IT's SYMPTOMS

Diabetes mellitus is commonly known as diabetes. Diabetes is a chronic degenerative disease. Insulin is not produced for low use.(As per Fig. 1)

There are many types of diabetes:

- Type-1
- Type-2
- During pregnancy

- Other types(NPTEL, n.d.).

Fig. 2 shows diabetes symptoms.

Figure 2a. Diabetes symptoms (NPTEL, n.d.)

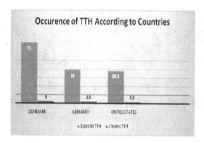

Figure 2b. Diabetes symptoms (NPTEL, n.d.)

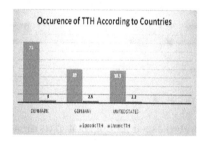

TYPE-1 DIABETES

Type-1 diabetes is generally thought to be caused, if not directly, by the destruction of immune-related insulin-producing pancreatic beta cells. As this view has changed over the past decade, age at onset of symptoms is no longer a limiting factor. It is less in adolescents, and in adults (Ahmed, 2002; Bluestone et al., 2010; Rastogi, Chaturvedi, Satya, Arora, Sirohi et al, 2018).

TYPE-2 DIABETES

Diabetes (DM) is probably one of the oldest human diseases. It was first mentioned in the Egyptian version 3000 years ago. In 1936, the difference between type-1 and DM2 was confirmed. Insulin-dependent DM is the most common type of DM with hyperglycemia, insulin resistance, and insulin deficiency (Chen et al., 2011; Kumar et al., 2016).

CVD, CAN & CAD

Cardiovascular disease (CVD) is one of the main causes of mortality and morbidity in diabetic patients, and the main purpose of the next diabetes is to reduce vascular dysfunction and fertility related diabetes. There are the most common ways to prevent CVD in diabetics, lower blood pressure and LDL cholesterol, and improve glycemic control. However, CMD is very common and is the leading cause of death in DM patients. Therefore, better understanding of the causes of CVD is important to achieve new therapeutic goals. (Goyal & Yusuf, 2006; Grundy et al., 1999; Maser et al., 1990; Shah & Mathur, 2010; Yusuf et al., 2001)

Cardiac independence disorder (CAN) is a often overlooked and overlooked diabetes-related disorder that has important implications for CVD, DMD for death and disease. With a deeper understanding of cannibalism and its role, CVD offers new therapeutic goals that can lower blood pressure in diabetics. The purpose of this test is to provide an overview of epidemiology, causes, cardiovascular disorders, diagnosis and treatment. Particular emphasis has been placed on recent developments in this area.

Coronary artery disease (CAD) is a condition caused by the accumulation of atherosclerotic plaques in the pericardial coronary artery leading to myocardial ischemia. It is a common and diverse public health crisis today, and is a major cause of morbidity and mortality in developing and developed countries. (Ajay & Prabhakaran, 2010) Heart disease affects millions of people in both developed and producing countries. In the developed world over the past few decades, mortality rates have been reduced due to this disease, which nevertheless is a major case of destruction and causes huge social and economic sacrifices at the world level.

CAD risk factors are extremely variable and classified as non-convertible risk factors. Moderate risk factors include high blood pressure, diabetes mellitus, dyslipidemia, obesity and smoking. Non-convertible risk factors include CAD age, gender, race and family story. A systematic coronary risk assessment scheme is recommended to evaluate the individual's overall cardiovascular risk. CAD is closely linked to lifestyle and modifiable physiological factors, and correction of risk factors has been demonstrated to reduce cardiovascular morbidity and death rate(Ajay & Prabhakaran, 2010; Biggers et al., 2019).

INSULIN

Insulin is a peptide hormone secreted by pancreatic beta cells that determines levels of insulin resistance by increasing its growth and development through regulation of carbohydrate, fat and protein metabolism and promotion of glucose and normal glucose levels. High levels of insulin increase poor biological response, which is classically associated with sensitivity to glucose exclusion (Cefalu, 2001; Reaven, 2004).

HYPOGLYCEMIA

Unconscious hypoglycemia (HU) is defined as the onset of nerve hypoglycemia before the onset of an autoimmune warning sign. This is a big limitation to achieving severe diabetes and poor animation. Hypoglycaemia usually has a glucose concentration lower than 70 mg / dL (3.9 mmol / L) (Rastogi, Chaturvedi, Satya, Arora, Yadav et al, 2018). Because flu is permanently dependent on glucose, a powerful mechanism for fast regulation of blood glucose and protection of the human body results from the negative effects of hypoglycemia (Desouza et al., 2010; Diderichsena & Andersena, 2018; Gulati et al., 2019).

DEPRESSION

Depression is a very significant public health disorder in conditions of its morbidity and suffering, dysfunction, morbidity and financial load. Depression is more usual in adult females than men. In terms of morbidity, low as a disorder has always been the focus of researchers in India. Several authors will study their prevalence, oncology problems, psychosocial risk factors, including life events, symptom measurement in cultural context, complications, neuropsychiatric biology, treatment, outcome, prevention, disorders and burdens It has been. Some subjects are likewise attempting to address several matters (Haddock et al., 1997; Singh et al., 2019).

OBESITY

Obesity is a public health problem that is widespread throughout the world. Overweight and obesity are the leading movements in products that include type-2 diabetes, cardiovascular disease, various cancers, and other health problems that can increase mortality and morbidity. Overweight and obesity are the leading movements in products that include type-2 diabetes, cardiovascular disease, various cancers, and other health problems that can increase mortality and morbidity. (Gill, 2006; Satya et al., 2018).

DIETS FOR DIAGNOSING THE TYPE-2 DIABETES

Treating diabetes is essential. Daily consumption requires a fixed exchange system. Food Feed List: A list of groups that can measure similar calories and similar proteins, fats, tea foods and replace each other in a diet plan. Dietary fibers and foods containing complex carbohydrates are useful for diabetics. Go down, required requirements, Serum cholesterol and triglyceride levels & weight control and hypotension (HTN). Nutrition is an important part of treatment. Treatment includes medication, nutritional management, and exercise (NPTEL, n.d.).(As per Fig. 3 and Fig. 4)

LITERATURE SURVEY

According to Alana Biggersa, Lisa K. Sharp, Hataikarn Nimitphong, Sunee Saetung, Nantaporn Siwasaranond, Areesa Manodpitipong, Stephanie J. Crowley, Megan M. Hood, Ben S. Gerber, Sirimon Reutrakulc (Biggers et al., 2019)

Hypoglycemia is one of the most important complications of type-2 diabetes and is associated with insulin and other hypoglycemic agents. The risk of hypoglycemia depends on diabetes, genes such as insulin and sulfonylureas, loss of kidney function, aging and other complications.

They examined two groups of people with type-2 diabetes to find out their relationship with depression, quality of sleep and a history of low blood sugar.

Figure 3. Food exchange list to help the patients (NPTEL, n.d.)

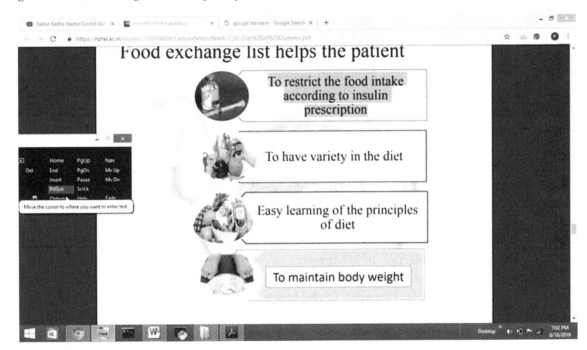

They used this method in which two adults in Chicago and Bangkok responded to a questionnaire to assess sleep quality, symptoms of depression, and the frequency of hypoglycemia with type-2 diabetes. Effective barriers to regression models are established for each adjustment group for treatment duration, insulin and sulfonylurea management and other factors.

They believe that people of both age groups with hypoglycemia respond more to long-term diabetes, lower insulin use, and less sleep quality. Chicago homosexual groups were less likely to use sulfonylureas, but had higher depression scores. In Thai groups, sulfonylureas are most commonly used. In Thailand's final regression model, depressive symptoms were independently associated with a high incidence of hypoglycemia. In the final models of Chicago and Thailand, sleep quality was not associated with the prevalence of hypoglycemia.

Figure 4. Eating habbits and possible minerals (NPTEL, n.d.)

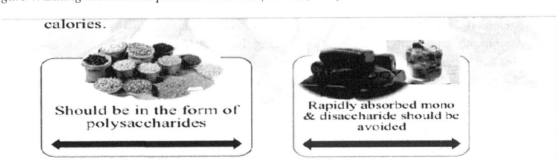

For more information on these complex relationships, Alena Bigrosa, Lisa Carey Sharp, use remote monitoring of blood glucose levels, sleep, and ecological momentum assessment. In the Thai group, symptoms of depression were associated with hypoglycemia.

The paper written by Daniela Chinnici, Angela Middlehurst, Nikhil Tandon, Monika Arora, Anne Belton, Denise Reis Franco, Glaucia Margonari Bechara, Fernanda Castelo Branco, Tina Rawal, Radhika Shrivastav, Els Sung, Maeva Germe, David Chaney, David Cavan(Bruen et al., 2017) Improving Children's Diabetes School Experience: Assessing Children's Project.(Rastogi, Chaturvedi, Satya, Arora, Singhal et al, 2018; Sharma et al., 2018)

According to Daniel Chinichi, Angela Midhlhurst and Nickel Todon, the school staff, their children and their parents are created from diabetes, and children's projects are deepening knowledge about diabetes. They chose a school for Brazilian and Indian students. A qualitative methodology was used. School staff, their children and their parents were asked. They can cause diabetes and more. Spectators came a month or three after the children were executed. For analysis of big data collection (Bruen et al., 2017).

They identified the limits of the future are to raise awareness and to reveal more people for not having diabetes. Limits: Data collection in IoT involves an annual exam at school and summer vacation, and results were collected for the second round of interviews at unusual points. Due to the small sample size, big data saturation is limited to parents of children with diabetes, and for administrative issues, do not interview Indian public schools.

Therefore, the author decided that the project would have positive feedback from the material. The proposed package is said to be useful, informative, attractive and created. The project brought the need for diabetes intervention in schools. Brazilian parents are diabetic and they believe they have gained new knowledge, but it was believed that their parents in India did not receive new information due to the small sample size.

Usama M. Alkholya., and Abdalmonema, N (Alkholya et al., 2017) has discussed the condition of Q10 and vitamin E in children with type-1 diabetes is being studied. They found that the levels of intracellular cell carcinoma of vitamin E and plasma Q10 in children with T1D and A1% C were significantly higher in children with diabetes. Children with poor glycemic control showed platelet vitamin E, coenzyme Q 10, FPG, WC / HC etc.They introduced the following method. It includes many children with type-1 diabetes that have been selected and then compared to 48 healthy children. # Hantente Reland Fitness (for height) and scale balance (for weight). Each measurement was performed on an average of three consecutive measurements, with a standard instrument and an international biological program.

The authors suggested that further research on the therapeutic potential of both vitamin E and coenzyme Q 10 in the prevention and prevention of vascular disease is needed(Alkholya et al., 2017).

They thought that patients with type-1 diabetes, mainly those with low intake, had high levels of vitamin E and Q10 collagen, and lowered platelet levels in the coenzyme Q10 vaccine.

Finn Diderichsena and Ingelise Andersen (Diderichsena & Andersena, 2018) told that there is not enough meaning to depression of diabetes and obesity. Low education and violence, obesity due to various illnesses. Obesity is a major cause of diabetes. Low income is another issue. Violence against women also contributes to the economic crisis. They used the proposed method, a multiclass family study method using a three-step random sampling method.

According to Ingelise Andersen (Diderichsena & Andersena, 2018) the main unit-National census machine. Secondary unit-household. Third level-people who live in a household 18 years of age or older. The Human Development Index was used in 27 states of Brazil to measure the content of socioeconomic development. Logistic regression is often used, but here is a generalized binary linear model of IBM SPSS, V 25 for regression analysis.

They recommended creating a better environment with less violence to educate the public about various issues. Decreased obesity (Diderichsena & Andersena, 2018; Gupta et al., 2019).

Finally, they concluded that obesity also led to my wife and my depression. The diabetes and obesity cluster may be due to obesity. Both depression and diabetes, particularly in the case of adult women, in connection with education and income.

The paper written by Juan José´ Gagliardino, Jean-Marc Chantelot, Catherine Domenger, Hasan Ilkova, Ambady Ramachandran, Ghaida Kaddaha, Jean Claude Mbanya, Juliana Chang, Pablo Aschner, on behalf of the IDMPS, the Guidance Committee is called Diabetes Education and Health Insurance. Based on the healthcare provided to people with type-1 diabetes in Latin America, information from the International Study on Diabetes (IDMPS)(Gaglardio et al., 2009) says that by agreeing to the sources, the goal was to examine the impact of access to diabetes education and health insurance in Latin America.

Juan José´ Gagliardino (Gaglardio et al., 2009) has revealed this study shows that diabetes education is important as a growing and important healthcare provider. Health officials need a lot of medical care in the relationship between unexpected diabetes and long-term complications, medical care is needed to reduce the social and economic burden of type-1 diabetes, and it is necessary to receive education There is (Gaglardio et al., 2009).

M Ghassibe-sabbagh (Ghassibe-Sabbagh et al., 2019) has described diabetes is one of the most common and dangerous diseases in today era. Around 425 million people of this world suffer from diabetes.

He revealed a report says that in 2040 the number will surpass 629 million people. Type-2 diabetes (T2DM) is very dangerous to health and causes long-term vascular damage, blindness and other disorders. Nephropathy, diabetic ganglia and cardiovascular. To control the T2DM, patients need to manage and maintain their lifestyle, Self-management and self-control are the most common things that need to follow by every patient. Peers support also play an important role as some of the problems faced by the diabetic patient can only be shared by him/her.

According to him, this study is done in Japan and almost 80,000 diabetic patients are enrolled in the self-help group where they can share and discuss their problem and gets benefitted. The whole framework is Human belief models are psychological models that shape human behavior. This model helps to establish relationships between T2DM patients (Ghassibe-Sabbagh et al., 2019).

He used the following methodology, Questionnaire and Research Plan was sent to many medical places and asked to collect the big data from the diabetic patient using IoT tools. Any serious Patients were not selected for the study, only patients who have difficulty in giving answer of the question, Patients with gestational diabetes etc. There were no age Criteria in this study. Scaling criteria was introduced by HBM framework. Four teachers and nurse were appointed who will evaluate how well the items 57 has been selected. Adding all the scores, this was a total score It is evaluated to roll out with confidence T2DM(Ghassibe-Sabbagh et al., 2019; Singhal et al., 2019).

He has resulted this approach is very beneficial for everyone in this world who suffers from diabetic. Japan successfully conducted this research and showed some new and innovative way of helping the diabetic patient. Self-Management, Self-Control and Peer- Support these are the some of the techniques which can change the shape of the diabetic patient in the coming future.

He also described the limitation of this study; the only limitation that can be formed from the study is the area. This research is done in Japan only and the result can vary from place to place.

The author concluded that the study done was successful and questioners were sent to 378 patients out of which 377 collected, out of which only those surveys was selected which have RCT2DM answer. After this only 289 survey used for the final result. With the help of RCT2DM, we can measure awareness of patients with T2DM. Initially, the relationship was built by four factors. "The merits of the relationship" "Severity Diabetes mellitus," "Obstacle related" And Attitude to communication".

The paper 'Diabetes detection using deep learning algorithms' written by the following authors Swapna G, Vinayakumar R, Soman K.P.[54].

According to him, diabetes is a metabolic disease that affects many people around the world. The outbreak is great every year. Without treatment, many important pelvic visceral complications of

Diabetes can be devastating. Early diagnosis of diabetes is very important for timely treatment that can stop the disease before such effects. RR parameter signals known as HRV signals (derived from electrocardiogram signals) (ECGs) can be used effectively to diagnose non-invasive diabetes.

Extract planning and dynamic features of HRV input data using Swapna G, Vinayakumar R, Soman K.P. (Swapna et al., 2018) short-term memory (LSTM), convolutional neural network (CNN), and combinations thereof. These features are supported by vector vectors.

They found that CNN and CNN-LSTM architectures show three & six% margins, respectively, compared to the recent work of non-SVM. The proposed classification scheme can help clinicians use the ECG signal to diagnose diabetes with a very high accuracy of 96%.

Thus, early diagnosis of diabetes is very important. Diabetic neuropathy affects neurological function. In the proposed study, HRV big data was analyzed for the diagnosis of diabetes using deep learning techniques. CNN 5-LSTM achieved the highest accuracy value of 95.7% using the SVM network. This is the highest published value for the automated diagnosis of diabetes using HRV as input. A flexible, recyclable system without compromise can be a real tool for doctors to discover diabetes. Improve accuracy with very large input data. If the input data is sufficient for research, the deep learning potential is truly terrible, and detection of anomalies in difficult and unpredictable areas in the future can be greatly improved. By extracting the dynamic nature of the input data, unexpected predictions of the input data that may not be unreasonable may be performed. Predictive information acts not only as a patient, but also as a warning signal for doctors to counter and prevent it.

RESULTS, INTERPRETATION AND DISCUSSION

Diabetes is known as hyperglycaemia. In this position, the body is ineffective to make adequate insulin and it has to be controlled. Diabetes is incurable. Now every person in this world is facing headache and stress related problems as well as physically challenged with curse of diabetes in daily life.

IoT helps us in a way that the machine should judge on its own and can interact or judge some future information. This big data is being stored in the form of cloud which is being taken properly so that data cannot be misguided by someone. In the modern era, the volume of sample or raw big data has increased at a rapid rate. This data may be used for evaluation in many fields.

Big Data currently possesses latest method of implementation named as data analytics and it is a dynamic and trending field in today's information era, modern big data processing techniques are required to handle above issues of this ever growing raw or sample big data.

Figure 5. Gender-distribution in the sample

From the Hospitals of Delhi and NCR, sample of 30 subjects has been collected in random fashion who has been suffering from Diabetes from their Health Insurance Providers without disclosing any Personal Information (PI) or Sensitive Personal Information (SPI) by Law. To identify each case sample ids like S1, S2 etc. has been allotted to the subjects. Sample big data has been collected for following parameters:

1. Gender
2. Age
3. Diabetes Type
4. Subject on Insulin
5. Subject having Obesity
6. Subject having CAD
7. Subject having HTN
8. Subject suffering from TTH (a.ka. headache) / Migraine.

Our area of interest is on TTH/ Migraine parameter. The study focuses on finding the role of diabetes in causing TTH and what are the peculiar probabilities/ pattern which do/can lead subject to TTH.

To find the pattern and relationship on different parameters, we first, analyzed the collected sample data with following parameters: TTH/ Migraine parameter, Diabetes Type & Insulin.

Table 1. Age group distribution in the sample

Age Group	% of Total Number of Subjects	Number of Subjects
<=25	16.666666667%	5
25-60	56.666666667%	17
60-100	26.666666667%	8

ABOUT THE STUDY AND ANALYSIS

GENDER - DISTRIBUTION

Sample contains the equal number of male and female subjects. It was not intentionally collected equal numbers but in random sampling it occurs by chance. So our sample is not prone to Gender bias.(As per Fig. 5)

Figure 6. Age group-distribution in the sample

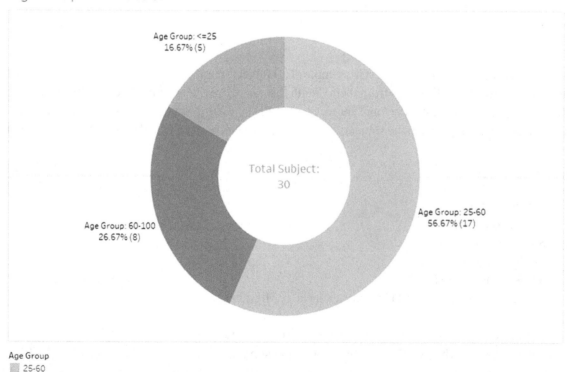

Table 2. Age group & gender- distribution

Age Group	Gender	Min. Age	% of Total Number of Subjects	Frequency
<=25	Male	15	13.333333333%	4
<=25	Female	18	3.333333333%	1
25-60	Male	34	20%	6
25-60	Female	32	36.666666667%	11
60-100	Male	65	16.666666667%	5
60-100	Female	62	10%	3

AGE GROUP-DISTRIBUTION

In order to study the distribution of diabetes and related diseases across the different ages, sample has been grouped in different age bins. The percentage and frequency of subjects are shown in below (As per Table 1)

It can be clearly observed from the donut chart study that the 25-60 age group is more prone towards diabetes. So it has been observed middle age is having more diabetic cases than other ages. The possible cause can be bad food habit, less exercises, stress and irregular sleeping. It is the age group in which subjects are found comparative focus less on health and daily routines due to which they catch life time illness like diabetes.(As per Fig. 6)

AGE GROUP & GENDER- DISTRIBUTION

It became important to understand the distribution of gender across the ages. On analyzing the frequency stacked columnar graph, it can be easily seen that females of age group 25-60 are the highest in frequency in the collected sample. On studying articles related to diabetes it can be said that the possible cause can be the pregnancy in females, irregular sleeping and daily habits etc.(As per Fig. 7) and (As per Table 2)

ANALYSIS: TTH DISTRIBUTION IN THE SAMPLE

In the sample total 26.67% subjects are reported of having TTH. This number becomes significant as it is saying that out 4 diabetic patient 1 is suffering from TTH. Diabetic patients are generally reported of having TTH due to stress and mental demotivation caused due to problems like diabetes. (As per Fig. 8)

On analyzing this ratio distribution within the gender, it has been found that males are more prone to TTH than as compare to females. 25% more males are reported having TTH than females. On detailed look into the big data and subjected to discussion it has been found that sampled males are working while females are less working so there is possibility of work stress which is causing more frequent headache. (As per Fig. 9a and 9b)

Figure 7. Age group & gender-distribution in the sample

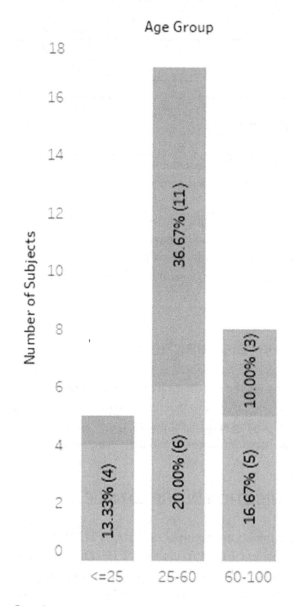

Figure 8. TTH distribution among the subjects of the sample

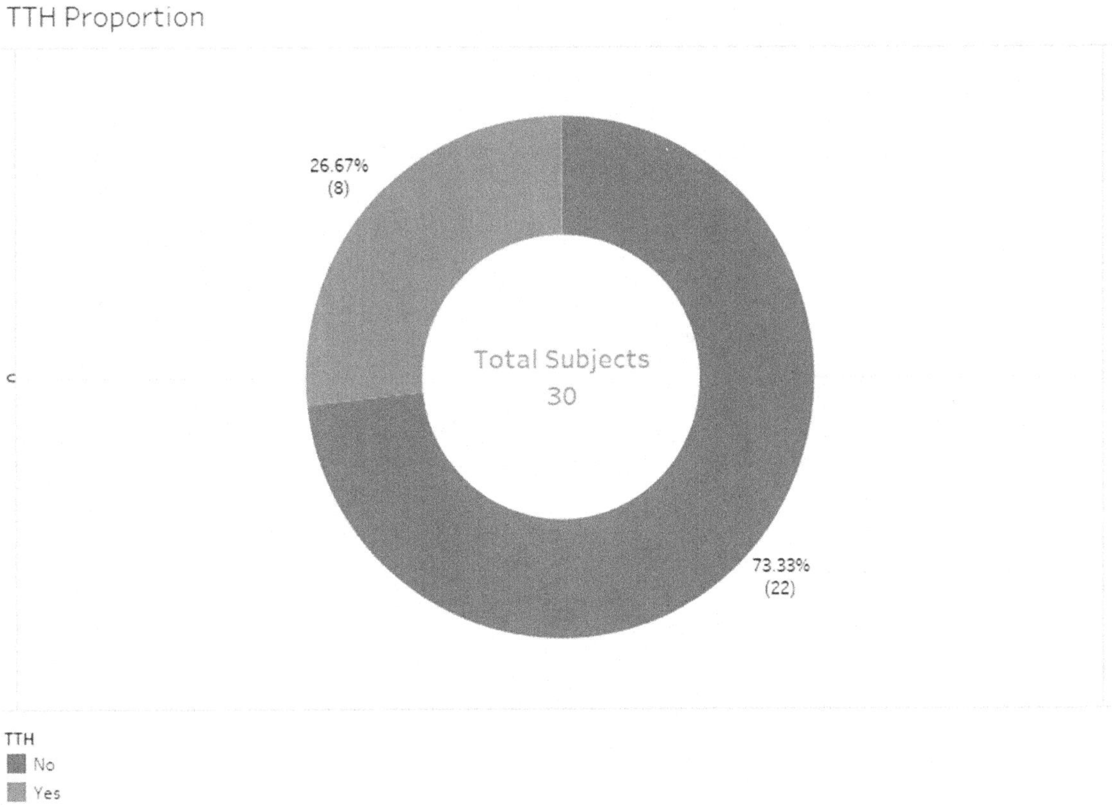

TTH Proportion

TTH
■ No
■ Yes

In order to understand the patterns occurring with the age group, frequency of having headache with age group is plotted to reveal the pattern and interestingly the pattern found with the TTH is different as of Diabetic case. TTH is increasing in the patient with the increase in their age and the increase is significantly important. This can be understood as the nervous system weakens due to aging effect causing the incapability of body to cope up with the tensions effectively and resulting into headache. So, the aged diabetic patient should be more cautious and should take preventive actions for TTH as 50% of aged group () diabetic patient has been reported of having headache i.e 1 out of every second person is suffering from TTH. (As per Fig. 10a and 10b)

The overall age group with gender and number of subject having TTH or not is plotted in below grouped stacked columnar chart. It can be observed that very few cases are observed for TTH for the males below 60 but the number get increased dramatically as age goes beyond 60. This signifies old age men are having highest probability among all segregation having TTH. (As per Fig. 11)

Also, for females increasing trends of TTH can be observed upto age of 60 beyond that cases of TTH decreases. This is in line with the overall pattern of diabetic subject variation with age group.

In order visualize this pattern keenly, above graph is plotted only for TTH subjects and below graph is obtained. (As per Fig. 11)

Figure 9. TTH pattern with Age group and frequency of headache with Age and Gender for 2 samples

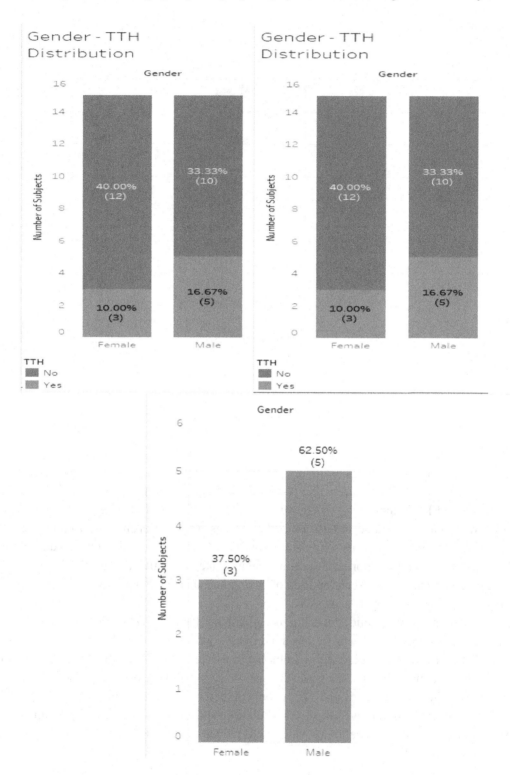

Figure 10. Overall age group with gender and number of subjects having TTH for 2 samples

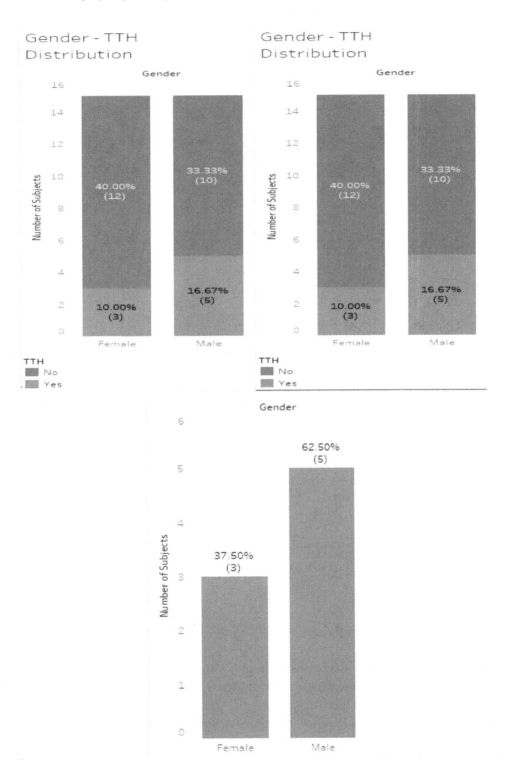

Figure 11. Age group & gender as per TTH distribution

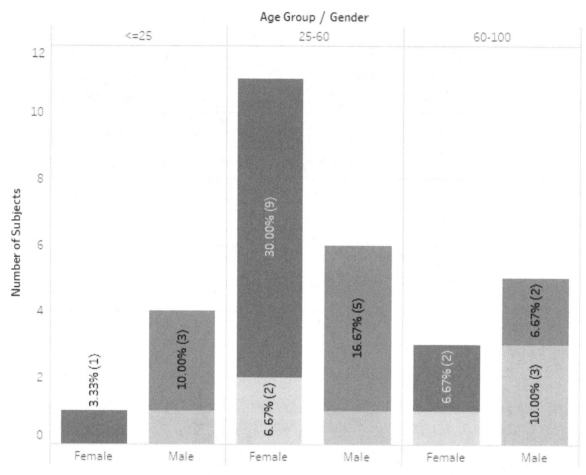

Age Group & Gender-TTH Distribution

In conclusion, it can be said that TTH cases increasing with age in case of males and not following the pattern of Diabetes variation with age while in case of female TTH pattern variation is same as diabetes i.e increasing trend up to age of 60 then decreasing.

In order to gain more in-sight and to know the role of diabetic type in causing the TTH, a stacked bar relationship of diabetes type and TTH is plotted and it has been observed that type-I diabetic is almost no contribution in TTH. In other words subject suffering from type-I is reported very less about TTH. It can be justified as type-I subjects are of younger age groups so they are able to cope up with tense situation or it might be the case they do not have such significant level of tension that can cause the TTH.

Figure 12. Correlation of TTH as per gender, number of subjects and age

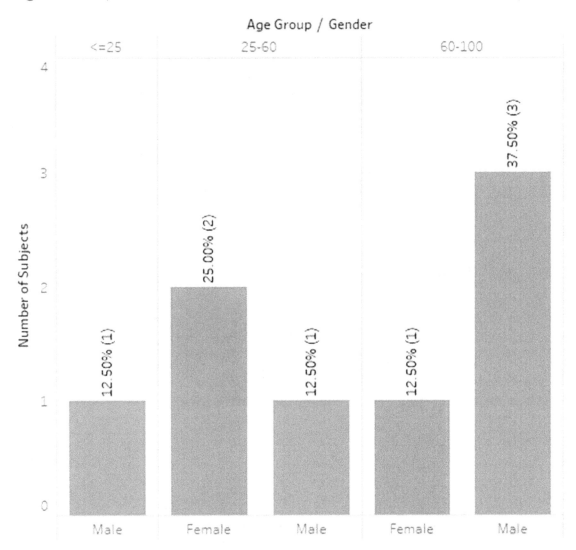

Figure 13. Diabetes distribution over available subjects

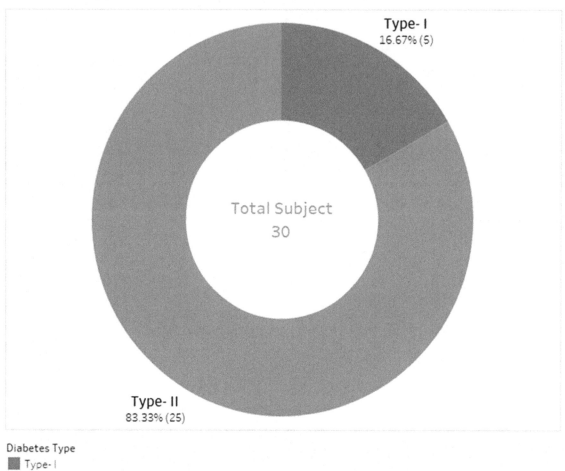

DIABETES TYPE – DISTRIBUTION IN THE SAMPLE

Diabetes has two categories:

1. Type-I
2. Type-II(As per Fig. 12)

It is clearly shown by the donut chart that Type-II diabetes is most commonly found diabetes. This type of diabetes are mainly caused due to bad life styles – irregular sleeps, wrong food habit. In this type of diabetes some cases may or may not require insulin. In the initial stage such subject can control it by correcting their life style, doing yoga or exercises.

Figure 14. Diabetes type & insulin consumption as per Type-1 & Type -2 distribution

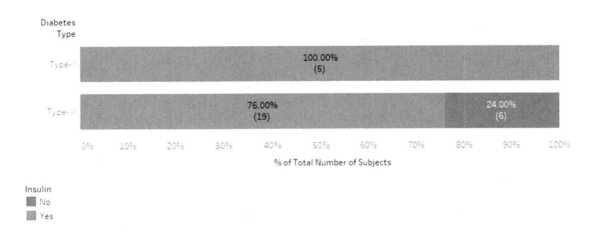

DIABETES & INSULIN CONSUMPTION

In type-I, external insulin consumption is must. It is due to the fact because body of subject either stopped insulin production or producing very less insulin so external consumption of insulin is must. It can be by birth or hereditary.

In type-II it can be clearly seen in the stacked bar chart sample contains 76% of type-II subject which consumes insulin that means subject either not focusing on alternate of insulin like correcting life style, food habits etc or the case is so worsen that body is now dependent on external insulin. (As per Fig. 13)

Figure 15. Diabetes type & gender as per Type-1 & Type-2 distribution

Diabetes Type & Gender - Distribution

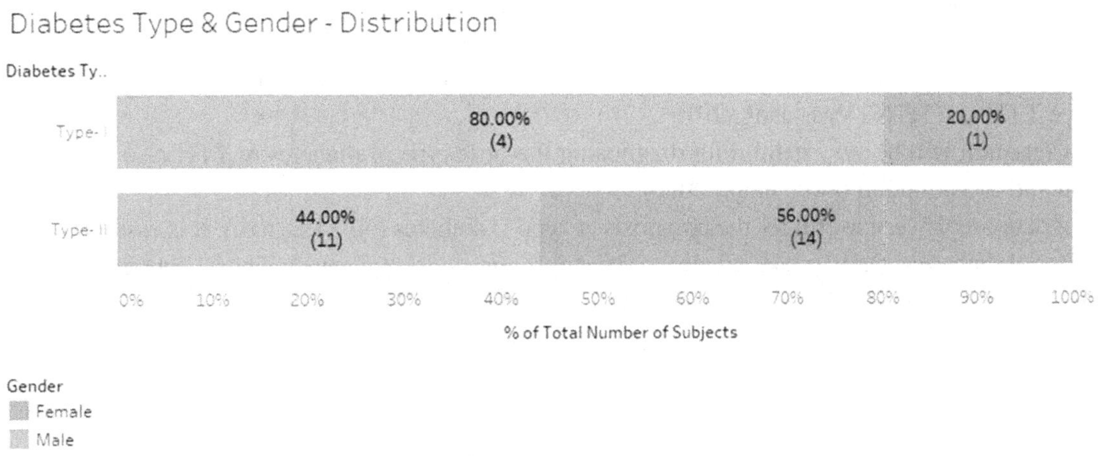

Table 3. Summary for the diabetes type, gender & age group –distribution in the sample

Diabetes Type, Gender & Age Group - Distribution								
				Age Group				
		<=25		25-60		60-100		
Diabetes Type	Gender	% of Total Number of Subjects	Number of Subjects	% of Total Number of Subjects	Number of Subjects	% of Total Number of Subjects	Number of Subjects	
Type-I	Female	20.00%	1.00					
	Male	60.00%	3.00	20.00%	1.00			
Type-II	Female			44.00%	11.00	12.00%	3.00	
	Male	4.00%	1.00	20.00%	5.00	20.00%	5.00	

DIABETES TYPE & GENDER – DISTRIBUTION

It can be seen clearly that the in Type-I category, male is having 80% of total type-I subjects that is indicating that males are more prone to hereditary diabetes transfer as compare to females. Since the sample size is less so to conclude it into final remark one should study larger sample size for type-I diabetes patient. This fact is supported by the big data using IoT devices when we look deeper into the details then we found that even in type-I case only female subject is of middle age while all male subjects are below 25 year of age group.

In type-II category female seems to dominate by 16% that indicates females are having more bad habits for food, life style etc. When we look into insight of gender with age group distribution it has been found that in every age group females are dominating.

Interesting observation in both these graphs shows that none of our female subject having diabetes are below 25 years i.e. early age diabetes cases are very less comparative to males subjected to the case sampling should not be impacted for age group gender biasing. (As per Fig. 14) and (As per Table 3)

NOVETY IN OUR WORK

In the current scenario the problem of Diabetes & stress in Male &female with different age group (<=25, 25-60 and 60-100) has emerged out to be as a big problem (Gautam, 2016; Gautam, 2017; Gautam et al., 2018; Todd, 2010).

The People in any class or society are affected by the problem of diabetes. Therefore, they are stressed and face TTH and HTN (Vyas et al., 2018) .

Our research will be very helpful for diagnosing the both type of diabetes & TTH also insulin production and consumption (Saini et al., 2018).

Diet planning is very useful for the diagnosis of type-2 diabetes (NPTEL, n.d.). It is essential for the treatment of diabetics. Daily intake requires a fixed exchange system. Dietary Fiber: Diets rich in dietary fiber and complex carbohydrates are beneficial for diabetics It will be lower:

Table 4. TTH variation with the variation of other disease

- Required amount of insulin (Cefalu, 2001; Reaven, 2004)
- Serum cholesterol and triglyceride levels
- Help weight control and lower blood pressure
- Whole grains, fruits, vegetables, fenugreek seeds are rich in complex carbohydrates
- Pregnant women may need vitamin and mineral supplements
- Alcohol: Moderate alcohol use does not adversely affect diabetes in well-controlled patients (NPTEL, n.d.).

In the initial stage such subject can control it by correcting their life style, doing yoga or exercises. Nutrition is the Fundamental part of treatment (NPTEL, n.d.).

Treatment involves medication, nutritional management & exercise. This type of research is of great benefit to the community, which is increasing more and more suffering.

We have used the Tableau s/w for the Analysis of Diabetes and Correlation of Stress on Human Health on Various Medical Parameters. The Tableau platform helps you turn your data into insights that drive action. As rightly said, Big Data everywhere & tableau for everyone.

FUTURE SCOPE, LIMITATIONS AND POSSIBLE APPLICATIONS

This study has a scintillating future scope which can overcome its limitations. We have found from our sample analysis our sample is not prone to Gender bias. Which can be used efficiently in future for analyzing large data sample.

It is clearly shown by the donut chart that Type-II diabetes is most commonly found diabetes. This type of diabetes is mainly caused due to bad life styles – irregular sleeps wrong food habit. In this type of diabetes some cases may or may not require insulin. In the initial stage such subject can control it by correcting their life style, doing yoga or exercises(Chen et al., 2011).

Since the sample size is less so to conclude it into final remark one should study larger sample size for type-I diabetes patient residing in various regions.TTH variation with the variation of other disease in subject shown below. (As per Table 4)

We can easily find TTH variation with the variation of other disease like Obesity & many more in subject using Tableau s/w for the large datasets(Gill, 2006; Saini et al., 2018).

This TTH& both type of diabetes depends on various factors like age, gender, Diabetes Type, Subject on Insulin, Subject having Obesity, Subject having CAD Subject having HTN&subject suffering from TTH (a.ka. headache) / Migraine(Bluestone et al., 2010; Chen et al., 2011; Chobanian et al., 2003; Grundy et al., 1999; Vyas et al., 2018).

Diets plan can be very useful for diagnosing the type -2 Diabetes(Chen et al., 2011). It's an essential part of the treatment of diabetic patients.(Chaturvedi, 2015)

TABLEAU S/W, APPLICATIONS WITH BENEFITS

The board can see and understand anyone's information. Connect to most large databases, create visualizations, drag and drop, and share with one click.

Tableau Desktop: Tableau Desktop is a visualization of smart business tools and heavy data that anyone can use. It specializes in converting tedious table data into eye care tables and expressions.

Tabletop Desktop: A desktop server with all the features and mobile networking features of Tableau Desktop.

Tableau Online: This is the version of the Server Tableau host. It is typically designed to deliver software to everyone using cloud computing.

Tableau Reader: This is the free desktop version of Tableau. Its functionality is limited only by looking at the screenshots created on the board.

General tab: This is a free version of carpet software that can be used to create visualizations.

Exciting visualization: Provide a clean picture carpet on a scale. Get unorganized information and provide various visualizations to better understand the process.

●Detailed information

○ Easy to use

RECOMMENDATIONS AND FUTURE CONSIDERATIONS

The authors have distributed the parameters in the sample for better analysis like: Gender, age and Gender & age group. We have found our sample is not bias. It contains equals number of males and females. The result were taken using analysis parameters as mentioned above type of Diabetes Type I & II with different age groups <=25, 25-60 and 60-100. It has been observed middle age (25-60) is having more diabetic cases than other ages.The study may be increase for larger subjects.

In the Type-I category, male is having 80% of total type-I subjects that is indicating that males are more prone to hereditary diabetes transfer as compare to females. It was seen that females of age group 25-60 are the highest in frequency in the collected sample. On studying articles related to diabetes it can be said that the possible cause can be the pregnancy in females, irregular sleeping and daily habits etc. This fact is supported by the big data when we look deeper into the details then we found that even in type-I case only female subject is of middle age while all male subjects are below 25 year of age group. (Chaturvedi, 2019; Chaturvedi et al., 2015)

In type-II category female seems to dominate by 16% that indicates females are having more bad habits for food, life style etc. When we look into insight of gender with age group distribution it has been found that in every age group females are dominating. In conclusion, overall age group with gender and number of subject having TTH or not is plotted in below grouped stacked columnar chart.

It can be observed that very fewer cases are observed for TTH for the males below 60 but the number get increased dramatically as age goes beyond 60. This signifies old age men are having highest probability among all segregation having TTH.(Richa & Prakash, 2016a; Richa & Prakash, 2016b)

CONCLUSION

It was seen that with the starting of the sample analysis we had the sample From the Hospitals of Delhi and NCR, of 30 subjects in random fashion. Our sample is not prone to Gender bias. On seeing the result, it can be clearly observed from the donut chart study that the 25-60 age groups is more prone towards diabetes (NPTEL, n.d.; Todd, 2010).

On analyzing the frequency stacked columnar graph, it can be easily seen that females of age group 25-60 are the highest in frequency in the collected sample. On studying articles related to diabetes it can be said that the possible cause can be the pregnancy in females, irregular sleeping and daily habits etc.

It is clearly shown by the donut chart that Type-II diabetes is most commonly found diabetes(Chen et al., 2011). This type of diabetes is mainly caused due to bad life styles – irregular sleeps, wrong food habit. In this type of diabetes some cases may or may not require insulin. In the initial stage such subject can control it by correcting their life style, doing yoga or exercises.

In type-II it can be clearly seen in the stacked bar chart sample contains 76% of type-II subject which consumes insulin that means subject either not focusing on alternate of insulin like correcting life style, food habits etc or the case is so worsen that body is now dependent on external insulin(Cefalu, 2001; Chen et al., 2011; Reaven, 2004).

It can be seen clearly that the in Type-I category, male is having 80% of total type-I subjects that is indicating that males are more prone to hereditary diabetes transfer as compare to females(Ahmed, 2002; Bluestone et al., 2010).

This fact is supported by the big data when we look deeper into the details then we found that even in type-I case only female subject is of middle age while all male subjects are below 25 year of age group.

On analyzing this ratio distribution within the gender, it has been found that males are more prone to TTH than as compare to females. 25% more males are reported having TTH than females. On detailed look into the big data and subjected to discussion it has been found that sampled males are working while females are less working so there is possibility of work stress which is causing more frequent headache (Chaturvedi et al., 2018; Chobanian et al., 2003; Rastogi, Chaturvedi, Satya, Arora, Yadav et al, 2018; Satya et al., 2019).

During our research interesting observation that none of our female subject having diabetes is below 25 years i.e. early age diabetes cases are very less comparative to males subjected to the case sampling should not be impacted for age group gender biasing.(Chaturvedi et al., 2012; Tsai et al., 2013)

In Conclusion, overall age group with gender and number of subject having TTH or not is plotted in below grouped stacked columnar chart. It can be observed that very less cases are observed for TTH for the males below 60 but the number get increased dramatically as age goes beyond 60. This signifies old age men are having highest probability among all segregation having TTH (Saini et al., 2018; Vyas et al., 2018).

REFERENCES

Ahmed, A. M. (2002, April). History of diabetes mellitus. *Saudi Medical Journal*, *23*(4), 373–378. PMID:11953758

Ajay, V. S., & Prabhakaran, D. (2010). Coronary heart disease in Indians: Implications of the INTER-HEART study. *The Indian Journal of Medical Research*, *132*, 561–566. PMID:21150008

Alkholya, Abdalmonema, Zaki, Mohamed, Elkoumi, Abu Hashima, & Maha. (2017). *Basset a, Hossam E. Salahc The antioxidant status of coenzyme Q10 and vitamin E in children with type-1 diabetes*. Academic Press.

Arora, N., Rastogi, R., Chaturvedi, D. K., Satya, S., Gupta, M., Yadav, V., Chauhan, S., & Sharma, P. (2019). Chronic TTH Analysis by EMG & GSR Biofeedback on Various Modes and Various Medical Symptoms Using IoT. Big Data Analytics for Intelligent Healthcare Management. doi:10.1016/B978-0-12-818146-1.00005-2

Bansal, I., Rastogi, R., Chaturvedi, D. K., Satya, S., Arora, N., & Yadav, V. (2018). Intelligent Analysis for Detection of Complex Human Personality by Clinical Reliable Psychological Surveys on Various Indicators. *National Conference on 3rd MDNCPDR-2018*.

Biggers, A., Lisa, K., Sharp, B., Nimitphong, H., Saetung, S., Siwasaranond, N., Manodpitipong, A., Crowley, S., Hood, M., Gerber, S., & Reutrakulc, S. (2019). Relationship between depression, sleep quality, and hypoglycemia among persons with type-2 diabetes. *J Clin Transl Endocrinol.*, *15*, 62–64. . doi:10.1016/j.jcte.2018.12.007

Bluestone, J. A., Herold, K., & Eisenbarth, G. (2010, April 29). Genetics, pathogenesis and clinical interventions in type-1 diabetes. *Nature*, *464*(7293), 1293–1300. doi:10.1038/nature08933 PMID:20432533

Bruen, D., Delaney, C., Florea, L., & Diamond, D. (2017). Glucose Sensing for Diabetes Monitoring: Recent Developments. *Sensors (Basel)*, *17*(8), 1866. doi:10.339017081866 PMID:28805693

Cefalu, W. T. (2001). Insulin resistance: Cellular and clinical concepts. *Experimental Biology and Medicine (Maywood, N.J.)*, *226*(1), 13–26. doi:10.1177/153537020122600103 PMID:11368233

Chaturvedi, D. K. (2019). Relationship between Chakra Energy and Consciousness. *Biomedical Journal of Scientific and Technical Research, 15*(3), 1-3. doi:10.26717/BJSTR.2019.15.002705

Chaturvedi, D.K. (2015). Dayalbagh Way of Life for Better Worldliness. *Journal of Research in Humanities and Social Science, 3*(5), 16-23.

Chatruvedi, D.K. (2014a). Correlation between Energy Distribution profile and Level of Consciousness. *International Journal of Education, 4*(1), 1–9.

Chaturvedi, D. K. (2014b). The correlation between Student Performance and Consciousness Level. *International Journal of Computing Science and Communication Technologies, 6*(2), 936-939.

Chaturvedi, D. K. (2013a). Correlation between Human Performance and Consciousness. *IEEE-International Conference on Human Computer Interaction.*

Chaturvedi, D. K. (2013b). The Correlation between Student Performance and Consciousness Level. *International Conference on Advanced Computing and Communication Technologies (ICACCT™-2013),* 200-203.

Chaturvedi, D. K. (2013c). A Study of Correlation between Consciousness Level and Performance of Worker. *Industrial Engineering Journal, 6*(8), 40–43.

Chaturvedi, D. K. (2012). Human Rights and Consciousness. *International Seminar on Prominence of Human Rights in the Criminal Justice System (ISPUR 2012),* 33.

Chaturvedi, D. K. (2004). *Science, Religion and Spiritual Quest.* DEI Press.

Chaturvedi, D. K., Kumar, J., & Bhardwaj, R. (2015, September). Effect of meditation on Chakra Energy and Hemodynamic parameters. *International Journal of Computers and Applications, 126*(12), 52–59. doi:10.5120/ijca2015906304

Chaturvedi, D. K., & Lajwanti, T. H. CKohli, H.P. (2012). Energy Distribution Profile of Human Influences the Level of Consciousness. *Towards a Science of Consciousness, Arizona Conference Proceeding.*

Chaturvedi, D. K., Rastogi, R., Arora, N., Trivedi, P., & Mishra, V. (2017). Swarm Intelligent Optimized Method of Development of Noble Life in the perspective of Indian Scientific Philosophy and Psychology. *Proceedings of NSC-2017 (National System Conference).*

Chaturvedi, D.K., Rastogi, R., Satya, S., Arora, N., Saini, H., Verma, H., Mehlyan K., & Varshney, Y. (2018). Statistical Analysis of EMG and GSR Therapy on Visual Mode and SF-36 Scores for Chronic TTH. *Proceedings of UPCON-2018.*

Chauhan, S., Rastogi, R., Chaturvedi, D. K., Satya, S., Arora, N., Yadav, V., & Sharma, P. (2018). Analytical Comparison of Efficacy for Electromyography and Galvanic Skin Resistance Biofeedback on Audio-Visual Mode for Chronic TTH on Various Attributes. Proceedings of the ICCIDA-2018.

Chen, L., Magliano, D. J., & Zimmet, P. Z. (2011). The worldwide epidemiology of type-2 diabetes mellitus: present and future perspectives. *Nature Reviews Endocrinology.* www.nature.com/uidfinder

Chobanian, A. V., Bakris, G. L., Black, H. R., Cushman, W. C., Green, L. A., Izzo, J. L. Jr, Jones, D. W., Materson, B. J., Oparil, S., Wright, J. T. Jr, & Roccella, E. J. (2003, December). Joint National Committee on Prevention, Detection, Evaluation, and Treatment of High Blood Pressure. *Hypertension, 42*(6), 1206–1252. doi:10.1161/01.HYP.0000107251.49515.c2 PMID:14656957

Cryer, P. E. (2001). Hypoglycemia-associated autonomic failure in diabetes. *American Journal of Physiology. Endocrinology and Metabolism, 17*(8), 678–695. PMID:11701423

Desouza, C. V., Bolli, G. B., & Fonseca, V. (2010). Hypoglycemia, diabetes, and cardiovascular events. *Diabetes Care, 33*(6), 1389–1394. doi:10.2337/dc09-2082 PMID:20508232

Diderichsena, B.F., & Andersena, I. (2018). The syndemics of diabetes and depression in Brazil – An epidemiological analysis. *SSM Popul Health.* . doi:10.1016/j.ssmph.2018.11.002

Erem, C., Hacihasanoglu, A., Kocak, M., Deger, O., & Topbas, M. J. (2009, March). Prevalence of prehypertension and hypertension and associated risk factors among Turkish adults: Trabzon Hypertension Study. *Public Health (Oxf), 31*(1), 47–58. doi:10.1093/pubmed/fdn078 PMID:18829520

Gaglardio, J. J., Chantelot, J. M., & Domenger, C. (2009, February). Hhasan ilkova on behalf of the IDMPS steering committee. *Diabetes Care, 32*(2), 227–233. doi:10.2337/dc08-0435 PMID:19033410

Gautam, S. (2016). Healthline Editorial Team. In *Automated ML based analyses of diabetes and correlation of stress on human health on various medical parameter.* https://www.healthline.com/health/whats-your-stress-type

Gautam, S. R. (2017). *Automated ML based analyses of diabetes and correlation of stress on human health on various medical parameter.* https://www.healthline.com/health/migraine/migraine-vs-headache

Gautam, S., Valencia, H., & Kristeen, C. (2018). Automated ML based analyses of diabetes and correlation of stress on human health on various medical parameter. *Clinical Forum for Nurse Anesthetists, 5*(February). https://www.healthline.com/health/tension-headache

Ghassibe-Sabbagh, M., Mehanna, Z., Farraj, L. A., Salloum, A. K., & Zalloua, P. A. (2019, February 20). Gestational diabetes mellitus and macrosomia predispose to diabetes in the Lebanese population. *Journal of Clinical & Translational Endocrinology, 16*, 100185. doi:10.1016/j.jcte.2019.100185

Gill, T. (2006). Epidemiology and health impact of obesity: An Asia Pacific perspective. *Asia Pacific Journal of Clinical Nutrition, 15*, 3–14. PMID:16928656

Goyal, A., & Yusuf, S. (2006). The burden of cardiovascular disease in the Indian subcontinent. *The Indian Journal of Medical Research, 124*, 235–244. PMID:17085827

Grundy, S. M., Benjamin, I. J., Burke, G. L., Chait, A., Eckel, R. H., Howard, B. V., Mitch, W., Smith, S. C. Jr, & Sowers, J. R. (1999). Diabetes and cardiovascular disease. *Circulation, 100*(10), 1134–1146. doi:10.1161/01.CIR.100.10.1134 PMID:10477542

Gulati, M., Rastogi, R., Chaturvedi, D. K., Sharma, P., Yadav, V., Chauhan, S., Gupta, M., & Singhal, P. (2019). Statistical Resultant Analysis of Psychosomatic Survey on Various Human Personality Indicators: Statistical Survey to Map Stress and Mental Health. In *Handbook of Research on Learning in the Age of Transhumanism.* Hershey, PA: IGI Global. doi:10.4018/978-1-5225-8431-5.ch022

Gupta, M., Rastogi, R., Chaturvedi, D. K., & Satya, S. (2019). Comparative Study of Trends Observed During Different Medications by Subjects under EMG & GSR Biofeedback. *IJITEE, 8*(6S), 748-756. https://www.ijitee.org/download/volume-8-issue-6S/

Haddock, C. K., Rowan, A. B., Andrasik, F., Wilson, P. G., Talcott, G. W., & Stein, R. J. (1997). Home-based behavioural Treatments for chronic benign headache: A meta-analysis of controlled trials. *Cephalalgia, 17*, 113–118. doi:10.1046/j.1468-2982.1997.1702113.x PMID:9137849

Kumar, M. R., Shankar, R., & Singh, S. (2016). Hypertension among the adults in rural Varanasi: A cross-sectional study on prevalence and health seeking behavior. *Indian Journal of Preventive and Social Medicine, 47*(1-2), 78–83.

Low, S., Chin, M. C., & Deurenberg-Yap, M. (2009). Review on epidemic of obesity. *Annals of the Academy of Medicine, Singapore, 38*, 57–59. PMID:19221672

Maser, R. E., Lenhard, J. M., & DeCherney, S. G. (2000). Cardiovascular Autonomic Neuropathy. *The Endocrinologist, 10*(1), 27–33. doi:10.1097/00019616-200010010-00006

Maser, R. E., Pfeifer, M. A., Dorman, J. S., Kuller, L. H., Becker, D. J., & Orchard, T. J. (1990). Diabetic autonomic neuropathy and cardiovascular risk. Pittsburgh Epidemiology of Diabetes Complications Study III. *Archives of Internal Medicine, 150*(6), 1218–1222. doi:10.1001/archinte.1990.00390180056009 PMID:2353855

McCrory, D., Penzien, D. B., Hasselblad, V., & Gray, R. (2001). Behavioural and physical treatments for tension Type and cervocogenic headaches. *Foundation for Chiropractic Education and Research, 5*(3), 51.

Mullaly, J. W., Hall, K., & Goldstein, R. (2009, November/December). Efficacy of BF in the Treatment of Migraine and Tension Type Headaches. *Pain Physician, 12*, 1005–1011. PMID:19935987

NPTEL. (n.d.). https://nptel.ac.in/courses/126104004/LectureNotes/Week-7_05-Diet%20in%20Diabetes.pdf

Rastogi, R., Chaturvedi, D. K., Satya, S., Arora, N., & Chauhan, S. (2018). An Optimized Biofeedback Therapy for Chronic TTH between Electromyography and Galvanic Skin Resistance Biofeedback on Audio, Visual and Audio Visual Modes on Various Medical Symptoms. *National Conference on 3rd MDNCPDR-2018 at DEI.*

Rastogi, R., Chaturvedi, D. K., Satya, S., Arora, N., Singhal, P., & Gulati, M. (2018). Statistical Resultant Analysis of Spiritual & Psychosomatic Stress Survey on Various Human Personality Indicators. *International Conference Proceedings of ICCI 2018.* 10.1007/978-981-13-8222-2_25

Rastogi R. Chaturvedi D. K. Satya S. Arora N. Sirohi H. Singh M. Verma P. Singh V. (2018). Which One is Best: Electromyography Biofeedback Efficacy Analysis on Audio, Visual and Audio-Visual Modes for Chronic TTH on Different Characteristics. *Proceedings of ICCIIoT- 2018.* https://ssrn.com/abstract=3354375

Rastogi, R., Chaturvedi, D. K., Satya, S., Arora, N., Yadav, V., Chauhan, S., & Sharma, P. (2018). SF-36 Scores Analysis for EMG and GSR Therapy on Audio, Visual and Audio Visual Modes for Chronic TTH. In Proceedings of the ICCIDA-2018. Springer.

Reaven, G. (2004). The metabolic syndrome or the insulin resistance syndrome? Different names, different concepts, and different goals. *Endocrinology and Metabolism Clinics of North America, 33*(2), 283–303. doi:10.1016/j.ecl.2004.03.002 PMID:15158520

Reddy, K. S. (2004). Cardiovascular disease in non-western countries. *The New England Journal of Medicine, 350*(24), 2438–2440. doi:10.1056/NEJMp048024 PMID:15190135

Richa, D. K. C., & Prakash, S. (2016a). The consciousness in Mosquito. *Journal of Mosquito Research, 6*(34), 1-9.

Richa, D. K. C., & Prakash, S. (2016b). Role of Electric and Magnetic Energy Emission in Intra and Interspecies Interaction in Microbes. *American Journal of Research Communication, 4*(12), 1-22.

Saini, H., Rastogi, R., Chaturvedi, D. K., Satya, S., Arora, N., Gupta, M., & Verma, H. (2019). An Optimized Biofeedback EMG and GSR Biofeedback Therapy for Chronic TTH on SF-36 Scores of Different MMBD Modes on Various Medical Symptoms. In Hybrid Machine Intelligence for Medical Image Analysis, Studies Comp. Intelligence (Vol. 841). Springer Nature Singapore Pte Ltd. doi:10.1007/978-981-13-8930-6_8

SainiH.RastogiR.ChaturvediD. K.SatyaS.AroraN.VermaH.MehlyanK. (2018). Comparative Efficacy Analysis of Electromyography and Galvanic Skin Resistance Biofeedback on Audio Mode for Chronic TTH on Various Indicators. *Proceedings of ICCIIoT- 2018.* https://ssrn.com/abstract=3354371

Satya, S., Arora, N., Trivedi, P., Singh, A., Sharma, A., Singh, A., Rastogi, R., & Chaturvedi, D. K. (2019). *Intelligent Analysis for Personality Detection on Various Indicators by Clinical Reliable Psychological TTH and Stress Surveys. In Proceedings of CIPR 2019 at Indian Institute of Engineering Science and Technology.* Springer-AISC Series.

Satya, S., Rastogi, R., Chaturvedi, D. K., Arora, N., Singh, P., & Vyas, P. (2018). Statistical Analysis for Effect of Positive Thinking on Stress Management and Creative Problem Solving for Adolescents. *Proceedings of the 12th INDIA-Com,* 245-251.

Shah, B., & Mathur, P. (2010). Surveillance of cardiovascular disease risk factors in India. *The Indian Journal of Medical Research, 132,* 634–642. PMID:21150017

Sharma, S., Rastogi, R., Chaturvedi, D. K., Bansal, A., & Agrawal, A. (2018). Audio Visual EMG & GSR Biofeedback Analysis for Effect of Spiritual Techniques on Human Behavior and Psychic Challenges. *Proceedings of the 12th INDIACom,* 252-258.

Singh, A., Rastogi, R., Chaturvedi, D. K., Satya, S., Arora, N., Sharma, A., & Singh, A. (2019). Intelligent Personality Analysis on Indicators in IoT-MMBD Enabled Environment. In *Multimedia Big Data Computing for IoT Applications: Concepts, Paradigms, and Solutions.* Springer. Advance online publication. doi:10.1007/978-981-13-8759-3_7

Singhal, P., Rastogi, R., Chaturvedi, D. K., Satya, S., Arora, N., Gupta, M., Singhal, P., & Gulati, M. (2019). Statistical Analysis of Exponential and Polynomial Models of EMG & GSR Biofeedback for Correlation between Subjects Medications Movement & Medication Scores. *IJITEE, 8*(6S), 625-635. https://www.ijitee.org/download/volume-8-issue-6S/

Swapna, G., Vinayakumar, R., & Soman, K. P. (2018). Diabetes detection using deep learning algorithms. *ICT Express*, 243–246. www.elsevier.com/locate/icte

Todd, J. A. (2010, April 23). Etiology of type-1 diabetes. *Immunity*, *32*(4), 457–467. doi:10.1016/j.immuni.2010.04.001 PMID:20412756

Tsai, Cohly, & Chaturvedi. (2013). Towards the Consciousness of the Mind. *Towards a Science of Consciousness, Dayalbagh Conference Proceeding*.

Vyas, P., Rastogi, R., Chaturvedi, D. K., Arora, N., Trivedi, P., & Singh, P. (2018). Study on Efficacy of Electromyography and Electroencephalography Biofeedback with Mindful Meditation on Mental health of Youths. *Proceedings of the 12th INDIA-Com*, 84-89.

Yadav, V., Rastogi, R., Chaturvedi, D. K., Satya, S., Arora, N., Yadav, V., Sharma, P., & Chauhan, S. (2018). Statistical Analysis of EMG & GSR Biofeedback Efficacy on Different Modes for Chronic TTH on Various Indicators. *Int. J. Advanced Intelligence Paradigms*, *13*(1), 251–275. doi:10.1504/IJAIP.2019.10021825

Yusuf, S., Reddy, S., Ounpuu, S., & Anand, S. (2001). Global burden of cardiovascular diseases: Part II: Variations in cardiovascular disease by specific ethnic groups and geographic regions and prevention strategies. *Circulation*, *104*(23), 2855–2864. doi:10.1161/hc4701.099488 PMID:11733407

Compilation of References

Berral-García, J. L. (2016). *A quick view on current techniques and machine learning algorithms for big data analytics.* ICTON Trento. doi:10.1109/ICTON.2016.7550517

Mullaly, J. W., Hall, K., & Goldstein, R. (2009, November/December). Efficacy of BF in the Treatment of Migraine and Tension Type Headaches. *Pain Physician*, *12*, 1005–1011. PMID:19935987

Shelby, Z., Hartke, K., & Bormann, C. (2014). *The Constrained Application Protocol (CoAP).* RFC 7252.

Xiao, Xie, Chen, & Dai. (2016). A mobile offloading game against smart attacks. *IEEE Access*, *4*, 2281–2291.

Arora, N., Rastogi, R., Chaturvedi, D. K., Satya, S., Gupta, M., Yadav, V., Chauhan, S., & Sharma, P. (2019). Chronic TTH Analysis by EMG & GSR Biofeedback on Various Modes and Various Medical Symptoms Using IoT. Big Data Analytics for Intelligent Healthcare Management. doi:10.1016/B978-0-12-818146-1.00005-2

Bormann, C., Hartke, K., & Shelby, Z. (2015). *The Constrained Application Protocol (CoAP).* RFC 7252. https://www.rfc-editor.org/rfc/rfc7252.txt

Tang, Sun, Liu, & Gaudiot. (n.d.). Enabling Deep Learning on IoT Devices. *Computer*, 92 – 96.

Xiao, L., Yan, Q., Lou, W., Chen, G., & Hou, Y. T. (2013). Proximity-based security techniques for mobile users in wireless networks. *IEEE Transactions on Information Forensics and Security*, *8*(12), 2089–2100. doi:10.1109/TIFS.2013.2286269

Erem, C., Hacihasanoglu, A., Kocak, M., Deger, O., & Topbas, M. J. (2009, March). Prevalence of prehypertension and hypertension and associated risk factors among Turkish adults: Trabzon Hypertension Study. *Public Health (Oxf)*, *31*(1), 47–58. doi:10.1093/pubmed/fdn078 PMID:18829520

McDonald. (2019). *The Internet of Things requires machine learning and AI.* Retrieved from https://www.ibm.com/blogs/internet-of-things/iot-the-internet-of-things-requires-machine-learning/

Skytta, V. (2017). Lightweight Machine to Machine Protocol as Part of Multiprotocol Device Management System. Communication and Information Sciences, Aalto University.

Xiao, L., Wan, X., & Han, Z. (2018). PHY-Layer Authentication With Multiple Landmarks With Reduced Overhead. *IEEE Transactions on Wireless Communications*, *17*(3), 1676–1687. doi:10.1109/TWC.2017.2784431

Bertino, E., & Islam, N. (2017). Botnets and Internet of Things Security. *Computer,IEEE*, *50*(2), 76–79. doi:10.1109/MC.2017.62

Vyas, P., Rastogi, R., Chaturvedi, D. K., Arora, N., Trivedi, P., & Singh, P. (2018). Study on Efficacy of Electromyography and Electroencephalography Biofeedback with Mindful Meditation on Mental health of Youths. *Proceedings of the 12th INDIA-Com*, 84-89.

Wang, Ma, Zhang, Gao, & Wu. (2018). Deep learning for smart manufacturing: Methods and applications. *J. Manuf. Syst.*, *48*, 144-156.

Xiao, L., Li, Y., Han, G., Liu, G., & Zhuang, W. (2016). PHY-layer spoofing detection with reinforcement learning in wireless networks. *IEEE Transactions on Vehicular Technology*, *65*(12), 10037–10047. doi:10.1109/TVT.2016.2524258

Chang, W.-G., & Lin, F. J. (2016). Challenges of incorporating OMA LWM2M gateway in M2M standard architecture. *IEEE Conference on Standards for Communications and Networking (CSCN)*, 1–6. 10.1109/CSCN.2016.7785166

Kwon, D., Park, S., Baek, S., Malaiya, R. K., Yoon, G., & Ryu, J. T. (2018). A study on development of the blind spot detection system for the IoT-based smart connected car. *Proceedings of the 2018 IEEE International Conference on Consumer Electronics (ICCE)*, 1–4. 10.1109/ICCE.2018.8326077

SainiH.RastogiR.ChaturvediD. K.SatyaS.AroraN.VermaH.MehlyanK. (2018). Comparative Efficacy Analysis of Electromyography and Galvanic Skin Resistance Biofeedback on Audio Mode for Chronic TTH on Various Indicators. *Proceedings of ICCIIoT- 2018.* https://ssrn.com/abstract=3354371

Xiao, L., Li, Y., Huang, X., & Du, X. J. (2017). Cloud-based malware detection game for mobile devices with offloading. *IEEE Transactions on Mobile Computing*, *16*(10), 2742–2750. doi:10.1109/TMC.2017.2687918

Li, H., Ota, K., & Dong, M. (2018). Learning IoT in Edge: Deep Learning for the Internet of Things with Edge Computing. *IEEE Network*, *32*(1), 96–101. doi:10.1109/MNET.2018.1700202

Todd, J. A. (2010, April 23). Etiology of type-1 diabetes. *Immunity*, *32*(4), 457–467. doi:10.1016/j.immuni.2010.04.001 PMID:20412756

Vermillard, J. (2015). *Bootstrapping device security with lightweight M2M.* https://medium.com/@vrmvrm/device-key-distribution-with-lightweight-m2m-36cdc12e5711

Xia, Wan, Lu, & Zhang. (2018). IoT Security Techniques Based on Machine Learning. Academic Press.

Abu Alsheikh, Lin, Niyato, & Tan. (2014). Machine learning in wireless sensor networks: Algorithms,strategies, and applications. *IEEE Commun. Surveys and Tutorials*, *16*(4), 1996–2018.

IoT Device Management Protocols: LwM2M, OMA-DM and TR-069. (2019). https://www.muutech.com/en/iot-device-management-protocols-lwm2m-oma-dm-and-tr-069

Yadav, V., Rastogi, R., Chaturvedi, D. K., Satya, S., Arora, N., Yadav, V., Sharma, P., & Chauhan, S. (2018). Statistical Analysis of EMG & GSR Biofeedback Efficacy on Different Modes for Chronic TTH on Various Indicators. *Int. J. Advanced Intelligence Paradigms*, *13*(1), 251–275. doi:10.1504/IJAIP.2019.10021825

NPTEL. (n.d.). https://nptel.ac.in/courses/126104004/LectureNotes/Week-7_05-Diet%20in%20Diabetes.pdf

Open Mobile Alliance. (2016). *OMA Device Management Protocol.* http://www.openmobilealliance.org/release/DM/V2_0-20160209-A/OMA-TS-DM_Protocol-V2_0-20160209-A.pdf

Ozay, Esnaola, Yarman Vural, Kulkarni, & Poor. (2015). Machine learning methods for attack detection in the smart grid. *IEEE Transactions on Neural Networks and Learning Systems*, *27*(8), 1773–1786. PMID:25807571

Tanskanen, M. (n.d.). *Applying machine learning to IoT data.* Retrieved from https://www.sas.com/en_us/ insights/articles/big-data/machine-learning-brings-concrete-aspect-to-iot.html

Bluestone, J. A., Herold, K., & Eisenbarth, G. (2010, April 29). Genetics, pathogenesis and clinical interventions in type-1 diabetes. *Nature*, *464*(7293), 1293–1300. doi:10.1038/nature08933 PMID:20432533

Mahdavinejad, Rezvan, Barekatain, Adibi, Barnaghi, & Sheth. (2018). Machine learning for internet of things data analysis: a survey. *Digital Communications and Networks*, 161-175.

Open Mobile Alliance. (2019). *Lightweight Machine to Machine Technical Specification*. http://www.openmobilealliance. org/release/LightweightM2M/Lightweight_Machine_to_Machine-v1_1-OMASpecworks.pdf

Roman, R., Lopez, J., & Mambo, M. (2018). Mobile edge computing, Fog et al.: A survey and analysis of security threats and challenges. *Future Generation Computer Systems*, *78*(3), 680–698. doi:10.1016/j.future.2016.11.009

Ahmed, A. M. (2002, April). History of diabetes mellitus. *Saudi Medical Journal*, *23*(4), 373–378. PMID:11953758

Antonia, C., Putera, L., & Lin, F. J. (2015). Incorporating OMA Lightweight M2M protocol in IoT/M2M standard architecture. *IEEE 2nd World Forum on Internet of Things (WF-IoT)*, 559– 564.

Kulkarni, & Venayagamoorthy. (2009). Neural network based secure media access control protocol for wireless sensor networks. *Proc. Int'l Joint Conf. Neural Networks*, 3437–3444.

Buczak, & Guven. (2015). A survey of data mining and machine learning methods for cyber security intrusion detection. *IEEE Communications Surveys and Tutorials*, *18*(2), 1153–1176.

Rastogi, R., Chaturvedi, D. K., Satya, S., Arora, N., Yadav, V., Chauhan, S., & Sharma, P. (2018). SF-36 Scores Analysis for EMG and GSR Therapy on Audio, Visual and Audio Visual Modes for Chronic TTH. In Proceedings of the IC-CIDA-2018. Springer.

Sheng, Z., Mahapatra, C., Zhu, C., & Leung, V. C. M. (2015). Recent Advances in Industrial Wireless Sensor Networks toward Efficient Management in IoT. *IEEE Access: Practical Innovations, Open Solutions*, *3*, 622–637. doi:10.1109/ ACCESS.2015.2435000

Smola, & Vishwanathan. (2008). *Introduction to Machine Learning*. Cambridge University Press.

Chaturvedi, D. K., Rastogi, R., Arora, N., Trivedi, P., & Mishra, V. (2017). Swarm Intelligent Optimized Method of Development of Noble Life in the perspective of Indian Scientific Philosophy and Psychology. *Proceedings of NSC-2017 (National System Conference)*.

Cristianini. (n.d.). *An introduction to support vector machines: And the kernel-based learning methods*. Cambridge University Press.

Rao, S., Chendanda, D., Deshpande, C., & Lakkundi, V. (n.d.). Implementing LWM2M in Constrained IoT Devices. *IEEE Conference on Wireless Sensors (ICWiSe)*, 52–57. 10.1109/ICWISE.2015.7380353

Wang, T., Wen, C.-K., Wang, H., Gao, F., Jiang, T., & Jin, S. (2017). Deep Learning for Wireless Physical Layer: Opportunities and Challenges. *IEEE China Communication*, *14*(11), 92–111. doi:10.1109/CC.2017.8233654

Choudhury, Gupta, Pradhan, Kumar, & Rathore. (2017). Privacy and Security of Cloud-Based Internet of Things (IoT). *2017 International Conference on Computational Intelligence and Networks*, 41-45.

Kesavan, S., & Kalambettu, G. K. (2018). IOT enabled comprehensive, plug and play gateway framework for smart health. *International Conference on Advances in Electronics, Computers and Communications (ICAECC)*, 1-5. 10.1109/ ICAECC.2018.8479431

Rastogi R. Chaturvedi D. K. Satya S. Arora N. Sirohi H. Singh M. Verma P. Singh V. (2018). Which One is Best: Electromyography Biofeedback Efficacy Analysis on Audio, Visual and Audio-Visual Modes for Chronic TTH on Different Characteristics. *Proceedings of ICCIIoT- 2018*. https://ssrn.com/abstract=3354375

Sianaki, O. A., Yousefi, A., Tabesh, A. R., & Mahdavi, M. (2018). Internet of Everything and Machine Learning Applications: Issues and Challenges. *2018 32nd International Conference on Advanced Information Networking and Applications Workshops (WAINA)*.

Chen, L., Magliano, D. J., & Zimmet, P. Z. (2011). The worldwide epidemiology of type-2 diabetes mellitus: present and future perspectives. *Nature Reviews Endocrinology*. www.nature.com/uidfinder

Drotar & Smeakal. (n.d.). Comparative Study of Machine Learning Techniques for Supervised classification of Biomedical Data. *Acta Electrotechnica et Informatica, 14*, 5–10.

Slovetskiy, S., Magadevan, P., Zhang, Y., & Akhouri, S. (2018). *Managing Non-IP Devices in Cellular IoT Networks*. https://www.omaspecworks.org/wp-content/uploads/2018/10/Whitepaper-11.1.18.pdf

Tan, Jamdagni, He, Nanda, & Liu. (2013). A system for Denial-of-Service attack detection based on multivariate correlation analysis. *IEEE Transactions on Parallel and Distributed Systems, 25*(2), 447–456.

Grundy, S. M., Benjamin, I. J., Burke, G. L., Chait, A., Eckel, R. H., Howard, B. V., Mitch, W., Smith, S. C. Jr, & Sowers, J. R. (1999). Diabetes and cardiovascular disease. *Circulation, 100*(10), 1134–1146. doi:10.1161/01.CIR.100.10.1134 PMID:10477542

Katzir, R. (2019). *Distributing a machine learning algorithm across IoT devices, edge and cloud*. Retrieved from https://medium.com/digital-catapult/distributing-a-machine-learning-algorithm-across-iot-device-edge-and-cloud-731480bfcceb

Maser, R. E., Pfeifer, M. A., Dorman, J. S., Kuller, L. H., Becker, D. J., & Orchard, T. J. (1990). Diabetic autonomic neuropathy and cardiovascular risk. Pittsburgh Epidemiology of Diabetes Complications Study III. *Archives of Internal Medicine, 150*(6), 1218–1222. doi:10.1001/archinte.1990.00390180056009 PMID:2353855

Michalski. (n.d.). *Machine learning an artificial intelligence approach*. Springer.

Maser, R. E., Lenhard, J. M., & DeCherney, S. G. (2000). Cardiovascular Autonomic Neuropathy. *The Endocrinologist, 10*(1), 27–33. doi:10.1097/00019616-200010010-00006

Ravinder Reddy, R., Mamatha, Ch., & Govardhan Reddy, R. (2018). A Review on Machine Learning Trends, Application and Challenges in Internet of Things. *International Conference on Advances in Computing, Communications and Informatics (ICACCI)*.

Far. (2019). *IoT and Machine Learning/Deep Learning*. Retrieved from https://medium.com/datadriveninvestor/iot-and-machine-learning-deep-learning-f102bf578c99

Reddy, K. S. (2004). Cardiovascular disease in non-western countries. *The New England Journal of Medicine, 350*(24), 2438–2440. doi:10.1056/NEJMp048024 PMID:15190135

Gupta, S., Agrawal, A., Gopalakrishnan, K., & Narayanan, P. (2015). Deep learning with limited numerical precision. *International Conference on Machine Learning*.

Shah, B., & Mathur, P. (2010). Surveillance of cardiovascular disease risk factors in India. *The Indian Journal of Medical Research, 132*, 634–642. PMID:21150017

Ajay, V. S., & Prabhakaran, D. (2010). Coronary heart disease in Indians: Implications of the INTERHEART study. *The Indian Journal of Medical Research, 132*, 561–566. PMID:21150008

Han, Mao, & Dally. (2015). *Deep compression: Compressing deep neural networks with pruning, trained quantization and Huffman coding*. Academic Press.

Goyal, A., & Yusuf, S. (2006). The burden of cardiovascular disease in the Indian subcontinent. *The Indian Journal of Medical Research*, *124*, 235–244. PMID:17085827

Marsland. (n.d.). *Machine learning: An algorithmic perspective*. Boca Raton: Chapman & Hall/CRC.

Ba, J., Mnih, V., & Kavukcuoglu, K. (2014). *Multiple object recognition with visual attention*. arXiv:1412.7755

Gautam, S., Valencia, H., & Kristeen, C. (2018). Automated ML based analyses of diabetes and correlation of stress on human health on various medical parameter. *Clinical Forum for Nurse Anesthetists*, *5*(February). https://www.healthline.com/health/tension-headache

Ha, M., & Lindh, T. (2018). Enabling Dynamic and Lightweight Management of Distributed Bluetooth Low Energy Devices. *International Conference on Computing, Networking and Communications (ICNC): Wireless Ad hoc and Sensor Networks*, 615-619. 10.1109/ICCNC.2018.8390355

Wirth, Akrour, Neumann, & Frnkranz. (2017). A Survey of Preference-Based Reinforcement Learning Methods. *Journal of Machine Learning Research*, *18*, 1–46.

Steinwart, & Christmann. (2008). *Support vector machines*. Springer-Verlag.

Yusuf, S., Reddy, S., Ounpuu, S., & Anand, S. (2001). Global burden of cardiovascular diseases: Part II: Variations in cardiovascular disease by specific ethnic groups and geographic regions and prevention strategies. *Circulation*, *104*(23), 2855–2864. doi:10.1161/hc4701.099488 PMID:11733407

Cefalu, W. T. (2001). Insulin resistance: Cellular and clinical concepts. *Experimental Biology and Medicine (Maywood, N.J.)*, *226*(1), 13–26. doi:10.1177/153537020122600103 PMID:11368233

Szegedy, C., Liu, W., Jia, Y., Sermanet, P., Reed, S., Anguelov, D., Erhan, D., Vanhoucke, V., & Rabinovich, A. (2015) Going deeper with convolutions. *Proceedings of the IEEE Conference on Computer Vision and Pattern Recognition*, 1–9.

Reaven, G. (2004). The metabolic syndrome or the insulin resistance syndrome? Different names, different concepts, and different goals. *Endocrinology and Metabolism Clinics of North America*, *33*(2), 283–303. doi:10.1016/j.ecl.2004.03.002 PMID:15158520

Vapnik, V. (n.d.). Support vector clustering. *Journal of Machine Learning Research*, *2*, 125–137.

Desouza, C. V., Bolli, G. B., & Fonseca, V. (2010). Hypoglycemia, diabetes, and cardiovascular events. *Diabetes Care*, *33*(6), 1389–1394. doi:10.2337/dc09-2082 PMID:20508232

Haddock, C. K., Rowan, A. B., Andrasik, F., Wilson, P. G., Talcott, G. W., & Stein, R. J. (1997). Home- based behavioural Treatments for chronic benign headache: A meta-analysis of controlled trials. *Cephalalgia*, *17*, 113–118. doi:10.1046/j.1468-2982.1997.1702113.x PMID:9137849

Gill, T. (2006). Epidemiology and health impact of obesity: An Asia Pacific perspective. *Asia Pacific Journal of Clinical Nutrition*, *15*, 3–14. PMID:16928656

Low, S., Chin, M. C., & Deurenberg-Yap, M. (2009). Review on epidemic of obesity. *Annals of the Academy of Medicine, Singapore*, *38*, 57–59. PMID:19221672

Bansal, I., Rastogi, R., Chaturvedi, D. K., Satya, S., Arora, N., & Yadav, V. (2018). Intelligent Analysis for Detection of Complex Human Personality by Clinical Reliable Psychological Surveys on Various Indicators. *National Conference on 3rd MDNCPDR-2018*.

Cryer, P. E. (2001). Hypoglycemia-associated autonomic failure in diabetes. *American Journal of Physiology. Endocrinology and Metabolism*, *17*(8), 678–695. PMID:11701423

Kumar, M. R., Shankar, R., & Singh, S. (2016). Hypertension among the adults in rural Varanasi: A cross-sectional study on prevalence and health seeking behavior. *Indian Journal of Preventive and Social Medicine, 47*(1-2), 78–83.

Ambedkar. (2017). Reinforcement Learning Algorithms: Survey and Classification. *Indian Journal of Science and Technology, 10,* 1–8.

Bankole, A., & Ajila, S. (n.d.). Predicting cloud resource provisioning using machine learning techniques. *26th Annual IEEE Canadian Conference on Electrical and Computer Engineering,* 1–4. 10.1109/CCECE.2013.6567848

Gautam, S. (2016). Healthline Editorial Team. In *Automated ML based analyses of diabetes and correlation of stress on human health on various medical parameter.* https://www.healthline.com/health/whats-your-stress-type

Silva, Rodrigues, Saleem, Kozlov, & Rabêlo. (2019). M4DN.IoT - A Networks and Devices Management Platform for Internet of Things. *IEEE Access, 7,* 53305-53313.

Gulati, M., Rastogi, R., Chaturvedi, D. K., Sharma, P., Yadav, V., Chauhan, S., Gupta, M., & Singhal, P. (2019). Statistical Resultant Analysis of Psychosomatic Survey on Various Human Personality Indicators: Statistical Survey to Map Stress and Mental Health. In *Handbook of Research on Learning in the Age of Transhumanism.* Hershey, PA: IGI Global. doi:10.4018/978-1-5225-8431-5.ch022

Biggers, A., Lisa, K., Sharp, B., Nimitphong, H., Saetung, S., Siwasaranond, N., Manodpitipong, A., Crowley, S., Hood, M., Gerber, S., & Reutrakulc, S. (2019). Relationship between depression, sleep quality, and hypoglycemia among persons with type-2 diabetes. *J Clin Transl Endocrinol., 15,* 62–64. . doi:10.1016/j.jcte.2018.12.007

Singh, A., Rastogi, R., Chaturvedi, D. K., Satya, S., Arora, N., Sharma, A., & Singh, A. (2019). Intelligent Personality Analysis on Indicators in IoT-MMBD Enabled Environment. In *Multimedia Big Data Computing for IoT Applications: Concepts, Paradigms, and Solutions.* Springer. Advance online publication. doi:10.1007/978-981-13-8759-3_7

Bruen, D., Delaney, C., Florea, L., & Diamond, D. (2017). Glucose Sensing for Diabetes Monitoring: Recent Developments. *Sensors (Basel), 17*(8), 1866. doi:10.339017081866 PMID:28805693

Satya, S., Rastogi, R., Chaturvedi, D. K., Arora, N., Singh, P., & Vyas, P. (2018). Statistical Analysis for Effect of Positive Thinking on Stress Management and Creative Problem Solving for Adolescents. *Proceedings of the 12th INDIA-Com,* 245-251.

Alkholya, Abdalmonema, Zaki, Mohamed, Elkoumi, Abu Hashima, & Maha. (2017). *Basset a, Hossam E. Salahc The antioxidant status of coenzyme Q10 and vitamin E in children with type-1 diabetes.* Academic Press.

Rastogi, R., Chaturvedi, D. K., Satya, S., Arora, N., Singhal, P., & Gulati, M. (2018). Statistical Resultant Analysis of Spiritual & Psychosomatic Stress Survey on Various Human Personality Indicators. *International Conference Proceedings of ICCI 2018.* 10.1007/978-981-13-8222-2_25

Diderichsena, B.F., & Andersena, I. (2018). The syndemics of diabetes and depression in Brazil – An epidemiological analysis. *SSM Popul Health.* . doi:10.1016/j.ssmph.2018.11.002

Sharma, S., Rastogi, R., Chaturvedi, D. K., Bansal, A., & Agrawal, A. (2018). Audio Visual EMG & GSR Biofeedback Analysis for Effect of Spiritual Techniques on Human Behavior and Psychic Challenges. *Proceedings of the 12th INDIACom,* 252-258.

Chaturvedi, D.K., Rastogi, R., Satya, S., Arora, N., Saini, H., Verma, H., Mehlyan K., & Varshney, Y. (2018). Statistical Analysis of EMG and GSR Therapy on Visual Mode and SF-36 Scores for Chronic TTH. *Proceedings of UPCON-2018.*

Cortes, C., & Vapnik, V. (1995, September). Support-vector networks. *Machine Learning, 20*(3), 273–297. doi:10.1007/BF00994018

Narudin, F. A., Feizollah, A., Anuar, N. B., & Gani, A. (2016). Evaluation of machine learning classifiers for mobile malware detection. *Soft Computing*, *20*(1), 343–357. doi:10.100700500-014-1511-6

Umar, B., Hejazi, H., Lengyel, L., & Farkas, K. (2018). *Evaluation of IoT Device Management Tools*. The Third International Conference on Advances in Computation, Communications and Services, Barcelona, Spain.

Gaglardio, J. J., Chantelot, J. M., & Domenger, C. (2009, February). Hhasan ilkova on behalf of the IDMPS steering committee. *Diabetes Care*, *32*(2), 227–233. doi:10.2337/dc08-0435 PMID:19033410

Gupta, M., Rastogi, R., Chaturvedi, D. K., & Satya, S. (2019). Comparative Study of Trends Observed During Different Medications by Subjects under EMG & GSR Biofeedback. *IJITEE*, *8*(6S), 748-756. https://www.ijitee.org/download/volume-8-issue-6S/

Ghassibe-Sabbagh, M., Mehanna, Z., Farraj, L. A., Salloum, A. K., & Zalloua, P. A. (2019, February 20). Gestational diabetes mellitus and macrosomia predispose to diabetes in the Lebanese population. *Journal of Clinical & Translational Endocrinology*, *16*, 100185. doi:10.1016/j.jcte.2019.100185

Singhal, P., Rastogi, R., Chaturvedi, D. K., Satya, S., Arora, N., Gupta, M., Singhal, P., & Gulati, M. (2019). Statistical Analysis of Exponential and Polynomial Models of EMG & GSR Biofeedback for Correlation between Subjects Medications Movement & Medication Scores. *IJITEE*, *8*(6S), 625-635. https://www.ijitee.org/download/volume-8-issue-6S/

Swapna, G., Vinayakumar, R., & Soman, K. P. (2018). Diabetes detection using deep learning algorithms. *ICT Express*, 243–246. www.elsevier.com/locate/icte

Saini, H., Rastogi, R., Chaturvedi, D. K., Satya, S., Arora, N., Gupta, M., & Verma, H. (2019). An Optimized Biofeedback EMG and GSR Biofeedback Therapy for Chronic TTH on SF-36 Scores of Different MMBD Modes on Various Medical Symptoms. In Hybrid Machine Intelligence for Medical Image Analysis, Studies Comp. Intelligence (Vol. 841). Springer Nature Singapore Pte Ltd. doi:10.1007/978-981-13-8930-6_8

McCrory, D., Penzien, D. B., Hasselblad, V., & Gray, R. (2001). Behavioural and physical treatments for tension Type and cervocogenic headaches. *Foundation for Chiropractic Education and Research*, *5*(3), 51.

Chaturvedi, D. K. (2012). Human Rights and Consciousness. *International Seminar on Prominence of Human Rights in the Criminal Justice System (ISPUR 2012)*, 33.

Chaturvedi, D. K. (2013a). Correlation between Human Performance and Consciousness. *IEEE-International Conference on Human Computer Interaction.*

Chaturvedi, D. K. (2013b). The Correlation between Student Performance and Consciousness Level. *International Conference on Advanced Computing and Communication Technologies (ICACCT™-2013)*, 200-203.

Azure IoT Device Management. (2019). Retrieved from https://docs.microsoft.com/en-us/azure/iot-hub/iot-hub-device-management-overview

Bishop. (n.d.). *Pattern recognition and machine learning (information science and statistics)*. New York: Springer-Verlag.

Gautam, S. R. (2017). *Automated ML based analyses of diabetes and correlation of stress on human health on various medical parameter*. https://www.healthline.com/health/migraine/migraine-vs-headache

Hussain, Hussain, Hassan, & Hossain. (2019). Machine Learning in IoT Security: Current Solutions and Future Challenges. Academic Press.

Chaturvedi, D. K. (2004). *Science, Religion and Spiritual Quest*. DEI Press.

Chaturvedi, D. K. (2014b). The correlation between Student Performance and Consciousness Level. *International Journal of Computing Science and Communication Technologies, 6*(2), 936-939.

Chatruvedi, D.K. (2014a). Correlation between Energy Distribution profile and Level of Consciousness. *International Journal of Education, 4*(1), 1–9.

Chaturvedi, D.K. (2013c). A Study of Correlation between Consciousness Level and Performance of Worker. *Industrial Engineering Journal, 6*(8), 40–43.

Chaturvedi, D.K. (2015). Dayalbagh Way of Life for Better Worldliness. *Journal of Research in Humanities and Social Science, 3*(5), 16-23.

Chaturvedi, D. K., Kumar, J., & Bhardwaj, R. (2015, September). Effect of meditation on Chakra Energy and Hemodynamic parameters. *International Journal of Computers and Applications, 126*(12), 52–59. doi:10.5120/ijca2015906304

Chaturvedi, D. K. (2019). Relationship between Chakra Energy and Consciousness. *Biomedical Journal of Scientific and Technical Research, 15*(3), 1-3. doi:10.26717/BJSTR.2019.15.002705

Richa, D. K. C., & Prakash, S. (2016a). The consciousness in Mosquito. *Journal of Mosquito Research, 6*(34), 1-9.

Richa, D. K. C., & Prakash, S. (2016b). Role of Electric and Magnetic Energy Emission in Intra and Interspecies Interaction in Microbes. *American Journal of Research Communication, 4*(12), 1-22.

Chaturvedi, D. K., & Lajwanti, T. H. CKohli, H.P. (2012). Energy Distribution Profile of Human Influences the Level of Consciousness. *Towards a Science of Consciousness*, *Arizona Conference Proceeding*.

AWS Device Management. (2019). Retrieved from https://aws.amazon.com/iot-device-management/

Branch, J. W., Giannella, C., Szymanski, B., Wolff, R., & Kargupta, H. (2013). In-network outlier detection in wireless sensor networks. *Knowledge and Information Systems, 34*(1), 23–54. doi:10.100710115-011-0474-5

Fusco, G., Colombaroni, C., Comelli, L., & Isaenko, N. (2015). Short-term traffic predictions on large urban traffic networks: Applications of network-based machine learning models and dynamic traffic assignment models. *Proceedings of the 2015 IEEE International Conference on Models and Technologies for Intelligent Transportation Systems (MT-ITS)*, 93–101. 10.1109/MTITS.2015.7223242

Rastogi, R., Chaturvedi, D. K., Satya, S., Arora, N., & Chauhan, S. (2018). An Optimized Biofeedback Therapy for Chronic TTH between Electromyography and Galvanic Skin Resistance Biofeedback on Audio, Visual and Audio Visual Modes on Various Medical Symptoms. *National Conference on 3rd MDNCPDR-2018 at DEI*.

Tsai, Cohly, & Chaturvedi. (2013). Towards the Consciousness of the Mind. *Towards a Science of Consciousness*, *Dayalbagh Conference Proceeding*.

Chobanian, A. V., Bakris, G. L., Black, H. R., Cushman, W. C., Green, L. A., Izzo, J. L. Jr, Jones, D. W., Materson, B. J., Oparil, S., Wright, J. T. Jr, & Roccella, E. J. (2003, December). Joint National Committee on Prevention, Detection, Evaluation, and Treatment of High Blood Pressure. *Hypertension, 42*(6), 1206–1252. doi:10.1161/01.HYP.0000107251.49515. c2 PMID:14656957

Gers, F.A., Schraudolph, N.N., & Schmidhuber, J. (n.d.). Learning precise timing with LSTM recurrent networks. *Journal of Machine Learning Research*, 115-143.

Sarikaya, B., Sethi, M., & Garcia-Carillo, D. (2018). *Secure IoT Bootstrapping: A Survey* https://tools.ietf.org/id/draft-sarikaya-t2trg-sbootstrapping-05.html

Yu, J., Lee, H., Kim, M.-S., & Park, D. (2008). Traffic flooding attack detection with SNMP MIB using SVM. *Computer Communications, 31*(17), 4212–4219. doi:10.1016/j.comcom.2008.09.018

L. (2015). DeepEar: robust smartphone audio sensing in unconstrained acoustic environments using deep learning. *ACM International Conference on Pervasive and Ubiquitous Computing, 1*, 283–294.

Pritikin, M., Richardson, M., Behringer, M., Bjarnason, S., & Watsen, K. (2018). *Bootstrapping Remote Secure Key Infrastructures (BRSKI).* Internet-Draft draft-ietf-anima-bootstrapping-keyinfra-16.

Rish, I. (n.d.). An empirical study of the naive Bayes classifier. *IJCAI Workshop on Empirical Methods in AI.*

Satya, S., Arora, N., Trivedi, P., Singh, A., Sharma, A., Singh, A., Rastogi, R., & Chaturvedi, D. K. (2019). *Intelligent Analysis for Personality Detection on Various Indicators by Clinical Reliable Psychological TTH and Stress Surveys. In Proceedings of CIPR 2019 at Indian Institute of Engineering Science and Technology.* Springer-AISC Series.

Chauhan, S., Rastogi, R., Chaturvedi, D. K., Satya, S., Arora, N., Yadav, V., & Sharma, P. (2018). Analytical Comparison of Efficacy for Electromyography and Galvanic Skin Resistance Biofeedback on Audio-Visual Mode for Chronic TTH on Various Attributes. Proceedings of the ICCIDA-2018.

Jamshidi, P., Ahmad, A., & Pahl, C. (2014) Autonomic resource provisioning for cloud-based software. *Proceedings of the 9th international symposium on software engineering for adaptive and self-managing systems*, 95-104.

L. (2014). Tagoram: Real-time tracking of mobile RFID tags to high precision using COTS devices. *ACM International Conference on Mobile Computing and Networking, 1*, 237–248.

Watsen, K., Abrahamsson, M., & Farrer, I. (2018). *Zero Touch Provisioning for Networking Devices.* Internet-Draft draft-ietf-netconf-zerotouch-25.

Abadi, M., Chu, A., Goodfellow, I., McMahan, H. B., Mironov, I., Talwar, K., & Zhang, L. (2016, October). Deep learning with differential privacy. In *Proceedings of the 2016 ACM SIGSAC Conference on Computer and Communications Security* (pp. 308-318). ACM. 10.1145/2976749.2978318

Abbott, L. F. (1997). Synaptic depression and cortical gain control. *Science, 275*(5297), 220–224. doi:10.1126cience.275.5297.221 PMID:8985017

Abbott, L. F., & Kepler, T. B. (1990). Model neurons: From hodgkin-huxley to Hopfield. *Statistical Mechanics of Neural Networks, 18*, 5–18.

Abdelbar, A. M., & Hedetniemi, S. M. (1998). The complexity of approximating MAP explanation. *Artificial Intelligence, 102*, 21–38. doi:10.1016/S0004-3702(98)00043-5

Abdullah, A. M. K., & Mitul, A. F. (2013). Design and Implementation of Touchscreen and Remote Control Based Home Automation System. *Proceedings of 2013 2nd International Conference on Advances in Electrical Engineering (ICAEE 2013),* 347-352.

Achariya & Ahmed. (2016). A survey on big data analytics: challenges, open research issues & tools. *IJACSA, 7*(2).

Adadi, A., & Berrada, M. (2018). Peeking Inside the Black-Box: A Survey on Explainable Artificial Intelligence (XAI). *IEEE Access: Practical Innovations, Open Solutions, 6*, 52138–52160. doi:10.1109/ACCESS.2018.2870052

Ahmad & Mazhar Rathore. (2016). *Real time intrusion detection system for Ultra-high-speed big data environments.* Springer Science+Business Media.

Ahmad, A., & Mazhar Rathore, M. (2016). Defining Human Behaviors using Big Data Analytics In Social Internet of Things. *IEEE 30th International Conference on Advanced Information Networking and Applications*, 1102-1107. 10.1109/AINA.2016.104

Ahmed, K., Abbas, N. A., Al-haideri, & Bashikh, A.A. (2019). Implementing artificial neural networks and support vector machines to predict lost circulation. *Egyptian Journal of Petroleum.* doi:10.1016/j.ejpe.2019.06.006

Ahmed, A., & Ahmed, E. (2016, January). A survey on mobile edge computing. *Proc. 10th Int. Conf. Intell. Syst. Control (ISCO)*, 1-8.

Ahmed, M. (2019). A novel big data analytics framework for smart cities. *Future Generation Computer Systems, 91*, 620–633. doi:10.1016/j.future.2018.06.046

Akbar, S. R., Amron, K., Mulya, H., & Hanifah, S. (2017, November). Message queue telemetry transport protocols implementation for wireless sensor networks communication—A performance review. In *2017 International Conference on Sustainable Information Engineering and Technology (SIET)* (pp. 107-112). IEEE. 10.1109/SIET.2017.8304118

Akgul, O., Penekli, H. I., & Genc, Y. (2016). Applying deep learning in augmented reality tracking. In *2016 12th International Conference on Signal-Image Technology & Internet-Based Systems (SITIS)* (pp. 47-54). IEEE. 10.1109/SITIS.2016.17

Alansari, Z., Anuar, N. B., Kamsin, A., Soomro, S., Belgaum, M. R., Mira, M. H., & Alshaer, J. (2018). Challenges of Internet of Things and Big Data Integration. *International Conference on International Conference on Emerging Technologies in Computing.* 10.1007/978-3-319-95450-9_4

Al-Fuqaha, A., Guizani, M., Mohammadi, M., Aledhari, M., & Ayyash, M. (2015). Internet of things: A survey on enabling technologies, protocols, and applications. *IEEE Communications Surveys and Tutorials, 17*(4), 2347–2376. doi:10.1109/COMST.2015.2444095

Alli, A. A., & Alam, M. M. (2019). SecOFF-FCIoT: Machine learning-based secure offloading in Fog-Cloud of things for smart city applications. *Internet of Things, 7*, 100070. doi:10.1016/j.iot.2019.100070

Alom, M. Z., Taha, T. M., Yakopcic, C., Westberg, S., Sidike, P., Nasrin, M. S., Hasan, M., Van Essen, B. C., Awwal, A. A. S., & Asari, V. K. (2019). A state-of-the-art survey on deep learning theory and architectures. *Electronics (Basel), 8*(3), 292. doi:10.3390/electronics8030292

Alotaibi, K. H. (2015). Threat in Cloud-Denial of Service (DoS) and Distributed Denial of Service (DDoS) Attack, and Security Measures. *Journal of Emerging Trends in Computing and Information Sciences, 6*(5), 241–244.

Alsheikh, M. A., Niyato, D., Lin, S., Tan, H. P., & Han, Z. (2016). Mobile big data analytics using deep learning and apache spark. *IEEE Network, 30*(3), 22–29. doi:10.1109/MNET.2016.7474340

Alur, R. (2016). *Systems computing challenges in the Internet of Things.* arXiv preprint arXiv:1604.02980

Aman, M. N. (2019). Hardware Primitives-Based Security Protocols for the Internet of Things. In Cryptographic Security Solutions for the Internet of Things. IGI Global.

Amazon, A. W. S. (2015). *Amazon Web Services Overview of Security Processes.* Author.

Amir Gandomi, A. (2015). Beyond the hype: Big data concepts, methods, and analytics. *International Journal of Information Management, 35*(2), 137–144. doi:10.1016/j.ijinfomgt.2014.10.007

Anita, P., Mary, M., & Josephine, M.S. (2018). Analysis and Forecasting Of Electrical Energy a Literature Review. *International Journal of Pure and Applied Mathematics, 119*(15), 289–293.

Artola, C., Pinto, F., & Pedraza, P. D. (2015). Can internet searches forecast tourism inflows? *International Journal of Manpower*, *36*(1), 103–116. doi:10.1108/IJM-12-2014-0259

Asano, S., Yashiro, T., & Sakamura, K. (2016). Device collaboration framework in IoT-aggregator for realizing smart environment. *TRON Symposium (TRONSHOW)*, 1-9. 10.1109/TRONSHOW.2016.7842886

Askar, A. (2019). *Internet of things (IoT) device registration*. Google Patents.

Assante, D. (2018). Internet of Things education: Labor market training needs and national policies. In *2018 IEEE Global Engineering Education Conference (EDUCON)*. IEEE. 10.1109/EDUCON.2018.8363459

Atlam, H., Alenezi, A., Alharthi, A., Walters, R., & Wills, G. (2017). Integration of cloud computing with internet of things: challenges and open issues. Academic Press.

Atzori, L., Iera, A., & Morabito, G. (2010). The internet of things: A survey. *Computer Networks*, *54*(15), 2787–2805. doi:10.1016/j.comnet.2010.05.010

Audun, J., & Jochen, H. (2007, April). *Dirichlet Reputation Systems*. Paper presented at the Second International Conference on Availability, Reliability and Security (ARES'07), Vienna, Austria

Aydin, N. (2015). Cloud Computing for E-Commerce. *Journal of Mobile Computing and Application*, *2*(1), 27–31.

Balachandra & Prasad. (2017). *Challenges and Benefits of Deploying Big data analytics in the cloud for business intelligence international conference on knowledge based & intelligent information & engineering systems*. Elsevier.

Balaji, L., Dhanalakshmi, A., & Chellaswamy, C. (2017). A variance distortion rate control scheme for combined spatial-temporal scalable video coding. *Journal of Mobile Multimedia*, *13*, 277–290.

Baldi, P. (2012, June). Autoencoders, unsupervised learning, and deep architectures. In *Proceedings of ICML workshop on unsupervised and transfer learning* (pp. 37-49). Academic Press.

Barnaghi, P. M. (2015). Challenges for Quality of Data in Smart Cities. *J. Data and Information Quality, 6*(2-3), 6:1-6:4.

Basumatary, Pratap, Singh, Brijendra, & Gore. (2018, January). *Demand Side Management of a University Load in Smart Grid Environment*. Paper presented at the Workshops ICDCN '18, Varanasi, India.

Bechtsis, D., Tsolakis, N., Vlachos, D., & Iakovou, E. (2017). Sustainable supply chain management in the digitalisation era: The impact of Automated Guided Vehicles. *Journal of Cleaner Production*, *142*, 3970–3984. doi:10.1016/j.jclepro.2016.10.057

Bengio, Y. (2009). Learning deep architectures for AI. *Foundations and trends® in Machine Learning, 2*(1), 1-127.

Bilal, K., & Erbad, A. (2017). Edge Computing for Interactive Media and Video Streaming. *IEEE International Conference on Fog and Mobile Edge Computing (FMEC)*, 1-6. 10.1109/FMEC.2017.7946410

Birendrakumar, S., Tejashree, R., Akibjaved, T., & Ranjeet, P. (2017). IoT Based Smart Energy Meter. *International Research Journal of Engineering Technology*, *4*(4), 96–102.

Birk, A., & Carpin, S. (2006). Merging occupancy grid maps from multiple robots. *Proceedings of the IEEE*, *94*(7), 1384–1397. doi:10.1109/JPROC.2006.876965

Borkowski, M., Schulte, S., & Hochreiner, C. (2016, December). Predicting cloud resource utilization. In *2016 IEEE/ACM 9th International Conference on Utility and Cloud Computing (UCC)* (pp. 37-42). IEEE. 10.1145/2996890.2996907

Bourzac, K. (2017). Speck-size computers: Now with deep learning [news]. *IEEE Spectrum*, *54*(4), 13–15. doi:10.1109/MSPEC.2017.7880447

Boyen, X., & Koller, D. (1998). Tractable inference for complex stochastic processes. *UAI98 – Proceedings of the Fourteenth Conference on Uncertainty in Uncertainty in Artificial Intelligence*, 33–42.

Bradley, J. E., Korfiatis, P., Akkus, Z., Kline, T., & Philbrick, K. (2017). *Toolkits and Libraries for Deep Learning*. Retrieved from https://www.ncbi.nlm.nih.gov/pmc/articles/PMC5537091/

Bradley, J., Barbier, J., & Handler, D. (2013). *Embracing the Internet of everything to capture your share of $14.4 trillion*. White Paper, Cisco.

Cepheli, Ö. (2016). Hybrid intrusion detection system for ddos attacks. *Journal of Electrical and Computer Engineering*.

Chellaswamy, C., Chinnammal, V., Dhanalakshmi, A., & Malarvizhi, C. (2017). An IoT based frontal collision avoidance system for railways. *IEEE International Conference on Power, Control, Signals &Instrumentation Engineering (ICPCSI)*, 1082-1087. 10.1109/ICPCSI.2017.8391877

Chellaswamy, C., Famitha, H., Anusiya, T., & Amirthavarshini, S. B. (2018b). IoT based humps and pothole detection on roads and information sharing. *IEEE International Conference on Power Energy Information and Communication (ICCPEIC)*, 84-90. 10.1109/ICCPEIC.2018.8525196

Chellaswamy, C., Sivakumar, K., Nisha, J., & Kaviya, R. (2018a). An IoT based dam water management system for agriculture. *IEEE International Conference on Recent Trends in Electrical, Control and Communication (RTECC-18)*, 51-56. 10.1109/RTECC.2018.8625696

Chen, X., Liu, X., & Peng, X. (2015). IoT- Based Air Pollution Monitoring and Forecasting System. *International Conference on Computer and Computational Sciences (ICCCS)*, 257-260.

Cheng, J., & Druzdzel, M. (2000). AIS-BN: An adaptive importance sampling algorithm for evidential reasoning in large Bayesian networks. *Journal of Artificial Intelligence Research*, *13*, 155–188. doi:10.1613/jair.764

Chen, T., Du, Z., Sun, N., Wang, J., Wu, C., Chen, Y., & Temam, O. (2014, February). Diannao: A small-footprint high-throughput accelerator for ubiquitous machine-learning. *ACM SIGPLAN Notices*, *49*(4), 269–284. doi:10.1145/2644865.2541967

Chi, C. (2019). *Best AI Chatbots for 2019*. Retrieved from https://blog.hubspot.com/marketing/best-ai-chatbot

Choi, Y. B., Kadakkuzha, B. M., Liu, X. A., Akhmedov, K., Kandel, E. R., & Puthanveettil, S. V. (2014). Huntingtin is critical both presynaptically and postsynaptically for long-term learning-related synaptic plasticity in Aplysia. *PLoS One*, *9*(7), e103004. doi:10.1371/journal.pone.0103004 PMID:25054562

Cisco. (n.d.). Retrieved September 24, 2019, from https://www.cisco.com/c/dam/en/us/products/collateral/se/internet-of-things/at-a-glance-c45-731471.pdf

Clemens, J., Pal, R., & Philip, P. (2016, October). Extending trust and attestation to the edge. In *2016 IEEE/ACM Symposium on Edge Computing (SEC)* (pp. 101-102). IEEE. 10.1109/SEC.2016.29

Coelho, I. M., Coelho, V. N., Luz, E. J. S., Ochi, L. S., Guimarães, F. G., & Rios, E. (2017). A GPU deep learning metaheuristic based model for time series forecasting. *Applied Energy*, *201*(1), 412–418. doi:10.1016/j.apenergy.2017.01.003

Côrte-Real, N. (2019). Leveraging internet of things and big data analytics initiatives in European and American firms: Is data quality a way to extract business value? *Information & Management*.

da Cruz, M. A., Rodrigues, J. J. P., Al-Muhtadi, J., Korotaev, V. V., & de Albuquerque, V. H. C. (2018). A reference model for internet of things middleware. *IEEE Internet of Things Journal*, *5*(2), 871–883. doi:10.1109/JIOT.2018.2796561

Dan, S., & Roger, C. (2010). Privacy and consumer risks in cloud computing. *Computer Law & Security Review, 26*(4), 391–397. doi:10.1016/j.clsr.2010.05.005

Datameer Inc. (2013). *The guide to big data analytics.* New York: Datameer.

Datameer. (2016). *Big data analytics and the internet of things.* Author.

David, J., & Thomas, C. (2015). DDoS attack detection using fast entropy approach on flow-based network traffic. *Procedia Computer Science, 50,* 30–36.

Dayan, P., & Abbott, L. F. (2001). Theoretical Neuroscience: Computational and Mathematical Modeling of Neural Systems. *Neuroscience, 39*(3), 460.

Deloitte. (2015). *Smart cities big data.* Deloitte.

Deng, L. (2014). A tutorial survey of architectures, algorithms, and applications for deep learning. *APSIPA Transactions on Signal and Information Processing, 3,* 3. doi:10.1017/atsip.2013.9

Deng, L., & Yu, D. (2014). Deep learning: Methods and applications. *Found. Trends Signal Process., 7*(3–4), 197–387. doi:10.1561/2000000039

Desai, S. (2010). Violence and surveillance: Some unintended consequences of CCTV monitoring within mental health hospital wards. *Surveillance & Society, 8*(1), 84–92. doi:10.24908s.v8i1.3475

Doersch, C. (2016). *Tutorial on variational autoencoders.* arXiv preprint arXiv:1606.05908

Dohler, M., Vilajosana, I., & Vilajosana, X., & Losa, J. (2011). Smart cities: An action plan. *Proceedings of Barcelona smart cities congress 2011.*

Dooley, R., Edmonds, A., Hancock, D. Y., Lowe, J. M., Skidmore, E., Adams, A. K., ... Knepper, R. (2018). *Security best practices for academic cloud service providers.* Academic Press.

Dragomir, D., Gheorghe, L., Costea, S., & Radovici, A. (2016, September). A survey on secure communication protocols for IoT systems. In *2016 International Workshop on Secure Internet of Things (SIoT)* (pp. 47-62). IEEE. 10.1109/SIoT.2016.012

Due, C., Connellan, K., & Riggs, D. (2012). *Surveillance, security and violence in a mental health ward: an ethnographic case-study of an Australian purpose-built unit.* Academic Press.

Du, M., Wang, K., Xia, Z., & Zhang, Y. (2020). Differential Privacy Preserving of Training Model in Wireless Big Data with Edge Computing. *IEEE Transactions on Big Data, Volume, 6*(2), 283–295.

Edn. (n.d.). Retrieved September 21, 2019, from https://www.edn.com/5G/4442859/The-basics-of-Bluetooth-Low-Energy--BLE--

Elragal & Elgendy. (2014). Big Data Analytics: A Literature Review Paper. *ICDM 2014: Advances in Data Mining. Applications and Theoretical Aspects,* 214-227.

Elsaeidy, A., & Kumudu, S. (2019). Intrusion detection in smart cities using Restricted Boltzmann Machines. *Journal of Network and Computer Applications, 135,* 76–83. doi:10.1016/j.jnca.2019.02.026

Enbysk, L. (2013). *Smart Cities Council.* https://smartcitiescouncil.com/article/smart-citiestechnology-market-top-20-billion-2020

Fady, A. M. I., & Elsayed, E. H. (2019). Trusted Cloud Computing Architectures for infrastructure as a service: Survey and systematic literature review. *Computers & Security, 82,* 196–226. doi:10.1016/j.cose.2018.12.014

Faizal, Zaki, Shahrin, Robiah, Rahayu, & Nazrulazhar. (2009). *Threshold verification technique for network intrusion detection system.* arXiv preprint arXiv:0906.3843

Faizal, M. A., Zaki, M. M., Shahrin, S., Robiah, Y., & Rahayu, S. S. (2010). Statistical Approach for Validating Static Threshold in Fast Attack Detection. *Journal of Advanced Manufacturing Technology, 4*(1), 53–72.

Far, S. B., & Rad, A. I. (2018). *Security Analysis of Big Data on Internet Things* (https://arxiv.org/abs/1808.09491).

Feng, P., & Wang, P. (2019). Matching Technology of Internet of Things Based on Multiple Linear Regression Model in Urban Management. *In The International Conference on Cyber Security Intelligence and Analytics.* Springer.

Fernandes, J. L., Lopes, I. C., Rodrigues, J. J., & Ullah, S. (2013, July). Performance evaluation of RESTful web services and AMQP protocol. In *2013 Fifth International Conference on Ubiquitous and Future Networks (ICUFN)* (pp. 810-815). IEEE. 10.1109/ICUFN.2013.6614932

François, J., Aib, I., & Boutaba, R. (2012). FireCol: A collaborative protection network for the detection of flooding DDoS attacks. *IEEE/ACM Transactions on Networking, 20*(6), 1828–1841. doi:10.1109/TNET.2012.2194508

Fumo, N., & Biswas, R. (2015). Regression analysis for prediction of residential energy consumption. *Elsevier Renewable and Sustainable Energy Reviews, 7*(47), 332–343.

Gangid, N., & Sharma, B. (2016). Cloud Computing and Robotics for Disaster Management. *IEEE Inter. Conference on Intelligent Systems. Modelling and Simulation*, 1-6.

Gani, Nasaruddin, & Marjani. (2017). Big IoT Data Analytics: Architecture, Opportunities, and Open Research Challenges. *IEEE Access, 5,* 5247-5260.

Gantz, J., & Reinsel, D. (2012). *The digital universe in 2020: Big data, bigger digital shadows, and biggest growth in the far east.* EMC Corporation.

Gardner, H. (1983). *Frames of Mind: The Theory of Multiple Intelligences.* Basic Books.

Geng, X., Zhang, Q., Wei, Q., Zhang, T., Cai, Y., Liang, Y., & Sun, X. (2019). *A Mobile Greenhouse Environment Monitoring System Based on the Internet of Things.* IEEE. doi:10.1109/ACCESS.2019.2941521

Gennaro, R., Gentry, C., & Parno, B. (2010, August). Non-interactive verifiable computing: Outsourcing computation to untrusted workers. In *Annual Cryptology Conference* (pp. 465-482). Springer. 10.1007/978-3-642-14623-7_25

Genovese, A., Labati, R. D., Piuri, V., & Scotti, F. (2011, September). Wildfire smoke detection using computational intelligence techniques. In *2011 IEEE International Conference on Computational Intelligence for Measurement Systems and Applications (CIMSA) Proceedings* (pp. 1-6). IEEE. 10.1109/CIMSA.2011.6059930

Ghosh, A., Chakraborty, D., & Law, A. (2018). Artificial intelligence in Internet of things. *CAAI Transactions on Intelligence Technology, 3*(4), 208–218. doi:10.1049/trit.2018.1008

Gilchrist, A. (2016). *Industry 4.0: the industrial internet of things.* Apress. doi:10.1007/978-1-4842-2047-4

Goeddel, R., & Olson, E. (2016, October). Learning semantic place labels from occupancy grids using CNNs. In 2016 IEEE/RSJ international conference on intelligent robots and systems (IROS) (pp. 3999-4004). IEEE. doi:10.1109/IROS.2016.7759589

Golchay, R. (2011). *Towards bridging IOT and cloud services: proposing smartphones as mobile and autonomic service gateways.* arXiv preprint arXiv:1107.4786

Gong, P., & Van Leeuwen, C. (2007). Dynamically maintained spike timing sequences in networks of pulse-coupled oscillators with delays. *Physical Review Letters. APS.*, *98*(4), 048104. doi:10.1103/PhysRevLett.98.048104 PMID:17358818

Goodfellow, I., Abadie, J. P., Mirza, M., Xu, B., Farley, D. W., Ozair, S., . . . Bengio, Y. (2014). Generative Adversarial Nets. https:// arxiv.org/abs/1406.2661

Goodfellow, I., Pouget-Abadie, J., Mirza, M., Xu, B., Warde-Farley, D., Ozair, S., . . . Bengio, Y. (2014). Generative adversarial nets. In Advances in neural information processing systems (pp. 2672-2680). Academic Press.

Gopalakrishnan, P. K. (2019). Live Demonstration: Autoencoder-Based Predictive Maintenance for IoT. In *2019 IEEE International Symposium on Circuits and Systems (ISCAS)*. IEEE. 10.1109/ISCAS.2019.8702230

Gouru, N., & Vadlamani, N. (2019). DistProv-Data Provenance in Distributed Cloud for Secure Transfer of Digital Assets with Ethereum Blockchain using ZKP. *International Journal of Open Source Software and Processes*, *10*(3), 1–18. doi:10.4018/IJOSSP.2019070101

Gubbi, J., Buyya, R., Marusic, S., & Palaniswami, M. (2013). Internet of Things (IoT): A vision, architectural elements, and future directions. *Future Generation Computer Systems*, *29*(7), 1645–1660. doi:10.1016/j.future.2013.01.010

Gunduz, H. (2019). Deep learning-based Parkinson's disease classification using vocal feature sets. *IEEE Access: Practical Innovations, Open Solutions*, *7*, 115540–115551. doi:10.1109/ACCESS.2019.2936564

Gupta, S., Kumar, P., & Abraham, A. (2013). A profile based network intrusion detection and prevention system for securing cloud environment. *International Journal of Distributed Sensor Networks*, *9*(3), 364575. doi:10.1155/2013/364575

Han, S., Pool, J., Tran, J., & Dally, W. (2015). Learning both weights and connections for efficient neural network. In Advances in neural information processing systems (pp. 1135-1143). Academic Press.

Han, B., Gopalakrishnan, V., Ji, L., & Lee, S. (2015). Network function virtualization: Challenges and opportunities for innovations. *IEEE Communications Magazine*, *53*(2), 90–97. doi:10.1109/MCOM.2015.7045396

Hao, H., & Rongxing, L., & Zonghua, Z. (2015, December). *Vtrust: A robust trust framework for relay selection in hybrid vehicular communications*, Paper presented at the IEEE Global Communications Conference, GLOBECOM 2015, San Diego, CA.

He, H., Kamburugamuve, S., Fox, G. C., & Zhao, W. (2016). Cloud based Real-time Multi-Robot Collision Avoidance for Swarm Robotics. *International Journal of Grid and Distributed Computing*, *9*(6), 339–358. doi:10.14257/ijgdc.2016.9.6.30

He, Y., Mendis, G. J., & Wei, J. (2017). Real-time detection of false data injection attacks in smart grid: A deep learning-based intelligent mechanism. *IEEE Transactions on Smart Grid*, *8*(5), 2505–2516. doi:10.1109/TSG.2017.2703842

Hlaing, W., Thepphaeng, S., Nontaboot, V., Tangsun, N., Sangsuwan, T., & Chaiyod, P. (2017, March). *Implementation of WiFi-based single phase smart meter for Internet of Things (IoT)*. Paper presented at the International Electrical Engineering Congress (iEECON), Pattaya, Thailand.

Hochreiter, S., & Schmidhuber, J. (1997). Long short-term memory. *Neural Computation, 9*(8), 1735-1780. Retrieved September 18, 2019, from https://machinelearningmastery.com/inspirational-applications-deep-learning/

Hollands, R. G. (2015). Critical Interventions into the Corporate Smart City. *Cambridge Journal of Regions, Economy and Society*, *8*(1), 61–77. doi:10.1093/cjres/rsu011

Huang, F., Xu, J., Gu, J., & Lou, Y. (2008). Optimum Design of Network Structures Based on Hybrid Intelligence of Genetic - Ant Colonies Algorithm. *International Conference on Intelligent Computation Technology and Automation (ICICTA)*, 116-120. 10.1109/ICICTA.2008.205

Hudaib, A., & Albdour, L. (2019). Fog Computing to Serve the Internet of Things Applications: A Patient Monitoring System. *International Journal of Fog Computing*, 2(2), 44–56. doi:10.4018/IJFC.2019070103

Hugo, J. E., Morales, E. F., & Sucar, L. E. (2016). A naïve Bayes baseline for early gesture recognition. *Pattern Recognition Letters*, *73*, 91–99. doi:10.1016/j.patrec.2016.01.013

Hwang, Y. H. (2015). Iot security & privacy: threats and challenges. In *Proceedings of the 1st ACM Workshop on IoT Privacy, Trust, and Security*. ACM. 10.1145/2732209.2732216

Hwang, K., Cai, M., Chen, Y., & Qin, M. (2007). Hybrid intrusion detection with weighted signature generation over anomalous internet episodes. *IEEE Transactions on Dependable and Secure Computing*, *4*(1), 41–55.

Iyer, B., & Patil, N. (2015). Health Monitoring and Tracking System For Soldiers Using Internet of Things (IoT). *International Conference on Computing, Communication and Automation (ICCCA2017)*.

Izhikevich, E. M., Gally, J. A., & Edelman, G. M. (2004). Spike-timing dynamics of neuronal groups. Cerebral Cortex, 14(8), 933–944. doi:10.1093/cercor/bhh053

Janssen, M., Luthra, S., Mangla, S., Rana, N. P., & Dwivedi, Y. K. (2019). Challenges for adopting and implementing IoT in smart cities. *Internet Research*, *29*(6), 1589–1616. doi:10.1108/INTR-06-2018-0252

Jararweh, Y., Doulat, A., AlQudah, O., Ahmed, E., Al-Ayyoub, M., & Benkhelifa, E. (2016, May). The future of mobile cloud computing: integrating cloudlets and mobile edge computing. In *2016 23rd International conference on telecommunications (ICT)* (pp. 1-5). IEEE. 10.1109/ICT.2016.7500486

Jararweh, Y., Doulat, A., Darabseh, A., Alsmirat, M., Al-Ayyoub, M., & Benkhelifa, E. (2016, April). SDMEC: Software defined system for mobile edge computing. In *2016 IEEE International Conference on Cloud Engineering Workshop (IC2EW)* (pp. 88-93). IEEE.

Jayashree, M. (2013). Data Mining: Exploring Big Data Using Hadoop and Map Reduce. *International Journal of Engineering Science Research*, *4*(1).

Jiang, Shi, & Zhou. (2019). A Privacy Security Risk Analysis Method for Medical Big Data in Urban Computing. *IEEE Access*, *7*, 143841-143854.

Jianliang, M., Haikun, S., & Ling, B. (2009). The Application on Intrusion Detection Based on K-means Cluster Algorithm. *International Forum on Information Technology and Applications*, 150-152.

Jin, H., Xiang, G., Zou, D., Wu, S., Zhao, F., Li, M., & Zheng, W. (2013). A VMM-based intrusion prevention system in cloud computing environment. *The Journal of Supercomputing*, *66*(3), 1133–1151.

Jin, I., Udo, H., Rayman, J. B., Puthanveettil, S., Kandel, E. R., & Hawkins, R. D. (2012). Spontaneous transmitter release recruits postsynaptic mechanisms of long-term and intermediate-term facilitation in Aplysia. *Proceedings of the National Academy of Sciences of the United States of America*, *109*(23), 9137–9142. doi:10.1073/pnas.1206846109 PMID:22619333

Jin, J., Gubbi, J., Marusic, S., & Palaniswami, M. (2014). An Information Framework for Creating a Smart City Through Internet of Things. *IEEE Internet of Things Journal*, *1*(2), 112–121. doi:10.1109/JIOT.2013.2296516

Jin, L., Xiao, Y., Zheng, X., Kim-Kwang, R. C., Liang, H., & Xiaohui, C. (2017). A cloud-based taxi trace mining framework for smart city. *Software, Practice & Experience*, *47*(8), 1081–1094.

Kamburugamuve, S., Christiansen, L., & Fox, G. (2015). A framework for real-time processing of sensor data in the cloud. *Journal of Sensors*, 1–12.

Kamilaris, A., & Ostermann, F. (2018). *Geospatial Analysis and Internet of Things in Environmental Informatics.* arXiv preprint arXiv:1808.01895

Keahey, K., Tsugawa, M., Matsunaga, A., & Fortes, J. (2009). Sky computing. *IEEE Internet Computing, 13*(5), 43–51. doi:10.1109/MIC.2009.94

Kehoe, B., Patil, S., Abbeel, P., & Goldberg, K. (2015). A Survey of Research on Cloud Robotics and Automation. IEEE Trans. On Automation & Eng., 12(2), 398-409.

Kempter, R., Gerstner, W., & Van Hemmen, J. (1999). Hebbian learning and spiking neurons. *Physical Review E. APS, 59*(4), 4498–4514. doi:10.1103/PhysRevE.59.4498

Khan, M., Wu, X., Xu, X., & Dou, W. (2017). Big Data Challenges and Opportunities in the Hype of Industry 4.0. *IEEE ICC 2017 SAC Symposium Big Data Networking Track.* 10.1109/ICC.2017.7996801

Klaine, P. V., Imran, M. A., Onireti, O., & Souza, R. D. (2017). A survey of machine learning techniques applied to self-organizing cellular networks. *IEEE Communications Surveys and Tutorials, 19*(4), 2392–2431.

Konduru, V. R., & Bharamagoudra, M. R. (2017, August). Challenges and solutions of interoperability on IoT: How far have we come in resolving the IoT interoperability issues. In *2017 International Conference On Smart Technologies For Smart Nation (SmartTechCon)* (pp. 572-576). IEEE. 10.1109/SmartTechCon.2017.8358436

Krizhevsky, A., Sutskever, I., & Hinton, G. E. (2012). Imagenet classification with deep convolutional neural networks. In Advances in neural information processing systems (pp. 1097-1105). Academic Press.

Kumar, D. (2019). All things considered: an analysis of IoT devices on home networks. *28th {USENIX} Security Symposium ({USENIX} Security 19.*

Kumar, B. (2016). Security threats and their mitigation in infrastructure as a service. *Perspectives in Science, 8,* 462–464. doi:10.1016/j.pisc.2016.05.001

Laeeq, K., & Shamsi, J. A. (2015). A study of security issues, vulnerabilities and challenges in internet of things. *Securing Cyber-Physical Systems, 10.*

Lahmiri, S., & Shmuel, A. (2019). Detection of Parkinson's disease based on voice patterns ranking and optimized support vector machine. *Biomedical Signal Processing and Control, 49,* 427–433. doi:10.1016/j.bspc.2018.08.029

Lar, S. U., Liao, X., & Abbas, S. A. (2011, August). Cloud computing privacy & security global issues, challenges, & mechanisms. In *2011 6th International ICST Conference on Communications and Networking in China (CHINACOM)* (pp. 1240-1245). IEEE.

LeCun, Y., Bengio, Y., & Hinton, G. (2015). Deep learning. *Nature, 521*(7553), 436–444. doi:10.1038/nature14539 PMID:26017442

Lee, I., & Lee, K. (2015). The Internet of Things (IoT): Applications, investments, and challenges for enterprises. *Business Horizons, 58*(4), 431–440.

Lee, J.-H., Park, M.-W., Eom, J.-H., & Chung, T.-M. (2011). Multi-level intrusion detection system and log management in cloud computing. In *13th International Conference on Advanced Communication Technology (ICACT2011),* (pp. 552-555). IEEE.

Lee, J., Wang, J., Crandall, D., Šabanović, S., & Fox, G. (2017, April). Real-time, cloud-based object detection for unmanned aerial vehicles. In *2017 First IEEE International Conference on Robotic Computing (IRC)* (pp. 36-43). IEEE.

Lerche, C., Hartke, K., & Kovatsch, M. (2012, September). Industry adoption of the Internet of Things: A constrained application protocol survey. In *Proceedings of 2012 IEEE 17th International Conference on Emerging Technologies & Factory Automation (ETFA 2012)* (pp. 1-6). IEEE. 10.1109/ETFA.2012.6489787

Li, Deng, & Cai. (2019). Statistical analysis of tourist flow in tourist spots based on big data platform and DA-HKRVM algorithms. In *Personal and Ubiquitous Computing*. Springer.

Liang, G., Hong, H., Xie, W., & Zheng, L. (2019). Combining Convolutional Neural Network With Recursive Neural Network for Blood Cell Image Classification. *IEEE Access: Practical Innovations, Open Solutions, 6*, 36188–36197. doi:10.1109/ACCESS.2018.2846685

Liang, M., Li, Z., Chen, T., & Zeng, J. (2015). Integrative Data Analysis of Multi-Platform Cancer Data with a Multimodal Deep Learning Approach. *IEEE/ACM Transactions on Computational Biology and Bioinformatics, 12*(4), 928–937. doi:10.1109/TCBB.2014.2377729 PMID:26357333

Li, H., Ota, K., & Dong, M. (2018). Learning IoT in edge: Deep learning for the Internet of Things with edge computing. *IEEE Network, 32*(1), 96–101.

Lin, Z., Mu, S., Huang, F., Mateen, K. A., Wang, M., Gao, W., & Jia, J. (2019). A Unified Matrix-Based Convolutional Neural Network for Fine-Grained Image Classification of Wheat Leaf Diseases. *IEEE Access: Practical Innovations, Open Solutions, 7*, 11570–11590. doi:10.1109/ACCESS.2019.2891739

Liono, J., Jayaraman, P. P., Qin, A. K., Nguyen, T., & Salim, F. D. (2019). QDaS: Quality driven data summarisation for effective storage management in Internet of Things. *Journal of Parallel and Distributed Computing, 127*, 196–208. doi:10.1016/j.jpdc.2018.03.013

Liu, X., Lam, K. H., Zhu, K., Zheng, C., Li, X., Du, Y., . . . Pong, P. W. (2016). *Overview of spintronic sensors, Internet of Things, and smart living.* arXiv preprint arXiv:1611.00317

Liu, Y., Dong, B., Guo, B., Yang, J., & Peng, W. (2015). Combination of Cloud Computing and Internet of Things (IoT) in Medical Monitoring Systems. *International Journal of Hybrid Information Technology, 8*(12), 367–376. doi:10.14257/ijhit.2015.8.12.28

Liu, Y., Sun, Y. L., Ryoo, J., Rizvi, S., & Vasilakos, A. V. (2015). A survey of security and privacy challenges in cloud computing: Solutions and future directions. *Journal of Computing Science and Engineering: JCSE, 9*(3), 119–133. doi:10.5626/JCSE.2015.9.3.119

Li, Y. (2016). The concept of smart tourism in the context of tourism information services. *Tourism Management*, 1–8. doi:10.1016/j.tourman.2016.03.014

Lopez-Martin, M., Carro, B., Sanchez-Esguevillas, A., & Lloret, J. (2019). Network Traffic Classifier With Convolutional and Recurrent Neural Networks for Internet of Things. *IEEE Access: Practical Innovations, Open Solutions, 5*, 18042–18050. doi:10.1109/ACCESS.2017.2747560

Louridas, P., & Ebert, C. (2016). Machine learning. *IEEE Software, 33*(5), 110–115. doi:10.1109/MS.2016.114

Lucas, A., Williams, A. T., & Cabrales, P. (2019). Prediction of Recovery From Severe Hemorrhagic Shock Using Logistic Regression. *IEEE Journal of Translational Engineering in Health and Medicine, 7*, 1–9. doi:10.1109/JTEHM.2019.2924011 PMID:31367491

Ma, M. (2013). Data management for internet of things: Challenges, approaches and opportunities. In *2013 IEEE International conference on green computing and communications and IEEE Internet of Things and IEEE cyber, physical and social computing.* IEEE. 10.1109/GreenCom-iThings-CPSCom.2013.199

Mahmud, M., Kaiser, M. S., Hussain, A., & Vassanelli, S. (2018). Applications of Deep Learning and Reinforcement Learning to Biological Data. *IEEE Transactions on Neural Networks and Learning Systems*, *29*(6), 2063–2079. doi:10.1109/TNNLS.2018.2790388 PMID:29771663

Malche, T., & Maheshwary, P. (2015). Harnessing the Internet of things (IoT): A review. *International Journal (Toronto, Ont.)*, *5*(8).

Manju Sharma. (2016). Big data analytics challenges & solutions in cloud. *American Journal of Engineering Research*, *6*(4), 46-51.

Manoj, B. S., & Baker, A. H. (2007). Communication challenges in emergency response. *Communications of the ACM*, *50*(3), 51–53. doi:10.1145/1226736.1226765

Maqsood, H., Mehmood, I., Maqsood, M., Yasir, M., Afzal, S., Aadil, F., Selim, M. M., & Muhammad, K. (2020). A local and global event sentiment based efficient stock exchange forecasting using deep learning. *International Journal of Information Management*, *50*, 432–451. doi:10.1016/j.ijinfomgt.2019.07.011

Maria, K. (2018). *Big Data in Tourism*. Semantic Scholar.

Markram, H. (1997). Regulation of synaptic efficacy by coincidence of postsynaptic APs and EPSPs. *Science. AAAS.*, *275*(5297), 213–215. doi:10.1126cience.275.5297.213 PMID:8985014

Masek, P., Fujdiak, R., Zeman, K., Hosek, J., & Muthanna, A. (2016, April). Remote networking technology for IoT: Cloud-based access for AllJoyn-enabled devices. In *2016 18th Conference of Open Innovations Association and Seminar on Information Security and Protection of Information Technology (FRUCT-ISPIT)* (pp. 200-205). IEEE.

Mathew, A. R., & Al Hajj, A. (2017). Secure Communications on IoT and Big Data. *in Indian Journal of Science and Technology*, *10*(11).

Mezgár, I., & Rauschecker, U. (2014). The challenge of networked enterprises for cloud computing interoperability. *Computers in Industry*, *65*(4), 657–674. doi:10.1016/j.compind.2014.01.017

Mhadhbi, Z., Zairi, S., Gueguen, C., & Zouari, B. (2018). Validation of a Distributed Energy Management Approach for Smart Grid Based on a Generic Colored Petri Nets Model. *Journal of Clean Energy Technologies*, *6*(1), 20–25.

Michael Wittig. (2018). https://cloudonaut.io/encrypting-sensitive-data-stored-on-s3/

Michie, D., Spiegelhalter, D., Taylor, C., & Campbell, J. (1994). *Machine Learning, Neural and Statistical Classification*. Ellis Horwood.

Miori, V., & Russo, D. (2014). Domotic evolution towards the IoT. In *2014 28th International Conference on Advanced Information Networking and Applications Workshops*. IEEE. 10.1109/WAINA.2014.128

Mohammadi, A., Al-Fuqaha, M., Sorour, S., & Guizani, M. (2018). Deep Learning for IoT Big Data and Streaming Analytics: A Survey. *IEEE Communications Surveys and Tutorials*, *20*(4), 2923–2960. doi:10.1109/COMST.2018.2844341

Mohammadi, M., & Al-Fuqaha, A. (2018). Enabling cognitive smart cities using big data and machine learning: Approaches and challenges. *IEEE Communications Magazine*, *56*(2), 94–101.

Mohammadi, M., Al-Fuqaha, A., Sorour, S., & Guizani, M. (2018). Deep learning for IoT big data and streaming analytics: A survey. *IEEE Communications Surveys and Tutorials*, *20*(4), 2923–2960.

Mohammad, M. (2018). A hybrid algorithm using a genetic algorithm and multiagent reinforcement learning heuristic to solve the traveling salesman problem. *Neural Computing & Applications*, *30*(9), 2935–2951. doi:10.100700521-017-2880-4

Mohd, M. R. S., Herman, S. H., & Sharif, Z. (2017). Application of K-Means clustering in hot spot detection for thermal infrared images. *2017 IEEE Symposium on Computer Applications & Industrial Electronics (ISCAIE),* 107-110. 10.1109/ISCAIE.2017.8074959

Morrison, A., Diesmann, M., & Gerstner, W. (2008). Phenomenological models of synaptic plasticity based on spike timing. *Biological Cybernetics, 98*(6), 459–478. doi:10.100700422-008-0233-1 PMID:18491160

Muhammad, K., Khan, S., Palade, V., Mehmood, V., & De Albuquerque, V. H. C. (2019). Edge Intelligence-Assisted Smoke Detection in Foggy Surveillance Environments. *IEEE Transactions on Industrial Informatics.* . doi:10.1109/TII.2019.2915592

Muralitharan, K., Sakthivel, R., & Shi, Y. (2015). Multi objective Optimization Technique for Demand Side Management with Load Balancing Approach in Smart Grid. *Elsevier Neurocomputing, 177,* 110–119.

Nabipour, M., Nayyeri, P., Jabani, H., & Mosavi, A. (2020). Predicting Stock Market Trends Using Machine Learning and Deep Learning Algorithms Via Continuous and Binary Data; a Comparative Analysis. *IEEE Access: Practical Innovations, Open Solutions, 8,* 150199–150212. doi:10.1109/ACCESS.2020.3015966

Naik, N. (2017, October). Choice of effective messaging protocols for IoT systems: MQTT, CoAP, AMQP and HTTP. In *2017 IEEE international systems engineering symposium (ISSE)* (pp. 1-7). IEEE.

Naskar, S. (2020). A literature review of the emerging field of IoT using RFID and its applications in supply chain management. In Securing the Internet of Things: Concepts, Methodologies, Tools, and Applications. IGI Global.

Nathiya, T. (2017). Reducing D DOS Attack Techniques in Cloud Computing Network Technology. *International Journal of Innovative Research in Applied Sciences and Engineering, 1*(1), 23–29. doi:10.29027/IJIRASE.v1.i1.2017.23-29

Neelakandan, S. (2019). *Robotic process automation for supply chain management operations.* Google Patents.

Neirotti, P., Marco, A. D., Cagliano, A. C., Mangano, G., & Scorrano, F. (2014). Current Trends in Smart City Initiatives: Some Stylised Facts. *Cities (London, England), 38*(5), 25–36. doi:10.1016/j.cities.2013.12.010

Nguyen, G., Dlugolinsky, S., Bobák, M., Tran, V., López García, Á., Heredia, I., Malík, P., & Hluchý, L. (2019). Machine Learning and Deep Learning frameworks and libraries for large-scale data mining: A survey. *Artificial Intelligence Review, 52*(1), 77–124. doi:10.100710462-018-09679-z

Nguyen, T. T., Camacho, D., & Jung, J. E. (2016). Identifying and ranking cultural heritage resources on geotagged social media for smart cultural tourism services. *Personal and Ubiquitous Computing.* Advance online publication. doi:10.100700779-016-0992-y

Nicholls, J.G. (2001). *From Neuron to Brain.* Academic Press.

Nolan, K. A., & Volavka, J. (2006). Video recording in the assessment of violent incidents in psychiatric hospitals. *Journal of Psychiatric Practice, 12*(1), 58–63. doi:10.1097/00131746-200601000-00010 PMID:16432448

Novikov, A., Podoprikhin, D., Osokin, A., & Vetrov, D. P. (2015). Tensorizing neural networks. In Advances in neural information processing systems (pp. 442-450). Academic Press.

Okafor, K. C., Ononiwu, G. C., & Precious, U. (2017). Development of Arduino Based IoT Metering System for On-Demand Energy Monitoring. *International Journal of Mechatronics. Electrical and Computer Technology, 7*(23), 3208–3224.

Olsen, D. P. (1998). Ethical considerations of video monitoring psychiatric patients in seclusion and restraint. *Archives of Psychiatric Nursing, 12*(2), 90–94. doi:10.1016/S0883-9417(98)80058-7 PMID:9573636

Ordóñez, F., & Roggen, D. (2016). Deep convolutional and lstm recurrent neural networks for multimodal wearable activity recognition. *Sensors (Basel)*, *16*(1), 115.

Ouadou, M, (2019). A Data-Filtering Approach for Large-Scale Integrated RFID and Sensor Networks. In *International Conference on Mobile, Secure, and Programmable Networking*. Springer. 10.1007/978-3-030-22885-9_7

Page, J., Bain, M., & Mukhlish, F. (2018). The Risks of Low Level Narrow Artificial Intelligence. *IEEE International Conference on Intelligence and Safety for Robotics (ISR)*, 1-6. 10.1109/IISR.2018.8535903

Parkhi, O. M., Vedaldi, A., & Zisserman, A. (2015, September). Deep face recognition. In BMVC (Vol. 1, No. 3, p. 6). Academic Press.

Pascanu, R., Gulcehre, C., Cho, K., & Bengio, Y. (2013). *How to construct deep recurrent neural networks.* arXiv preprint arXiv:1312.6026

Patel & Patel. (2016). Internet of things-IOT: definition, characteristics, architecture, enabling technologies, application & future challenges. *International Journal of Engineering Science and Computing, 6*(5).

Patel, K. K., & Patel, S. M. (2016). Internet of things-IOT: definition, characteristics, architecture, enabling technologies, application & future challenges. *International Journal of Engineering Science and Computing, 6*(5).

Pecht & Kang. (2019). *Predictive Maintenance in the IoT Era.* Academic Press.

Perera, C., Zaslavsky, A., Christen, P., & Georgakopoulos, D. (2013). Context aware computing for the internet of things: A survey. *IEEE Communications Surveys and Tutorials*, *16*(1), 414–454.

Pfister, J. P., & Gerstner, W. (2006). Triplets of spikes in a model of spike timing-dependent plasticity. *Journal of Neuroscience. Social Neuroscience*, *26*(38), 9673–9682. PMID:16988038

Pooja, T. D., & Kulkarni, S. B. (2016). IOT Based Energy Meter Reading. *International Journal of Recent Trends in Engineering & Research*, *2*(6), 586–591.

Pratt, G. A., & Williamson, M. M. (1995). Series elastic actuators. In *Proceedings 1995 IEEE/RSJ International Conference on Intelligent Robots and Systems. Human Robot Interaction and Cooperative Robots*. IEEE. 10.1109/IROS.1995.525827

Priya, I. P., & Tripathi, A. (n.d.). *Big Data, Cloud and IoT: An Assimilation* (Unpublished doctoral dissertation).

Qi, . (2018). Passenger travel regularity analysis based on a large scale smart card data. *Journal of Advanced Transportation*, *2018*, 1–11.

Qin, S., Man, J., Wang, X., Li, C., Dong, H., & Ge, X. (2019). Applying big data analytics to monitor tourist flow for the scenic area operation management. *Discrete Dynamics in Nature and Society*, 1-11. doi:10.1155/2019/8239047

Rajandekar, A., & Sikdar, B. (2015). A survey of MAC layer issues and protocols for machine-to-machine communications. *IEEE Internet of Things Journal*, *2*(2), 175–186. doi:10.1109/JIOT.2015.2394438

Rajendran, P. K. (2015). Hybrid intrusion detection algorithm for private cloud. *Indian Journal of Science and Technology*, *8*(35), 1–10.

Rajeshwari, S., Santhoshs, H., & Varaprasad, G. (2015). Implementing Intelligent Traffic Control System for Congestion Control, Ambulance Clearance, and Stolen Vehicle Detection. *IEEE Sensors Journal*, *15*(2), 1109 – 1113.

Rajput, R., & Gupta, A. (2018). Power Grid System Management through Smart Grid inIndia. *International Journal on Recent Technologies in Mechanical and Electrical Engineering*, *5*(1), 17–26.

Raju, P. S., Mahalingam, M., & Rajendran, R. A. (2020). Review of Intellectual Video Surveillance through Internet of Things. In *The Cognitive Approach in Cloud Computing and Internet of Things Technologies for Surveillance Tracking Systems* (pp. 141–155). Academic Press. doi:10.1016/B978-0-12-816385-6.00010-6

Ramanan, R. G., Manikandaraj, S., & Kamaleshwar, R. (2017, February). *Implementation of Machine Learning Algorithm for Predicting User Behavior and Smart Energy Management.* Paper presented at the International Conference on Data Management, Analytics and Innovation, Pune, India.

Rashidi, B., Sharifi, M., & Jafari, T. (2013). A survey on interoperability in the cloud computing environments. *International Journal of Modern Education and Computer Science*, *5*(6), 17–23. doi:10.5815/ijmecs.2013.06.03

Rashmi, H., Rohith, S. R., & Indira, M. S. (2013). RFID and GPS based automatic lane clearance system for ambulance. *International Journal of Advanced Electrical and Electronics Engineering, (IJAEEE), 2*(3), 102–107.

Raychaudhuri, D., Nagaraja, K., & Venkataramani, A. (2012). Mobilityfirst: A robust and trustworthy mobility-centric architecture for the future internet. *Mobile Computing and Communications Review*, *16*(3), 2–13. doi:10.1145/2412096.2412098

Richhariya, B., & Tanveer, M. (2018). EEG signal classification using universum support vector machine. *Expert Systems with Applications*, *106*, 169–182. doi:10.1016/j.eswa.2018.03.053

Rinat, G. (2020). *Brain machine interface: the accurate interpretation of neurotransmitters' signals targeting the muscles.* International Journal of Applied Research in Bioinformatics. doi:10.4018/IJARB.2020 0102

Rinat, G., & Vardan, M. (2019A). Math model of neuron and nervous system research, based on AI constructor creating virtual neural circuits: Theoretical and Methodological Aspects. In V. Mkrttchian, E. Aleshina, & L. Gamidullaeva (Eds.), *Avatar-Based Control, Estimation, Communications, and Development of Neuron Multi-Functional Technology Platforms* (pp. 320–344). IGI Global. doi:10.4018/978-1-7998-1581-5.ch015

Rinat, G., & Vardan, M. (2019B). Brain machine interface – for Avatar Control & Estimation in Educational purposes Based on Neural AI plugs: Theoretical and Methodological Aspects. In V. Mkrttchian, E. Aleshina, & L. Gamidullaeva (Eds.), *Avatar-Based Control, Estimation, Communications, and Development of Neuron Multi-Functional Technology Platforms* (pp. 345–360). IGI Global. doi:10.4018/978-1-7998-1581-5.ch016

Rose, K., Eldridge, S., & Chapin, L. (2015). The internet of things: An overview. *The Internet Society (ISOC), 80.*

Rossi, F. D. (2019). Network Support for IoT Ecosystems. In Enabling Technologies and Architectures for Next-Generation Networking Capabilities. IGI Global.

Said, O., & Masud, M. (2013). Towards internet of things: Survey and future vision. *International Journal of Computer Networks*, *5*(1), 1–17.

Salah, K., Rehman, M. H. U., Nizamuddin, N., & Al-Fuqaha, A. (2019). Blockchain for AI: Review and Open Research Challenges. *IEEE Access: Practical Innovations, Open Solutions*, *7*, 10127–10149. doi:10.1109/ACCESS.2018.2890507

Salas-Vega, S., Haimann, A., & Mossialos, E. (2015). Big data and health care: Challenges and opportunities for coordinated policy development in the EU. *Health Systems and Reform*, *1*(4), 285–300. doi:10.1080/23288604.2015.1091 538 PMID:31519092

Salim, F., & Haque, U. (2015). Urban Computing in the Wild: A Survey on Large Scale Participation and Citizen Engagement with Ubiquitous Computing, Cyber Physical Systems, and Internet of Things. *International Journal of Human-Computer Studies*, *8*(1), 31–48. doi:10.1016/j.ijhcs.2015.03.003

Sambandam Raju, P., Mahalingam, M., & Arumugam Rajendran, R. (2019). Design, Implementation and Power Analysis of Pervasive Adaptive Resourceful Smart Lighting and Alerting Devices in Developing Countries Supporting Incandescent and LED Light Bulbs. *Sensors (Basel)*, *19*(9), 2032. doi:10.339019092032 PMID:31052250

Sas. (2017). https://www.sas.com/en_us/insights/analytics/big-data-analytics.html

Satyanarayanan, M. (2017). Edge Computing for Situational Awareness. *IEEE International Symposium on Local and Metropolitan Area Networks (LANMAN)*, 1-6.

Schmidt, M. (2019). Wireless power supply for a RFID based sensor platform. In *Smart Systems Integration; 13th International Conference and Exhibition on Integration Issues of Miniaturized Systems*. VDE.

Schütze, M. (2011). *Examination of the Attitudes of Mental Health Patients Towards Video Monitoring on a Secure Psychiatric Ward* (Doctoral dissertation). Bochum, Germany, Ruhr University Bochum Faculty of Medicine. http://www-brs.ub.ruhruni-bochum.de/netahtml/HSS/Diss/SchuetzeMorana/diss.pdf

Sha, M., Hackmann, G., & Lu, C. (2013, April). Energy-efficient low power listening for wireless sensor networks in noisy environments. In *Proceedings of the 12th international conference on Information processing in sensor networks* (pp. 277-288). 10.1145/2461381.2461415

Sharma, P., & Navdeti, C. (2014). Securing Big Data Hadoop: A Review of Security Issues, Threats and Solution. *IJCSIT*, *5*(2), 2126–2131.

Shrestha, A., & Mahmood, A. (2019). Review of Deep Learning Algorithms and Architectures. *IEEE Access: Practical Innovations, Open Solutions*, *7*, 53040–53065. doi:10.1109/ACCESS.2019.2912200

Shuijing, H. (2014, January). Data security: the challenges of cloud computing. In *2014 Sixth International Conference on Measuring Technology and Mechatronics Automation* (pp. 203-206). IEEE. 10.1109/ICMTMA.2014.52

Silva, D. F. (2018). *Desafios na implementação de projetos de internet das coisas e ações para superá-los*. Academic Press.

Singh & Panda. (2015). Defending Against DDOS Flooding Attacks-A Data Streaming Approach. *International Journal of Computer & IT*, 38-44.

Singh & Reddy. (2014). A survey on platforms for big data analytics. *Journal of Big Data, 2*.

Singla, A., & Sachdeva, R. (2013). Review on security issues and attacks in wireless sensor networks. *International Journal of Advanced Research in Computer Science and Software Engineering*, *3*(4).

Sintef, O. V., & Norway, P. F. (2014). *Internet of Things–From Research and Innovation to Market Deployment*. Academic Press.

Soyata, T., Muraleedharan, R., Langdon, J., Funai, C., Ames, S., Kwon, M., & Heinzelman, W. (2012, May). COMBAT: mobile-Cloud-based cOmpute/coMmunications infrastructure for BATtlefield applications. In Modeling and Simulation for Defense Systems and Applications VII (Vol. 8403, p. 84030K). International Society for Optics and Photonics.

Stefania, C. (2017). Resource management in cloud platform as a service systems: Analysis and opportunities. *Journal of Systems and Software*, *132*, 98–118. doi:10.1016/j.jss.2017.05.035

Stent, G. S. (1973). A physiological mechanism for Hebb's postulate of learning. *Proceedings of the National Academy of Sciences of the United States of America*, *70*(4), 997–1001. 10.1073/pnas.70.4.997

Steve Lohr. (2010). *The New York Times*. Retrieved from https://www.nytimes.com/2010/03/13/technology/13netflix.html

Stolovy, T., Melamed, Y., & Afek, A. (2015). Video surveillance in mental health facilities: Is it ethical? The Israel Medical Association journal. *The Israel Medical Association Journal, 17*(5), 274–276. PMID:26137651

Subrahmanya Sarma & Raghupathi. (2018). Security Issues Of Big Data In IoT Based Applications. *International Journal of Pure and Applied Mathematics, 118*(14).

Sun, G., Chang, V., Ramachandran, M., Sun, Z., Li, G., Yu, H., & Liao, D. (2017). Efficient location privacy algorithm for Internet of Things (IoT) services and applications. *Journal of Network and Computer Applications, 89*, 3–13. doi:10.1016/j.jnca.2016.10.011

Sun, N., Sun, B., Lin, J., & Wu, M. (2018). Lossless Pruned Naive Bayes for Big Data Classifications. *Big Data Research, 14*, 27–36. doi:10.1016/j.bdr.2018.05.007

Taher, N. C., Mallat, I., Agoulmine, N., & El-Mawass, N. (2019). An IoT-Cloud Based Solution for Real-Time and Batch Processing of Big Data: Application in Healthcare. *3rd International Conference on Bio-engineering for Smart Technologies.*

Takabi, H., Joshi, J. B., & Ahn, G. J. (2010). Security and privacy challenges in cloud computing environments. *IEEE Security and Privacy, 8*(6), 24–31. doi:10.1109/MSP.2010.186

Talia, D. (2013). *Clouds for scalable big data analytics.* IEEE Computer Science. doi:10.1109/MC.2013.162

Tang, C., Tang, A., Lee, E., & Tao, L. (2015). Mitigating HTTP Flooding Attacks with Meta-data Analysis. In *2015 IEEE 17th International Conference on High Performance Computing and Communications, 2015 IEEE 7th International Symposium on Cyberspace Safety and Security, and 2015 IEEE 12th International Conference on Embedded Software and Systems,* (pp. 1406-1411). IEEE. 10.1109/HPCC-CSS-ICESS.2015.203

Tang, J., Sun, D., Liu, S., & Gaudiot, J. (2017). Enabling Deep Learning on IoT Devices. *Computer, 50*(10), 92–96. doi:10.1109/MC.2017.3641648

The national intelligence council sponsor workshop. (2008). *Intelligence, S. C. B., 2008. Disruptive Civil Technologies. Six Technologies with Potential Impacts on US Interests out to 2025.* Available: https://fas.org/irp/nic/disruptive.pdf

Tsodyks, M., Uziel, A., & Markram, H. (2000). Synchrony generation in recurrent networks with frequency-dependent synapses. The Journal of Neuroscience, 20(1).

Turab, N. M., Taleb, A. A., & Masadeh, S. R. (2013). Cloud computing challenges and solutions. *International Journal of Computer Networks & Communications, 5*(5), 209–216. doi:10.5121/ijcnc.2013.5515

Uddin, M. Z. (2019). A wearable sensor-based activity prediction system to facilitate edge computing in smart healthcare system. *Journal of Parallel and Distributed Computing, 123*, 46–53. doi:10.1016/j.jpdc.2018.08.010

Valpola, H. (2015). From neural PCA to deep unsupervised learning. In *Advances in Independent Component Analysis and Learning Machines* (pp. 143–171). Academic Press.

Vanolo, A. (2014). Smart mentality: The Smart City as Disciplinary Strategy. *Urban Studies (Edinburgh, Scotland), 51*(5), 883–898. doi:10.1177/0042098013494427

Varghese, B., Wang, N., Barbhuiya, S., Kilpatrick, P., & Nikolopoulos, D. S. (2016, November). Challenges and opportunities in edge computing. In *2016 IEEE International Conference on Smart Cloud (SmartCloud)* (pp. 20-26). IEEE. 10.1109/SmartCloud.2016.18

Vartiainen, H., & Hakola, P. (1994). The effects of TV monitoring on ward atmosphere in a security hospital. *International Journal of Law and Psychiatry, 17*(4), 443–449. doi:10.1016/0160-2527(94)90019-1 PMID:7890477

Venkataramani, S., Ranjan, A., Roy, K., & Raghunathan, A. (2014, August). AxNN: energy-efficient neuromorphic systems using approximate computing. In *Proceedings of the 2014 international symposium on Low power electronics and design* (pp. 27-32). ACM.

Verizon. (n.d.). Retrieved September 26, 2019, from https://www.verizon.com/cs/groups/public/documents/adacct/hmc_smartphone051212_1.pdf

Vermesan, O., & Friess, P. (Eds.). (2013). *Internet of things: converging technologies for smart environments and integrated ecosystems.* River publishers.

Vignesh, G., Vishal, N., Prakash, S., & Sivakumar, V. (2016, May). *Automated Traffic Light Control System and Stolen Vehicle Detection.* Paper presented at the 2016 IEEE International Conference on Recent Trends in Electronics, Information & Communication Technology (RTEICT), Bangalore, India.

Vijayalakshmi, A. V., & Arockiam, L. (2016). A study on security issues and challenges in IoT. *International Journal of Engineering Sciences & Management Research, 3*(11), 1–9.

Vinoski, S. (2006). Advanced message queuing protocol. *IEEE Internet Computing, 10*(6), 87–89. doi:10.1109/MIC.2006.116

Visuwasam & Raj. (2018). NMA: integrating big data into a novel mobile application using knowledge extraction for big data analytics. In *Cluster Computing.* Springer Nature.

Wadhwa, A. V., & Gupta, S. (2015). Study of security issues in cloud computing. *International Journal of Computer Science and Mobile Computing IJCSMC, 4*(6), 230–234.

Wang, L., & Alexander, C. A. (2016). Big Data Analytics and Cloud Computing in Internet of Things. *American Journal of Information Science and Computer Engineering, 2*(6), 70–78.

Wang, S., Bonomi, L., Dai, W., Chen, F., Cheung, C., Bloss, C. S., Cheng, S., & Jiang, X. (2020). Big Data Privacy in Biomedical Research. *IEEE Transactions on Big Data, Volume, 6*(2), 296–308.

Wang, S., Zhan, T.-M., Chen, Y., Zhang, Y., Yang, M., Lu, H.-M., Wang, H.-N., Liu, B., & Phillips, P. (2016). Multiple Sclerosis Detection Based on Biorthogonal Wavelet Transform, RBF Kernel Principal Component Analysis, and Logistic Regression. *IEEE Access: Practical Innovations, Open Solutions, 4*, 7567–7576. doi:10.1109/ACCESS.2016.2620996

Wang, W., Lee, J., Harrou, F., & Sun, Y. (2020). Early Detection of Parkinson's Disease Using Deep Learning and Machine Learning. *IEEE Access: Practical Innovations, Open Solutions, 8*, 147635–147646. doi:10.1109/ACCESS.2020.3016062

Wang, Y., Kinsner, W., & Zhang, D. (2009). Contemporary Cybernetics and Its Facets of Cognitive Informatics and Computational Intelligence. *IEEE Transactions on Systems, Man, and Cybernetics. Part B, Cybernetics, 39*(4), 823–833. doi:10.1109/TSMCB.2009.2013721 PMID:19349246

Warr, J., Page, M., & Crossen-White, H. (2005). *The appropriate use of CCTV observation in a secure unit.* Bournemouth University.

Werbos, P. J. (1990). Backpropagation through time: What it does and how to do it. *Proceedings of the IEEE, 78*(10), 1550–1560.

Wortmann, F., & Flüchter, K. (2015). Internet of things. *Business & Information Systems Engineering, 57*(3), 221–224. doi:10.100712599-015-0383-3

Xiao, G. (2014). User interoperability with heterogeneous IoT devices through transformation. *IEEE Transactions on Industrial Informatics, 10*(2), 1486–1496. doi:10.1109/TII.2014.2306772

Xiao, P., Qu, W., Qi, H., & Li, Z. (2015). Detecting DDoS attacks against data center with correlation analysis. *Computer Communications*, *67*, 66–74.

Xie, J., Yu, F. R., Huang, T., Xie, R., Liu, J., Wang, C., & Liu, Y. (2019). A Survey of Machine Learning Techniques Applied to Software Defined Networking (SDN): Research Issues and Challenges. *IEEE Communications Surveys and Tutorials*, *21*(1), 393–430. doi:10.1109/COMST.2018.2866942

Xin, Y., Kong, L., Liu, Z., Chen, Y., Li, Y., Zhu, H., Gao, M., Hou, H., & Wang, C. (2018). Machine Learning and Deep Learning Methods for Cyber security. *IEEE Access: Practical Innovations, Open Solutions*, *6*, 35365–35381. doi:10.1109/ACCESS.2018.2836950

Xu, X., Lie, Y., Zhang, Z., & Zhu, S. (2017). Study and Implementation on the Monitor of Liquid Level of Liquid Scintillator. *Second International Conference on Mechanical, Control and Computer Engineering*, 131-134.

Yang, H., & Wang, F. (2019). Wireless Network Intrusion Detection Based on Improved Convolutional Neural Network. *IEEE Access: Practical Innovations, Open Solutions*, *7*, 64366–64374. doi:10.1109/ACCESS.2019.2917299

Yang, Z. (2011). Study and application on the architecture and key technologies for IOT. In *2011 International Conference on Multimedia Technology*. IEEE. 10.1109/ICMT.2011.6002149

Yao, S., Hu, S., Zhao, Y., Zhang, A., & Abdelzhar, T. (2017). DeepSense: A Unified Deep Learning Framework for Time-Series Mobile Sensing Data Processing. *Proc. 26th Int'l Conf. World Wide Web*, 351–360. 10.1145/3038912.3052577

Yao, S., Zhao, Y., Shao, H., Zhang, A., Zhang, C., Li, S., & Abdelzhar, T. (2018). RDeepSense: Reliable Deep Mobile Computing Models with Uncertainty Estimations. *Proceedings of the ACM on Interactive, Mobile, Wearable and Ubiquitous Technologies*, *1*(4), 173. doi:10.1145/3161181

Yao, S., Zhao, Y., Zhang, A., Hu, S., Shao, H., Zhang, C., Su, L., & Abdelzhar, T. (2018). Deep Learning for the Internet of Things. *Computer*, *51*(5), 32–41. doi:10.1109/MC.2018.2381131

Yao, S., Zhao, Y., Zhang, A., Su, L., & Abdelzhar, T. (2017). DeepIoT: Compressing Deep Neural Network Structures for Sensing Systems with a Compressor Critic Framework. *Proc. 15th ACM Conf. Embedded Network Sensor System.* 10.1145/3131672.3131675

Yavuz, F. Y. (2018). *Deep learning in cyber security for internet of things* (Doctoral dissertation).

Yazici, M. T., Basurra, S., & Gaber, M. M. (2018). Edge Machine Learning: Enabling Smart Internet of Things Applications. *Big Data Cognitive Computing*, *2*(3), 26. doi:10.3390/bdcc2030026

Yunhe, P. (2016). Urban Big Data and the Development of City Intelligence. *Engineering*, *2*(2), 171–178. doi:10.1016/J.ENG.2016.02.003

Zhang & Li. (2019). Intelligent Travelling Visitor Estimation Model with Big Data Mining. *Enterprise Information Systems*, 1–14. doi:10.1080/17517575.2019.1590860

Zhang, M. X., Grolinger, K., & Capretz, A. M. (2018, December). *Forecasting Residential Energy Consumption: Single Household Perspective*, Paper presented at the 17th IEEE International Conference on Machine Learning and Applications (ICMLA), Orlando, FL.

Zhang, C., Patras, P., & Haddadi, H. (2019). Deep Learning in Mobile and Wireless Networking: A Survey. *IEEE Communications Surveys and Tutorials*, *21*(3), 2224–2287. doi:10.1109/COMST.2019.2904897

Zhang, C., Zhang, H., Qiao, J., Yuan, D., & Zhang, M. (2019). Deep Transfer Learning for Intelligent Cellular Traffic Prediction Based on Cross-Domain Big Data. *IEEE Journal on Selected Areas in Communications, 37*(6), 1389–1401. doi:10.1109/JSAC.2019.2904363

Zhang, D., Han, X., & Deng, C. (2018). Review on the research and practice of deep learning and reinforcement learning in smart grids. *CSEE Journal of Power and Energy Systems, 4*(3), 362–370. doi:10.17775/CSEEJPES.2018.00520

Zhang, L., Estrin, D., Burke, J., Jacobson, V., Thornton, J. D., Smetters, D. K., ... Papadopoulos, C. (2010). Named data networking (ndn) project. Relatório Técnico NDN-0001. *Xerox Palo Alto Research Center-PARC, 157*, 158.

Zhang, W., Liu, K., Zhang, W., Zhang, Y., & Gu, J. (2016). Deep neural networks for wireless localization in indoor and outdoor environments. *Neurocomputing, 194*, 279–287.

Zhao, L., Chen, L., Ranjan, R., Choo, K. R., & He, J. (2016). Geographical information system parallelization for spatial big data processing: a review. *Cluster Computing, 19*(1), 139–152.

Zheng, Y., Capra, L., Wolfson, O., & Yang, H. (2014). Urban Computing: Concepts, Methodologies, and Applications. *ACM Transactions on Intelligent Systems and Technology, 5*(3), 1–55.

Zheng, Y., Wu, W., Chen, Y., Qu, H., & Ni, L. M. (2016). Visual Analytics in Urban Computing: An Overview. *IEEE Transactions on Big Data, 2*(3), 276–296. doi:10.1109/TBDATA.2016.2586447

Zhou, L., Pan, S., Wang, J., & Vasilakos, A. V. (2017). Machine Learning on Big Data: Opportunities and Challenges. *Neurocomputing, 237*, 350-361.

Zhou, X., Gong, W., Fu, W., & Du, F. (2017). Application of deep learning in object detection. *2017 IEEE/ACIS 16th International Conference on Computer and Information Science (ICIS),* 631-634.

Zhu, Q. (2010). Iot gateway: Bridgingwireless sensor networks into internet of things. In *2010 IEEE/IFIP International Conference on Embedded and Ubiquitous Computing. IEEE.* 10.1109/EUC.2010.58

About the Contributors

Sathiyamoorthi Velayutham is currently working as an Associate Professor in Computer Science and Engineering Department at Sona College of Technology, Salem, Tamil Nadu, India. He was born on June 21, 1983, at Omalur in Salem District, Tamil Nadu, India. He received his Bachelor of Engineering degree in Information Technology from Periyar University, Salem with First Class. He obtained his Master of Engineering degree in Computer Science and Engineering from Anna University, Chennai with Distinction and secured 30th University Rank. He received his Ph.D degree from Anna University, Chennai in Web Mining. His areas of specialization include Web Usage Mining, Data Structures, Design and Analysis of Algorithm and Operating System. He has published many papers in International Journals and conferences. He has published many books and book chapters in various renowned international publishers. He has also participated in various National level Workshops and Seminars conducted by various reputed institutions.

* * *

Adam A. Alli is a PhD. in Computer Science and Engineering fellow at Islamic University of Technology (IUT), Board Bazar, Gazipur-1704, Bangladesh. He received his MSc. in Computer Science (2008) at the University of Mysore India, B.Sc. in Computer Science (2002) at Islamic University in Uganda. He also received a postgraduate diploma in Management and Teaching at Higher Education (2015) at Islamic University in Uganda, and a Graduate Diploma in ICT Leadership and Knowledge Society (2013) at Dublin City University through the GeSCI program. He was Dean Faculty of Science at Islamic University in Uganda from 2011 to 2016. He is a lecturer of Computer Science and Engineering at both Islamic University in Uganda and Uganda Technical College (UTC) Bushenyi. He is a lead researcher for Islamic University in Uganda ICT4D group.

Chidhambara Rajan B. obtained his Bachelors degree in Electronics & Communications engineering, Masters degree in Microwave & Optical engineering from Madurai Kamaraj University and a Ph.D. from Anna University, Chennai. He has 29 years of teaching experience in government and reputed private institutions. He is a member of professional societies like IEEE, IETE, IEI, ISTE, CSI, ISOI, etc. He has published several technical papers in national and international journals and conferences.

Chellaswamy C. received the B.E degree in electronics and communication engineering from Madurai Kamaraj University, Tamilnadu, India, in 1994, the Post the graduate degree in applied electronics from Sathyabama University, Chennai, India, in 2005, and the Ph.D. degree in electronics and communication engineering from St. Peters University, Chennai, India, in 2017. He is currently with the Lords Institute of Technology, Hyderabad as Professor and Head of electronics and communication engineering department. His professional services include - but are not limited to - Industry Consultations, a Workshops Chair, a Technical Program Committee Member, and a Reviewer for several international journals and conferences. He has authored over 60 scientific research articles in referred international journals and conferences. His research interests include energy management systems, solar PV systems, intelligent autonomous systems; remote monitoring, IoT based system design, and inspired optimization algorithms.

D. K. Chaturvedi is working in Dept. of Elect. Engg, Faculty of Engg, D.E.I., Dayalbagh, Agra since 1989. Presently he is Professor. He did his B.E. from Govt. Engineering College Ujjain, M.P. then he did his M.Tech. and Ph.D. from D.E.I. Dayalbagh. He is gold medalist and received Young Scientists Fellowship from DST, Government of India in 2001-2002 for post doctorial research at Univ. of Calgary, Canada. Also, he had research collaboration with different organizations at national and international level. He is the Fellow - The Institution of Engineers (India), Fellow - Aeronautical Society of India, Fellow - IETE, Sr. Member IEEE, USA and Member of many National and International professional bodies such as IET, U.K., ISTE, Delhi, ISCE, Roorkee, IIIE, Mumbai and SSI etc. The IEE, U.K. recognized his work in the area of Power System Stabilizer and awarded honorary membership to him in 2006. He did many R&D projects of MHRD, UGC, AICTE etc. and consultancy projects of DRDO. He contributed in the national mission of ICT of Govt. of India as Virtual Power Lab Developer. He has guided 10 Ph.Ds., 65 M.Tech. Dissertations and published more than 300 International and National Papers. He has chaired and Co-Chaired many International and National Conferences. He is referee of many International Journals including IEE Proceedings and IEEE Transactions. He is Head of Dept. of Footwear Technology, Convener, Faculty Training and Placement Cell, and Advisor, IEI Students' Chapter (Elect. Engg.), D.E.I. Dayalbagh, Agra.

Bhuvana D. S. is pursuing her masters in Computer Science and Engineering, Dayananda Sagar University Bangalore on Big Data Analysis. She did BTech in Computer Science and engineering from Maharaja Institute of Technology, Mysore and was an IEEE student member for 4 years. Her areas of interest are Big Data Analytics, Internet of Things and Image Processing.

Shaila G. is an Associate Professor in the Department of Computer Science & Engineering in Dayananda Sagar University. She did her Ph. D. from National Institute of Technology, Tiruchirapalli, Tamil Nadu in the area of Multimedia Information Retrieval in Distributed System. She has totally 14 years of teaching and research experience. She has also worked for Central Power Research Institute as a Trainee Engineer for one year and later she worked as a Junior Research Fellow for DST project for the period of 2 year 8 months. She has also worked as a member of Student Exchange program for the "Obama-Singh Knowledge Initiative Program UNLV, Las Vegas, US ", an Indo-US collaborated Project. Her areas of interest are Information Retrieval, Image Processing, Cognitive Science and Pattern Recognition.

Rinat Galiautdinov is a Principal Software Developer and Architect having the expertise in Information Technology and Computer Science. Mr. Galiautdinov is also an expert in Banking/Financial industry as well as in Neurobiological sphere. Mr. Rinat Galiautdinov works on the number of highly important researches as an independent researcher.

Sowmya H. D. is pursuing her M.Tech from Dayanand Sagar University Bangalore on Big Data. She has completed her B.E from The Oxford College of Engineering, VTU University. Her area of interest are Big Data Analytics and Machine Learning.

Divya K. is pursuing her M.Tech from Dayanand Sagar University Bangalore on Big data . She has completed her B.E from Dr Sri Shivakumara Mahaswamy college of engineering (Dr.smce), Bangalore. Her area of interest are Big Data analytics and Artificial Intelligence.

Karthika K. has received her B.Tech degree in the year 2009 from Lord Venkateshwara engineering college, Kanchepuram and ME degree in the year 2013 from Multimedia Technology anna University,Guindy,Chennai. Currently she is pursuing her Pursuing Ph.D. in Anna University, Chennai, in the field of Data Mining and Security. She has 7 years of teaching experience and she is working as Assistant Professor in Department of Information Technology at Adhiyamaan College of Engineering, Hosur, Tamilnadu.

Arthi Kalidasan received the Bachelor of Engineering in the field of Electronics and Communication Engineering from Adhiyamaan College of engineering in 2010 and Master of engineering in the field of VLSI Design from SKR Engineering College in 2012. She is currently pursuing the Ph.D. Degree with the Information and Communication engineering, Anna University. She is currently working as an Assistant Professor with the Department of Electronics and communication engineering, in SRM Valliammai engineering college. Her research interests include IoT, Machine Learning and VLSI Design. She is a Member of Computer Society of India and IETE.

Monish L. is pursuing his Masters in Computer Science and Engineering at Dayananda Sagar University Bangalore on Big Data Analytics and he did Btech in Computer Science Engineering from The Oxford College of Engineering, has been awarded as topper in the college. His areas of interest are, Big data Analytics, Internet of Things and Machine Learning.

Murugan Mahalingam graduated in E&CE from the University of Madras in 1989. Received his Masters in E & TC Engg. (Microwave) in 2001 and Ph.D. in 2010 respectively from the University of Pune. Presently he is serving as the Professor of ECE Dept. and the Vice Principal of Valliammai Engineering College, Kattankulathur, Tamil Nadu. Having over 30 years of teaching, his fields of interests are Antennas, Microwave, SatCom, OptiComm and EMI&C. He is a Fellow of IETE, Life Member of ISTE, IEI, ISOI, SEMCEI, SSI and Member of CSI and ISCA. Over one hundred papers are published in the International / National repute Conferences/Journals and written four text books. In 2016, he received the prestigious ISTE's Anna University National Award for an Outstanding Academic.

Nambobi Mutwalibi is a research assistant at Motion Analysis Research Lab, Islamic University in Uganda. He is also working as the Head of Science and Technology, Labour College of East Africa. He was a research assistant in Technical and Vocational Education (TVE) specializing in computer science and engineering at Islamic University of Technology (IUT, 2018). He holds MBA (Virtual University of Uganda, Muyenga, Kampala), BSc. Technical Education (Islamic University of Technology, Dhaka, Bangladesh). His research interest on TVET, Disruptive Innovations, Wargaming Strategy, Game theory,

Coopetition, Blue Ocean Strategy, Blended learning, Green Skills, and ICTs in a developing country. He can be reached via his website: www.nambobi.com.

J. Fenila Naomi was born in Coimbatore, TamilNadu, India, in 1993. She received M.Tech degree from PSG College of Technology in the year 2018, Coimbatore. She has secured TANCET scholarship during her P.G. course. She received B.E degree from Hindusthan College of Engineering and Technology. Currently she is working as Assistant Professor at Sri Krishna College of Engineering and Technology, Coimbatore. Her research areas are cloud computing, data mining and IoT. She has published research papers in International and National Journals.

Shanthi Bala P. received her Ph.D from Pondicherry University. She is presently working as a Assistant Professor in Department of Computer Science, Pondicherry University, Puducherry. She has around 10 years of teaching and 6 years of research experience. Her research interests include Knowledge Engineering, Artificial intelligence, Ontology and Networks. She has published more than 30 papers in International Journal and conferences.

Rajlaxmi Patil is pursuing her M.Tech from Dayanand Sagar University Bangalore on Big data. She has completed her B.Tech from Guru Nanak Institute of Technology, JNTU university. She has 4 years of work experience. Her area of interest are Big Data analytics, Machine Learning and Artificial Intelligence.

Swathi R. has received Master of Philosophy in Computer Science under Vels University, Chennai during the year 2014. She completed Master of Computer Applications under Bharathidasan University, Tiruchirappalli, India during the year 2010. More than 4 years of experience in Teaching. Currently working as Assistant Professor & Head of the Department of Computer Science in Sree Abiraami Arts and Science College for Women, Thiruvalluvar University, Vellore, India. Previously she has worked as Assistant Professor in St.Joseph's Arts and Science College, Kovur, Chennai, India. Her research areas include Wireless Networks, Internet of Things, Data Science, Cloud Computing, Big Data Analytics and Machine Learning. She has published 2 papers in the reputed International journals and presented 2 research publications in the International & National conferences.

Revathi Rajendran is working as Associate Professor in Valliammai Engineering College. She has completed Ph.D. in Video Processing from Anna University, Chennai. She has 18 years of teaching experience from Anna University affiliated colleges. She filed patent and has published several technical papers in National and International journals, conferences and text book. She has guided many projects in various domains like RFID, Image Processing, Mobile Computing, Video Processing etc., She has gone through various Seminars, Workshops and FDPs to various colleges. She also delivered Guest Lectures in Anna University and their affiliated colleges. She has a member of professional societies like IEEE, ISTE, ACM and CSI. Mentor of 'Introduction to Psychology' (Year-2016), 'Great experiments in Psychology' (Year-2017), 'Introduction to IoT' (Year-2017) & 'Real time Operating System' (Year-2018) courses in online NPTEL course. Published 3 national articles, 10 International/National Journals paper & presented 10 International/ National Conferences. Filed a patent in the title of "Locomotive Detection of Idols" in 2018.

Devi Priya Rangasamy is an Associate Professor in the Department of Information Technology, Kongu Engineering College. She has received her PhD from Anna University, Chennai in 2013. She has Published about 75 papers in national and International Conferences and Journals. Her research interests are Data Warehousing and Mining and Nature Inspired Algorithms.

Rohit Rastogi received his B.E. degree in Computer Science and Engineering from C.C.S.Univ. Meerut in 2003, the M.E. degree in Computer Science from NITTTR-Chandigarh (National Institute of Technical Teachers Training and Research-affiliated to MHRD, Govt. of India), Punjab Univ. Chandigarh in 2010. Currently he is pursuing his Ph.D. In computer science from Dayalbagh Educational Institute, Agra under renowned professor of Electrical Engineering Dr. D.K. Chaturvedi in area of spiritual consciousness. Dr. Santosh Satya of IIT-Delhi and dr. Navneet Arora of IIT-Roorkee have happily consented him to co supervise. He is also working presently with Dr. Piyush Trivedi of DSVV Hardwar, India in center of Scientific spirituality. He is a Associate Professor of CSE Dept. in ABES Engineering. College, Ghaziabad (U.P.-India), affiliated to Dr. A.P. J. Abdul Kalam Technical Univ. Lucknow (earlier Uttar Pradesh Tech. University). Also, He is preparing some interesting algorithms on Swarm Intelligence approaches like PSO, ACO and BCO etc. Rohit Rastogi is involved actively with Vichaar Krnati Abhiyaan and strongly believe that transformation starts within self.

Kanyana Ruth is a physicist pursuing MSc. in Physics at Kampala International University. She holds a BSc. in Technology-physics from Kyambogo University, Uganda (2015). She worked with security systems at smart security Ltd (2019). She is currently working with Kampala International University in the Directorate of research, Innovation, Consultancy and Extension department. Her research interests include integration of IoT in radiation safety and management.

Lavanya S. is pursuing her M.Tech from Dayanand sagar university Bangalore on Big data. She has completed her B. Tech from Vemana Institute of technology, VTU University. She has published paper in international conference and journal. Her area of interest are big data, cloud computing, image processing.

Padmadevi S. received B.E in Computer science and engineering (2004) from Madurai Kamaraj University, Tamilnadu, India and M.E in Computer science and Engineering (2007) from Anna University, Tamilnadu, India. Currently she is working as Assistant Professor at Department of Computer science and engineering, Velammal college of Engineering and Technology, Tamilnadu. Her research interests include Wireless networks, Mobile Computing, Adhoc networks and VANET. She has published research papers at national and international journals, conference proceedings as well as chapters of books.

Rashmi S. earned her Ph.D in Computer Science and Engineering from Visvesvaraya Technological University, Belgaum for her work in the area of Cloud Computing, in the year 2019. She has nearly 16 years of teaching experience in engineering colleges/University. She is serving as an associate professor for the Department of Information Science and Engineering in Dayananda Sagar College of Engineering, Bengaluru. She has formerly worked as an Assistant Professor in Dayananda Sagar University, East Point College of Engineering and Technology and National Institute of Engineering, Mysuru. After graduating from Mysore University in 2001, she specialized in Computer Network Engineering from National Institute of Engineering. Her main research interests include Cloud Computing, Machine Learning and Analytics, IOT and Cyber security. She has authored many Journal and conferences papers, both National and International.

Sathishkumar S. has received his B.E (Computer Science and Engineering) degree in the year 2006 from Nandha Engineering College, Erode and M.E., (Computer Science and Engineering) degree in the year 2012 from Paavai Engineering College, Namakkal. Currently he is pursuing his Ph.D. in Anna University, Chennai, in the field of Data Mining. He has 7 years of teaching experience and he is working as Assistant Professor in Department of Information Technology at Adhiyamaan College of Engineering, Hosur, Tamilnadu.

Murali Saktheeswaran completed B.E.(CSE) at 2008 from PSR Engineering College, Sivakasi and M.E. (CSE) at 2016 from Anna University Regional Centre, Madurai.

Preethi Sambandam Raju graduated in Electronics and Communication Engineering from Anand Institute of Higher Technology in 2012. She received her Masters degree from St.Joseph's College of Engineering in 2014. Presently, she is pursuing her Ph.D in Anna University. She is a life member of ISTE and CSI. Currently, having 5 years of teaching experience and her research interests include video surveillance, Internet of Things, Artificial Intelligence.

Roopashree Shailendra is pursuing PhD from Visveswaraya Technical University, Belagavi. Research area includes Machine Learning, Cloud computing and Computer Vision. Nearly 12 years of experience in both IT industry and reputed engineering colleges / University. Has earned Master of Technology specialised in Computer Science and Engineering from Visveswaraya Technical University, Belagavi and Bachelor of Engineering in Computer Science and Engineering from Mysore University, Mysuru. Currently working as Assistant Professor in Department of Computer Science and Engineering in Dayananda Sagar University. Life member of Computer Society of India. Published an Indian Patent in Machine Learning and Image Processing. Worked as Assistant Professor in a reputed engineering college for eight years and as software developer for four years in MNC companies under embedded systems and PLM platform. Published papers in Journals, International and National Conferences. Area of interest include Machine Learning, IOT, Image Processing, Cloud computing and Pattern Recognition.

Parul Singhal received her B.Tech degree from AKTU Univ. Presently She is M.Tech. Second Year student of CSE in ABESEC, Ghaziabad. She is a Teaching Assistant in the CSE department of ABES Engineering. Ghaziabad, India. She is working presently on data mining (DM) and machine learning (ML). She is also working on TTH and stress. She has keen interest in Google surfing. Her hobbies is playing badminton and reading books. She is young, talented and dynamic.

Rajab Ssemwogerere is pursuing a Master's of science in Computer Science at Makerere University (MUK) Kampala, Uganda since 2019. He received his honors B.Sc. in Computer Science (2018) and a diploma in Computer science and Information Technology (2014) at the Islamic University in Uganda. He also gained certificates (Introduction to cybersecurity, Introduction to the internet of things and digital transformation (2018) from CISCO networking Academy, Building Database Applications in PHP, Building Web Applications in PHP, Google Cloud Platform Big Data and Machine Learning Fundamentals, Google Cloud Platform Fundamentals and Core Infrastructure, IT Project Management, Introduction to

Git and GitHub, Troubleshooting and Debugging Techniques, Using Python to Interact with the Operating System, Crash Course on Python, Technical Support Fundamentals and Fundamentals of Digital Marketing, from google. Currently, he works as a research assistant in the Motion Analysis Research Lab as well as an IT technical Support Officer based at the Islamic University in Uganda. He Led a team of six that developed an autonomous smart office system that later won the Rector's award at Islamic University in Uganda (2018). And in the year 2019, he also contributed on the Wearable Monitoring Frameworks for the Elderly and Children project in the Motion Analysis Research Lab (MARL) . His research interests are; computer vision, Artificial intelligence, Machine learning and Internet of Things.

Sivakumar V. has completed Ph.D. under Anna University, Chennai, M.E. degree in Computer Science and Engineering from the Anna University Coimbatore, Coimbatore, India, in 2010 and B.E. degree in Computer Science and Engineering from Anna University, Chennai, India, in 2006. Currently he is working as Assistant Professor in the Department of Computer Science and Engineering at Dayananda Sagar Academy of Technology and Management, Bangalore, Karnataka, India. Previously he was worked as Assistant Professor in Adhiyamaan College of Engineering (Autonomous), Hosur from 2010 to 2019. His research interests include Networks, Mobile Ad hoc networks, Data Analytics, Cloud Computing, Storage Management. He has published 12 in the reputed International journals including Elsevier and Springer & more than 21 papers are presented at National & International Conferences.

Yuvaraj V. has received B.E. degree in Electronics and Communication Engineering from Anna University, Chennai, India, in 2008. Currently he is working as Technical Solution Manager in Shenzhen Center Power Tech Co. Ltd. Shenzhen, China. Previously he was worked as Senior Service Engineer in Exicom Telesystems Ltd, Mumbai, India. He have more than 12 years experience in Lithium ion batteries. His research interests include Battery System Management, BMS operation logics, Fault finding in batteries and BMS, Energy Storage System, EV battery, e-mobility, Fuel Cells.

M. Chandra Vadhana is pursuing her master degree in Pondicherry University in the stream of Network and Information Security. she completed her bachelor degree in Sri Manakula Vinayagar Engineering College in the stream of Information Technology. Her area of interest is Network Security, Cyber Forensics.

Immanuel Zion Ramdinthara is a Research Scholar, Dept. of Computer Science and Engineering under the guidance Dr. P. Shanthi Bala in the area of "Machine Learning and IoT in Agriculture domain.

Index

Ensure Quality Research is Introduced to the Academic Community

Become an IGI Global Reviewer for Authored Book Projects

Premier Reference Source

Emerging GIS Applications for Emergency and Disaster Management

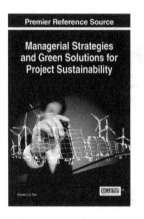

Premier Reference Source

Managerial Strategies and Green Solutions for Project Sustainability

Premier Reference Source

Comparative Approaches to Using R and Python for Statistical Data Analysis

Premier Reference Source

Solutions for High-Touch Communications in a High-Tech World

The overall success of an authored book project is dependent on quality and timely reviews.

In this competitive age of scholarly publishing, constructive and timely feedback significantly expedites the turnaround time of manuscripts from submission to acceptance, allowing the publication and discovery of forward-thinking research at a much more expeditious rate. Several IGI Global authored book projects are currently seeking highly-qualified experts in the field to fill vacancies on their respective editorial review boards:

Applications and Inquiries may be sent to:
development@igi-global.com

Applicants must have a doctorate (or an equivalent degree) as well as publishing and reviewing experience. Reviewers are asked to complete the open-ended evaluation questions with as much detail as possible in a timely, collegial, and constructive manner. All reviewers' tenures run for one-year terms on the editorial review boards and are expected to complete at least three reviews per term. Upon successful completion of this term, reviewers can be considered for an additional term.

If you have a colleague that may be interested in this opportunity, we encourage you to share this information with them.

IGI Global's Transformative Open Access (OA) Model:
How to Turn Your University Library's Database Acquisitions Into a Source of OA Funding

In response to the OA movement and well in advance of Plan S, IGI Global, early last year, unveiled their OA Fee Waiver (Read & Publish) Initiative.

Under this initiative, librarians who invest in IGI Global's InfoSci-Books (5,300+ reference books) and/or InfoSci-Journals (185+ scholarly journals) databases will be able to subsidize their patron's OA article processing charges (APC) when their work is submitted and accepted (after the peer review process) into an IGI Global journal. *See website for details.

How Does it Work?

1. When a library subscribes or perpetually purchases IGI Global's InfoSci-Databases and/or their discipline/subject-focused subsets, IGI Global will match the library's investment with a fund of equal value to go toward subsidizing the OA article processing charges (APCs) for their patrons.

   Researchers: **Be sure to recommend the InfoSci-Books and InfoSci-Journals to take advantage of this initiative.**

2. When a student, faculty, or staff member submits a paper and it is accepted (following the peer review) into one of IGI Global's 185+ scholarly journals, the author will have the option to have their paper published under a traditional publishing model or as OA.

3. When the author chooses to have their paper published under OA, IGI Global will notify them of the OA Fee Waiver (Read and Publish) Initiative. If the author decides they would like to take advantage of this initiative, IGI Global will deduct the US$ 2,000 APC from the created fund.

4. This fund will be offered on an annual basis and will renew as the subscription is renewed for each year thereafter. IGI Global will manage the fund and award the APC waivers unless the librarian has a preference as to how the funds should be managed.

Hear From the Experts on This Initiative:

"I'm very happy to have been able to make one of my recent research contributions, "Visualizing the Social Media Conversations of a National Information Technology Professional Association" featured in the *International Journal of Human Capital and Information Technology Professionals*, freely available along with having access to the valuable resources found within IGI Global's InfoSci-Journals database."

– **Prof. Stuart Palmer**,
Deakin University, Australia

For More Information, Visit: www.igi-global.com/publish/contributor-resources/open-access/read-publish-model
or contact IGI Global's Database Team at eresources@igi-global.com.

InfoSci®-OnDemand

Continuously updated with new material on a weekly basis, InfoSci®-OnDemand offers the ability to search through thousands of quality full-text research papers. Users can narrow each search by identifying key topic areas of interest, then display a complete listing of relevant papers, and purchase materials specific to their research needs.

Comprehensive Service
- Over 125,000+ journal articles, book chapters, and case studies.
- All content is downloadable in PDF and HTML format and can be stored locally for future use.

No Subscription Fees
- One time fee of $37.50 per PDF download.

Instant Access
- Receive a download link immediately after order completion!

"It really provides an excellent entry into the research literature of the field. It presents a manageable number of highly relevant sources on topics of interest to a wide range of researchers. The sources are scholarly, but also accessible to 'practitioners'."

- Lisa Stimatz, MLS, University of North Carolina at Chapel Hill, USA

"It is an excellent and well designed database which will facilitate research, publication, and teaching. It is a very useful tool to have."

- George Ditsa, PhD, University of Wollongong, Australia

"I have accessed the database and find it to be a valuable tool to the IT/IS community. I found valuable articles meeting my search criteria 95% of the time."

- Prof. Lynda Louis, Xavier University of Louisiana, USA

Recommended for use by researchers who wish to immediately download PDFs of individual chapters or articles.

www.igi-global.com/e-resources/infosci-ondemand

www.igi-global.com

Printed in the United States
By Bookmasters